WITHDRAWN

DATE DUE

MAY 0 1 '96			
DEC 0 2 1998			
APR 1 1 2001			
APR 0 3 2002			

#47-0108 Peel Off Pressure Sensitive

DUQUESNE STUDIES
Philosophical Series

17

PHENOMENOLOGY
AND ATHEISM

DUQUESNE STUDIES
Philosophical Series

17

PHENOMENOLOGY AND ATHEISM

by

WILLIAM A. LUIJPEN, O.S.A., PH.D.

DUQUESNE UNIVERSITY PRESS
Pittsburgh, Pa.

Editions E. NAUWELAERTS, LOUVAIN

1964

Library of Congress Catalog Card Number 64-17127

All rights reserved
© 1964, by Duquesne University
Printed in the United States of America by
The Ad Press, Ltd., New York, N. Y.

iv

DUQUESNE STUDIES

Philosophical Series

Volume Thirteen—*Andrew G. van Melsen*, SCIENCE AND TECH-NOLOGY. Pp. X and 373. Price: paper $6.20, cloth $6.95. Published also in Dutch and German.

Volume Fourteen—*P. Henry van Laer*, PHILOSOPHY OF SCIENCE. Part Two: A Study of the Division and Nature of Various Groups of Sciences. Pp. XIII and 342. Price: paper $5.75, cloth, $6.50.

Volume Fifteen—*Remy C. Kwant*, THE PHENOMENOLOGICAL PHILOSOPHY OF MERLEAU-PONTY. Pp. IX and 257. Price: paper $4.50, cloth $5.25.

Volume Sixteen—*John A. Peters*, METAPHYSICS: A SYSTEMATIC SURVEY. Pp. XVIII and 529. Price: paper $9.00, cloth $9.75.

Volume Seventeen—*William A. Luijpen*, PHENOMENOLOGY AND ATHEISM. Pp. XIV and 343. Price: paper $5.75, cloth $6.50.

IN PREPARATION:

Joseph A. Kockelmanns, *Phenomenology and Physical Science*

Martin G. Plattel—*Social Philosophy*

Andrew G. van Melsen—*Evolution and Philosophy*

DUQUESNE STUDIES are published in the following series: African, Philological, Philosophical, Psychological, Spiritan and Theological.

Periodical publications of Duquesne University Press:

Annuale Mediaevale ($4.00 per year); Duquesne Hispanic Review ($3.00 per year); Duquesne Review. A Journal of the Social Sciences ($2.25 per year); Duquesne Science Counselor ($3.00 per year; $3.25 outside U.S.); Journal of Ecumenical Studies ($6.00 per year; outside U.S. $6.50); Review of Existential Psychology and Psychiatry ($5.00 per year).

"Lord, I am not trying to invade and
pry into Your Majesty, for I do not
liken my knowledge to It in the least.
But I long for a glimpse of the truth
that is believed and loved by my heart."
St. Anselm

CONTENTS

ix

PREFACE

The voices of contemporary atheists must sound strange—like sounds coming from a distant world or from strange times—to those whose existence is deeply rooted in an established philosophical theodicy or in a system of theology. Nonetheless, that world and that era are also the very world and era of these believers in God. This fact indicates not only that an increasing number of their fellow-men are atheists but also, and even especially, that atheism is a possibility that lies concealed in their own existence. Such an admission, however, is more than these philosophers and theologians are able or willing to acknowledge, and for this reason the voices of the atheists continue to make a strange impression on them.

Nevertheless, it is a fact that cannot be disregarded: Atheism is more than a system of propositions denying God held to be true by atheists. It is not merely a way of life in which God is denied or in which He is consciously and deliberately neglected. Atheism is first and foremost, the actualization of *a fundamental human potentiality*. This potentiality is so fundamental that it is surreptitiously actuated in the existence *also* of those who justly consider themselves theists or believers.

Atheism is a fundamental human possibility because it is fundamentally *impossible* for man to see God in the same way as he sees the world. God is a transcendent God. He who says that he sees God just as he sees the world is an atheist just as much as one who bluntly denies God. Both the denial and the "affirmation" of God may therefore originate in an atheistic attitude. This truth, however, escapes those whose existence is deeply rooted in an established theodicy or theological system. They do not realize that, for them, the affirmation of God practically comes down to the acceptance of a number of theses concerning God. The affirmation of a thesis stating that there is a God *seems* to affirm nothing else but God. For this reason one who has "established" himself in a system is unable to see that his affirmation may contain also the affirmation of a pseudo-god.

If we want to realize the truth of this assertion, we must be willing to place ourselves on the soil from which all *real* affirmations and confirmations spring; we must be ready to enter the realm of a *personal* confirmation of *reality*. Only then shall we realize that we are no longer able to use the simple little word "is" in the usual way, when there is question of "affirming" a transcendent God. We shall also simultaneously realize that he is an atheist who says *unqualifiedly* that God "is."

An important consequence of this realization is the insight that not all those who say that God "is not" are atheists. There is a "good" kind of atheism—the kind that discards pseudo-gods, gods about whom it is said *unqualifiedly* that they "are."

Should it surprise anyone, then, that "atheism is a fundamental human possibility"? Should one be surprised to hear that this potentiality is actualized—surreptitiously, of course—in the existence of those who call themselves theists and believers and are truly such? One who realizes that this possibility exists will no longer think of the voices of contemporary atheists as sounds coming from a distant world and from a strange era. The modern atheists appear to be very close to him, and their voices sound as coming from his own existence.

What we have briefly outlined here indicates the sphere in which we want to discuss atheism in the present work. Evidently, it is not our claim that there are no true atheists. We do not maintain that all "atheists" are merely intent on discarding pseudo-gods and are in reality theists who fail to understand themselves. But we agree with Jean Lacroix when he says that, whereas formerly it was the custom to emphasize the implicit faith of unbelievers, the time has come for pointing out the implicit unbelief of believers. Contemporary atheism can make an inestimable contribution to the task of unmasking this unbelief and purifying faith.

It is not our intention merely to present an accurate description of contemporary atheism. We shall also try to define our own position and adopt a personal attitude which contains a judgment of values. We wish to do this as philosophers and it would thus be impossible without a personal philosophical conviction. Our philosophical conviction is that of existential phenomenology,[1] and this conviction expresses itself in the title of this book.

It is our sincere hope that this book will not be read solely by professional philosophers and theologians. It is possible, however, that non-specialists might lose courage when reading the first chapter.

---

[1]See the author's book *Existential Phenomenology,* Pittsburgh, 4th impr., 1965. Tr.

We suggest that they omit it and begin reading with the second chapter. Our sole wish is that the present work may be beneficial to all who really want to think and reflect. Their valuable critique will be sincerely appreciated.

William A. Luijpen, O.S.A.

The American edition differs only slightly from the original Dutch text. A few passages have been modified somewhat, subtitles have been added to facilitate reading, and indexes of names and subject matter have been appended. Our thanks are due to the Reverend Walter van de Putte, C.S.Sp., for making the initial translation of this book from the Dutch, to the author who has personally read the finished product and suggested a few improvements, and to Reverend Michael A. Machado for reading the text and making a number of literary revisions.

Duquesne University

Henry J. Koren, C.S.Sp.

CHAPTER ONE

AGNOSTICISM AND THE EXISTENCE
OF GOD—KANT

It is almost a commonplace nowadays to maintain that Kant's agnosticism constitutes one of the most important foundation stones of present-day atheism. It is therefore absolutely necessary to know Kant's views if we wish to understand contemporary atheism.

However, one cannot simply say that Kant's agnosticism is the foundation of contemporary atheism. First of all, Kant himself was not an atheist; just the opposite is true. On the theoretical level, he was convinced, throughout his life, of the validity of Newton's physics as a science and, on the practical plane, he accepted the validity of the categorical imperative of ethics. This imperative, Kant held, implied God's existence as a postulate. Kant, then, was not an atheist.

Secondly, the interpretation of Kant's doctrine and especially his *Critique of Pure Reason* remains a matter of dispute. Is it right to call Kant an agnostic? His philosophical stature seems sufficiently large to lend itself to diverse interpretations. Every phase of the history of philosophy seems to yield its own particular interpretation of Kant.

For our purpose, however, it is sufficient to show that Kant actually has been interpreted in a way which provided one of the strongest foundations for modern atheism. It is this interpretation that we shall reproduce in relation to the theme of contemporary atheism. We ourselves disagree with this interpretation, but this point is provisionally unimportant. The criticism will come later.

1. HISTORICAL ANTECEDENTS OF THE KANTIAN PROBLEMATICS

Kant always believed that he had been successful in his search for a way out of the impasse into which philosophy had fallen as a result of the battle between rationalism and empiricism. This struggle is, in reality, as old as philosophy itself. Plato and Heraclitus were already powerful representatives of those two mutually antagonistic currents of thought. Fundamentally both currents result from diverse views

1

about the true nature of knowledge. Both also acknowledge the distinction between sense knowledge and intellectual knowledge, but they differ in their appreciation of these forms of knowledge.[1]

Rationalism

According to the rationalist, *true* knowledge consists in thinking by means of necessary and universal concepts. Realizing that the senses sometimes mislead us, the rationalist is prompted to distrust sense knowledge. If the senses *sometimes* deceive us, they are capable of *always* deceiving us. The rationalist attaches importance solely to thinking and its necessary and universal concepts. He dogmatically accepts that whatever reason can coherently conceive does also actually exist. Necessary and universal concepts have *ipso facto* ontological value. Consequently, when we start from an indubitable principle, we may feel sure that the results of all logical deductions will be in agreement with reality. The rationalist accepts dogmatically that the order of being is constructed according to the same laws as the order of knowledge. It stands to reason that, in this view of philosophy, mathematics has always been considered the model of thinking. Unsurprisingly, such a confidence in reason and its power of thinking led to a divinization of reason in pantheism.[2]

Descartes, Spinoza, Leibniz and Wolff were the principal representatives of the modern rationalistic tradition before the advent of Kant. Wolff deserves particular notice, not because he was the most brilliant of these thinkers, but because Kant was, at first, greatly influenced by him. According to Wolff, philosophy was the science of essences, conceived as possibilities. That is possible which can be thought without contradiction; hence, according to Wolff, this must also be accepted as reality. Using the rationalist's terminology, it can be said that, according to Wolff, the *rationes cognoscendi* are perfectly identical with the *rationes essendi*.[3]

According to Wolff, speculative philosophy, constructed in a geometrical manner, is divided into two sections: general and special metaphysics. Special metaphysics has three subdivisions: cosmology, which deals with the world; rational psychology which deals with

[1] F. Sassen, *Geschiedenis van de nieuwere wijsbegeerte tot Kant*, Nijmegen, 1946, pp. 131-134.
[2] F. J. Thonnard, *A Short History of Philosophy*, tr. by Edward A. Maziarz, New York, 1955, no. 355.
[3] H. J. De Vleeschauwer, *Immanuel Kant*, Antwerpen 1931, p. 59.

the soul; natural theology which treats of God. Kant would say later that this metaphysics does not deserve to be called a true science.

Empiricism

There is, of course, very little room for a genuine appreciation of sense experience in the view of rationalism. Most rationalists attached some value to sense experience, but it was concerned exclusively with practical value and not with truth value. For the rationalist, genuine knowledge consists in thinking by means of universal and necessary concepts.

Since, according to the rationalist, no truth value could be attributed to sense experience, he likewise found it impossible to accept that sense experience should be held to be a source of knowledge. He was thus forced to seek refuge in innatism, the doctrine of innate ideas.

It was at this point that empiricism rose in revolt.[4] The empiricist refused to accept any innate idea and claimed that, on the contrary, man's cognitive power is like a blank paper on which nothing has been written.[5] Hence it is necessary that something be written upon it from outside before this power can actually know anything. Now, according to empiricism, this "writing" is produced solely by means of sense experience.[6]

Knowledge as Mirroring

Primary and Secondary Sense Qualities. Thus far we have indicated only in what respect rationalism and empiricism differ from each other. Alongside these mutually exclusive views, however, they are in fundamental, though unexpressed, agreement regarding the definition of human knowledge. The distinction which Locke makes between the primary and secondary qualities of things will make it easier for us to explain more fully this fundamental definition of

---

[4]John Locke, *An Essay Concerning Human Understanding,* bk I, chaps. 2-4, in *The Philosophical Works of John Locke,* ed. by J. A. St. John, London, 1902, vol. 1, pp. 134 ff.

[5]"Let us then suppose the mind to be, as we say, white paper, void of all characters, without any ideas; how comes it to be furnished?" Locke, *Essay,* bk. II, ch. 1, no. 2, p. 204.

[6]"Whence has it all the materials of reason and knowledge? To this I answer in one word, From experience: in that all our knowledge is founded." Locke, *ibid.*

knowledge.[7] It is necessary to grasp that definition if we wish to understand Kant's thought.

Primary qualities are qualities which can be reached by several senses. For example, the shape of an apple can be grasped by the sense of sight and that of touch. Those qualities were called "common sensibles" by the Scholastics.

In contrast with them there are secondary qualities, called "proper sensibles" by the Scholastics, which are the proper objects of the various senses. The color of an apple is the proper object of sight, its smell is the object of the olfactory sense. Moreover, Locke distinguishes between "ideas in the mind" and "qualities in bodies." He calls "idea" that which consciousness becomes aware of in itself; and the idea is produced in consciousness by certain powers of things, so-called "qualities."[8] According to Locke, the "ideas" of the primary qualities are objective, whereas those of secondary qualities are subjective. For, water heated to a particular degree can produce the sensation of heat in one hand while being felt as cold by the other; but a particular shape never leads to the "idea" of square through one hand and to that of a circle through the other.[9]

Implications of the Distinction. This distinction seems, at first sight, to be rather innocuous. In reality this is not so. The differentiation between secondary qualities and primary qualities introduces an implicit theory about the nature of human knowledge. For as long as knowledge is conceived as a way of existing, hence as the immediate presence of a knowing subject to a present reality, it is impossible to maintain that the primary qualities are objective, but not the secondary ones. When a knowing subject is immediately present to an apple, both its shape and its smell and color are given as present realities, as objective. Nevertheless, Locke maintains that the shape is objective but that smell and color are not. What, then, does his viewpoint imply?

The implication is that knowledge is *not* conceived as the immediate presence of the knower to a present reality. It leaves hardly any other possibility in regard to the theory of human knowledge than to consider it as a purely passive re-flection or mirroring of a world that

---

[7]Locke, *Essay,* bk. II, ch. 8, nos. 9-10, *loc. cit.,* pp. 243 ff.

[8]"Whatsoever the mind perceives in itself, or is the immediate object of perception, thought, or understanding, that I call 'idea'; and the power to produce any idea in our mind I call 'quality' of the subject wherein that power is." Locke, *Essay* bk. II, ch. 8, no. 8, *loc. cit.* p. 243.

[9]Locke, *Essay,* bk. II, ch. 8, no. 21, *loc. cit.,* p. 249.

is detached from the knower. According to this view, the knowing subject is conceived not as an existence, but as a passive, worldless subject. And the world is conceived as a collection of "things in themselves," a "world in itself," as brute reality, i.e., as a world in which the knowing subject is not involved, in which he does not live and with which he has in principle no dealings. It is then possible to say that the primary qualities alone are objective, i.e., "accuracy" belongs exclusively to the re-flection or mirroring of quantitative aspects. It was thought impossible to have an accurate mirroring of the secondary qualities,[10] because the knower would spoil the mirror-like reflection by "subjective additions."[11]

Descartes and Locke. Descartes' methodic doubt had led to the same theory. By "putting in brackets," i.e., suspending judgment concerning everything that can be doubted, he isolated the knowing subject entirely from man's body and from the world. The *Cogito* is the only indubitable fact according to Descartes. By doubting the reality of the world, however, Descartes did not get rid of the human world, but merely reduced it to being the content of his *Cogito*. The human world, the world the knowing subject deals with and in which he lives, was qualified merely as a "thought-about" world.[12] For, even if the pen with which I write and the paper on which I write and the chair on which I sit and the room in which I live were not realities, it would still remain incontrovertible that, when I write with a pen on paper and sit on a chair in a room, I nevertheless have the pen-*idea*, the paper-*idea,* the chair-*idea* and the room-*idea*. It is impossible to doubt the *Cogito* and its contents.

But then the question naturally comes to mind whether the contents of the *Cogito* have any objectivity, any reality. To what extent does something correspond to the ideas contained in the *Cogito*?

---

[10]"What I have said concerning colours and smells may be understood also of tastes and sounds, and other like sensible qualities; which, whatever reality we by mistake attribute to them, are in truth nothing in the objects themselves, but powers to produce various sensations in us, and depend on those primary qualities, viz., bulk, figure, texture, and motion of parts, as I have said." Locke, *Essay,* bk. II, ch. 8, no. 14, *loc. cit.,* p. 246.

[11]"From whence I think it is easy to draw this observation, that ideas of primary qualities of bodies are resemblances of them, and their patterns do really exist in the bodies themselves; but the ideas produced in us by those secondary qualities have no resemblance of them at all. There is nothing like our ideas existing in the bodies themselves." Locke, *Essay,* bk. II, ch. 8, no. 15, *loc. cit.,* p. 246.

[12]Maurice Merleau-Ponty, *Phenomenology of Perception,* New York (The Humanities Press), 1962, Preface, p. ix.

Descartes, of course, felt unable to assert that nothing existed except the *Cogito* and its contents. It is evident, nevertheless, that in the Cartesian view the "objectivity," the "reality," to which some ideas correspond can no longer be conceived as a *human* world, for the human world is reduced to the content of the *Cogito*. When the knowing subject is totally divorced from the world, we must of necessity conceive the world as totally divorced from the knowing subject. The "objective" world is then conceived as a collection of "things in themselves," as a "world in itself," whose existence has to be proved. Moreover, Descartes maintained that there exists only one clear idea of the world, namely, the idea of "quantity"; therefore, according to him, the quantitative world alone is "objective."

There are, of course, differences between Descartes and Locke, but these philosophers fundamentally agree on the definition of human knowledge: knowledge re-flects, mirrors a subject-less world in a world-less subject. Physical science is the system of objective mirror-like reflections because it deals only with categories of quantity.[13]

The Scepticism of Hume

Knowledge is Knowledge of Impressions. The above-mentioned view of knowledge, which was generally accepted since Descartes and Locke, was responsible, it is commonly believed, for the philosophical scepticism of Hume. Being an empiricist, Hume always rejected innate ideas; all knowledge, according to him, is knowledge of sense experience.[14] As an empiricist, he likewise never accepted an active *Cogito*. For him, knowledge is purely passive, a mere receiving of "impressions," i.e., "messages," so to say, from a world in which the knower does not live.

From this standpoint, there is no hesitation about the answer to the question of *what* the knower knows. For Descartes the answer is that he knows thoughts, and for Hume that he knows "impressions." Both therefore agree that what is known is contents of consciousness.

---

[13]Later Husserl will call this view the "natural attitude," but not in the sense that it is the correct view of knowledge. What Husserl means is that this faulty view has become so common in Western thought that it may be called a "second nature."

[14]"And therefore we shall here content ourselves with establishing one general proposition. That all our simple ideas in their first appearance are deriv'd from simple impressions, which are correspondent to them, and which they exactly represent." David Hume, *A Treatise on Human Nature*, bk. I, part I, sect. 1; in L. A. Selby—Bigge ed., Oxford, 1951, p. 4.

Descartes' answer is dictated by his methodic doubt. For, when he is asked what the knower knows, he can reply only "what has not been put in brackets," is indubitable.

Hume's answer, as is true of all empiricists, is dictated by the fact that the world is conceived as separated from the knowing subject. For how could any one seriously maintain that the knower knows the things of the world *themselves* if he first posits the subject and the world as separated realities? Locke had already proclaimed that *what* the knower knows is the *ideas* themselves.[15] Consciousness is thought of as a kind of "cabinet" in which the contents of consciousness are stored.[16] The "cabinet" itself is totally separated from the world from which "messages" are received. Taking over this view, Hume could hardly avoid the idea that those "messages" from the world in which the knower does *not* live, constitute the object of knowledge. What the knower knows is phenomena, subjective impressions within his own inner sanctum.[17]

There had been philosophers before Hume who tried to reach that which lies beyond the phenomenon by means of the principle of causality. Hume brands such an attempt as philosophical nonsense.[18] For the idea of causality is merely the result of the experience that impressions follow one another in regular succession, which experience leads to the subjective expectation that one kind of impression will be followed by another. Examine things carefully, Hume suggests, and you will realize that a sense experience yields nothing more than the impression that the movement of a billiard ball *B* takes place *after* the collision of a billiard ball *A*

---

[15]"Every man being conscious to himself, that he thinks, and that which his mind is applied about, whilst thinking, being the ideas that are there, it is past doubt that men have in their mind several ideas, such as are those expressed by the words, 'whiteness, hardness, sweetness, thinking, motion, man, elephant, army, drunkenness', and others." Locke, *Essay,* bk. I, no. 1, *loc. cit.,* p. 205.

[16]"The senses at first let in particular ideas, and furnish the yet empty cabinet: and the mind by degrees growing familiar with some of them, they are lodged in the memory, and names got to them." Locke, *Essay,* bk. I, ch. 2, no. 15, *loc. cit.,* p. 142.

[17]"Only, in characterizing Hume's doctrine, it must not be forgotten that this absolutely certain matter-of-fact quality, which belongs to impressions, is solely that of their presence as mental states. In this meaning and restriction, intuitive knowledge embraces not only the facts of inner experience, but also those of outer experience, but at the price of recognising that the latter are properly only species of the former,—a knowledge, that is, of mental states." Wilhelm Windelband, *A History of Philosophy,* vol. II, Part V, Ch. I, par. 34, Harper Torch books, New York, 1958, p. 472.

[18]"All our knowledge is limited to the ascertaining and verifying of impressions, and to the relations of these mental states to each other." Windelband, *loc. cit.,* p. 473.

with billiard ball *B*. If this experience is repeated, there results a subjective expectation that it will always happen in the same way. And there comes finally the thought that the movement of the billiard ball *B* has in reality been *produced* by billiard ball *A*. But the attempt to confirm the *existence* of a cause and its operation *in reality* transgresses the possibilities of any genuine and responsible confirmation, for responsible confirmation is exclusively concerned with subjective impressions.[19] Any attempt to confirm and justify that claims to transcend subjective impressions is an expression of a "faith" which can be useful for daily life[20] but is unable to stand the light of a critical examination. A critical attitude must necessarily end in radical phenomenalism.[21]

Hume's own contemporaries did not hesitate to call his phenomenalism a radical brand of scepticism,[22] for there remains no possibility whatsoever to know "reality."

Hume's Scepticism and the Mirror Theory of Knowledge. We cannot refrain from remarking that Hume's scepticism is the inevitable and logical consequence of every theory that makes knowledge consist of a mirror-like reflection and refuses to conceive it as the immediate presence of the knowing subject to a present real world. In such a theory the "real" world functions as a world-without-a-subject. It is a world of which no subject is aware, about which no subject actually speaks, with which no subject really has dealings, in which no subject really lives and which no subject really affirms. Such a world, of course, can never be affirmed. Hume concludes from it that we never affirm anything except our impressions.[24]

There were philosophers before Hume who conceived the world as an "inhuman" or subject-less world, and nonetheless affirmed its "existence." Hume is right when he thinks that a justified and real affirmation of an unaffirmed world is an impossibility. The surprising point is that philosophy had to wait until Hume before it sank

---

19Wilhelm Windelband, *loc. cit.,* p. 476.
20D. Hume, *op. cit.,* bk. I, part IV, sect. VII, pp. 268 f.
21"With this, all theory, all examination of cause, all doctrine of the 'true being' behind 'phenomena' is excluded." Windelband, *loc. cit.,* p. 476.
22Wilhelm Windelband, *loc. cit.,* pp. 476 f.
24"The idea of existence, then, is the very same with the idea of what we conceive to be existent. To reflect on any thing simply, and to reflect on it as existent, are nothing different from each other. . . . Now since nothing is ever present to the mind but its perceptions and since all ideas are derived from something antecedently present to the mind; it follows, that 'tis impossible so much as to conceive or form an idea of any thing specifically different from ideas and impressions." Hume, *op. cit.,* bk. I, part II, sect. VI, pp. 66 f.

into this so-called scepticism. Hume is right also when he thinks it impossible to save the reality of the world by means of the principle of causality. For, if "to exist in reality" is declared to have no other meaning than "to exist in a world that is not affirmed," there remains no possibility to affirm that causal operations "are" in "reality."

Hume was the first philosopher who actually drew the ultimate consequences of the empiricist mirror theory of knowledge. The same cannot be said of Locke. The latter conceives the world of things as separate from the knowing subject, but he nevertheless calls the *ideas* of primary qualities objective. The *ideas* themselves are the objects of knowledge, and yet Locke thinks that it lies in his power to affirm that some ideas manifest themselves as "resemblances" of the things themselves. But according to Locke's theory things "themselves" are unaffirmed, unknown things. The things that are affirmed and known are the *ideas*. Locke does not realize that, when he proclaims the ideas of primary qualities to be accurate mirrorings, he presupposes that he is able to compare the *ideas,* i.e., the affirmed and known things, with the *bodies themselves,* i.e., with things that are not affirmed and not known. But such a comparison is evidently impossible, and hence the distinction between the *ideas* of primary and of secondary qualities is without foundation.[25] The subject cannot "see" whether or not the *ideas* mirror the unknown qualities of the *bodies themselves.*

No such ambiguities can be found in Hume, In his opinion, justified affirmations are concerned exclusively with subjective impressions on consciousness. For him, "existing reality," that is, the "unaffirmed and unknown world," is unattainable. The so-called scepticism of Hume is a very intelligent sort of scepticism.

Hume and Kant

Hume's teaching made an immense impression on Kant. Kant had grown up in the dogmatic rationalism of Wolff, although he had never let himself become entirely enslaved by it.[26] For example,

---

[25] "I assert, that instead of explaining the operations of external objects by its means, we utterly annihilate all these objects, and reduce ourselves to the opinions of the most extravagant scepticism concerning them. If colours, sounds, tastes, and smells be merely perceptions, nothing we can conceive is possest of a real, continu'd, and independent existence; not even motion extension and solidity, which are the primary qualities chiefly insisted on." D. Hume, *op. cit.,* bk. I, part IV, sect. IV, pp. 227 f.
[26] H. J. De Vleeschauwer, *Immanuel Kant,* Antwerpen-Nijmegen 1931, p. 88.

he had always rejected the ontological proof of God that was commonly used by rationalism. Neither was he convinced that the concepts of space proposed by Leibniz and Wolff were correct. According to these two philosophers, space is a pure idea, it is simply that which we feel forced to conceive as a condition for being able to think of the material monads as a whole. Kant found a different concept of space in Newton. The latter conceived space as the "real," though empty surroundings within which the power of attraction between things develops and within which things exercise a "real" influence upon one another.[27] Kant preferred Newton's concept to that of Leibniz and Wolff.

It took Kant some time to free himself from dogmatizing rationalism. He finally realized that necessity-of-thought cannot be simply identified with reality, and that the conceptual operations of logic tell us nothing about reality. In his view metaphysicians are builders of thought-worlds that have no connection with reality.[28] Kant was thus led to seek the connection with reality in the concepts of empiricism that are born from experience, instead of looking for this connection in the innate ideas of rationalism. In this way he replaced one form of dogmatism by another. According to his own testimony,[29] however, it was the scepticism of Hume that aroused him from the slumber of empirical dogmatism.[30] But if, as Hume claims, the concept of causality has no objective validity and is nothing more than a subjective expectation aroused by the mechanism of association, it follows that, likewise, the concepts which, according to empiricism, are given us by experience, do not provide any possibility of knowing reality.

At any rate, the reading of Hume convinced Kant that, if Hume's concept of human knowledge was true, it would inevitably preclude the possibility of any kind of *scientific* thinking. If man is incapable of knowing anything besides changeable and concrete "impressions," then there is no room for the necessary and universal judgments of

---

27F. J. Thonnard, *A Short History of Philosophy*, no. 369.

28Windelband, *op. cit.*, vol. 1, p. 537.

29"I freely admit: it was David Hume's remark that first, many years ago, interrupted my dogmatic slumber and gave a completely different direction to my enquiries in the field of speculative philosophy." Kant, *Prolegomena to Any Future Metaphysics*, ed. by Peter G. Lucas, Manchester University Press, 1953, p. 9.

30It is for the most part disregarded that [Kant] characterized as dogmatic not only rationalism, but also the empiricism of the earlier theory of knowledge. . . . The dogmatism from which . . . Kant declared that he had been freed through Hume *was that of empiricism*." Windelband, *op. cit.*, p. 537, footnote 4.

science. For such judgments imply more in the process of knowledge than Hume is willing to admit when he reduces the whole of knowledge to the registration of changeable and concrete "impressions." Kant, however, felt sure that the fact that physical science exists could not be denied, for Newton's physics did exist. Hence to speak about human knowledge in a way that makes physics as a science *impossible* was nonsense. Kant was absolutely convinced that Newton's physics was valid.[31]

But the situation was quite different with respect to metaphysics. It was certain that the latter had not yet found the sure road to science.[32] And if metaphysics is to find that way, he argued, it is necessary to begin with an examination of the necessary conditions required to make human knowledge in general possible. This task cannot be impossible, for *de facto* mathematics and physics do exist as sciences. It was this examination that Kant undertook in his *Critique of Pure Reason.*

2. KANT'S CRITIQUE OF PURE REASON

Kant's purpose in this capital work consisted in providing a doctrine of transcendental method. This doctrine is not metaphysics itself but a preparation for metaphysics; it examines the prerequisite possibilities of all knowledge and thus also of metaphysical knowledge.[33] Herein lies the meaning of the qualification which he calls "transcendental." Kant calls transcendental the knowledge that is not concerned with objects but with the way we know objects. If we know objects in one way or in another, this fact implies surely that knowledge is *a priori* possible.[34] What must we accept *a priori* in order that knowledge at least *can* be what it actually is?

Kant's method is characterized as "transcendental" in contrast to the psychological method of Locke. The latter thought that he could solve the problem of knowledge by a psychological analysis of knowledge and an explanation of its genesis.[35] Kant starts from knowledge as it exists and the object of knowledge as it exists and tries to

---

[31]H. J. De Vleeschauwer, *op. cit.,* p. 61.

[32]Kant, *Critique of Pure Reason,* ed. by Norman Kemp Smith, New York, 1950, p. 21.

[33]*Op. cit.,* p. 9.

[34]"I entitle *transcendental* all knowledge which is occupied not so much with objects as with the mode of our knowledge of objects insofar as this mode of knowledge is to be possible *a priori.*" *Op. cit.,* p. 59.

[35]Locke, *An Essay Concerning Human Understanding,* Introduction, *loc. cit.,* Vol. I, pp. 128 ff.

examine the conditions for this possibility, in order to determine whether, and in what sense, metaphysical thinking is possible.

Synthetic a Priori Judgments

Kant formulated the task he set himself as the question concerning the possibility of synthetic *a priori* judgments.[36] For, according to him, these are the kind of judgments that are used by the sciences, namely, mathematics, physics and metaphysics.

Kant makes a distinction between analytic and synthetic judgments. Those judgments are analytic that yield the predicate by a mere analysis of the subject of the judgment, because the concept of the predicate is implicitly contained in the concept of the subject. Thus the judgment, "all bodies have extension," is analytic because the concept of body includes the concept of extension. Analytic judgments do not increase our knowledge; they are, strictly speaking, tautological. The predicate merely clarifies the subject.[37]

Synthetic judgments, on the other hand, add to our knowledge. In a synthetic judgment the predicate adds something to the subject, and the predicated concept is not contained in the concept of the subject. The judgment, "all bodies are heavy," is a synthetic judgment, for the analysis of the concept of "body" does not yield the concept "heavy."

Next, Kant makes a distinction between *a priori* and *a posteriori* knowledge. Purely *a priori* knowledge is *totally* independent of experience. When it is stated that he who undermines the foundations of his house knows *a priori* that it will collapse, we are not permitted to call that knowledge purely *a priori*. True, such an individual does not have to wait for the experience of the actual collapse of his house to know that such a thing will happen. Nevertheless, he knows from experience that an unsupported object falls or collapses.[38] Purely *a priori* knowledge, on the contrary, is totally independent of experience. It follows therefore that knowledge which is

---

[36]It is striking that for Kant knowledge is identical with what can be expressed in the form of a judgment. Husserl's phenomenology will delve much more deeply. Husserl launched his phenomenology precisely for the purpose of finding a foundation for knowledge expressed in the form of a judgment since a judgment, as such, does not have a ground in itself. Kant's argument in favor of the judgment is based on his conception of the "place of truth." Truth, he held, lies in the judgment. While phenomenology does not deny this point, it stresses that such an assertion can be made only if one admits a more profound idea of truth—namely, that truth is "unconcealedness."

[37]*Critique of Pure Reason*, p. 48.

[38]*Op. cit.*, pp. 41 f.

totally independent of all the contingencies of experience will have a *necessary* and *universal* value. Its opposite is *a posteriori* knowledge, which depends on experience and hence is never *necessarily* and *universally* valid.

Many synthetic judgments are evidently *a posteriori* judgments. They are judgments in which a contingent connection is established between the subject and the predicate. When I say, e.g., that Descartes was a philosopher, I am stating a synthetic *a posteriori* judgment, for my judgment can only be based upon experience and consequently the connection between subject and predicate is contingent. Descartes was not necessarily a philosopher.

But there are also synthetic *a priori* judgments. Though presupposing experience, such judgments transcend experience because they include and express necessity and universality. The judgment, "whatever happens has a cause" is evidently synthetic, for the analysis of the concept "to happen" does not include the concept "to have a cause." This judgment, then, is synthetic and it is possible only on the basis of experience. Nevertheless, this judgment expresses that the predicate universally and necessarily belongs to the subject. Hence it contains an *a priori* element of knowledge, for the contingent character of experience cannot yield a basis for universality and necessity. Accordingly, although that judgment presupposes experience, it nonetheless transcends experience.[39]

The Sciences

According to Kant, synthetic *a priori* judgments are used in all theoretical sciences.[40] The contrary would be unthinkable. For analytic judgments merely clarify the concept of the subject of the judgment, that is, they are really tautologies; hence such judgments do not broaden or enrich our knowledge. But scientific judgments are enriching. It follows, then, that they are synthetic. They are, moreover, characterized by necessity and universality. The connection between subject and predicate in scientific judgments is not contingent. Being synthetic they presuppose experience, but being also universal and necessary they transcend experience and are on that account *a priori* and not *a posteriori*.

Kant mentions mathematics, physics and metaphysics as the theoretical sciences that make use of the synthetic *a priori* judgments.

---

[39]*Op. cit.* pp. 48 ff.
[40]*Op. cit.,* pp. 52 ff.

The mathematical judgment, "7 + 5 = 12," is synthetic *a priori* because, according to Kant, the concept 12 is not discovered by the analysis of "7 + 5." The concept "7 + 5" contains only the "union of two numbers into one number," and no amount of analysis will yield the concept "12."[41] In order to find this concept, it is necessary to make this relation of numbers perceptible, for example, by using one's fingers or looking at so many dots; in other words the judgment is synthetic.[42] But it is also *a priori* since it is universally and necessarily valid. Similarly the judment, "a straight line is the shortest connection between two points," is synthetic *a priori*.[43]

In physics, the judgment, "the quantity of matter remains the same amidst all the changes that take place in the physical world," is synthetic *a priori*.

With respect to metaphysics, it should be possible to state likewise that it makes use of synthetic *a priori* judgments. It cannot press its claim to be a science if it consists merely of an analysis of *a priori* concepts, for in such a case it does not give new knowledge. Metaphysics can only be accepted as a science if, starting from experience, it transcends experience, that is, if it makes use of synthetic *a priori* judgments. The judgment, "the world must have had a beginning," should be capable of being accepted as a synthetic *a priori* judgment. At least, it is the *intention* of metaphysics to pronounce synthetic *a priori* judgments.[44]

Doubts About the Possibility of Metaphysics

The history of metaphysics reveals that it has periods of bloom and decay. The reason for this is, according to Kant, that philosophers have never recognized the necessity first to elaborate a doctrine of transcendental method. And yet the need for it is evident.[45] For, if mathematics and physics are rightly called successful sciences, whereas metaphysics is thus far unsuccessful, the reason must be found in the fact that man, in his mathematical and physical studies, took care to fulfill the conditions on which the possibility of such knowledge is based but neglected to do the same with respect to metaphysical thinking.

41*Op. cit.*, p. 52.
42*Op. cit.*, p. 53.
43*Op. cit.*, pp. 53 f.
44*Op. cit.*, p. 55.
45*Op. cit.*, pp. 55 f.

Hence, according to Kant, the problem of metaphysics cannot be solved unless, as a prerequisite to metaphysical thinking, man first attempts to solve this problem: What conditions must be fulfilled in order that scientific knowledge in general *can* be what it is, or, which comes to the same thing, in order that the object of science *be able* to appear as it does? Now, to ask "What are the conditions which make science in general possible?" is identical with asking "What conditions make synthetic *a priori* judgments possible?" For these judgments are the elements that constitute the sciences. According to Kant, there is no danger that an investigation concerning the possibility of synthetic *a priori* judgments in the fields of mathematics and physics may end in the negative, for these sciences are actually given; they really exist.[46] But when we recall the failure of metaphysics, there are reasons for doubting its possibility.[47]

Some Necessary Distinctions

It is not possible to show that there are synthetic *a priori* judgments unless the critique, on the one hand, establishes that the process of knowledge contains elements gathered from experience and, on the other, manages to discern in it elements transcending experience, so that the judgment can become universal and necessary. If a judgment contains no elements from experience, it is purely tautological. If it lacks *a priori* elements of knowledge, it cannot have universal and necessary validity, hence it cannot be called scientific.

From the very beginning of his Introduction Kant feels certain that all human knowledge begins with experience.[48] For our cognitive power would not be aroused to exercise its activity if objects did not stimulate our senses and did not put our mind in motion.[49]

This, however, says Kant, does not mean that all knowledge arises out of experience. There is a possibility that our knowledge might be a synthesis, namely, the synthesis of sense impressions to which are "added" elements supplied by the cognitive power. Perhaps we are not immediately able clearly to distinguish those "addi-

---

[46]*Op. cit.*, p. 56.

[47]"But the poor progress which has hitherto been made in metaphysics, and the fact that no system yet propounded can, in view of the essential purpose of metaphysics, be said really to exist, leaves everyone sufficient ground for doubting as to its possibility." *Op. cit.*, p. 56.

[48]"There can be no doubt that all our knowledge begins with experience." *Op. cit.*, p. 41.

[49]*Ibid.*

tions" from the "raw material." Much practice may be needed to distinguish the one from the other.[50] The body of Kant's work is devoted to substantiating this surmise.

The task of doing this is complex, for it is necessary to distinguish and examine several levels of knowledge. There are two branches of knowledge, namely, sensibility and understanding. By means of sensibility objects are "given" to us. By understanding we "think" them.[51] In his *Transcendental Aesthetic,* Kant tries to isolate the *a priori* forms of sensibility, that is, the forms that constitute the conditions under which objects are given to us. In his *Transcendental Logic,* he deals with the *a priori* forms of understanding, that is, the forms by means of which we "think the object."[52]

Space and Time as a Priori Forms of Sensibility

Whatever may be the manner in which the cognitive act is related to objects, it is undeniable that intuition (*Anschauung*) is that through which there is an *immediate* relation between the knower and the objects. Objects are "given" to us in the act of sense cognition. But this reception is possible only when objects "affect," "excite" our mind (*Gemut*). We speak of sensibility (*Sinnlichkeit*) to indicate the receptivity of the knowing subject for the influence of the objects. When an object affects us in this way we have a "sensation" (*Empfindung*). An intuition is said to be "empirical" when it is related to an object by means of sensation. The undetermined object of an empirical intuition is called "appearance" (*Erscheinung*). By the "matter" of sensation Kant means that element in the appearance which sensation offers to sensibility.[53] This "matter" is given to us *a posteriori.*

It is undeniably true that we represent to ourselves objects as ordered in space, and inner states of our mind as ordered in time.

---

[50] "But though all our knowledge begins with experience, it does not follow that it all arises out of experience. For it may well be that even our empirical knowledge is made up of what we receive through impressions and of what our own faculty of knowledge (sensible impressions merely serving as the occasion) supplies from itself. If our faculty of knowledge makes any such addition, it may be that we are not in a position to distinguish it from the raw material, until with long practice of attention we have become skilled in separating it." *Op. cit.,* pp. 41 f.

[51] "By way of introduction or anticipation we need only say that there are two stems of human knowledge, namely, *sensibility* and *understanding,* which perhaps spring from a common, but to us unknown, root. Through the former, objects are given to us; through the latter, they are thought." *Op. cit.,* p. 61 f.

[52] *Op. cit.,* p. 62.

[53] *Op. cit.,* pp. 65 f.

We represent the objects to ourselves as being outside of us, as placed in space, as having a determined shape and size, and as having determined relations to one another.[54] We represent to ourselves the states of our mind as occurring in succession, as preceding and following, that is, as ordered in time. Hence space and time are "forms," or principles, that give order to our sensibility. The question, then, is whether these forms or principles are given *a posteriori*, just as the matter of sense knowledge is given *a posteriori*.

Kant's reply is a categorical denial.[55] We shall confine ourselves to Kant's remarks concerning space, for they give a more complete expression of his thought, and what he says about space is fundamentally applicable to time.

Unlike the "matter" of sense knowledge, space as a principle of order cannot itself be the result of external experience. For, to be able to refer particular sensations to something outside me (that is, something in another part of space than that occupied by myself) and to be able to represent to myself objects as being outside and alongside one another, i.e., as occupying diverse places, I must necessarily have at my disposal the representation of space. For, this representation is a necessary prerequisite for the appearance of the objects in space.[56] That in which the sensations are arranged in orderly fashion and which is a prerequisite of these sensations cannot itself be the result of a sensation.[57]

Empiricist Background of Kant's a Priori Forms of Intuition

If we wish to understand Kant's argument and his claim that the forms or principles that impart order to intuition are not the product of sensation or the result of external experience, we must keep in mind the empiricist theory of sense experience known by Kant. For, he put forward his *a priori* forms of intuition for the purpose of overcoming empiricism, and the empiricist doctrine of knowledge certainly presents enormous difficulties if one wants to hold that the representations of space and time are *a posteriori*.[58]

---

[54]*Op. cit.*, p. 67.

[55]"That in which alone the sensations can be posited and ordered in a certain form, cannot itself be sensation; and therefore, while the matter of all appearance is given to us *a posteriori* only, its form must lie ready for the sensations *a priori* in the mind, and so must allow of being considered apart from all sensation." *Op. cit.*, p. 66.

[56]*Op. cit.*, p. 68.

[57]*Op. cit.*, p. 66.

[58]We make use here of A. J. De Sopper's excellent work, *Wat is philosophie?*, Haarlem, 1950, pp. 42-50.

Sense-knowledge, according to empiricism, is the purely passive reproduction, in a kind of conscious mirror, of objects that are separate from the knower. One who accepts this view and nothing else, is unable to account for the representation of time, that is, of the pattern "earlier—later," or "before—after." To clarify the point, let us suppose that three successive light signals coming from the external world are received by the conscious mirror. If we suppose that the mirror reflects the external world in a purely passive way, it is impossible to account for the fact that the second light signal is experienced as following the first, and the third as following the second. For the first signal no longer exists when the second light signal arrives and, since sense knowledge is supposed to be a passive reflection, we are forced to say that nothing of the first light signal remains in the conscious mirror after the light has disappeared. But if nothing of the first signal remains in the mirror, how can we say that we experience the second signal as coming *after* the first? The first is simply *nothing* when the second signal is received. If we adopt the empiricist concept of sense experience, "after the first signal" simply means "after nothing," and this is not really "after."[59]

Almost the same remarks apply to the representation of space, i.e., of the pattern "alongside—outside." If sense experience is merely a passive mirroring, three dots alongside and outside one another cannot be experienced as such. The passive reflection of three dots alongside and outside one another yields nothing more than the impression of "a dot," "a dot," "a dot." The realization that they are alongside and outside one another requires more than passive mirroring; it requires that those three dots are *brought* into relation with one another. This is more than passivity, just as relating one light signal to others by retaining the first implies more than passivity.[60]

Kant had the empiricist theory of knowledge in mind when he maintained that the forms of space and time are not themselves the result of sense experience and therefore not *a posteriori* representations. But he presented also positive arguments to prove that they are *a priori* forms. For example, if we take away from a body everything that our intellect thinks about it, such as substance, energy, and divisibility, as well as everything that belongs to the sensation, such as impenetrability, hardness, and color, there still remains something

---

[59] De Sopper, *op. cit.*, pp. 44-45.
[60] De Sopper, *op. cit.*, pp. 46-47.

of this empirical intuition—namely, extension and shape, i.e., "spatiality."[61] The same can be said about time. Space and time, then, are *a priori* forms of intuition. There are, therefore, also non-empirical, pure intuitions, in which there is nothing that belongs to sensation.[62]

We conclude with Kant that empirical intuition is a synthesis of the *a posteriori* matter of sensations and the *a priori* forms of intuition. The *a priori* ordering principles of space and time are impressed on the matter of the sensation, so that the objects of sense knowledge are perceived as ordered in space and time.

Vindication of the Possibility of Mathematics

It is easy to explain the possibility of mathematics when we admit the validity of the *a priori* forms of intuition. Mathematics is the science which determines the properties of space in synthetic *a priori* judgments.[63] These properties cannot be explained through a mere analysis of concepts. From concepts of line and triangle one cannot deduce that the two sides of a triangle together are longer than the third side.[64] Mathematical judgments therefore are synthetic. On the other hand, mathematical judgments are necessary and universal. Because necessity and universality cannot be produced by the contingent and concrete data of experience, they point to an *a priori* element in the mathematical judgment.

This *a priori* element is the ordering principle of space. Being *a priori,* it creates order of necessity and therefore affects *all* experiences. In this way it gives rise to the necessity and universality that are expressed in the mathematical judgment.[65] A great light dawned upon the first man who constructed an isosceles triangle and realized that his determination of its properties did not express what he saw in that figure but what he himself had *put* into it.[66] Only when this point was understood, was mathematics able to walk on the royal road of science.

---

[61] Kant, *op. cit.,* p. 66.

[62] "These belong to pure intuition, which, even without any actual object of the senses or of sensation, exists in the mind as a mere form of sensibility." *Op. cit.,* p. 66.

[63] *Op. cit.,* p. 70.

[64] *Op. cit.,* p 69

[65] "Our explanation is thus the only explanation that makes intelligible the *possibility* of geometry, as a body of *a priori* synthetic knowledge". *Op. cit.,* p. 71.

[66] *Op. cit.,* p. 19.

Kant's "Copernican Revolution"

A revolution which Kant himself called "Copernican," manifests itself in the theory of knowledge when we study his conception of the *a priori* forms of intuition. Copernicus realized that he was not making any progress in his attempt to explain the movement of the heavenly bodies as long as he began with the hypothesis that the stars were moving around the observer. He then investigated whether he could not be more successful if he supposed that the stars stood still whereas the spectator moved around them.[67]

We find something similar in Kant's theory of knowledge. He is unable to see how he can account for the necessity and universality contained in mathematical judgments if he has to suppose that knowledge conforms to objects. For the action of objects on the knower can only yield a chaos of contingent and concrete impressions. Would it not be better to suppose that the objects conform to the rules of knowledge? If we admit that the objects conform to the forms of intuition, the necessity and universality of mathematical judgments are no longer problems.[68] For, in that case, the necessary and universal forms of intuition imprint themselves on the matter of the sensations, ordering them in space and time. Accordingly, the determination of the properties of space is but the expression of what the knower has previously put in the figures.

Objective Value of the a Priori Forms of Intuition and the Existence of the "Thing in Itself"

All this shows clearly that space, according to Kant, should not be conceived as a property of things in themselves. It would be a mistake to imagine that space belongs to things in themselves and remains when we abstract from the *a priori* forms of intuition.[69] And the same must be said about time.[70]

Space and time are impressed upon things to the extent that they appear; hence they have objective value only for objects of sensi-

---

[67] *Op. cit.,* p. 22.

[68] "If intuition must conform to the constitution of objects, I do not see how we could know anything of the latter *a priori;* but if the object (as object of the senses) must conform to the constitution of our faculty of intuition, I have no difficulty in conceiving such a possibility." *Op. cit.,* p. 22.

[69] "Space does not represent any property of things in themselves, nor does it represent them in their relation to one another. That is to say, space does not represent any determination that attaches to the objects themselves, and which remains even when abstraction is made of all subjective conditions of intuition." *Op. cit.,* p. 71.

[70] *Op. cit.,* p. 65.

bility.[71] The proposition, "All things are side by side in space," is valid only in the sense that "All things, as outer appearances, are side by side in space."[72] Kant, then, teaches the *reality* or objective value of space and time only with regard to appearances; but he upholds their *ideality* in respect of things in themselves.[73] The thing in itself, therefore, is never known and cannot be known; and no question about it ever comes up in experience.[74]

One may justly ask what can be the sense of affirming the thing in itself when at the same time it is said that this thing is unknowable. This question was voiced even by Kant's contemporaries and he took account of it in the second edition of his work; moreover, he added to it an extensive refutation of idealism.[75]

Even in the first edition Kant clearly indicated that his statement "Things in themselves are unknowable and *a priori* forms of intuition have objective value only for the appearances" does not imply that the knower has an illusion, that is, that he knows things only as they "seem" to be.[76] Things do not *seem* to be outside me, but they *appear* as outside me. Of things that do *not* appear I am unable to say that in themselves they are outside me.[77]

Intuition and Thought

These remarks do not express all the conditions required to explain fully the possibility of knowledge. They do not mention all the conditions that are required by the appearance of the object of knowledge.

Let us recall once more that, when Kant speaks of knowledge, he has in mind our "knowledge of physical science." We then realize that by referring to sensations and to *a priori* forms of intuition one does not yet explain the possibility of physical science as a science or the appearance of the cognitive object of physical science. We have merely explained what Kant thinks about intuition by means of which objects are *given*. Our knowledge, however, arises from two

---

[71]*Op. cit.*, p. 72.
[72]*Ibid.*
[73]*Ibid.*
[74]*Op. cit.*, p. 74.
[75]*Op. cit.*, pp. 244-256.
[76]*Op. cit.*, pp. 88 f.
[77]"Thus when I maintain that the quality of space and of time, in conformity with which as a condition of their existence, I posit both bodies and my own soul, lies in my mode of intuition and not in those objects themselves, I am not saying that bodies merely *seem* to be outside me, or that my soul only *seems* to be given in my self-consciousness." *Op. cit.*, pp. 88 f.

sources; receptivity for impressions and spontaneity in the production of concepts.[78] Through the second the object is *thought*.[79]

The nature spoken of by the physical sciences is not a mere conglomeration of data that are arranged in space and time, but an interconnected whole man *thinks* by means of concepts. Physical science presupposes a number of general propositions regarding this interconnection of the things of nature, such as "Whatever happens has a cause." The question therefore is: how are such synthetic *a priori* judgments possible?

A Priori Forms of Thinking. Wholly in line with his "Transcendental Aesthetic," Kant believes he can solve this problem by accepting *a priori* forms of understanding. These forms are impressed on the manifold data of intuition and these manifold data are then reduced to a unity. The intellect imposes laws upon nature by means of *a priori* forms.[80] We must disregard the possibility that the opposite might occur and that nature might impose laws upon the understanding. Necessary and universal knowledge cannot possibly come from experience, as the latter was understood by empiricism, for experience yields only the contingent and the concrete. The necessary and universal judgments of physical science are possible only through the *a priori* character of the forms.[81]

The sensible aspect of our human knowledge is distinguished from thought by its receptivity. The understanding, on the contrary, is marked by spontaneity. But we must keep in mind that both elements *together* yield human knowledge as it presents itself to us. If there is no receptivity of the sensitivity, no objects of knowledge are given, so that the concepts are "empty," i.e., they do not refer to anything. If there are no concepts, the intuitions are blind,[82] that is, they have no intelligible object. Hence concepts must receive their object from intuition and the data of intuition must be brought

---

[78]*Op. cit.*, p. 92.

[79]"The faculty . . . which enables us to *think* the object of sensible intuition is the understanding." *Op. cit.*, p. 93.

[80]"Categories are concepts which prescribe laws *a priori* to appearances and therefore to nature, the sum of all appearances." *Op. cit.*, p. 172.

[81]"Now this *empirical* derivation, in which both philosophers [Locke and Hume] agree, cannot be reconciled with the scientific *a priori* knowledge which we actually do possess, namely, *pure mathematics* and *general science of nature;* and this fact suffices to disprove such derivation." *Op. cit.*, p. 128.

[82]"Thoughts without content are empty, intuitions without concepts are blind." *Op. cit.*, p. 93.

under concepts.[83] Intuition and concept together constitute the elements of our knowledge so that neither concepts without intuition nor intuition without concepts can yield knowledge.[84]

It follows that we must not confuse the contribution of intuition to knowledge with that of the concepts. We saw how Kant conceives intuition by following his explanations in the *Transcendental Aesthetic.* The science of the *a priori* forms of the intellect he calls *Transcendental Logic.*[85] The latter he divides into *Transcendental Analytic,* which considers the elements of pure understanding, i.e., concepts and fundamental principles,[86] and *Transcendental Dialectic,* which serves as a means to prevent the elements of pure knowledge of the understanding from being used beyond the realm in which they are objectively valid.[87]

The Categories as a Priori Forms of the Understanding

In his *Transcendental Analytic,* Kant intends primarily to trace the elementary, non-derived, non-composed concepts back to their very roots in the human understanding.[88] It is not permissible to proceed here in a discretionary way or to rely on chance.[89] Kant thinks he can avoid such a faulty procedure.

The understanding can make use of its concepts only when it makes judgments; it is the faculty of judgment.[90] Kant found in formal logic a classical division of judgments according to quantity, quality, relation and modality which give a total of twelve kinds of judgments. Adopting this division, Kant thinks that it is possible to distinguish twelve corresponding elementary concepts by means of which the objects given by intuition are unified and are thought. These concepts he calls "categories."[91]

---

[83]"It is, therefore, just as necessary to make our concept sensible, that is, to add the object to them in intuition, as to make our intuitions intelligible, that is to bring them under concepts." *Ibid.*

[84]"Intuitions and concepts constitute, therefore, the elements of all our knowledge, so that neither concepts without an intuition in some way corresponding to them, or an intuition without concepts, can yield knowledge." *Op. cit.,* p. 92.

[85]*Ibid.*

[86]*Op. cit.,* p. 100.

[87]*Op. cit.,* pp. 100 f.

[88]*Op. cit.,* p. 103.

[89]*Op. cit.,* p. 104.

[90]"Now we can reduce all acts of understanding to judgments, and the *understanding* may therefore be represented as a *faculty of judgment.*" *Op. cit.,* p. 106.

[91]*Op. cit.,* p. 113.

Kant goes to much trouble to present the categories as a coherent and necessary whole, as a division that has the force of law. He calls these concepts "subsistence," "causality," "unity," "plurality," and so forth. It is not necessary to mention the entire list, for there is no one nowadays who still believes that Kant was successful in his attempt.

Neither shall we try to explain Kant's complementary theory regarding the necessity of schemata for the imagination. He formulates this theory because he considers it is impossible that the heterogeneous elements of intuition and concept can be reduced to a synthetic unity without special means. After all, he argues, there must be some reason why now one category, and now another, is used to make an object of knowledge become an object of knowledge. According to Kant, there are twelve schemata that act as necessary links between intuition and the application of the categories.[92] The schema exists as a kind of pre-formation in the appearances, as a kind of organization of them which anticipates the application of the categories. For example, the schema of succession which is proper to time leads to the application of the category of causality.

All this does not need to be dealt with extensively. It may be useful, however, to consider briefly the unifying function of the understanding which Kant calls "transcendental apperception."[93]

As we have seen, the knowledge of physical science and therefore also the object of this knowledge consists of syntheses, wholes formed by diverse operations and elements. However, the unity of the object of knowledge demands that we accept the unifying function of the subject, of the "I." For how would it be possible to speak of an object of knowledge if that object did not appear to us as a certain unity? This unity, however, becomes problematic as soon as we realize that it contains a multiplicity of elements and functions. This multiplicity of elements and functions must find a principle of unity in its origin, that is, in the knowing subject.[94] The object is not

---

[92] "Obviously there must be some third thing, which is homogeneous on the one hand with the category, and on the other hand with the appearance, and which thus makes the application of the former to the latter possible. This mediating representation must be pure, that is, void of all empirical content, and yet at the same time, while it must in one respect be *intellectual*, it must in another be *sensible*. Such a representation is the *transcendental schema*." *Op. cit.*, p. 181.

[93] "The transcendental unity of apperception is that unity through which all the manifold given in an intuition is united in a concept of the object." *Op. cit.*, p. 157.

[94] "It must be possible for the 'I think' to accompany all my representations." *Op. cit.*, p. 152.

really an object if it has no unity, but every object presupposes the subject in order to be able to be an object. Kant calls this unifying function of the "I" transcendental apperception or the "I think." The use, therefore, of the various categories by which in fact the unity of the object is constituted means that the unifying power of the transcendental apperception is particularized. But, says Kant, we should not think of a real unity of a substantial "I," a Cartesian "thinking thing," but merely of a necessary point of reference, as the transcendental condition for the unity of the object of knowledge.

Provisional Conclusion

The task which Kant set for himself was to determine the possibilities and limits of human knowledge and thus to decide whether traditional metaphysics was possible or not. The answer to both questions is implied in the results of Kant's above-mentioned speculations. Reviewing those results in a separate chapter, Kant touches a topic that was to occupy his attention for a long time, namely, the impossibility of traditional metaphysics.[95]

From what has been established thus far it is evident that the understanding may make only an empirical, and not a transcendental, use of its concepts.[96] In other words, the concepts of the understanding never refer to things in themselves, but only to appearances. For the object of a concept can be given only in an empirical intuition; hence the concept has no real given object without intuition, that is, it has no objective value.[97] But empirical intuition brings us only in contact with appearances. The use of concepts outside the intuitions is a mere play.[98] The pure thinking about things in themselves by the understanding, armed with its categories, is not a real *knowledge* of real objects.

At this point Kant introduces a number of new technical terms. He uses the term *noumenon* to designate the thing in itself and *phenomenon* to designate the appearances.[99] The noumenon, then, is not the object given in the intuition but purely that which is thought

---

[95]*Op. cit.*, pp. 257-275.

[96]*Op. cit.*, p. 259.

[97]"Now the object cannot be given to a concept otherwise than in intuition; for though a pure intuition can indeed precede the object *a priori*, even this intuition can acquire its object, and therefore objective validity, only through the empirical intuition of which it is the mere form." *Ibid.*

[98]"Apart from this relation they have no objective validity, and in respect of their representations are a mere play of the imagination or of understanding." *Ibid.*

[99]Op. cit., pp. 266 f.

of by the understanding; it is the noumenon in the negative sense.[100]
We should recall here, that, according to Kant, there is no
other intuition than sense intuition. Hence the categories of the understanding are only applicable to objects as given in sense intuition,
that is, to phenomena, and it is only for these that they are objectively valid.[101] On the contrary, the noumenon could be a given
object for a non-sensitive, or intellectual intuition. This is the
noumenon in the positive sense. But for us, human beings, intuition is
always of the sensitive kind. We haven't the least idea of what those
intellectual intuitions and the positive noumenon could be.[102] Hence
whenever Kant speaks of the noumenon, he always uses the term in
the negative sense.[103]

Kant considers the noumenon as a "limiting concept"; it is indispensable for us if we wish to be conscious of the limits of our knowledge. It prevents sense intuition from any attempt to reach things in
themselves.[104] At the same time, however, the understanding sets
limits for itself by the concept of the noumenon and prevents itself
from applying its categories to the noumenon. The noumenon can
only be thought of as an unknown X.[105]

In us, human beings, it is only the combination of the understanding and sensibility that can constitute objects. If they are divorced, we have intuitions without concepts or concepts without intuitions; in both cases, therefore, we have representations that cannot be referred to any definite object.[106]

That means that, in principle, the fate of traditional metaphysics
has been sealed. Traditional metaphysics, which deals with the world
or the universe (cosmology), the soul and the "I" (rational psychology), and God (natural theology), is not possible as a science since
it deals with objects that cannot be given by intuition. Metaphysical
"knowledge" is therefore not true knowledge. It is an "empty" way
of thinking about the supersensible, without any relation to a given

---

[100]*Op. cit.*, p. 268.
[101]*Op. cit.*, pp. 268 f.
[102]"But if we understand by it an *object* of a *non-sensible intuition*, we
thereby presuppose a special mode of intuition, namely, the intellectual, which
is not that which we possess, and of which we cannot comprehend even the
possibility." *Op. cit.*, p. 268.
[103]*Op. cit.*, p. 270.
[104]"Further, the concept of a noumenon is necessary, to prevent sensible
intuition from being extended to things in themselves, and thus to limit the
objective validity." *Op. cit.*, pp. 271 f.
[105]*Op. cit.*, p. 272.
[106]*Op. cit.*, p. 274.

object. True, the knowing subject is necessitated to think about the supersensible, but when he conceives it as a given object, he gets entangled in what Kant calls a transcendental illusion. Hence lies the explanation of the impasse in which traditional metaphysics has fallen.

The Ideas of Reason

From all that Kant has said thus far about knowledge, it is evident that the *a priori* forms of intuition and the categories exercise a unifying function. The union of sensations with intuitions is accomplished by means of the *a priori* forms of space and time, and the fusion of the intuitions into knowledge of objects is made by means of the categories of the understanding. But all this does not yet attain the highest kind of synthesis. The understanding is prompted to aim at an ever higher form of synthesis which in metaphysical thinking is reached by means of the "ideas" of reason. Let us see what Kant means by this assertion.

In and through the knowledge we have in physical science phenomena are connected in such a way that one phenomenon appears as the condition of another. In the judgment, "all bodies are alterable," we declare that "being a body" contains the condition for their alterability. The condition of the body's alterability can be clarified by means of reasoning. In this way the judgment in question is justified. This judgment then appears as the conclusion of a sequence of major and minor premises. The conclusion, "bodies are alterable," is drawn from the premises: "everything composite is alterable," and "bodies are composite." Being-composed is thus revealed as the condition for the alterability of bodies which is then expressed in the conclusion.[107] In this way reason proceeds in a certain "ascending" movement. But the ascending movement can be continued.[108] The major premise expresses that "being composed" involves the condition on which alterability depends. And reason quite naturally wants to ascend to a higher synthesis. This it does by looking upon the major premise as being itself a conclusion, and reason then searches for a proposition under which the subject of the conclusion can be used as a minor term. The mind can thus build an ascending series of reasonings in which it expresses how one phenomenon is the condition of another and so on *ad infinitum.*

---

[107] *Op. cit.,* pp. 320 f.
[108] *Op. cit.,* pp. 321 f.

We can also construct a descending series of reasonings, but the ascending series is more important. For in a conclusion we formulate knowledge that is dependent on a condition and this condition in its turn depends on a previous condition and so on. Reason is thus forced to look upon the ascending series of conditions as completed and given in their totality.[109] For otherwise none of the conclusions could be accepted as valid. The case is somewhat different in regard to a descending series since the truth of the conclusions that are found on a higher level does not depend on those that lie below.[110]

The ascending series of reasonings ends at the summit in something unconditional, which Kant calls a "concept of reason," and he thinks that there are three: the idea of the universe, the idea of the soul or "I," and the idea of God.[111] For we necessarily think of all appearances in nature in relation to an all-embracing world or universe. We necessarily think of whatever appears in our consciousness as in relation to the soul, to the ever-identical "I." We also unavoidably think of absolutely everything as being the effect of an absolute cause or God. It is not important for our purpose to examine here how Kant arrived at this classification of ideas.[112]

Normative Function of Ideas. However, it is of the utmost importance to realize that the ideas of reason should not be conceived as referring to subsistent realities. The "world," the "I," and "God" are not really *known,* but we must of necessity *think* them. They are not *given* in and through knowledge but are *set* as tasks for us by our thinking.[113] We conceive the reduction of all intellectual knowledge to the ultimate unconditioned as an *accomplished* task. But such a reduction is really never finished because the phenomena in space and time are endless. If such a task were actually accomp-

---

109"If, therefore, knowledge be viewed as conditioned, reason is constrained to regard the series of conditions in the ascending line as completed and as given in their totality." *Op. cit.,* p. 321.

110*Op. cit.,* pp. 321 f.

111*Op. cit.,* p. 323.

112Cf. H. Van Oyen, *Philosophia,* vol. II, 1949, pp. 169-177; W. Windelbond, *History of Philosophy,* vol. 2, pp. 548 ff.; J. Maréchal, *Le point de départ de la métaphysique,* Cahier III, La Critique de Kant, Bruxelles, 1944, pp. 220-225.

113"The pure concepts of reason—of totality in the synthesis of conditions—are thus at least necessary as setting as the task of extending the unity of understanding, where possible, up to the unconditioned, and are grounded in the nature of human reason. These transcendental concepts may, however, be without any suitable corresponding employment *in concreto,* and may therefore have no other utility than that of so directing the understanding, that, while it is extended to the uttermost, it is also at the same time brought into complete consistency with itself." *Op. cit.,* p. 316.

lished, the "world," the "I," and God would be *given* objects. But no objects are given to us except in and through intuition which, according to Kant, is exclusively sensitive.[114] Hence to consider ideas as validly relating to objects is always unjustified.[115]

Nevertheless, when it is said that the ideas are "merely" ideas, we should not conclude that they are superfluous.[116] That they are "merely ideas" means that they are inapplicable to objects; nevertheless they are indispensable. They are absolutely necessary guidelines that prompt the mind to ascend to an ever higher synthesis of knowledge. The ideas, then, have "only" a normative value but this value is indispensable.

Now, according to Kant, traditional metaphysics made the mistake of "ontologizing" the ideas of reason. It conceived the world, the "I," and God as realities existing in themselves and as objects of knowledge. The metaphysician thus became entangled in a "transcendental illusion" and deceived himself.[117] It is the task of dialectics to break through this illusion and to unmask the self-deception of the metaphysician. But this dialectics is not that of logic in which, abstracting from the content of knowledge, we merely try to discover the faults committed against the rules of reasoning; it is, on the contrary, a "transcendental" dialectics which unmasks the illegimate use of concepts in realms that lie beyond their application.[118]

Regarding traditional psychology, Kant thinks that he can point to four paralogisms because, in its reasoning, this branch of metaphysics became the victim of a hidden four term construction. It conceived the logical subject as a truly existing, immaterial substance and thus made all its conclusions false, for a fourth term was surreptitiously introduced.[119] The traditional cosmology must likewise be rejected, for it is possible to express contradictory propositions about the universe, considered as an object of knowledge.[120]

---

[114]"I understand by idea a necessary concept of reason to which no corresponding object can be given in sense experience." *Op. cit.,* p. 318.

[115]*Op. cit.,* p. 319.

[116]*Op. cit.,* pp. 319 f.

[117]*Op. cit.,* pp. 297 ff.

[118]"We are not at present concerned with logical dialectic, which abstracts from all content of knowledge and confines itself to exploring the fallacies concealed in the form of syllogisms, but with a transcendental dialectic which has to contain, completely *a priori,* the origin of certain modes of knowledge derived from pure reason as well as of certain inferred concepts, the object of which can never be given empirically and which therefore lie entirely outside [the sphere of] the faculty of pure understanding." *Op. cit.,* p. 323.

[119]*Op. cit..* pp. 327 ff.

[120]*Op. cit.,* pp. 384 ff.

We shall not develop these points further, but confine ourselves to the examination of Kant's critique of the traditional proofs for the existence of God.

3. KANT'S CRITIQUE OF THE TRADITIONAL PROOFS FOR THE EXISTENCE OF GOD

Beginning this new section, we feel that it might suffice to be content with writing a simple corollary. For whoever has understood Kant's teaching thus far will readily see that Kant's critique of the traditional proofs for God's existence is but an application of the principles established by Kant. Everything is already settled, for Kant has already decided that every affirmation of objects that are not given in and by sense-intuition transcends the possibility of any *real* confirmation. It is therefore to be expected that Kant will describe the proofs of God's existence as so many ways in which the metaphysician deceives himself and gets caught in "transcendental illusion" since it is his intention to confirm the existence of God as a reality by means of his proofs. But it is evident that God can never be given as an object of sense-intuition; hence the proofs for God's existence as proposed by the metaphysician have no objective value.

The attempt, therefore, to prove the existence of God is doomed to failure. True, the idea of God, as an ideal of knowledge, is indispensable; it is even unavoidable.[121] But that idea cannot objectively be applied to a supreme reality (*ens realissimum*), no matter how one wants to describe this most real Being.[122] Kant then shows in what way that idea of God arises and how it even arises necessarily.[123] After that, he demolishes the traditional proofs, offered as valid demonstrations for the *reality* contained in the idea of God. For Kant sees that everything that traditional metaphysics has attributed

---

[121]"It is therefore a transcendental *ideal* which serves as a basis for the complete determination which necessarily belongs to all that exists. This ideal is the supreme and complete material condition of the possibility of all that exists—the condition to which all thought of objects, so far as their content is concerned, has to be traced back." *Op. cit.*, pp. 490 f.

[122]"The object of the ideal of reason, an object which is present to us only in and through reason, is therefore entitled the *primordial being (ens originarium)*. As it has nothing above it, it is also entitled the *highest being (ens summum)*; and as everything that is conditioned is subject to it, the *being of beings (ens entium)*. These terms are not, however, to be taken as signifying the objective relation of an actual object to other things, but of an *idea* to *concepts*. We are left entirely without knowledge as to the existence of a being of such outstanding pre-eminence." *Op. cit.*, p. 492.

[123]*Op. cit.*, pp. 485-495.

to the reality of God is contained in the idea of God as the ideal of human knowledge.

The Invalidity of the Ontological Proof for God's Existence

The essential point of the ontological proof for God's existence is the passage from the *idea* of absolute perfection to necessary *existence*. This proof, variously expressed, is found in St. Anselm, Descartes and Leibniz, but Kant mentions only Descartes.[124]

The proof can be summarized as follows: We have an idea of God as Absolute Perfection; but it is more perfect to exist than not to exist; therefore God exists and He does so necessarily.

Illicit Transition from the Logical to the Ontological Order. Kant's objections are fundamentally in line with the critique that has been formulated by all those who oppose the validity of this proof. They can be reduced to the objection that there is an illegitimate transition from the order of thought to the order of being. The only legitimate conclusion ought to read: Therefore we *think* of God as necessarily existing. But this conclusion leaves the problem of His *real* existence unsolved.

We can now outline Kant's own critique in greater detail. If we accept the reasoning used in the ontological proof for God's existence, it would be a contradiction to accept the subject of the conclusion while rejecting the predicate. In other words, there is a necessary connection between the predicate and the subject of the conclusion. There are, however, many judgments which express a necessity. In the past, efforts were made to clarify the concept of "necessary existence" by means of the necessity that is found, for example, in geometric judgments.[125] But the result was rather an obscuration than a clarification. In the judgment, "A triangle has three angles," there is a necessary connection between predicate and subject, but the necessity in question is evidently a necessity of *judgment* and not a necessity of the thing. In other words, as soon as I posit the subject "triangle" in the judgment, I am forced to affirm the predicate "having three angles." If I deny the predicate I likewise deny the subject. It is a contradiction to deny the predicate while accepting the subject.

---

[124]*Op. cit.,* p. 507.
[125]*Op. cit.,* pp. 501 f.

However, the necessity that is contained in the judgment does not imply that a triangle is of necessity *given*.[126] It is evidently a contradiction to deny the predicate and at the same time to affirm the subject, but it is not contradictory to reject both the predicate and the subject, for nothing is then left in which there would be a contradiction.[127]

Accordingly, when we reject the predicate while accepting the subject of the judgment, "The absolutely Perfect is necessarily existing," we are guilty of contradiction. But there is no contradiction in rejecting both the subject and the predicate. "God is almighty" is a necessary judgment. We are guilty of contradiction if we affirm God and deny His almighty power, but there is no contradiction in rejecting both God and His almighty power.[128]

Absolute Perfection and Necessary Existence. However, someone might try to find a loophole by saying that there is one subject that cannot be denied, namely the concept of "absolute Perfection." Hence it would be contradictory to deny its "necessary existence." In reply, Kant refuses to admit that this subject cannot be denied and, secondly, that the conclusion "God exists of necessity" follows necessarily.[129]

First of all, Kant is certain that the concept of real existence is never contained in the concept of anything whatsoever.[130] The concept of one hundred real dollars is not different from the concept of one hundred possible dollars. If, after expressing all the characteristics and as many predicates of a thing as I want, I finally state that the thing "is," I thereby do not add a new predicate, but merely affirm that the thing "is given" and is not merely possible. But the real, considered conceptually, does not contain more than the possible.[131]

All this sheds light on the conclusion of the ontological proof for God's existence. When I affirm that the absolute Perfection necessarily exists, the judgment is either analytic or synthetic. I can call it analytic only if I first unjustifiably think that the predicate

---

[126]"The unconditioned necessity of the judgment is not the same as an absolute necessity of things." *Op. cit.,* p. 501.

[127]"If we reject subject and predicate alike, there is no contradiction; for nothing is then left that can be contradicted." *Op. cit.,* p. 502.

[128]*Ibid.*

[129]*Op. cit.,* pp. 503 f.

[130]"'*Being*' is obviously not a real predicate; that is it is not a concept of something which could be added to the concept of a thing." *Op. cit.,* p. 504.

[131]"The real contains no more than the possible." *Op. cit.,* p. 505.

"necessary existence" is contained in the subject. Such an assumption is not justified, for the concept "existence" is not a part of the content of the subject. If, in spite of that, I incorporate the concept of existence in the subject and conclude that absolute Perfection really exists, I am guilty of pure tautology. In reality I affirm nothing about the real existence of God, for I have first unjustifiably included the predicate in the subject—a predicate that I find in the subject by means of analysis. If, then, I wish to affirm something about the existence of God, I must make a judgment that is synthetic. But if it is synthetic, one can no longer claim that the denial of the predicate contains a contradiction. The predicate "necessary existence" can now be denied without contradiction, for it does not belong to the content of the subject.[132]

Kant is willing to accept that the judgmental subject "absolute Perfection" includes the possibility of a real existence; but this is a purely *logical* possibility, that is, the predicate "existence" can without contradiction be affirmed of the subject "absolute Perfection." But the absence of contradiction between two concepts is something other than the *ontological* possibility of things. We are not allowed to conclude directly from the one to the other.[133]

So when we conceive God as absolute Perfection and see that real existence does not contradict this concept, there still remains the question whether such a being really exists or not.[134] Kant thinks that it is impossible to solve that question, for man can only confirm the existence of objects that are given in sense-intuition and God is not that kind of object.[135] Therefore it is, in principle, impossible to establish the existence of God and it is useless to try to prove His existence "ontologically." He who tries to enlarge his knowledge through the concept of "absolute Perfection" by affirming God's real existence is as foolish as a merchant who believes he can increase his fortune by adding a couple of zeros to his cash account.[136]

---

[132]If we admit, as every reasonable person must, that all existential propositions are synthetic, how can we profess to maintain that the predicate of existence cannot be rejected without contradiction? This is a feature which is found only in analytic propositions, and is indeed precisely what constitutes their analytic character." *Op. cit.,* p. 504.

[133]*Op. cit.,* pp. 503 f.

[134]"When I think a being as the supreme reality, without any defect, the question still remains whether it exists or not." *Op. cit.,* pp. 505 f.

[135]*Op. cit.,* pp. 506 f.

[136]*Op. cit.,* p. 507.

Invalidity of the Cosmological Proof for God's Existence

From Experience to Uncaused Cause. While there is, in the onto-logical proof, an illegitimate transition from the logical order to the order of real existence, the defenders of the cosmological proof for the existence of God try to get around the difficulty by starting from the experience of the contingency of things.

This proof, traditionally considered, is as follows. There exist contingent things, i.e., things that do not necessarily exist. Since they do not exist of necessity, they do not have the reason for their existence in themselves. Hence they exist through the influence of something else; they are caused. If this "something else" is likewise contingent, it also is caused. But ultimately there must exist a necessary Being, the unconditional cause of all contingent things.[137]

The proof, then, begins with experience and is therefore not wholly "ontological." It is called "cosmological" because the object of all possible experience is called "cosmos" (world).[138]

Uncaused Cause and Absolute Perfection. Kant maintains that the proof is not yet complete when it concludes to the existence of a necessary Being. It is still necessary to show that this Being is God, that is, absolute Perfection. Only when we realize that an absolutely necessary Being can be conceived only as absolute Perfection are we permitted to conclude that God exists.[139]

According to Kant, then, we must distinguish several steps in that proof. First, the conclusion to the existence of a necessary Being is drawn from the existence of contingent things; then, the necessary Being is identified with absolute Perfection, God.

This, according to him, is a masterpiece of dialectical skill by which reason involves man in a transcendental illusion and thus deceives him. Those who use this proof start from experience in order to escape the difficulties of the ontological proof.[140] Experience, however, is used only in order to conclude to a necessary Being. But Kant had already shown, when he dealt with the antinomies of reason, that the "absolutely necessary Being," which experience

---

[137]*Op. cit.*, pp. 507 ff.
[138]*Op. cit.*, p. 508.
[139]"There is only one possible concept which determines a thing completely *a priori*, namely the concept of the *ens realissimum*. The concept of the *ens realissimum* is therefore the only concept through which a necessary being can be thought, in other words, a supreme being necessarily exists." *Op. cit.*, p. 509.
[140]*Ibid.*

prompts us to accept, can only be affirmed as an idea of reason and not as an existing reality.

What, however, happens to the cosmological proof for God's existence? To prove that the absolutely necessary Being is God, the argument appeals to the concept "absolute Perfection." It is claimed that only the concept of "absolute Perfection" adequately expresses the concept of "necessary Being." But we have here once more the same kind of play with concepts as in the ontological proof for God's existence.[141] For he who says that the concept "absolute Perfection" is the only one that adequately and properly expresses the necessary Being must also admit that this concept can be deduced from the concept "absolute Perfection."[142] This is precisely what is done in the ontological proof for God's existence, which does not provide any possibility to establish the real existence of God.

Accordingly, no matter how much the cosmological proof may appear to avoid the difficulties attached to the ontological proof, in the end, it is forced to have recourse to it; hence it is just as inconclusive as the ontological proof.[143]

Finally, in order to make his thought perfectly clear, Kant expresses his objection in a rigidly logical form. If the proposition "Every absolutely necessary being is absolute perfection" is true, we should be allowed to convert it *per accidens* so that it would read "Some absolute perfections are absolutely necessary." Now, since absolute perfections cannot differ from one another in any respect, we can likewise say, "Every absolute perfection is a necessary being." It is to this conclusion that the cosmological proof of God's existence leads us in its first stage. But here we have exactly the same combination of concepts as in the ontological proof of God's existence, and hence it proves nothing regarding God's existence.[144]

Critique of the First Stage of the Proof. Kant also offers fundamental objections against the first stage of the cosmological proof.

---

[141]"The cosmological proof uses this experience only for a single step in the argument, namely, to conclude to a necessary being. What properties this being may have, the empirical premise cannot tell us. Reason therefore abandons experience altogether, and endeavors to discover from such concepts what properties an absolutely necessary being must have." *Ibid.*

[142]"If I say, the concept of the *ens realissimum* is a concept, and indeed the only concept which is appropriate and adequate to necessary existence, I must also admit that necessary existence can be inferred from this concept." *Op. cit.*, p. 510.

[143]*Op. cit.*, pp. 510 f.

[144]*Ibid.*

It makes use of the principle of causality. This principle is used to pass beyond the world of the senses to the affirmation of the real existence of an absolutely necessary Being as the cause of contingent things. According to Kant's principles, this is, of course, a perfectly illegitimate use of the concept of cause, for the principle of causality is valid only within the realm of the sensible world.[145]

Moreover, the absolutely necessary Being appears in the first stage of the cosmological proof for God's existence as if it were the necessary limit of the series of contingent beings. But, if we remain within the field of the sensible world in which true knowledge is possible, it is absurd to claim to have reached the limit and to maintain that an infinite series is an impossibility. The sciences themselves refer us from one cause to another.

Invalidity of the Teleological or Physico-theological Proof for the Existence of God

The Proof. Without any confidence or hope of success Kant examines the value of the proof for God's existence based on the harmony and order in the world. How could such a proof establish the real existence of God? What is expressed in the ideas of reason can never be given in and by sense-intuition. Yet this is required if we want to establish the actual existence of that Being.[146] If the highest Being is considered a member of the chain of conditions, it is not the highest Being, since it is only a conditioned being. If it is placed outside the chain, how can reason build a bridge that will enable it to reach the highest Being.[147]

The world is an immeasurable stage of multiplicity, order, finality, beauty and harmony. All this is so impressive that man is struck dumb with utter amazement. Everywhere we see chains of effects and causes, of ends and purposes, and regularity in coming to be and passing away. Nothing has of itself come into the condition in which we find it to exist, but everything refers to something else as its cause, and this in turn necessarily refers again to something else. Everything would sink into nothingness if there were no absolute Origin, a highest Cause in virtue of which contingent beings exist

---

[145]*Op. cit.,* p. 511.

[146]"In view of what has already been said, it is evident that we can count upon a quite easy and, conclusive answer to this inquiry. For how can any experience ever be adequate to an idea? The peculiar nature of the latter consists just in the fact that no experience can ever be equal to it." *Op. cit.,* p. 518.

[147]*Op. cit.,* pp. 518 f.

and continue to exist.[148] This Cause, as cause of purposiveness, must be a rational Being, a Being endowed with intellect and will.[149]

How great is the perfection that we ought to attribute to highest Cause? What prevents us from attributing to it a degree of perfection that is higher than anything we can affirm and that contains all perfection in itself? Such a concept is not self-contradictory, nor is there anything in experience that contradicts it.[150]

Kant believes that this proof deserves the highest esteem. It is the oldest, clearest and most easily understood of the traditional proofs. Yet, it fails to yield apodictic certainty. Kant gives several reasons for this failure.

Kant's Critique. First of all, the proof too willingly accepts the analogy between a product of nature and an artifact. But we are not permitted to attribute greater certitude to the conclusion than the analogy itself possesses. Hence the conclusion is certainly not apodictic.[151]

We can say that order, finality, and harmony refer to the *form* of the world and therefore require as their source a Being which has mind and will. But the analogy with artifacts does not permit us to claim that the same can be said of the order, the finality, and harmony that are found in the *matter* and substance of the world. We would still have to prove that the things themselves cannot cause such an order without being in their turn the product of the highest possible Wisdom. And of what use is the concept of analogy when we try to solve that problem?[152] The utmost therefore that the argument can prove is the existence of a *architect* of the world who has pre-existing matter at his disposal, but it cannot establish a *Creator* of the world to whom all things are subject.[153]

Moreover, the concept of a supreme cause cannot be rendered determinate unless we borrow from the cosmological proof for God's

---

[148]*Op. cit.,* p. 519.

[149]"There exists, therefore, a sublime and wise cause (or more than one), which must be the cause of the world not merely as a blindly working all-powerful nature, by *fecundity,* but as intelligence, through *freedom.*" *Op. cit.,* p. 521.

[150]*Op. cit.,* pp. 519 f.

[151]*Op. cit.,* pp. 520 f.

[152]"To prove the latter we should have to demonstrate that the things in the world would not of themselves be capable of such order and harmony, in accordance with universal laws, if they were not *in their substance* the product of supreme wisdom. But to prove this we should require quite other grounds of proof than those which are derived from the analogy with human art." *Op. cit.,* p. 522.

[153]*Ibid.*

existence. For it is clear that the proof from order, finality, and harmony intends to establish the existence of a Cause which, as cause of those characteristics of the world, is proportioned to them.[154] The concept of such a being must then be a *determinate* one, for indefinite predicates, such as "a very great power" or "astounding eminence," do not give us a sufficient foundation for calling that Cause to which we conclude a proportioned Cause. The predicates we have just mentioned are not truly *determinate,* for such terms have meaning only insofar as they indicate that the power or eminence in question is great in comparison with the speaker's own power and eminence. Basing ourselves on such a comparison, we call that eminent power, which is to be made determinate, "very great" or "astounding."[155] But the concept of a Cause that is proportioned to the order, finality, and harmony cannot be such an indeterminate concept. It must be a determinate concept and this concept can be only the concept "absolute Perfection." As a matter of fact, the proof really wants to conclude to the absolute perfection of the supreme Cause. However, we must ask how this conclusion can be reached.

According to Kant it cannot be done. Nonetheless, the physico-theological proof attempts to conclude to the existence of absolute Perfection.[156] Its proponents either do not see or do not want to see that, after starting from the experience of order, finality, and harmony that exist in the world, they switch to the train of thought proper to the cosmological argument because they realize that they should arrive at the absolute Perfection. The physico-theological proof cannot lead man beyond admiration of the greatness, power and wisdom of the world's Cause. To proceed farther, he switches to the contingency of the world in his proof; from there he tries to attain the absolutely necessary Being, and finally absolute Perfection. The proof, then, begins with experience and when, as expected, it comes to an impasse, it switches to the cosmological proof; thus it ultimately depends upon the ontological proof because the cosmological proof itself is useless without the ontological argument.[157]

---

[154]"The inference, therefore, is that the order and purposiveness everywhere observable throughout the world may be regarded as a completely contingent arrangement, and that we may argue to the existence of a cause *proportioned* to it." *Op. cit.,* p. 522.

[155]*Op. cit.,* p. 523.

[156]"To advance to absolute totality by the empirical road is impossible. None the less this is what is attempted in the physico-theological proof." *Ibid.*

[157]*Ibid.*

In this way Kant arrives at the conclusion that there is only one proof for God's existence, namely, the ontological proof, and this proof is invalid.[158]

Kant's Critique of Natural Theology

When this state is reached, Kant has told us a hundred times that our concepts have objective validity only in the field of sense experience. An object is given as really existing only in sense-intuition. In a final section he summarily criticizes traditional natural theology. This critique consists chiefly of repeating ten times more what we have heard already a hundred times.

No Possibility of Theoretical Knowledge of God. According to Kant, theoretical knowledge of God is not possible. He calls "theoretical" the knowledge that expresses "what *is*." It stands in contrast to "practical" knowledge which expresses "what *ought to be*."[159] Theoretical knowledge is either "natural" or "speculative." It is "natural" when it speaks of objects that are given in sense experience. It is "speculative" when it makes affirmations that go beyond the objects given in experience.[160]

According to that terminology, the traditional theoretical knowledge of God is purely speculative. The speculative use of reason, however, in relation to natural theology is perfectly fruitless and by its very nature null and void.[161] This is easily understood. For if the law of causality leads to a First Being, this First Being would be a member of the series of objects of sense experience and it would no more be the First Being than any other member of the series. If we place the First Being above the series of objects of sense experience, it means that we have used the law of causality in a field in which it has no objective validity. The conclusion, then, is inevitable: our knowledge of God is purely speculative, that is, it has no objective value.[162]

Kant challenges anyone who puts more trust in the traditional proofs than in his critique to show him the reasons that justify going beyond sense experience by making use of pure ideas. He excuses himself from the task of considering new proofs or improve-

[158]*Op. cit.*, p. 524.
[159]*Op. cit.*, p. 526.
[160]*Op. cit.*, p. 527.
[161]*Op. cit.*, p. 528.
[162]*Ibid.*

ments of the traditional ones, for he knows that they will in any case make use of pure "ideas" in their attempt to transcend sense experience, and the only question is how such a transcendence is possible.[163]

Theoretical Reason Can Neither Affirm Nor Deny God. The highest Being remains an ideal for the use of speculative reason, an ideal that terminates and crowns the whole of human knowledge, but its objective reality cannot be demonstrated. The same reasons, however, that make us say that the objective reality of the highest Being cannot be proved, force us to admit that its reality cannot be rejected.[164] Both the denial and the acknowledgment of that Being transcend the possibilities of reason. Moreover, it is not excluded that there might be another way, not by means of reason, to confirm the real existence of a supreme Being. Kant here refers to morality, the possibility of which postulates the existence of God. In that case the traditional theology would have value to determine the concept of the supreme Being postulated by ethics. Only theoretical reason can keep away the aberrations of atheism, deism and anthropomorphism, by pointing out that they pass beyond the possibilities of speculative reason in their affirmations.[165] Only theoretical reason can act as a constant censor and show that they are led into error by sense deception.[166] And if practical reason postulates the affirmation of the real existence of the supreme Being, it is only theoretical reason that can more closely determine the necessity, infinity, unity, transcendence, eternity, almighty power, and so forth, of that Being.[167]

4. CRITICAL CONSIDERATIONS

At the beginning of this chapter we mentioned that, in Kant's agnosticism regarding theoretical reason, contemporary atheism thinks

---

[163] *Op. cit.*, p. 529.
[164] "Thus while for the merely speculative employment of reason the supreme being remains a mere ideal, it is yet *an ideal without a flaw,* a concept which completes and crowns the whole of human knowledge. Its objective reality cannot indeed be proved, but also cannot be disproved, by merely speculative reason." *Op. cit.*, p. 531.
[165] *Ibid.*
[166] "If, then, there should be a moral theology, transcendental theology, which before was problematic only, will prove itself indispensable in determining the concept of this supreme being and in constantly testing reason, which is so often deceived by sensibility, and which is frequently out of harmony with its own ideas." *Ibid.*
[167] *Op. cit.*, p. 531.

it possible to find an argument for the rejection of God. Those who defend such a view assume a certain position in regard to Kant's *Critique of Practical Reason,* but this position is open to numerous objections. If Kant in his *Critique of Pure Reason* comes to the conclusion that theoretical reason can only yield problematic judgments regarding God, his *Critique of Practical Reason* maintains that the undeniable existence of morality prompts and justifies assertoric judgments about God.[168] In his first *Critique* Kant asks: What must we unconditionally admit in order that natural science can be what it actually is? In his second *Critique* he is faced with an analogous question: What must we unconditionally accept in order that morality can be what it undeniably is?

Postulates of Practical Reason. For Kant morality is a *fact,* just as natural science is a *fact.* Morality brings with it laws and obligations which are universal and necessary. Just as the universality and necessity of scientific judgments are explained by the *a priori* forms of the intellect, so the universality and necessity of moral obligations have their explanation in the existence of an *a priori* form of the practical reason, which Kant calls the "categorical imperative." This imperative imposes itself on all human actions, and brings with it the "absolute" obligation which properly constitutes morality and is not derived from experience.

All this, according to Kant, presupposes certain "postulates." Morality surely cannot be what it undeniably is unless man's freedom, the immortality of the soul, and the existence of God are affirmed.[169] These are problematic concepts for theoretical reason, which is unable to prove the real existence of the realities to which these problematic concepts correspond. But the undeniable existence of the moral "ought" forces practical reason to accept that existing realities correspond to those concepts, for morality cannot be what it undeniably is without freedom, the immortality of the soul, and the

---

[168]"Therefore, through the practical law, which requires the existence of the highest good possible in the world, there is postulated the possibility of objects of pure speculative reason whose objective reality could not be assured by speculative reason. By this, then, the theoretical knowledge of pure reason does obtain an accession, but it consists only in this—that those concepts which for it are otherwise problematical (merely thinkable) are now described assertorically as actually having objects because practical reason inexorably requires the existence of these objects. *Critique of Practical Reason,* tr. by Lewis White, Liberal Arts Press, New York, 1956, p. 139.

[169]*Op. cit.,* pp. 126 ff.

existence of God.[170] Hence certain affirmations which cannot be made legitimately by theoretical reason are legitimate as coming from practical reason.

Kant, however, speaks emphatically of "postulates." Freedom, the immortality of the soul, and God's existence are not objects of "knowledge." Nevertheless, we must affirm them as existing realities. They are, then, according to Kant, objects of faith.[171] The ideas of theoretical reason are merely regulative principles, closing and crowning our experimental knowledge. What is expressed in these ideas is never given in sense-intuition; hence its real existence can never be affirmed by theoretical reason, but it can be affirmed by practical reason. However, once again, this assertion, does not mean that the thinking of theoretical reason is raised to the dignity of "knowledge."[172] The categorical imperative of practical reason does indeed give to the ideas of theoretical reason their corresponding objects, but these are not attained in an act of knowledge but in an act of faith.[173]

Importance of Kant's Second Critique. Those who try to justify their atheism by means of Kant's criticism have to belittle the significance of his *Critique of Practical Reason.* They claim that the "true" Kant is found in the first *Critique* where he appears as an agnostic in respect to the existence of God. Kant, it would seem, was frightened by the consequences of the principles he had laid down in his first *Critique.* Through weakness or cowardice he apparently tried to soften the harmful effects of his first *Critique,* and

---

[170]"The moral law led, in the foregoing analysis, to a practical problem which is assigned solely by pure reasons and without any concurrence of sensuous incentives. It is the problem of the completeness of the first and principal part of the highest good, viz. morality; since this problem can be solved only in eternity, it led to the postulate of immortality. The same law must also lead to affirm the possibility of the second element of the highest good, i.e., happiness proportional to that morality, it must do so as disinterestedly as heretofore, by a purely impartial reason. This it can do on the supposition of the existence of a cause adequate to this effect, i.e., it must postulate the existence of God as necessarily belonging to the possibility of the highest good." *Op. cit.,* pp. 128 f.

[171]*Op. cit.,* p. 130.

[172]*Op. cit.,* pp. 139 ff.

[173]"The three aforementioned ideas of speculative reason are not themselves cognitions; they are, nevertheless, transcendent thoughts in which there is nothing impossible. Now through an apodictic practical law, they, as necessary conditions of the possibility of that which this law requires to be made an object, acquire objective reality. That is to say, they show by this that they have objects, but we cannot yet indicate how their concept refers to an object; this, too, is not yet knowledge of these objects." *Op. cit.,* p. 140.

hence had written his second *Critique*. We find such an opinion already in Heinrich Heine. He pictures Kant as destroying everything to which man is attached and by which he lives. But then comes the day when Kant realizes that Lampe, his old servant, finds it impossible to live any longer in such a situation: "Poor old Lampe has to have a God, for without Him he cannot be happy."[174] This, they claim, was the reason why Kant wrote his second *Critique*.

This explanation, however, is naive. Though it is true that Kant wrote his *Critique of Practical Reason* after the *Critique of Pure Reason*, it is certain that he conceived the plan for both at the same time. In many places of his first *Critique* he hints that the agnosticism of the theoretical reason does not say the last word regarding the existence of God. Even in the first *Critique* it is evident to him that practical reason overcomes the agnosticism of theoretical reason.[175] But if this is so, why should one prefer the agnosticism of the theoretical reason to the denial of agnosticism professed by the practical reason?

Kant's Historical Importance. It must be evident to the reader that Kant's work contains profound philosophical thought. It cost Kant much trouble to find his way, but once he had found it, he proved himself capable of laying bare great regions of reality on the basis of the "primitive fact" or the "central reference point" of his thought. As is usually the case with a genius, Kant was for a time either adored or despised.

Things are more peaceful at present. His work now belongs to perennial philosophy. Those who follow him do it with reserve, and those who do not follow him are now more intent on discovering what Kant actually "saw" than on trying to refute him. All are convinced that the philosophy of our own time cannot permit itself to proceed as if Kant had never written his works. Any philosophy that wants to be up to date must always contain *also* something of Kantian inspiration.

The contemporary philosopher, then, cannot simply disregard Kant. When, for example, Kant tells us that the "thing in itself" is unknowable, it is not sufficient to make the opposite assertion.

---

[174]Quoted by A. J. De Sopper, *Wat is philosophie?*, Haarlem, 1950, p. 103.
[175]Cf. H. J. De Vleeschauwer, *Immanuel Kant*, Antwerpen, 1931, pp. 281-285.

Moreover, the philosopher of today realizes that, if it is possible for him to criticize Kant, he can do so principally because today's philosopher views things from a standpoint of philosophical thought that was made possible by Kant himself. Speaking more concretely, the contemporary philosophy of existential phenomenology has a number of objections against Kant's way of conceiving things. But there is not one phenomenologist who does not acknowledge that the dialectical perspective of thought, which is at work in existential phenomenology as a "primitive fact," was foreshadowed in Kant. Phenomenology rejects the *a priori* forms of sense intuition and the *a priori* forms of understanding. But when the phenomenologist stresses the significance which human subjectivity with its many attitudes has with respect to the constitution of meaning, he recognizes at the same time that it was precisely Kant who revealed that subjectivity. It is also undeniable that, since Kant, true knowledge cannot be defined as the accurate mirroring of a world divorced from the subject in a conscious looking-glass.

Kant's Presuppositions

The reader of Kant's works cannot help being impressed by the enormous systematizing power of his thought. And yet there is something in the work that constantly annoys the reader. He gets the impression that all that Kant supposedly "discovers" is really something that is already "established beforehand." If we could only convince ourselves that this impression is merely the result of the way Kant develops his thought and teaches us! A teacher, of course, is already supposed to know; but in the realm of philosophy to teach has no other meaning than to "let others see." But we do not have the impression that this is what Kant is doing. It seems rather that he draws conclusions from a few presuppositions, which he accepts as certain, without examining them, and this gives us an unpleasant feeling.

For instance, Kant accepts without examination that objects can be given to us solely in sense-intuitions. Whatever does not appear to the mind as ordered in space and time cannot be affirmed to exist in reality. Kant mentions this point in passing when he devotes one half of a page to explain the meaning of various terms he intends to use.[176] But in the meantime the fate of metaphysical questions

---

[176]*Critique of Pure Reason,* p. 65.

is irrevocably sealed. For example, that it is impossible to establish the real existence of the soul or ego-subject is evident at once when one first decrees that only that can be considered as "given" and really existing which is ordered in space and time and appears as such in sense-intuition. It is evident, of course, that the "being given" of an ego-subject differs very much from the "being given" of a material object; but may we conclude from it that the ego-subject is *not* given? This conclusion can only be maintained if we take the terms "to be given" and "to be established as a fact" in a very narrow sense. The question, however, is precisely whether or not such a claim is legitimate. But for Kant there is no problem, and we do not have to look very far to find the reasons for that lack of critical sense.

Prior to any critique, one thing is undeniably true for Kant, namely, that *knowledge,* genuine knowledge, experience in the *full* sense of the term, is to be found only in the physical sciences. By knowledge here is meant the kind of knowledge proper to physical science; and, for Kant, "really to establish something" means exclusively to establish things as is done in physical science.

We readily understand that one who is struck by the fruitfulness of the physical sciences might be prompted to make such a claim, and we would then expect him to apply himself to the kind of research that is proper to physical science. But it does not seem reasonable to maintain that knowledge, in an unqualified sense, is found only in physical science and then to go to work in a realm of knowledge that is foreign to physical science. He who makes such a claim cannot even engage in a critique of physical science, for his critical reflections would *not* be a pursuit of this science. Nevertheless, he would equate physical science with knowledge in an unqualified sense.

In spite of all this, Kant started from the assumption that knowledge in an unqualified sense is knowledge as it is found in physical science. The obvious and immediate conclusion is, of course, that reality in an unqualified sense is that which is revealed by physical science; consequently, only that can be accepted as reality which is given in sense-intuition. Hence metaphysical knowledge is not true knowledge and metaphysical proofs do not establish any realities as given. Kant looks upon all these propositions as "conclusions," but on closer inspection they are all simply presupposed. Varying Kant's assertions a little we could say that, according to him, we know in reality only what we ourselves have put into it, and that therefore Kant likewise knows in "knowledge" only what he himself has put into it. The question that presents itself here at once is: Where does Kant get the right to proceed as he does?

Was Kant a Scientistic or an Anti-Scientistic Thinker?

One may be tempted once more to put Kant aside, remarking this time that he is a victim of scientism. His agnosticism regarding the existence of God would be merely the result of his scientistic concept of knowledge, and his scientism would simply imply all the contradictions from which no kind of scientism can escape.

Kant, however, declares that the affirmation of God's existence is both possible and necessary. The undeniable fact of the existence of morality forces man to make assertoric judgments about God's real existence. How are these judgments possible? We know his answer: they are possible, not for theoretical reason, but for practical reason. What does such a reply mean?

As we have noted, even those who do not follow Kant are presently more interested in trying to find out what Kant really "saw," what animated him and what guided him—perhaps even without his noticing it—than in refuting him. We said also that we do not think it proper to believe that Kant wrote his second *Critique* only as a farce. On the contrary, we suspect that we face here one of the most important elements of Kant's "inspiration." Several things seem to point to the truth of this suspicion. We should at least try to understand the nature of that "inspiration."

Meaning of the Term "Knowledge" for Kant. An opportunity to do so is provided by Kant's claim that the affirmation of God's existence never is or becomes *knowledge*. This affirmation is an act of faith, of "rational faith."[177] It has often been said that Kant has undermined all theoretical foundation for the affirmation of God's existence. But we ask ourselves whether the accusation is justified when we take into account that, for Kant, genuine knowledge in regard to the theoretical mind means the knowledge of physical science. For how could Kant have maintained that the proof of God's existence can be given by this science? Physical science tries to grasp reality by means of quantitative categories; hence, if it were to speak about God, it would affirm the existence of nothing more

---

[177]*Critique of Practical Reason*, p. 130.

than a quantitative God, i.e., a pseudo-God. Kant, however, considers the affirmation of God's existence possible provided it is not an affirmation expressed by theoretical knowledge, and, in his terminology, this means on condition that the affirmation is *not* conceived as an affirmation belonging to the realm of physical science. Such a non-"scientific" (in the sense of physical science) affirmation Kant calls "faith." He thereby affirms without any ambiguity that man can make affirmations which transcend the possibilities of physical science but which nonetheless are justified affirmations of objective reality. Faith therefore means "knowledge" for Kant, but it is knowledge pertaining to reason more broadly conceived.

It would, of course, have been better if Kant had been more circumspect in the way he expressed himself, especially in his *Critique of Pure Reason*. But we should not be too severe with him, for this is a point which philosophers, even of our own time, seem unable to grasp. There are, for instance, numerous phenomenologists who calmly assert that phenomenology is opposed to "objective," "rational" and "scientific" knowledge when they really want to reject only the pretensions and the absolutizing of objectivism, rationalism and scientism.[178] In a similar way Kant asserts that the affirmation of God's existence is not "knowledge," but he means that it is not a knowledge of the type proper to physical science. We thus come to the conclusion that Kant, in his first *Critique,* wished to open the way to a genuine affirmation of God's existence by discarding the pretensions of scientism. Kant "saw" that metaphysics cannot be pursued in the same way as physical science.

Kant's Rejection of Scientism. This interpretation of Kant's doctrine evidently implies that the second *Critique* was considered by him to be no less important than the first. But there are also indications in Kant's first *Critique* that he never became the victim of scientism. For a true follower of scientism no other realities exist save those that are discovered in the particular *science* he favors. All other alleged "realities" he dismisses and has to reject by virtue of his position. Kant, however, does not permit theoretical reason to reject God's existence. Theoretical reason cannot prove the existence of God, but for the same reasons it is also incapable of denying

---

[178]For instance, in his *Phenomenology of Perception*, New York, 1962, p. viii, Merleau-Ponty speaks about the "rejection of science," but really means the "rejection of scientism."

it.[179] This way of reasoning is not in line with scientism, for its followers deny what does not appear within their field of vision. Kant's view in reality boils down to this, that in his opinion physical science is incapable of saying anything for or against the existence of God.

It is our opinion that Kant himself has formulated his most fundamental intentions in the Preface to the Second Edition where he says: "I have therefore found it necessary to deny *knowledge,* in order to make room for *faith.*"[180] "Knowledge" here means the scientific knowledge proper to physical science. Kant, then, considered it necessary to cast out the pretensions of this knowledge and so made room for the affirmation of God, freedom and immortality.[181] For, as long as we cling to the pretensions of scientism—that the physical sciences alone can tell us something about the meaning of reality—there is no room for the affirmation of God, freedom and immortality. Yet these affirmations have to be made. They are, of course, also a kind of "knowing." But it is a very special kind of knowledge—not that of physical science; hence Kant gives to it the name of rational *faith.*

In this way we arrive at the conclusion that Kant was certainly not an agnostic with respect to the existence of God. He wanted to prevent the affirmation of God's existence from becoming the affirmation of a pseudo-God, which would be the case if it were thought to lie within the realm of physical science. For any "God" arrived at by physical science would be a pseudo-God.

---

[179] *Critique of Pure Reason,* p. 531.
[180] *Op. cit.,* p. 29.
[181] "Even the assumption—as made on behalf of the necessary practical employment of my reason—of *God, freedom* and *immortality* is not permissible unless at the same time speculative reason be deprived of its pretensions to transcendent insight. For in order to arrive at such insight it must make use of principles which, in fact, extend only to what cannot be an object of experience, and which, if also applied to what cannot be an object of experience, always really change this into an appearance, thus rendering all *practical extension* of pure reason impossible." *Op. cit.,* p. 29.

CHAPTER TWO

PHYSICAL SCIENCE, SCIENTISM, AND ATHEISM. THE PROOF OF GOD'S EXISTENCE

We ended the preceding chapter with the remark that physical science can only affirm a pseudo-God. This declaration may serve as a transition to a problematics which before our time could not be dealt with in a dispassionate and orderly fashion. It is sufficient to recall here that not so many years ago the pursuit of physical science was rather commonly thought to lead almost automatically to the denial of God's existence. Today we are able to make the necessary distinctions; we can keep in mind the different possibilities and limitations of distinct ways of knowing, and avoid confusion.

1. Physical Science and Theology—Galileo

On a certain date in history, a cleavage occurred between physical science and theology. It was at the moment when Galileo was forced to take an oath by which he sacrificed his scientific conviction and yielded to the mistakes of theologians.[1]

The world view defended by Galileo destroyed the traditional concepts in which propositions of physical science, philosophy, and theology constituted, as it were, one solid mass of truth. God was viewed as the Creator of the universe; the earth was considered to be the center of the universe because Christ had become man on earth and it was unthinkable that this would not have taken place at the center of the universe. The movements of the heavenly bodies were thought to be caused by angels. The things of nature, the substances, were examined in their God-given essence, and their operations were deduced from the natures of these substances. It was thought, for instance, that the fall of an unsupported stone could be deduced from the nature of the stone. It belonged to the nature of "heavy" objects that they should fall, and a stone was but a special illustration of this nature. Likewise, it belonged to the nature of a "light" object that it should rise; fire and light were only special examples of that nature. All essences had their natural place.[2]

---

[1]Cf. F. Dessauer, *Der Fall Galilei und wir*, Frankfurt am Main, 3rd ed., 1951, pp. 25-55.

[2]*Ibid.*, p. 61.

49

Before Galileo it was considered possible to draw up a complete picture of the world in a deductive way.

With Galileo everything changed. He *questioned* nature and tried to attain certitude by means of induction.[3] He saw that the operations of things cannot be deduced from their natures but that they are caused by forces that can be expressed in indisputable laws. The heavenly bodies are not moved by angels, and the earth is not at the center of the universe but is a poor little body that moves around the sun.[4]

Theologians opposed the rejection of the Aristotelian and Ptolemaic view of the cosmos, because they thought this rejection blasphemous and contrary to the data of Revelation. Galileo was forced to renounce his views and from then on it was impossible to pursue physical science according to its own inherent demands without being at least formally disobedient to the Church.[5] This situation lasted two hundred years, for it was only in 1835 that Galileo's *Discorsi* were removed from the Index of Forbidden Books.

Catastrophic Consequences. The results were catastrophic. When physical science was not allowed to develop within the atmosphere of faith, it went its own way outside. Its affirmations appeared undeniable, but when the theologians finally realized that the method of inquiry of the physical sciences was not blasphemous and that the results of its investigations were not contrary to the data of Revelation, the harm had already been done: a cleavage had been caused which appeared almost impossible to bridge. For a very long time anyone who had a scientific status and did not wish to expose his dignity was expected to deny the existence of God. For, God did not figure among the objects of physical science and it was not at all necessary to appeal to God as "cause" in order to give scientific explanations for the objects considered by this science. It may be well to add here that "pious" scientists, who did think otherwise and thought it necessary to appeal to God's causality in order to give scientific explanations of physical phenomena, merely increased the confusion.

Those who pursued scientific research had certainly the right to investigate nature through the methods of physical science. It was,

---

[3]*Ibid.*, p. 62.
[4]*Ibid.*, p. 78.
[5]*Ibid.*, pp. 96 f.

of course, unfortunate that they were obstructed in their right by
some theologians, who even resorted to power politics to impose
their own views.[6] But in combating the opposition of the theologians, the scientists did not always keep in mind what exactly they
were fighting for. Psychological factors may have played a role in
this respect. For, after all, what was the question involved in the
dispute? It was that the scientist had a right to question
nature, alongside and outside the speculations of theologians. But
the theologians' opposition led the scientists to a sort of absolutism;
physical science made the claim that *it* alone had the right to make
true statements about the world.

Later, when it appeared that the conclusions of the physical sciences could not be denied, it seemed that scientism, i.e., the absolutism of physical science, itself was guaranteed by the facts. As a
consequence, the theologians were then faced with the task of defending the right of theological considerations against scientists who
had become victims of scientism. The success of the physical sciences
and the discomfiture of leading theologians seemed to justify the
view that to affirm the existence of God was a sign of backwardness.

What has been described above should be viewed not so much as
a formally declared system but as a mentality which gradually became predominant. Nevertheless, no one will be surprised if such a
mentality produces also a protagonist who develops the mentality
into a full-fledged system. The success of the physical sciences and
the error of leading theologians led to a positivistic mentality, and it
was Auguste Comte who transformed it into a system, the system of
positivistic philosophy.

2. THE POSITIVISM OF COMTE

We do not intend to give a complete description of Comte's system, nor shall we indicate the consequences of his system for the
formation of society, but we shall confine ourselves to the ideas of
Comte that are important with respect to atheism. To these belong
especially Comte's theory about the stages of man's collective and
individual development in history before he attains the level of authentic manhood.

___
[6]*Ibid.*, p. 36.

The Law of the Three Stages

According to Comte, the human mind reaches maturity by passing through three stages: the theological stage, the metaphysical stage, and the stage of positive science.[7]

In the theological stage man looks upon all the phenomena of nature as dependent upon supernatural causes: God, gods or spirits. Comte calls this stage also the "fictitious stage" because in his attempt to refer the phenomena of nature to a transcendental cause man uses only his imagination. Comte does not mean to say that the first phase of the history of man's mind was unimportant. The opposite is true; for no other explanations were possible at that primitive stage of human thought. It was man's first step and it made possible the further development and the final maturity of the human mind.[8] Catholic religion takes first rank in that stage of development.[9]

It stands to reason that there could be no direct transition from the theological stage, in which the imagination is alone at work, to the positive scientific stage. Theology and physics are so diametrically opposed that a transitional phase is necessary to bridge the gap between the two. This phase is the phase of metaphysics.[10]

In this stage the supernatural influence of God, of gods and of spirits is replaced by mysterious essences, causes and substances. The explanation of the phenomena of nature is no longer dependent on causes that transcend nature but the causes are found in nature itself. But these are very subtle and abstract, and a sound mind is bound to come to the conclusion that he is merely giving strange names to phenomena. These phenomena themselves, however, remain unexplained,[11] since the so-called explanations are, and remain, products of the imagination. Nevertheless, this transitional phase is

---

[7]"Each one of us is aware if he looks back upon his own history that he was a *theologian* in his childhood, a *metaphysician* in his youth, and a *physicist* in his manhood." Auguste Comte, *Cours de Philosophie Positive,* Paris, 1830 ff., vol. 1, p. 4.

[8]*Op. cit.,* vol. I, p. 7.

[9]*Op. cit.,* vol. V, pp. 158-259.

[10]"Theology and physical science are so utterly incompatible, their conceptions are so radically opposed that before renouncing the ones and using exclusively the others, man's intelligence had to have recourse to intermediary conceptions of an amphibious nature; the very intermediate character of these ideas was calculated to bring about the transition in a gradual way. All this indicates the natural destiny of metaphysical conceptions." *Op. cit.,* vol. I, p. 7.

[11]*Op. cit.,* vol. I, pp. 7-8.

of great importance, even if it did nothing else except destroy the concepts of the theological stage and prepare the definitive phase of maturity.

In the stage of positive science things are totally different with respect to the development of the human mind. The mind now investigates the phenomena of nature by means of *experience*. The mind is no longer in search of transcendent or immanent causes but simply wishes to discover the empirically verifiable laws governing the interdependence of those phenomena.[12] Anyone who knows something about positive science, Comte thinks, realizes that its pursuit is the only method to be used by the mature human mind. In short, there is only one valid way of knowing, namely, that of physical science.

This means, of course, that positive philosophy, as a matter of principle, lays claim to all realms of phenomena. For it would be contradictory to suppose that the human spirit would, on the one hand, cling to a primitive way of philosophizing, while, on the other, it adopts a method of thought that is diametrically opposed to the primitive stage.[13] But the universality of positive philosophy has not yet been achieved.[14] There is still an enormous gap in the system, for there is not yet any *social* physics, which is precisely the thing that is needed most.[15]

When, however, all fundamental conceptions have become homogeneous, then philosophy will be definitively constituted. Its character will no longer undergo any changes; it will merely develop by accretion.[16] Positive philosophy, by virtue of its universality, will manifest its natural superiority and take the place of theology and

---

[12]"As we have seen, the first characteristic of positive philosophy is that it views all phenomena as subjected to invariable natural *laws*. The purpose of our efforts is—seeing how vain is our search for what are called *causes*, whether first or final—to make an accurate discovery of these laws and to reduce them to the smallest possible number." *Op. cit.*, vol. I, p. 8.

[13]*Op. cit.*, vol. I, p. 11.

[14]"Everything, then, can be reduced to a simple question of fact: Does positive philosophy, which in the last two centuries has gradually undergone so great a development, encompass today all realms of phenomena? It is evident that this is not the case; consequently, a great deal of scientific work remains to be done in order to give positive philosophy the character of universality that is necessary for its definitive constitution." *Op. cit.*, vol. I, p. 11.

[15]"There remains one science to complete the system of sciences of observation—*social physics*." *Op. cit.*, vol. I, p. 12.

[16]*Op. cit.*, vol. I, pp. 12-13.

metaphysics. For future generations these two will merely be interesting points of history.[17]

"Theology will necessarily vanish in the presence of physics."[18] Comte could not have expressed his thought more explicitly. It is not necessary to combat the affirmation of God's existence. Progress will be made in such a way that at a given moment people who are interested in history will wonder what happened to the former affirmation of God's existence. It will then be evident that the backwardness of the theological stage in the development of the human mind gave way, without a struggle against God, to positive philosophy. Theological fictions and metaphysical abstractions will have been replaced by the affirmations of the positive sciences. The kingdom of God will then be gone forever and God will have departed without leaving even one unanswered question after Him.[19]

The Positivistic Mentality

Evidently Comte did not suspect that, despite his vaunted maturity of the human mind, so much attention would be given to the philosophical significance of myths and sagas[20] one hundred years after the appearance of his chief work. And yet such myths and sagas belong to the "backward" period of the human mind. Neither could he have imagined that, at a time that is even more "enlightened" than his, eminent men of science would once more ask themselves what the relation is between physical science and theology, without making themselves ridiculous in the eyes of other scientists.[21] Finally, Comte would have recoiled at the thought that a time would come when it would be considered "backward" to believe that a philosophical system could be as "definitive" as he considered his own to be. Much indeed has changed since Comte wrote his *Course of Positive Philosophy.*

---

[17]"Having thus acquired the character of universality which is still lacking in it, positive philosophy will be able to supersede theological and metaphysical philosophy by its natural superiority. For these two now have only one advantage over positive philosophy, viz., their universality; but, once deprived of it, they will have only an historical existence for the succeeding generations." *Op. cit.,* vol. I, p. 13.

[18]*Op. cit.,* vol. IV, p. 108.

[19]Cf. H. De Lubac, *The Drama of Atheist Humanism,* New York, 1950, pp. 128-159.

[20]Cf. Mircea Eliade, *Myths, Dreams and Mysteries,* New York, 1961.

[21]Cf. F. Dessauer, *Religion im Lichte der heutigen Naturwissenschaft,* Frankfurt, 2nd ed., 1951.

The fact remains, however, that scientism has exercised enormous influence—and we use the term "scientism" here to designate the positivistic mentality, as is usually done in our own day. In many cases the pursuit of science led to scientism, and apparently few stopped to ask themselves whether or not this transition was legitimate. Unsurprisingly, many of those who pursued physical research as well as all adherents of scientism were atheists. In their view "to prove something" could only mean "to do what was done in natural science." "To know" could only mean "to know as in natural science." Hence atheism was inevitable. That is why Le Dantec asked himself how it was possible that some ingenious men of science were not atheists. It even made him suspect that such people were not really sincere; but on second thought he rejected this suspicion, for he realized that his opponents could think the same about him, and yet would be mistaken.[22]

Le Dantec as an Example of the Scientistic Mentality. We should like to consider briefly the work of Le Dantec (1869-1917), not because he is still of any importance, but because he so clearly exemplifies the mentality of scientism. Le Dantec knows that there are proofs for the existence of God. He calls himself an atheist and says explicitly that he is not ashamed of it. However, he is not proud of his atheism, for in his view one man is an atheist by virtue of the same laws by which another is hunchbacked.[23] Whatever a man is, results from a deterministic biological process. Why, then, should anyone be proud of such a result? Or why should he be ashamed of it? And yet there are people with humps who are ashamed of being hunchbacks. Atheism, then, seems to give more consolation than a twist in one's spinal column, for an atheist is not ashamed of his atheism.[24] "I am an atheist, just as I am a Breton, or, as one is brown or blond without having wished to be so."[25]

---

[22]"I know people endowed with excellent minds who have pursued the same kind of studies as I and who nonetheless have preserved their former belief. I must admit that this surprises me greatly. For a long time I must confess I did not believe that they were entirely sincere, for the evidence seemed so striking to me. However, they must have suspected my intellectual honesty too; and this consoles me for having had evil thoughts about them." F. Le Dantec, *L'Athéisme,* Paris, 1906, p. 15.

[23]F. Le Dantec, *op. cit.,* pp. 9 f.

[24]"Thus it appears that atheism is probably more consoling than being hunchbacked, for I am not ashamed of being an atheist. On the other hand, if I don't keep it secret, I am not proud of it either. And I am not interested in making converts as the fox in the fable who had his tail cut." *Op. cit.,* pp. 9 f.

[25]*Op. cit.,* p. 10.

Accordingly, Le Dantec defends a deterministic biologism.[26] Of all that marks man as a person, therefore, none has any value. Man has no soul and there is no immortality or free-will.[27] But all these attributes have been used in the proof for God's existence to construct an idea of God based on the order and harmony that exist in the world. This was simply an anthropomorphic transformation of human characteristics into the idea of a God. But those characteristics originated in old animistic theories—theories that were possible because physiology was still unknown.[28] Man is wholly a product of nature, the result of a cosmic process that is ruled by ironclad laws. And if there is anything we ought to admire, it is this determinism and nothing else.[29]

But why do these iron laws exist? Man is unable to give an answer to this question. He is himself the result of cosmic laws and is permitted to study the results of these laws. That is all! The admiration he feels in the presence of those laws is only a remnant, lingering in his brain, of ancestral theological belief. Those persistent traces are hard to erase, but it would be illogical to construct a God in order to explain determinism since determinism prompts us to deny God.[30]

What remains of the proofs for God's existence in the "light" of such a view? They remain irrefutable for those who make use of them, but for them alone. They prove that those who believe, do believe.[31] That is all! It is, of course, undeniable that a religious faith, closely related to a moral consciousness, has existed at all times and among all peoples; but this also proves nothing. For bees and ants also have moral consciousness. Theirs is even more developed than the moral consciousness of man, at least if we base ourselves on the perfect order that exists in their social life. Why did those remarkable insects not offer the supervision of their social laws—which are older than ours—to God, as men have done? What is more convenient than faith in a supreme Judge? It makes the police superfluous.[32]

---

[26]*Op. cit.*, p. 21.
[27]*Op. cit.*, pp. 44 f.
[28]*Op. cit.*, p. 41.
[29]"For me, who am a convinced determinist, nothing is worthy of admiration save determination itself." *Op. cit.*, p. 44.
[30]"I'd really be illogical if I invented a God to explain the very determinism which induces me to deny God." *Op. cit.*, p. 45.
[31]"All these proofs are irrefutable for those who make use of them. Unfortunately, however, they are so only for them. All they really prove is that their proponents *believe* in God and that is all." *Op. cit.*, p. 24.
[32]*Op. cit.*, p. 34.

The work of Le Dantec is only one example of what we mean by the scientistic mentality. In Germany Haeckel was the principal popularizer of scientism.[33] He addressed himself expressly to all who "seek for the truth" and bewailed the fact that there were still people who appealed to metaphysics for help though they lived in the century of the physical sciences.[34] Such people, he said, still refuse to see that God and the world are one; they are still living in backward superstition and are deceived by priests.[35]

There is no need to add more examples, for it always comes down to the same thing, namely, true knowledge is identical with physical science; the rest is phantasy, superstition, and crude deception.

3. Physical Science and the Affirmation of God's Existence

We have mentioned already that those whose defense of atheism is based on scientism make short work of the demands imposed by the critique of knowledge. For them it is *a priori* certain that knowledge can have no other acceptable meaning than physical science.

Numerous objections have, of course, always been made against this *a priori* position of scientism. Repeatedly its proponents have been reproached on the ground that, contrary to their claim, scientism itself is not an expression of an insight that belongs to physical science. Moreover, it was immediately recognized that the scientistic view of knowledge simply eliminates all ethics. For instance, it is impossible to account for the difference between a deceased man and a murdered man on the basis of physical science. Nevertheless, there is a difference.

Today scientism has become utterly indefensible because of the insights provided by phenomenology. Knowledge obtained in the fashion of physical science now appears to be merely one of the many ways of knowing within a very complex whole of knowledge; it is merely one way of inquiring into reality within the all-encompassing question of being, which is identical with man as existent subject. Let us clarify this assertion.

Our survey of the pre-history of Kantianism showed that both rationalism and empiricism conceived knowledge as the mirroring-in-the-subject of a world that was apart from the subject. The world, according to that view, has a meaning in itself which is mirrored

---

[33]Ernst Haeckel, *Die Welträtsel*, Leipzig, 10th ed., 1909. English edition, *The Riddles of the Universe*, New York, 1900.
[34]*Op. cit.*, Vorwort, pp. IV-VII.
[35]*Op. cit.*, pp. 311-312.

and represented accurately in the subject's "true" knowledge. Scientism added that only the system of the physical sciences mirrors *the* system in an "objective" and "true" way.

Knowledge as Intentionality. Phenomenology, on the contrary, holds that knowledge is not a mirror-like image but a presence.[36] The knowing subject is "immediate presence to a present reality." The knowing subject is a certain "light" through which the world has meaning and significance as unconcealed-for-the-subject. It is the "bodily presence" (*leibhafter Gegenwart*) of the unconcealed which is ultimately the basis of all statements. This is what phenomenology means when it calls consciousness and knowledge *intentionality*. Knowledge is not a mirrored reflection but the orientation of the subject to a present reality, and this reality is not something-in-the-subject, but is reality *itself*.

Reality *itself* therefore can no longer be conceived as the real being which Hume says can never be known. This so-called "real being" was conceived as being-apart-from-the-subject. Being-apart-from-the-subject is "real being" that is not known, not affirmed, not discussed. Obviously, such a being cannot be known, affirmed, or spoken of. Kant likewise is also mistaken when he asserts that the thing-in-itself cannot be known but that it has to be affirmed, for the reasons invoked to make us say that it cannot be known force us to assert that it cannot be affirmed.[37] The reality *itself* of the world about which phenomenology speaks, is not the "real being" of Hume; it is not a conglomeration of Kantian things-in-themselves, it is not a "world in itself."

If consciousness or knowledge, as intentionality, is tied to the world, the world also is tied to consciousness. For Husserl, this unity of mutual implication was principally a relationship of knowing, although he repeatedly insisted that this relationship can also be found on other levels than that of knowledge. Heidegger and Merleau-Ponty developed Husserl's concept of intentionality and conceive man, and all his ways of being man, as "existence." Man is a subject, but he is involved in the world on all levels of being-man and not only on the level of knowledge. Thus the existing subject is

---

[36]We realize that these brief remarks about the fundamental principles of phenomenology are not very illuminating to those who are ignorant of phenomenology. We will revert to this question in Chapter Four. For a brief explanation of the fundamental principles we may refer to our little book, *De fenomenologie is een humanisme*, Amsterdam, 2nd ed., 1962 and to Chapter Two of *Existential Phenomenology*, Pittsburgh, 3rd impr., 1963, pp. 74-175.

[37]*Existential Phenomenology*, pp. 89 ff.

the center of a vast and complicated system of meanings which Husserl calls *"Lebenswelt,"* the world in which the subject lives. This world is the true and objective being-for-the-subject of which phenomenology speaks.

This world is, therefore, radically human. It has not *one* meaning *in itself* but is a system of meanings that is *co*-constituted by the attitude of the subject. The subject is involved in the world by means of many "attitudes," and this explains why the world has so many objective appearances. It is necessary to keep this in mind if we wish to understand the proper character of the various sciences, physical science included.[38]

Existence as the Origin of the Sciences

The subject, as existing *Cogito,* is a pre-reflective awareness-of-the-world. This awareness is presupposed by the judgments of philosophy and of positive science, but itself is not a judgment. It is the foundation, the ground of all judgmental knowledge. For a judgment has a foundation only when it refers to an aspect of man's world of life *(Lebenswelt),* which in turn presupposes the existing subject as *Cogito.* In other words, the judgment has a foundation in existence.[39]

Reality and the Subject's Specific Standpoint. Even as the many attitudes of the existing subject co-constitute many worlds, so do the specific problems of specific sciences bring the specific realms of being to the forefront of the existent subject's field of presence. A science is what it is, namely, *this particular* science and no other, because it puts this particular and specific question to reality.[40] Just as nothing but sounds appear in the audible world, which is attached to my ears, and nothing but colors and perspective present themselves in the visible world attached to my eyes, so are the objects of a specific science connected with the specific question of a particular science. Colors are meaningless to my ears and sounds are bereft of meaning for my eyes. For this reason it is nonsensical to deny the existence of colors because we are unable to hear them.

If we apply this idea concretely to the sciences, we can say similarly that it is nonsense to deny the existence of the soul because it is

[38]*Op. cit.,* pp. 25 ff.
[39]*Op. cit.,* pp. 143 f.
[40]Cf. Joseph A. Kockelmans, *Phaenomenologie en natuurwetenschap,* Haarlem 1962, pp. 47-65 (to be published in *Duquesne Studies, Philosophical Series,* as *Phenomenology and Physical Science*).

impossible to affirm this existence by means of physical science. For physical science does not ask the kind of question that would make the reality of the soul appear to the scientist. Nevertheless the proponent of scientism claims that no other questions and answers are legitimate except those of physical science. Such a claim is self-contradictory: it presupposes another attitude of questioning and replying than the one that is characteristic of physical science, but denies precisely the possibility of another attitude. One who pursues a particular science lives in a particular world, the world that is attached to his attitude of asking questions. Those who pursue distinct sciences are thus incapable of entering into a dialogue with one another and if they do it nonetheless, while adhering to their own particular questioning attitude, they are doomed to talk nonsense.

Existence as Standpoint. We have said above that the judgments of the sciences ultimately rest on existence. This implies that the specific questions of specific sciences are contained as original "interests" in existence. A science arises when a specific question, which as "interest" lies in existence, is taken up critically, reflectively and systematically. An example will serve to clarify our meaning.

Our co-existence contains an original psychological attitude of being-interested. Men in their daily lives act toward one another in an evidently psychological or non-psychological manner. The behavior of a judge toward a delinquent, of a teacher toward his pupil, of a doctor toward his patient, of an applicant toward a personnel director, of a counsellor toward his clients, of a girl toward a boy—all these ways of behaving are clearly either psychological or non-psychological.[41] But, one may ask, what is psychology?

We do not have to answer this question here, but may be satisfied with saying that one thing is certain: no matter what psychology is, it has undoubtedly to cultivate and develop the mysterious, psychological "knowing" that is contained in co-existence; and this should be done by a critical, reasoned and systematic study of what "interests" man when he clearly acts in a psychological way.[42] In dealing with someone psychologically, *specific* questions are asked and *specific* answers are given in a way that is still non-explicit and non-thematic. A process of knowing takes place in which the subject

[41]Cf. B. J. Kouwer and J. Linschoten, *Inleiding tot de Psychologie,* Assen, 1951, pp. 7-101.
[42]Cf. J. H. v. d. Berg, *Kroniek der Psychologie,* 's-Gravenhage, 1954.

assumes a definite attitude, and this attitude at the same time determines the direction in which this knowledge will evolve into a science. If a science fails to take up the original attitude of questioning, it will not be able to develop as a science in such a way that those who pursue it feel that they are acquiring the kind of knowledge which their original interest made them endeavor to attain. In such a case it will be necessary to revise the fundamental principles of the science in question.[43]

The Subject's Standpoint and the Limitation of His Science. The original interest which is contained in existence puts into the foreground a *definite* realm of being, a *definite* landscape of reality, a *definite* field of presence, and stakes it off as a figure against an horizon of various possible meanings.[44] But in the pursuit of a science corresponding to a definite attitude of the existent subject, this delimitation takes place with more care and accuracy than in spontaneous existence. In this way the formal object, the method and the language of the particular science are fixed as a matter of principle; and this science, as it develops, will reveal itself constantly to be clearly different from other sciences in its formal object, method, and language.[45]

It is possible, of course, that a science is able to find its own attitude only after repeated trials, i.e., after repeated revisions of its fundamental concepts. We can once more refer to psychology to illustrate the point. At the time when physical science began to distinguish itself from the other sciences by the extraordinary fruitfulness of its way of questioning, the psychologists were hopeful that they would attain similar success in psychology if they adopted the methods of physical science. But the results were just the reverse.[46] Psychology was pursued as if it were a kind of mental physics or chemistry until it was realized that it was impossible to express in that way what—it was implicitly realized—ought to be expressed.[47] It

---

[43]"The real 'movement' of the sciences occurs when their fundamental concepts are submitted to a more or less radical revision which is transparent to itself." Martin Heidegger, *Sein und Zeit*, Tübingen, 6th ed., 1949, p. 9 (English ed., *Being and Time*, New York, 1962, p. 29).

[44]"The fundamental structures of the area have already been worked out to some extent in the pre-scientific experience and interpretation of the domain of being in which the area of inquiry is itself confined." Heidegger, *op. cit.*, p. 9 (English ed., p. 29).

[45]Cf. Kockelmans, *op. cit.*, pp. 227-248.

[46]Cf. Kockelmans, *op. cit.*, pp. 53-55.

[47]Cf. J. H. v. d. Berg and J. Linschoten, *Persoon en wereld*, Utrecht, 1953, pp. 1-10, 244-253.

is only in our own day that psychologists feel that they approach in their science the original interest or the attitude of questioning which is specifically proper to psychology. But to reach this point, they were obliged to steer away from physical science.

What we have said shows clearly that the scientistic aim of a kind of unified science is a utopian ideal. It is impossible to pursue all the sciences as one pursues physical science, and it is also self-contradictory to maintain that in that case only physical science should be preserved. There is not one world but there are many worlds, and these worlds are neither more nor yet less objective than the world of the physicist.[48] Each science has its own world.[49]

The Impossibility of Affirming the Existence of God by Way of Physical Science

The Closed Realm of the Physicist. The astonishing fruitfulness of physical science is to be attributed to the fact that the physicists remained faithful to their own questioning attitude and to the "thematizing project" proper to their science,[50] without letting themselves be diverted from it even by the objections of some theologians. The scientist wants to question the world solely by means of *measurements.* He thereby stakes off a *specific* field of meaning, a *specific* region of reality, a *specific* field of presence within which he operates. For the physicist this realm is the realm of what is quantitative.[51] And this approach determines the thematizing project of the physicist. "If the physicist remains faithful to the fundamental demand to study every wordly event only in the light of this fundamental approach, his arguments assume a rigorously coherent form, and he attains in them that exactitude which is characteristic of physical science."[52]

Having resolved to question the objects and phenomena of nature only from the standpoint of measurements, he delimitates his field of presence in such a way that nothing that is not quantitative *can* ever arise in it. In other words, the realm in which the physicist is interested is fundamentally closed. This does not mean that his dialogue with the world is ever finished and complete, but it means that his

---

[48]Cf. F. J. Buytendijk, "Vernieuwing in de wetenschap," *Annalen van het Thijmgenootschap*, vol. 42 (1954), p. 237.
[49]Cf. Kockelmans, *op. cit.*, pp. 59-60.
[50]Cf. Heidegger, *op. cit.*, p. 363 (English ed., p. 414).
[51]Cf. Kockelmans, *op. cit.*, p. 232.
[52]Cf. Kockelmans, *op. cit.*, p. 233.

realm is, as a matter of principle, delimited in such a way that, from the standpoint of the thematizing project of the physicist, nothing can ever come into view except the quantitative. If, nevertheless, the physicist introduces something else, he thereby abandons the questioning attitude that is characteristic of him. For instance, he can be impressed by the greatness of what he sees and call it beautiful, but he thus goes beyond his pursuit *as* a physicist. In physical science *itself* nothing is "great" or "beautiful." At the same time, however, it follows that on the basis of his physical science alone he can never *deny* that something is great or beautiful.

Consequences of This Limitation. Applying this consideration to the matter that occupies our attention, we see clearly that a physicist, *as* a physicist, is never able to prove that the noematic correlate of the object of his study is "created." He unveils the quantitative aspect of the world and tries to formulate laws regarding its regularity of operation. *As* a physicist, however, he does not know whether the objects of his research are created or not. If he affirms it anyhow, he goes beyond the questioning attitude that is proper to him. And he commits the same fault when, as a physicist, he denies that the matter about which he speaks is created. As a physicist, he does not even know what he denies.

All this clearly indicates that the physicist, on the basis of his science, lacks competence to deny the existence of the Creator-God, which is affirmed by the believer. The fact that such a denial has been made by scientists in the past, and is made even today, reveals a frightful want of insight into the nature of knowledge.[53] It may be interesting to mention here the answer which Laplace gave to Napoleon when the latter, after being informed of Laplace's nebula theory regarding the origin of the solar system, asked the scientist what he thought of God in connection with his theory. "Sir," Laplace replied, "God is a superfluous hypothesis." Leaving aside what Laplace really meant, we must say that the reply is open to a twofold interpretation.

---

[53]"In the beginning of the struggle between faith and science, the laws of nature were viewed as the greatest enemies of religion. For wherever these laws ruled God could not be in control. The miracle, the proof of God's omnipotence, was wholly eliminated. Since everything happened of necessity and according to fixed laws, God had lost his importance. Matter and energy, in eternal motion, united and separated according to fixed laws. Nothing else existed. Illness and death resulted from the same necessity as health and happiness. God as an intervening and acting being, had disappeared into thin air." A. L. Constandse, *Grondslagen van het atheisme*, Rotterdam, 1926, p. 203.

Laplace was right if he meant that physical science does not have to make an appeal to God in order to say what it has to say *as* physical science. Physical science *never* faces the necessity of affirming the existence of God as long it confines its attention to the noematic correlate of the thematization that is proper to its own approach. Everything that the physicist has to say *as* a physicist can be said without affirming the existence of God. In this sense "God is a superfluous hypothesis." But let us suppose that Laplace meant: it is absolutely impossible for man to say something about God because physical science cannot say anything about Him and all true affirmations are reserved exclusively to physical science. In that case his reply would have been self-contradictory, for such a statement itself lies wholly beyond the possibilities of physical science. Haeckel failed to see this distinction when he interpreted Laplace's answer in a scientistic and, therefore, atheistic way.[54]

4. The Proof for the Existence of God

The Medieval Situation. In the Middle Ages metaphysics tried to prove the existence of God. It was then a question of proving the existence of the God known by Christian Revelation. The philosopher did not want to replace faith by rational understanding and understood very well that reason would not be able to tell us as much as God had deigned to reveal about Himself. Nevertheless, philosophers tried to approach God by means of the natural light of human reason; they wanted to know how far man could go in his affirmations about God without making use of Revelation.

The situation in which the medieval metaphysician philosophized was one of faith. The same is still true today for Christian philosophers who try to prove God's existence. Man is a situated subject, and it is not possible for any one to relinquish his situation whatever it may be. No one who lives in this twentieth century can shake off the facticity of two thousand years of good and bad Christianity; and when he tries to do it anyhow, he gets involved once more in a situation. Sartre, and many with him, have rejected Christianity explicitly. They thereby planted themselves in the concrete situation of unbelievers and reacted against a global situation created by a long history of good and bad Christian thinking and acting. They too, therefore, are situated.

------

[54]Ernst Haeckel, *Die Welträtsel*, p. 275.

Situation and Philosophical Vision. We want to emphasize this point even at this stage in order to make it clear that it is unreasonable to try to reduce the *content* of a man's thinking completely and entirely to the simple fact that a thinker finds himself in this or that situation. This is important to prevent philosophy from being torpedoed and rendered impossible from its very beginning. The fact that a man is always situated in a particular way and the fact that this situation is always represented in his thinking should not lead to the conclusion that the *content* of his thought can be simply and totally reduced to the kind of situation in which he exists and that it can be fully "explained" by that situation. For otherwise it would be fundamentally impossible to distinguish genuine philosophical "seeing" from pseudo-philosophical "seeing," and consequently philosophy would become meaningless.

Some, of course, may object and say, for instance: this shows once more that philosophy has neither meaning nor foundation; therefore, we should confine ourselves to physical science. But this objection too fails to impress us, for to reject philosophy, for example, in favor of physical science, is to make a statement that does not belong to the pursuit of physical science, but is a kind of *philosophy*—albeit a very bad kind of philosophy.

Moreover, the declaration that "the *content* of every philosophy may totally be reduced to the situation of the philosopher" is destructive of this very declaration itself. For those who disagree with that statement will answer that this declaration *itself* is likewise a product of the situation of the philosopher who expressed it. The intention, however, of those who proclaim that "the content of a philosophy can be reduced to the situation of the philosopher," is to say that the *content* of this philosophy does not have to be accepted as philosophically true since it is only the product of a situation. Those who bring this thesis to bear against itself likewise *intend* to say that the thesis does not possess any philosophical *truth,* but this the defenders of the thesis must refuse to admit, for it is precisely their intimate intention to affirm that their thesis actually contains the *truth.*

Accordingly, the intimate intention of the defenders of the thesis is in contradiction with the explicit intention expressed by the words of their thesis. Now, he who denies the intimate intention of the defenders of the thesis and thus admits that the thesis also is *merely* the product of a situation—hence also is *untrue*—no longer maintains anything.

We must accept, therefore, that it is fundamentally possible in philosophy to distinguish between real and merely apparent philosophical "seeing," regardless of the philosopher's situation. The same is true of the situation of faith. The Christian philosopher who tries to prove the existence of God wants to see how far he can go in his attempt to approach God when he relies exclusively on the natural light of reason. He lives in a situation of faith but does not start from faith.[55] That means that faith does not enter into the content of his thought. Only what he "sees" philosophically enters into this content.

The Metaphysical Intention

Physics and Metaphysics. A philosopher is a man who searches because he realizes that there is something to be seen and something to be said.[56] There is something to be seen. We take this term in its widest sense, that is, as having a relation to the immediate presence of a subject to a present reality, no matter what sort of reality it may be. The subject as *Cogito* is a kind of "light"and this light lets a meaning manifest itself. The manifestation of meaning to the subject, and the fact that meanings speak to him, prompts the subject to express himself, to try to say what reality is. Because man is a subject, he can speak.

This speaking, however, can take place on several levels. There is pre-scientific speech and scientific speech. Scientific speech critically, reflectively, and systematically takes up and examines a definite intention of pre-scientific speech in order to "see" reality more clearly and with greater certainty.

The very fact that pre-scientific speaking contains not only one but several intentions, shows that the *term* "seeing" has more than one meaning. A consequence of this is that there is no such thing as "unified" science. There is a plurality of sciences, and each of them is characterized by a specific attitude of questioning, seeing and speaking. It is on this idea that the difference between physics and metaphysics is founded.

---

[55]Cf. H. Bouillard, "Le refus de la théologie naturelle dans la théologie protestante contemporaine," *L'existence de Dieu, Cahiers de l'actualité religieuse* vol. 16, 1961, pp. 95-108.

[56]"To philosophize is to seek, to imply that there are things to be seen and said." Merleau-Ponty, *Eloge de la philosophie*, Paris, 1953, p. 57.

It would be wrong to deny that the physicist searches because he is convinced that there is something to be seen and something to be said. He, too, is driven by this wonder about reality. But this wonder is not the same kind of wonder as that of the metaphysician, which is much more profound. There is a wonder which is unknown to the physicist, and which, as a physicist, he will not act upon even if he knows it. He will not worry about the questions that are raised by the metaphysician. A physicist never asks himself why there is something rather than nothing,[57] but takes it for granted and accepts, without further questioning, that something is.

Things are totally different for the metaphysician. He places himself at the center of all possible questions, at the heart of the wonder of all wonders,[58] because he is aware that there is something rather than nothing. This awareness is the metaphysician himself as existent *Cogito* in its deepest meaning. But at the same time he is also the "object" of this awareness, for the subject-as-*Cogito* is something and not nothing.[59]

Metaphysics, in the tradition of Western thought, has been tied to certain formulas. It is important to preserve them, provided they are not mechanically repeated but brought to life by evoking the experience which the traditional terms served to express. In this way it is said, for instance, that metaphysics is concerned with being *as* be-ing.[60] What, we must ask, does this mean?

The Metaphysical Field of Presence. Historically it was Parmenides who first conceived the possiblity and perspective of the question regarding be-ing *as* be-ing. He understood that, if one adopts a certain questioning attitude, every be-ing agrees with every other be-ing, so that a certain questioning attitude makes it possible

---

[57]"To philosophize is to ask 'Why are there essents [be-ings] rather than nothing?'" Heidegger, *An Introduction to Metaphysics,* New York, 1961, p. 6.

[58]Heidegger, "What is Metaphysics?" in *Existence and Being,* London, n.d., pp. 379 f.

[59]Heidegger, *An Introduction to Metaphysics,* p. 4.

[60]At this point it becomes crucial to find a suitable translation of the term "zijnde," which corresponds to Heidegger's *Seiendes.* Translations of Heidegger's works use *being, that which is, what-is, essent, existent,* and *entity.* It appears preferable to us to use *be-ing,* which aptly transliterates the term as the participle of the verb *to be* and therefore manages to maintain the close relationship with the verb in a readily intelligible fashion. The term "zijn" (German *Sein*) will be translated as *being* and occasionally as *to be.* For the metaphysician there is no difficulty involved if we have to speak sometimes about "the being of be-ings," and to the non-metaphysician the expression "the being of essents" does not give any greater clarity. In quotations from other books we have retained the terms used by them. Tr.

to put *everything* into question in a single question. Every science find its inspiration in a specific question; in this question a specific and homogeneous region of being, a specific field of meaning, becomes a focal point in the field of presence of the subject-as-*Cogito;* it is cut off from other regions of being, which are thus moved back to the horizon of the subject's field of presence. A specific region of being, a specific field of meaning, is connected with a specific question of the subject as its correlate. The questioned objects agree with one another within this specific region of being, so that, for instance, when we inquire into the essence of a material thing, it does not matter whether the question is addressed to one material thing or to another. It follows, then, that whatever can be said about a material thing as a material thing is true prior to any empirical verification concerning any material thing that appears here and now. The reason is that the statements about a material thing as a material thing are true for the specific region of being of the material thing, since in this region every material thing agrees with every other material thing.

In regard to the metaphysical question, however, the field of presence of the subject-as-*Cogito* shows a very special structure. This question is not concerned with a particular be-ing as corresponding with every other particular be-ing within a particular region of being, but concerns be-ing as be-ing,[61] as agreeing with any kind of be-ing whatsoever; it is concerned with the universe, not as the sum total of plants, animals, men, planets, stars and suns, but as the universality of all be-ings *as* be-ings, as not-nothing.[62] When I consider plants, animals, men, planets, stars, and suns *as* be-ings, I am not thinking of them as being-plants as such, or as being-stars as such, for that is not essential to the fact that they are be-ings, since animals and planets are be-ings without being plants or stars.[63]

Metaphysics and the Metaphysical Dimension. It may be useful to emphasize that the metaphysical question is not an invention of the

---

[61]"[Aristotle] says 'as being' because the other sciences, which deal with particular beings, do indeed consider being (for all the subjects of the sciences are beings), yet they do not consider being as being, but as some particular kind of being, for example, number or line or fire or the like." St. Thomas Aquinas, *Commentary on the Metaphysics* of *Aristotle,* tr. by John Rowan, Chicago, Regnery, 1961, vol. I. p. 216, no. 530.

[62]"The range of this question finds its limits only in nothing, in that which simply is not and never was." Heidegger, *An Introduction to Metaphysics,* p. 2.

[63]"In asking this question we keep our distance from every particular and individual essent, from every this and that." Heidegger, *op. cit.,* p. 3.

science of metaphysics, but lies contained within the existent subject-as-*Cogito*. The metaphysician finds it there and takes it up to examine it critically, reflectively and systematically. The subject himself as *Cogito* is a metaphysical "consciousness." There is in every man an implicit metaphysical consciousness because everyone "knows" that a plant, a child, or a meteor does not belong to reality, to the order of being, *by virtue of* their being a plant, a child or a meteor. This consciousness, that everything "belongs to reality," is made explicit and elaborated in metaphysics. This consciousness is the subject himself as *Cogito* and is presupposed by metaphysics. Metaphysics is based on a metaphysical experience, on a definite dimension of the immediate presence of the subject to a present reality—namely, the dimension in which the subject dwells in the universe of being. Metaphysics presupposes "the metaphysical" in man. It is a reflexive return to the metaphysical dimension of the existing subject as *Cogito* and expresses the implications of this dimension.[64]

The Metaphysical "Standpoint." As should be evident from these remarks, metaphysical questioning is truly "meta-physical."[65] It cannot at all be compared to the questions of the physicist, but totally transcends them. The field of meaning of the physicist is a limited region of being, namely, that in which be-ings reveal a quantitative aspect. In metaphysics it is impossible to make use of any of the concepts and proofs of the physicist, for he does not deal with be-ing as *be-ing* but as *quantified*. The physicist, *as* such, doesn't even know what the metaphysician is concerned with.

We must add that, properly speaking, it is not correct to say that the metaphysical is a "circumscribed" or "limited" attitude of asking questions. All non-metaphysical attitudes of questioning are limited intentions, because they single out a particular field of meaning, a particular region of being. They are occupied with a particular kind of be-ing as *particular*. Metaphysics, on the contrary, is not concerned with a particular meaning, a particular kind of being but with meaning *as* meaning and be-ing *as* be-ing. It aims at the universe of being, the universality of all be-ings *as* be-ings. The metaphysical

---

[64]A. Dondeyne, "L'expérience préphilosophique et les conditions anthropologiques de l'affirmation de Dieu," *L'existence de Dieu, Cahiers de l'actualité religieuse*, vol. 16, p. 148.

[65]"When in our thinking we open our minds to this question, we first of all cease to dwell in any of the familiar realms." Heidegger, *op. cit.*, p. 10.

intention is not a "particular" or "specific" questioning attitude, but
is all-encompassing. Metaphysics, in this sense, is concerned with
everything.[66]

The Way to the Transcendent Being

As we have mentioned before, classical metaphysics has always
tried to discover to what extent the light of natural reason is able to
approach the God of Christian Revelation. According to Christian
tradition, God has not only revealed Himself as Tri-une but also as
Creator, Origin and Cause of all things. Metaphysics has never tried
nor will it try to prove that God is Tri-une, but the same cannot be
asserted with respect to God as Creator, Transcendent Origin and
Cause of all things. The reality of God as Creator, which is an
undeniable aspect of Christian Revelation, is something that can be
considered in the light of natural reason, when one realizes the implications of be-ing as be-ing.

The Inescapable Character of the Most Fundamental Question.
"Why is there something rather than nothing?" This is the most
fundamental question man can ask. But what exactly does man want
to know when he asks this question? Does it make sense to ask it?
Cannot man simply fix his regard on the be-ings that are and accept
them as such?

The reply is that it is impossible for him to do so. Asking about
be-ing as be-ing, man asks for the "why" of be-ing; he asks for the
ground, the cause of be-ings.[67] He *must* ask this question for be-ing
reveals itself as without a ground of being within itself, and yet it is.

We realize this when we see that be-ings *are* not by virtue of
their own essence,[68] for otherwise they would be *pure* "to be." But
this is evidently not so, for there are many be-ings; they are alike in
being be-ings, but they do not coincide and consequently are different. But what else could "to be different" mean if not that one being has something that the other does not have? Hence the "to be"

---

[66]"For through this questioning the essent as a whole is for the first time
opened up as such with a view to its possible ground, and in the act of
questioning it is kept open." Heidegger, *op. cit.*, p. 4.
    [67]"The formulation of the question includes: 1) a definite indication of what
is put into question, of what is *questioned;* 2) an indication of what the
question is about, of what is asked. For it is clearly indicated what the
question is about, namely, the essent. What is asked after, that which is asked,
is the why, i.e., the ground." Heidegger, *op. cit.*, pp. 18 f.
    [68]Cf. Thomas Aquinas, *Being and Essence,* ch. 5.

of be-ings evidently implies a certain "not to be"; consequently, be-ings are not pure "to be." Be-ings *are* not their "to be" but *have* it.

And now the mind feels the need of questioning further. For as soon as we realize that be-ings are not by virtue of their own essence, we realize also that they must be by virtue of "something else," for it is impossible to admit that be-ing is not. "Nothing" would be much simpler than be-ing, but it is impossible to deny that be-ing is. Be-ing has no foundation of being in itself and yet it is. Classical metaphysics expresses this idea by saying that be-ing is contingent.[69] The contingency of be-ing as be-ing forces us to ask the question why there is something and not nothing, for in the light of the preceding considerations we see that be-ing *can* also not be.[70]

The wonder about be-ing and the question why there is something rather than nothing spring from the vague awareness that no be-ing of the universe has the ground of its being in itself: none is self-explanatory as be-ing. It is the metaphysician who makes explicit the implications of this awareness. The wonder about be-ing gives rise to a radical questioning—so radical, in fact, that every be-ing loses its obviousness.[71] The explicit consciousness of the contingency of the be-ings and of the universe of being causes be-ing to waver.[72]

---

[69]The reader will notice that we do not mention the five starting points used by Thomas Aquinas in his *Summa Theologica*. They have been omitted intentionally in order to avoid unnecessary complications. Such complications and the resulting confusion are not avoided when, unlike St. Thomas, one does not go at once beyond the original starting point to the metaphysical dimension with which St. Thomas is concerned. The proof of God's existence from motion does not start from motion in order to conclude to a first physical mover, but proceeds from motion to the contingency of be-ing as be-ing and argues from this contingency to the existence of God. One who remains on the physical level of motion remains within the realm of physics within which "going on to infinity" is an everyday occurrence and a "first mover" is meaningless. The Thomistic proofs have only one foundation, and this foundation is metaphysical. "This ultimate and unique foundation is the impossibility that the be-ings of our world of experience as well as man himself can account for, and give a basis to their being. Yet it is their being which makes them be whatever they are. This metaphysical foundation is the radical gratuity of the be-ings of this world as be-ings." D. De Petter, " Le caractère métaphysique de la preuve de l'existence de Dieu et la pensée contemporaine," *L'existence de Dieu* (see footnote 55), p. 167.

[70]"It is the evidence of this gratuity which makes us ask the inevitable question: Why is there something rather than nothing?" De Petter, *art. cit.,* p. 167.

[71]"With our question we place ourselves in the essent in such a way that it loses its self-evident character as essent." Heidegger, *op. cit.,* p. 24.

[72]"Now the essent is no longer that which just happens to be present; it begins to waver and oscillate, regardless of whether or not we recognize the essent in all certainty, regardless of whether or not we apprehend it in its full scope. Henceforth the essent as such oscillates, insofar as we draw it into the question." Heidegger, *op. cit.,* p. 23.

Many special sciences have gained solid knowledge about particular fields of meaning, particular regions of reality and clearly-defined "landscapes." Physical science and the technology made possible by it have given man dominion over the world. Nevertheless, everything wavers as soon as man dares to ask why there is something rather than nothing. The replies of the special sciences are meaningless here, for they cannot even ask the question that has to be answered since they do not dwell in the universe of being. The metaphysical question suspends everything in mid-air,[73] and that includes the questioning metaphysician himself, for he too is a contingent be-ing.[74]

The Search for the Cause of Be-ings. A be-ing which does not have the reason for its being in itself and yet *is,* must find its ground in something other than itself; it must be under the influence of something else, it must be caused.[75] The contingent be-ing *is,* but in such a way that it could also not be. Be-ing itself deserves and demands to be put into question, so much even that this problem can never be shaken off. Be-ings *are* but their being is also a possibility of not being. This possibility of not being is not an addition to be-ing made by man's thinking; be-ing reveals itself as "able not to be" to the questioning metaphysician.[76] Accordingly, "being caused" also is not something that man's thinking adds to be-ing but a be-ing's very being shows *itself* as "being caused," as being-through-the-influence-of-something-else. And the metaphysician inquires about this "influence," i.e., about the cause of be-ing, when he tries to understand why there is something rather than nothing.

But the search for the reason, the cause of be-ing as be-ing, easily gets on the wrong track. One could imagine that the question about the cause of be-ing as be-ing is like the questions, "Why are there

---

[73]Heidegger, *op. cit.,* p. 24.

[74]"The essent begins to waver between the broadest and most drastic extremes: 'either essents—or nothing?'—and thereby the questioning itself loses all solid foundation. Our questioning being-there is suspended, and in this suspense is nevertheless self-sustained." Heidegger, *op. cit.,* p. 24.

[75]"Whatever does not pertain to a being by virtue of this being itself, pertains to it through a cause." Thomas Aquinas, *Contra gentes,* bk. I, ch. I. "From the very fact that something is a being by participation, it follows that it is caused." *Summa theologica,* p. I, q. 44, a. 1 *ad* 1.

[76]"[The essent] cannot slough off the problematic fact that it might also *not* be what it is and as it is. We do not experience this possibility as something that we add to the essent by thinking; rather the essent itself elicits this possibility, and in this possibility reveals itself. Our questioning only opens up the horizon in order that the essent may dawn in such questionableness." Heidegger, *op. cit.,* p. 24.

lice in the vineyard?" or, "Why are my books mouldy?"[77] That would be a mistake. Kant's critique has rendered great services in making us avoid such an error.

It is true, of course, that those two questions also inquire about causes. But the attitude in which the questions are asked co-determines the *kind of causal influence* about which an answer is sought. The causal influence that is invoked is one that is valid within a definite region of reality, within a definite "landscape" of being, but not outside it. I can also ask, "What causes the movement of celestial bodies?" or "Why is it that one who never meets with kindness cannot indefinitely continue to cope with life?" In this case my questions refer to other regions of reality within which other types of causal influence are valid. The metaphysician, however, cannot borrow any of these types because they belong to a *particular* realm of being. As a metaphysician, he dwells in the universe and not in any particular realm of reality. He who wants to make use of a kind of causality that is valid only within a particular field of meaning in order to explain be-ing, is on the wrong track; he shows that he does not realize what he is supposed to explain.

The metaphysician inquires about the cause that draws be-ing from non-being and prevents it from sinking back into nothing, for of itself a be-ing is nothing and, as merely be-ing, it can also not be.[78] The biologist can explain why there are lice in the vineyard, but when he does that, he merely explains that the lice have won the battle against the chemicals sprayed on the vines; he does not explain that a battle has been won over non-being.[79] The physicist does not have to explain be-ing as be-ing, for that question is meaningless for him *as* a physicist. When, *as* a physicist, he rejects the explanation of the metaphysician, his denial is *per se* concerned with something else than that which is affirmed by the metaphysician.

From these considerations it should be easy to see why we have said that nothing is much more simple than be-ing. If there is nothing, no explanations at all are needed. But something *is,* and therefore we have to ask why it is. What could possibly be the cause

---

[77]Cf. Heidegger, *op. cit.,* p. 23.

[78]"Thereby the why takes on a very different power and penetration. Why is the essent torn away from the possibility of nonbeing? Why does it not simply fall back into nonbeing?" Heidegger, *op. cit.,* p. 23.

[79]"The search for the why undergoes a parallel change. It does not aim simply at providing an also present ground and explanation for what is present; now a ground is sought which will explain the emergence of the essent as an overcoming of nothingness." Heidegger, *op. cit.,* p. 23.

of the being of be-ing? Certainly not any be-ing that belongs to the universe. For no matter which be-ing of this universe one may wish to designate as the cause of be-ing as be-ing, it is always a mere be-ing, i.e., a contingent be-ing, hence a caused be-ing. It is not the cause of be-ing, for it is caused be-ing. Precisely from the viewpoint from which one would want to designate it as the cause of be-ing, namely, the viewpoint of be-ing, it is not cause but caused because it is a contingent be-ing.[80] The metaphysical questioning suspends everything "in mid-air." "Nothing" appears more simple than be-ing as soon as one realizes that the universe, in the sense of the universality of all be-ings, does not have the reason for its being in itself. But there is not nothing; there are be-ings, the universe is. Be-ing is a being-caused; it is under the influence of something else; hence it is impossible that this "influencing reality" *is* not, for then there would be nothing. But something is.

Affirmation or Negation?

Let us try to appraise the results of our metaphysical reflection on the implications of the fact that be-ings are merely be-ings. At this point we realize that, by accepting as undeniable that be-ing *is* within the universe, we have in fact already affirmed the real existence of an Origin and Cause of all be-ings outside the universe, we have affirmed a Transcendent Origin and Cause. For the be-ings of the universe show themselves as contingent and caused; hence it is no longer possible to deny the Cause while affirming the being of these be-ings. It is evident that the Cause of be-ings is not to be found within the universe; hence it is undeniable that this Cause is a reality outside the universe.

Can we say that God "is"? As we have seen, the God of Christianity has revealed Himself as the Transcendent Origin and Cause of all things. Thus the metaphysician has penetrated to a depth where he can affirm that there really is a God. And yet it is almost impossible for him to say that God *is*. As soon as he *has to* say it, he realizes that he *cannot* say so, at least not without qualification. For what is meant by the term "is"? The metaphysician has affirmed

---

[80]"This question "why" does not look for causes that are of the same kind and on the same level as the essent itself. This "why" does not move on any one plane but penetrates to the "underlying" realms and indeed to the very last of them, to the limit; turning away from the surface, from all shallowness, it strives toward the depths; this broadest of all questions is also the deepest." *Op. cit.*, p. 3.

that be-ing *is*. But it is obvious that he can now no longer say unqualifiedly that the Transcendent Being *is*, for if he affirmed the Transcendent Being in this way, he would affirm it as a be-ing and consequently would not do justice to it. The thinking of the metaphysician becomes a riddle to himself. That which he can really conceive is be-ing; hence is there still a possibility of conceiving God? In the strict sense of the terms it is not possible for man to "think" or "speak" about God, for human thought and speech are concerned with be-ings and God is not a be-ing.

The thought and speech of the metaphysician about God is a thought and speech that does not reach God in the way his thinking and speaking about be-ings reach be-ings. It is only an indirect thinking and speaking by means of concepts and terms that point beyond themselves, because be-ings point beyond themselves. Those concepts and terms are, as it were, road signs: they themselves do not go to the place to which they point.

To put it more concretely, every affirmation of God must be accompanied by a negation; without an immediately added negation every affirmation is blasphemous. Man cannot say without qualification that God *is*, that He *is* the Creator and Providence, that He *is* Good and Wise. All those expressions dishonor God unless a certain negation is immediately added to them.

What we have said shows that there is no part of philosophy in which it is so easy for man to go astray than when he speaks about God.[81] The inclination not to go beyond the "spoken word," that is, to repeat the spoken words of the past as an acquired "possession" of a community of speaking persons, instead of restoring it to life and making it a "speaking word," is always a dangerous threat to authentic philosophizing. Speech really says something only when he who speaks affirms reality through it. But such speech supposes first

---

[81]In a discussion with a religious humanist Prof. E. Schillebeeckx argues against the view that the Catholic does not attempt to understand life and the world on the basis of his human powers, but simply takes his faith in Revelation as his starting point. Schillebeeckx rightly point out that supernatural faith in the God of Christian Revelation presupposes the rational justification of God's existence by means of man's natural faculties and then proceeds to present a sketch of such a justification. However, it strikes us as intolerable that the author makes no mention whatsoever of the negative aspect contained in this dialectic justification, especially when one keeps in mind that he addresses himself to persons who do not without reason assume an agnostic attitude toward the possibility of affirming God's existence. Cf. E. Schillebeeckx, "De betekenis van het niet-godsdienstige humanisme voor het hedendaagse Katholicisme," *Modern niet-godsdienstig humanisme,* Nijmegen, 1961, pp. 74-112.

of all seeing in person. We emphasize "in person," for "seeing" is something done by man himself, and if he *himself* does not see, he does not *see* at all. Of course, it is much easier merely to repeat words than to speak.

All this applies in even greater measure to speaking about God. To speak authentically about God demands a personal involvement in a dialectics of "understanding" and "not understanding," of "affirming" and "denying," in order not to lose sight of the fact that concepts and terms have no more value than that of road signs with respect to God. This rule applies also to theologians. They, too, use the little word "is" hundreds of times. Yet, we may ask how often do they ask themselves what it means? He who refuses to ask this question may finally think that he really "knows" what he speaks about.

Character of the Proof for God's Existence. In regard to the philosophical approach to the existence of God it is customary to use the term "to prove." However, it will be useful to make some remarks about it in order to prevent misunderstandings, for the term is heavily burdened with all kinds of connotations inherited from the past.

From what we have said above, it would be evident that it is not possible to compare the "proof" for the existence of God to a mathematical deduction or a physical induction.[82] The "proof" for God's existence is *sui generis*. The term "proof" expresses the undeniable fact that the road to the affirmation of God's existence cannot consist in explicitating the content of an immediate, natural experience of God, for God is not a present Reality to which man is directly present. Hence the proof for God's existence cannot consist in pointing out God, for when someone is effectively "pointed out" we expect his reality to manifest *itself*.[83] But God does not manifest *Himself* to man.

The proof of God's existence brings man to the affirmation of His existence in virtue of a certain process of "reasoning." This process

---

[82] "No matter how one conceives the affirmation of God's reality, or of the fundamental act of faith, it is quite clear that both lie in an entirely different dimension and that the notions of exactness or rigor demand to be re-interpreted or transposed." Gabriel Marcel "L'athéisme philosophique et la dialectique de la conscience religieuse," *L'athéisme contemporain*, Geneva, n. d., pp. 73 f.

[83] Cf. A. Dondeyne, "L'expérience préphilosophique et les conditions anthropologiques de l'affirmation de Dieu," *L'existence de Dieu, Cahiers de l'actualité religieuse*, 1961, p. 153.

consists in this that one realizes what is implied in the being of the be-ings given in a metaphysical experience. But when one realizes this implication and concludes that God *is,* God has not manifested *Himself,* God is not a "datum," something given.[84] And because God is not something "given," atheism remains a fundamental possibility.[85]

Retrospect and Difficulties

Many objections have been made against the proof for the existence of God in the course of history. And yet the proof seems to have gained prestige rather than lost. Kant's criticism forced the metaphysicians to remove any kind of physicalism from the proof for God's existence. For it is evidently impossible to transcend the field of sense intuition when one uses a physical concept of causality. God does not manifest Himself within the field of sense intuition.

In our own day the objections presented against the proof of God's existence are no longer epistemological but rather, we may say, anthropological. They are made by phenomenologists and existentialists, not only by the atheists among them, but also by the theists.

Objection of Atheists. The atheists, of whom Sartre and Merleau-Ponty are the principal protagonists, *start* from the *terminus* of the proof of God's existence. They think they can show that the real existence of the *Esse necessarium* makes impossible the reality of man as a contingent be-ing. They acknowledge the contingency, the point of departure of the proof, but refuse to accept the terminus to which the proof of God's existence leads,[86] because such a terminus would destroy contingency.[87] It may be readily admitted that this objection is impressive and differs entirely from the epistemological

---

[84]"The meaning of this 'pointing out' is to permit the *encounter with the thing itself.* Unfortunately, God is not an object of encounter for the philosopher; otherwise, the problem of God would have been solved long ago because God would not even be a problem." Dondeyne, *op. cit.,* p. 153.

[85]Cf. E. Borne, *Dieu n'est pas mort. Essai sur l'athéisme contemporain,* Paris, 1956, p. 18.

[86]"Theology establishes the contingency of the human being for the sole purpose of deriving it from a necessary being, that is, in order to get rid of it." Merleau-Ponty, *Eloge de la philosophie,* Paris, 1953, p. 61.

[87]"Father de Lubac discusses an atheism which intends to get rid, he says, even of the problem which made God arise in consciousness. But this problem, far from being disregarded by the philosopher, is made most radical by him; he puts it above the solutions which choke it." Merleau-Ponty, *op. cit.,* p. 62.

difficulties of the past. We shall delay to our last chapter the thorough examination of that objection because we have not yet given the explanations that are required for the evaluation of the objection in its proper context.

Objection of Theists. Theists, on the other hand, object to the proof for God's existence on the basis of the demands of man's authentic religiousness. They say that the proof does not conclude to the reality that God is for the religious man. The proof concludes only to the real existence of an impersonal transcendent Being, but not to God as He really is for one who prays. Bergson expressed this difficulty by saying that, when the philosopher speaks about God, he is so little occupied with the God of whom most people think, that no one would recognize the philosophers' God if He came down and showed Himself to our eyes. And Marcel finds it impossible to love and pray to the God of the metaphysical proof.[88]

It is undeniable, of course, that God means much more to the religious man than what is expressed in the proof of God's existence. But the question is whether it is right to conclude that the God of the proof means *nothing* and that the religious man can do without it. It is our opinion that both parts of this conclusion go too far and are therefore unacceptable.

The Proof of God's Existence is Not Meaningless. The defenders of this objection against the proof mean by "religious man" not one who acknowledges man's natural orientation toward a Transcendent Reality but one who has entered into the Christian's religious relation with God. "Religiousness" for these objectors is the same as the supernatural life of faith. As we have mentioned, God means much more for the man of supernatural faith than what is expressed in the proof of God's existence. In prayer God means much more than the Transcendent Being, just as "my mother" means much more for me who loves her than for a biologist who considers her simply as the basis of my conception through certain biological processes.

On the other hand, it is also undeniably true that man has to enter the religious dimension and that this entrance has to be rationally justified, for otherwise there could not be question here of a *human* entrance into the religious dimension. This rational justification implies also that man becomes intellectually convinced of

---

[88]Cf. P. Colin, "Le théisme actuel et les preuves classiques de l'existence de Dieu," *L'existence de Dieu,* pp. 139-140.

God's existence[89]; otherwise his religiousness is meaningless.[90] The rational conviction that God exists, of which the proof is the "learned expression," in any case brings man so far that he can no longer divinize his own subjectivity as freedom, because he sees this subjectivity as not self-grounding, i.e., as of itself and in itself absolutely *nothing*. The proof of God's existence prompts man to make an act of humility, submission and adoration that can in no way refer to a mere be-ing but can be addressed to the Transcendent Being alone. The rational recognition of God's existence thus is the starting point of a religious life in which God can assume an ever greater importance.[91]

Even when God constantly assumes greater importance in man's supernatural relation of faith to Him, the proof of God's existence does not become superflous. For man does not have any automatic guarantee that his trusting prayer to God is authentic. Even prayer can degenerate into a pseudo-prayer, in which God is no longer spoken to as a Transcendent God. It is possible to reduce God to a worldly factor, a pseudo-God, even in prayer. For instance, the prayer of petition can become a crude or subtle form of magic. Obviously, in such a case a metaphysical reflection on God's transcendence can serve as a means to purify prayer. Taking once more the analogy given above, the fact that I cannot express the reality which "my mother" is by recalling the physiological processes of conception and birth, does not mean that those processes do not belong to the integral reality that constitutes "my mother." It could even happen that only physiology would be able to determine who is really "my mother." In a similar way it may happen that man may

---

[89]Accordingly, we would never want to claim that the possibility to become rationally convinced of God's existence is reserved for metaphysicians. Only the expression of this rational justification in "learned language" belongs to them. Cf. D. De Petter, *art. cit.* (footnote 69), p. 169.

[90]"Now this entrance into religious life or into faith demands a rational justification because it is human and in order to be authentically human. And this justification must aim before everything else at the real existence of that God to whom we surrender in religious life. For otherwise this life could not acquire any meaning and value in our eyes." De Petter, *art. cit.*, p. 177.

[91]In our book *Existential Phenomenology* (p. 68) we have said that the proof of God's existence *presupposes* religiousness and that this religiousness leads to the proof. These assertions are not contradicted by what we are saying here, for the religiousness mentioned in *Existential Phenomenology* referred to man's *natural* orientation to the transcendent, as should be abundantly clear from the context. Hence it would be silly to interpret this orientation in a *supernatural* sense and to conclude that we defend a "fideistic" viewpoint.

need metaphysics in order to determine who really is "his God" and which gods are false gods.[92]

5. Atheism Among Those Who Affirm God's Existence

History shows clearly that atheism does not lead an independent existence. It appears only as a phenomenon that accompanies the genuine or the pseudo-affirmation of God. In this sense there is bad and good atheism. Socrates was the defender of a good atheism because he rejected the pseudo-gods of Athens. He went against the "faith" of the Athenians, but their faith was a bad faith.

Of course, things are different now from what they were in Socrates' time. And yet they are not so totally different as to exclude the existence of "good" atheism. Atheism still accompanies the affirmation of God's existence, whether genuine or merely a pseudo-affirmation. In our day this means that atheism does not merely reject the affirmation of God contained in New Testament Revelation but also—and sometimes exclusively—that which presents itself as an affirmation of God's existence without really affirming Him. For there are ways of affirming God's existence that are not at all, or only slightly, different from the affirmation of a pseudo-God. As a negation of such a pseudo-God, atheism is good and has a purifying value. It may be useful to develop this point further.

"Scientific" Proofs for God's Existence

At the time when God was rather generally rejected because physical science was incapable of proving His existence, there were, of course, a few pious scientists who tried to show that the sciences are able to establish His existence. A well-known example is Clausius who based his proof on the principle of entropy. More recent examples were the proofs of Carrel and Lecomte de Nouy, which were borrowed from biology.[93]

Scientific Proofs are Fundamentally Impossible. We shall not present those proofs or discuss the objections made against them by positive science. Suffice it to say that this kind of proof is *bound to* fail in principle since it attempts the impossible by going beyond the fundamental possibilities of knowledge accessible to positive science.

[92]Cf. M.Sciacca, *Le problème de Dieu et de la religion dans la philosophie contemporaine,* Paris, 1950, pp. 203-204.

[93]Cf. R. Jolivet, *Le Dieu des philosophes et des savants,* Paris, 1956, pp. 76-78.

Beyond any doubt, the God of the New Testament is a transcendent God, whereas the positive sciences, in virtue of their own attitude, are in principle capable only of attaining immanent causes.[94] All the positive sciences are concerned with causes within the world and are in principle unable to refer to any transcendent reality or transcendent causal influence. With Kant we can say that it is not possible to go beyond the field of the sense intuition when one makes use only of causality as it is understood by positive science.

It is true, of course, that the sciences over and over again encounter enigmas in their research. There is then a great temptation to let the "light" of the affirmation of God shine in such a dark corner of science and to appeal to God as the cause. But such a God is a pseudo-God. This is evident when we recall the history of progress made by science. The god of thunder and lightning, the sun-god, the god of fertility, and many similar gods have been discarded long ago.[95] And rightly so, for within the field of presence circumscribed by a particular attitude of asking scientific questions, there are no enigmas whose solution is fundamentally beyond the reach of the science in question. And, in principle, the field of presence of each particular science is a *closed* field, that is, it is so delimited that nothing can ever appear within it except the correlate of a particular, specific, scientific thematization. For example, within the field of presence of physical science nothing else can ever appear except numbers of measurement. There is no room in it for the true God. To prove God's existence by means of physical science is equivalent to making him the first link in a chain of causes and effects which are real from the standpoint of physical science. Such a God loses His transcendence in man's thinking and is a pseudo-God.[96] Anyone who wants to make the affirmation of God accessible to physical science is, in reality, defending a pseudo-God and renders poor service to theism.

Physical Enigmas Are Not "Open Doors" Leading to God. How strange it must sound to scientists when theologians tell them with a

[94]"Positive knowledge, which is by definition knowledge of the world and of phenomena, cannot in any form have any metaphysical importance." Jolivet, *op. cit.*, p. 77.

[95]Cf. J. Lacroix, *Le sens de l'athéisme moderne*, Tournai, 1958, p. 20.

[96]"Undoubtedly, it is correct to note that the idea of God has been purified by being no longer used as a principle of explanation. For, to prove God's existence scientifically, is to make God the first link of an explanatory chain, to make Him therefore a homogeneous factor in the whole of the explanation, and to make Him no longer a subject but an object." Lacroix, *op. cit.*, pp. 19 f.

great display of eloquence that God stands, as it were, waiting behind every door opened by science. Physicists who understand the nature of their science and non-physicists who know what physicists try to do, realize that behind every "open door," that is, behind the physical solution of every physical problem, there is another physical problem, which clamors for another *physical* answer. Nothing can ever appear, except a reality of physical science, that is, a quantitative reality, to anyone who remains faithful to the attitude that characterizes the pursuit of this science. There is, of course, much more in reality than the quantitative aspect, but not for the *physicist as such*. It is misleading and untrue to hold that nothing exists except physical science and quantity, but it is equally misleading and untrue to hold that the non-quantitative can be revealed by the physicist and that it exists for him *as* physicist. Accordingly, the question concerning God as the Creator cannot occur in physical science, and this science can never affirm God as such, if it is true that God is transcendent and not a certain unit of quantity.

Again, there are some theologians who think that what modern physics says about the mutability of the world goes beyond a simple confirmation of the starting point of the first proof of God's existence. They almost attribute to it the structure of a proof based on physical science, a proof which is in great part new and more acceptable, convincing, and pleasing to many minds. However, the same difficulties as those we have mentioned above accompany this new proof. And if there are many for whom a proof of God's existence based on physical science is more acceptable, more convincing, and more agreeable, it shows no more and no less than that there are many who either are ignorant of what the physicist does or totally unaware of God's transcendence. A proof of physical science can only be more convincing and acceptable to them because they are more at home with a pseudo-God than with the true, the transcendent God.

The Physical Problem of the Origin of Matter Does Not Demand a Creator. Thirdly, it is quite possible that the physicist will recognize that he is in the presence of an enigma when he faces the problem about the origin of the primordial world matter. But it is a mistake to tell the physicist that the human mind, trained in philosophical thought, can penetrate deeper in *this* problem. For the metaphysical problem of creation is totally different from the physicist's problem regarding the origin of the world's primordial matter. The metaphysical problem of creation is concerned with the explanation of contingency of be-ing as be-ing, in regard to both its origin and its continued existence. Formally speaking, it has nothing to do with the question of the origin of primordial matter. Unlike physical science, metaphysical thinking does not move in a horizontal line. It establishes a vertical dependence on a transcendent Being, and this is a question which the thinking of the physicist, by virtue of his own questioning attitude, cannot even ask.[97] He who maintains that the philosopher can say something more in the same line where the physicist acknowledges he can say no more seems to think that philosophical thought—in this case metaphysical thought—lies in the same line as the thinking of physical science. One can imagine how strange such a claim must appear to the physicist.

In fact philosophy has *nothing* to say regarding the realm encompassed by the thematization of physical science, just as physical science has nothing to say regarding the domain of metaphysics. Hence the metaphysician cannot continue the dialogue when the physicist is "stuck," for *from the very beginning* they move in different realms of meaning. Hence the idea of creation is neither reconcilable nor irreconcilable with the results of physical science, for the results of metaphysics and those of physics are unrelated. Physicists who understand their field of knowledge will not bow before a physical argument for God's existence, and they are right! It is misleading to present matters as if modern science is moving more toward the acknowledgment of God than was the case formerly when those sciences were still in their infancy, for neither a primitive science nor a highly developed science has anything to do with the affirmation of God's existence.

It was shortsighted on the part of certain physicists of former times to assert that the hypothesis of God was absolutely irreconcilable with the results of science. But it is just as shortsighted for believers to maintain that, in view of the present high development

[97]"The metaphysical proof is a proof from the gratuitousness of the being of the things that *are*, and not a proof from the first and temporal origin of the world, even though it is true that the proof is rather often spontaneously presented in this form. Formally speaking, the proof has nothing to do with the order of succession of things in the world or with the horizontal relationships of dependence which link them together. Metaphysical dependence, on the contrary, is a vertical dependence on a Being which transcends the entire internal order of the world. This world and everything it contains depends on the transcendent Being for the *beginning* of its existence only because it depends on this Being for its existence at every moment of its temporal development." D. De Petter, *art. cit.* (footnote 69), p. 169.

of science, the idea of God is demanded by science, i.e., that science has reached new results which are more favorable to the faith than its former discoveries.[98] Scientific results are neither favorable nor unfavorable to the faith. They have nothing to do with it.

We render theism a bad service when we expect science to bring to mankind the message of the Creator. If the sciences preach a Creator, they preach only a pseudo-creator. A God, who according to Clausius' principle of entropy "explains" the compensation for the loss of energy undergone in the macrocosm, is as much a pseudo-God as Thor who "explains" thunder and lightning. If today's physical science is still unable to explain the compensation for the loss of energy in the universe, it may be able to do so tomorrow. Will another God then be eliminated, as Thor once was?

Ambiguity of the Concept "Cause." Scientistic atheism renders better services to theism than a theism that seeks refuge in a dark corner of physical science. Because of scientism, the theist knows that whatever science discovers can never deserve to be called God.[99]

"If the progress of science manages to block all avenues that allow us to find God anywhere in the world just as we find there the world itself, it will merely block the doors leading to a *finite* god, a god who is not God. It will merely have closed the gates of blind alleys."[100] In other words, the progress of science greatly helps in the work of purifying the affirmation of God's existence.

The well-informed reader will have noticed that we have spoken in general about the causes dealt with in the positive sciences without referring to the differences which the concept "cause" assumes in distinct sciences. For our purpose there was no need of making those distinctions. Nevertheless, it may be useful to say a few words about this point. For if distinct positive sciences make use of distinct concepts of causality, it is *a fortiori* necessary to distinguish the concept "cause" as used in the positive sciences from that of metaphysics.

---

[98]"Until the present it was pointed out that one can no longer argue against the belief in God and in a divine world order by appealing to an antiquated level of science, because meanwhile science has reached new results that are favorable to faith. . . ." H. Pfeil, *Der atheistische Humanismus der Gegenwart,* Aschaffenburg, 1961, p. 23.

[99]"It is true and of great importance: no matter what science may discover, it is always something which we cannot on any account call God." Lacroix, *op. cit.,* p. 20.

[100]E. Schillebeeckx, "God op de helling," *Tijdschrift voor geestelijk leven,* vol. XV (1959), p. 403.

The history of the sciences has gradually shown that, e.g., the positive sciences of sociology and biology, despite their positive character, are unable to use the methods of physical science. The biological realm revealed itself as a region of being whose proper character escaped considerations of a physico-chemical nature; other fundamental categories appeared to rule here and not those of physics and chemistry.[101] The sociologist likewise found it impossible to "gather facts" in the same way as the physicist. The more the positive sciences developed, the more also they drew away from other positive sciences.

Whoever realizes that such a separation was bound to happen,[102] knows also that one and the same term, for example "cause," has different senses in different sciences. *A fortiori,* as is easy to see, the metaphysician cannot work with the concepts of cause as they are used in the positive sciences. Those who pursue positive sciences, as such, cannot even know what the metaphysician means when he searches for the cause of be-ing as be-ing.[103]

The Absence of God

Man No Longer Needs God. It is almost commonplace to state that God is absent from the present world. As Léon Bloy expresses it, "God is absent as He has never been before." Formerly, so it is claimed, things were different and man did not find it hard to see God in creation. Formerly it would have been pure folly for any man, it is argued, not too recognize his dependence on God and give expression to that dependence. The mystery of God was visible everywhere and man could not help recognizing his own lowliness and God's greatness. Man's helplessness as he faced the world was so evident that he could leave all responsibility for the world to God. In good health and illness, in prosperity and need, amidst natural calamities and epidemics, man knew himself to be in God's hands. He saw God's providence everywhere and was able to connect whatever happened to him with God's governance. And so, it is

---

[101]Cf. Kockelmans, *op cit.,* p. 101.

[102]Cf. Luijpen, *De fenomenologie is een humanisme,* Amsterdam, 1961, pp. 42-46.

[103]"The search for the why undergoes a parallel change. It does not aim simply at providing an also present ground and explanation for what is present; now a ground is sought which will explain the emergence of the essent as an overcoming of nothingness." Heidegger, *Introduction to Metaphysics,* p. 23.

said, in the past, wherever man might be, he could encounter God. But now everything is entirely different.

Man nowadays is his own master. He has created physical science and has replaced the pre-scientific rationality of his labor by the disciplined and sure rationality of the sciences. By means of technology he has won dominion over the world, control over health and illness, prosperity and poverty, natural calamities and epidemics. He is "the master and owner of nature" (Descartes). Man needs only the sciences to explain the changes and events of the world. Thunder and lightning no longer point to an angry God—the lightning rod does its job infallibly.[104] Good health is no longer a sign of God's favor but a natural result of efficient health measures such as quarantine, vaccination and medicaments. The fruitfulness of the soil is the natural result of the application of scientific fertilizers. Why, then, should he still have recourse to religious processions through the fields to pray God for a bountiful harvest? And when there is a calamitous flood, man no longer considers it God's punishment for his sins but, blaming his lack of foresight or carelessness in building dams or dikes, attributes the catastrophe to his own failure.[105]

These few words briefly describe the mentality of modern man living in our technological culture. It is said man no longer feels the need of God because he has learned to save himself. The physical sciences have made technology possible; the achievement of technology makes man independent; hence man no longer needs God.

A Wrong Way of Replying to This Objection. The question here is not primarily the power of physical science to explain natural phenomena, but is concerned with the power which physical science has given man to save himself. Here also it is necessary to make careful distinctions. When scientism proclaimed that God was a superfluous hypothesis, there were "pious" scientists who tried to prove that God's existence was something that was demanded by physical science. They did theism a bad service, for what they affirmed was only a pseudo-God. Thus, they supplied added fuel to the fires of atheism. We would make a similar mistake if we were to point out that there are needs with respect to which man is helpless

---

[104]Cf. F. Dessauer, *Religion im Lichte der heutigen Naturwissenschaft*, p. 10.

[105]Cf. E. Schillebeeckx, *Op zoek naar de levende God*, Utrecht, 1958, p. 11.

and that, therefore, in spite of all his power, he continues to have need of God and to invoke His help.

Such an argument is a dangerous procedure. First of all, it implies a secret protest against every feeling of achievement that man has felt since he acquired power over nature. But it is not at all improper for man to have a *certain* feeling of achievement and even of self-satisfaction. We should not belittle the power which man has won over nature and the possibilities he has created to save himself. Such an attainment is a truly human good, and the best representatives of that power are aware of the fact that the expectation of a future world that is *totally* humanized is no longer an empty pipedream. We owe admiration and gratitude to those who try to exploit all the possibilities of man's power over nature, for only thus shall we reach the sort of human dignity for which the whole world is pining.

Secondly, it is beside the point to argue that there will always remain some human needs within our world and to conclude that therefore it remains necessary to invoke God's help and influence. For as long as we are concerned with needs within our own world, the potentialities of man's power are, in principle, unlimited. Where within this world does that alleged necessity begin? At what point are we forced to invoke God's help and influence?

The atheist will point out that the invocation of God in any case is never effective, that it is but the gesture of poor devils who are unable to save themselves, and that such a mentality, when it becomes dominant in man, merely serves to paralyze him in his endeavor to free himself. To invoke God's help, he claims, is a kind of alienation. But once again, we should make careful distinctions, for the total rejection of the standpoint of the atheist would once more furnish him with new weapons. For the statement of the atheist is not entirely groundless.

Human Powerlessness, Technology, and the Affirmation of God's Existence

Half-Gods and the Transcendent God. In a chapter consecrated to contemporary atheism, Albert Dondeyne discusses the presuppositions on which the atheists base their assertion that modern man, living in a time of technology, can no longer affirm God's existence.[106] Dondeyne gives a selection of texts borrowed from certain

---

[106]Dondeyne, *Faith and the World*, Pittsburgh, 1963, ch. IV (pp. 109-125).

Marxists in which they express the impossibility of reconciling technology with the affirmation of God. These texts show that those atheists view the acceptance of God as a sort of faith in primitive gods who were challenged by Prometheus when he stole the fire from heaven and brought it to earth in a reed, thus making it possible for man to develop techniques to free himself from slavery and from subservience to the gods. The atheists, of course, are right when they hold that man should side with Prometheus if he wishes to develop his own potentialities, for the gods of the Promethean myth are only half-gods and man's competitors. Anyone who today still clings to Zeus certainly lives in a state of alienation.[107]

However, things are quite different with respect to the God revealed in the New Testament. Many atheists do not realize this. The God of the Christians is a transcendent God, not half-god and half-man; He is not a competitor with man. So the question now is whether the antithesis of technology and the affirmation of God still makes sense when we recognize the transcendent character of the Christian God. A second question is whether it is true that it was a most obvious thing to affirm the existence of God when men were living in a primitive culture and did not possess technological means. And finally we must ask ourselves whether God is really absent from a technological civilization because man has supposedly overcome the need of invoking His help. It is not easy to answer that question.

The Atheism of Theists. Atheists are right, of course, when they protest against theists who are annoyed because technology really brings relief for some human needs and actually liberates man. This kind of objection today retains hardly more than a purely historical significance. But it cannot be denied that in the past some theists have objected, e.g., to the introduction of lightning rods, alleging that its use was "tempting God."

Such a "theistic" attitude contains an ugly admixture of atheism. For God's causality is surreptitiously conceived as a sort of electric charge, whose release is identical with God's will and, since the latter is holy and wholesome for man, he may not put obstacles in its way. A similar conviction was implied in the resistance of theists to inoculation and painless childbirth. God's causality must not be interfered with, they thought, but they did not realize that, if it were possible to counteract God's influence through technology, it would

---

[107]Dondeyne, *op. cit.,* p. 115.

mean that God's influence is not that of a transcendent Cause. There are numerous other examples of theists who for "theological" reasons object to operations, blood-transfusions or the use of incubators. The atheist's objection against this kind of "theology" is a welcome and good kind of atheism. It brings out the fact that God's influence cannot be conceived as a causality that is immanent in the world.

The situation is more complex with respect to the matter of prayer. Many atheists look down on Christians who pray to God for help in their needs. They consider it undignified to bow before God or gods in supplication. Most of the representative testimonies that illustrate the attitude of atheists regarding the relation of technology to the affirmation of God merely mention the prayer of petition to discard it immediately. Moreover, many atheists think that they can accuse Christians of inconsistency, since the latter make use of technology to get relief in their troubles. Such Christians, they say, do not seem to believe in their own prayers.

We do not intend to try to justify the Christian prayer of petition in our present work. We merely want to point out once more that atheism is a phenomenon that accompanies theism as a negation. In our time this means that atheism accompanies by denial the affirmation of the God of Christian Revelation. If it weren't for the Christian concept of God, the atheists would not know what they ought to deny. They back up their denial of God by specific arguments and these are all of a philosophical nature. It is only as such that they should be evaluated by other philosophers.

Let us now see the objection that man should not expect relief in his needs from prayers of petition to God but should seek the help of technology, i.e., help himself, and that it is a degradation of his authenticity as a human being to invoke divine assistance. In our opinion such supplications would indeed be degrading if his appeal were concerned with God's intervention as another immanent cause, existing *alongside* the causal influences which are controllable by technology in all its forms.

The development of the positive sciences has made possible various techniques that were formerly unknown in the realms of economics, sociology, medicine, agriculture, psychology, psychiatry, and so forth, and these are now at man's disposal. One who appeals to God and considers His influence to be on the same level as modern techniques, implicitly degrades God Himself and makes of

Him a kind of super-economist, super-physician, super-farmer, super-psychologist or super-psychiatrist. But God is the *transcendent* Cause of all things and we should never assimilate His influence to that of the immanent causality exercised by wordly causes. God's influence is not *just like* that of meteorological, medical, or psychological factors. The prayer of petition to God as *another* immanent cause would be a sort of atheism, for it would seek to make God operate as an earthly power just as we make other powers of nature work.

There are Christian believers who every year put aside a definite sum for Masses to draw down God's blessing upon their affairs, *just as* they put aside definite sums for advertising. They act as if the offering of Masses sets to work a similar mechanism as that which is put in motion by the initiatives of their advertising agency! For the same reason no Christian can pray for the success of a lawsuit which he wants to win *in spite* of the weakness of his case. The sad thing is that such people blame God when "their prayers are not heard," *just as* they blame the director of their advertising agency or their lawyer when they are dissatisfied with them. If atheists merely object to the invocation of that kind of "divine intervention," urging us to use the techniques devised by man himself within the world, their atheism would be a good atheism, for they are then merely doing away with a pseudo-God.[108]

The Purifying Role of Atheism. One who keeps all this in mind will realize that we must be very prudent in describing the mentality of past ages in respect to the affirmation of God's existence. It doesn't make sense and is definitely misleading to say that "in a primitive culture, in which technique was undeveloped, the whole life of the

---

[108]These words merely indicate in what sense it is meaningless to invoke God with respect to action within the world. They should not be understood as if there were no standpoint from which it is meaningful to pray to God for "temporal favors." The believer knows that it is meaningful, but he realizes also that he can never explain the reason to an atheist because he has to appeal to faith in God. Authentic faith, however, does not permit man to make God implicitly an immanent factor of the world when he prays to God with respect to actions to be done within the realm of the world (Cf. Schillebeeckx, "De goede levensleiding van God," *Tijdschrift voor geesteijk leven,* vol. XVI, 1960, pp. 583-592). We may add that for an atheist human needs are of necessity identical with immanent needs. It escapes him again that man knows also transcendent needs, we may even say, that man *is* a transcendent need. The meaning of prayers of petition with respect to this transcendent need is again something that cannot be explained to an atheist. It is impossible for us to develop this point here any further.

community was permeated with religious acts and practices."[109] For the crucial question is whether or not those religious acts and practices were truly directed to a transcendent God, i.e., were authentically religious. If later those religious acts and practices were abandoned *because* man could take care of himself by means of technology, then it follows that the "presence" of God in primitive culture was based on the affirmation of a pseudo-God, at least with respect to those acts and practices.

Careless expressions can furnish fuel to atheism. They can make Van Praag right when he claims that irreligion has increased since the invention of artificial fertilizer.[110] What Van Praag should have said instead is that pseudo-religiousness has been unmasked since the invention of scientific fertilizers. Farmers who prayed to God as if He were an agricultural factor, which can now be replaced by more efficient fertilizers, merely affirmed a pseudo-God in their prayers.

It is also untrue to say that God is absent in our modern world *because* man is now able to save himself by means of his techniques. For the alleged presence of God in a primitive culture which is exclusively based on man's lack of power in the affairs of his world is a pseudo-presence. If God is present in the world, He is present in it as an absent Presence, because He is present as a *transcendent* Creator, regardless of the primitive character or highly developed state of man's culture. However, in highly developed cultures that are aided by advanced technology it is no longer easy to present the affirmation of a pseudo-God as an authentic affirmation of the transcendent God. For this we owe in part, a debt of gratitude to atheism. Hence we may repeat with Jean La Croix that "atheism plays the role of the negative judgment in our knowledge of God."[111] True, the importance of the "negative way" has always been recognized in the past alongside the possibilities offered by the "affirmative way." However, that recognition was often more a question of principle than of practical value. Atheism evidently plays a "purifying role."[112]

---

[109]J. Plat. "Vertekening van het Godsbeeld en atheisme," *Ter elfder ure,* vol. IV (1957), p. 180.
[110]Quoted by Schillebeeckx, *op. cit.,* p. 3.
[111]J. Lacroix, *Le sens de l'athéisme moderne,* Tournai, 1958, p. 56.
[112]Lacroix, *op. cit.,* p. 55.

CHAPTER THREE

THE ATHEISM OF KARL MARX

Introductory Remarks. It remains a mystery to many atheists why so many, otherwise very intelligent, people—even men who are outstanding in some field of human endeavor—are not ashamed to join those who theoretically and practically acknowledge the reality of God. How is it possible that scientists, physicians, historians, in other words, people who can practice their art or pursue their science without appealing to God, "lower" themselves by bowing before God or at least trying to adhere to Him?

There is an answer to those questions which, however, will not make any impression on atheists. It reads as follows: It is merely the absolutism of science that renders the affirmation of God's existence impossible; but that absolutism itself is a contradiction in terms. For anyone who does not adhere to this absolutism there are innumerable possibilities to affirm other statements and the affirmation of God's existence is not the least of them.

Atheists, however, want to explain things differently. What strikes them and sometimes even angers them is the fact that, not infrequently, one and the same man exhibits a truly scientific attitude together with what they call a form of immaturity or infantilism. They see no other explanation for the theism of men of science than a psychological aberration.

Such a view of theism is not new. It is in fact so old that it has been transformed into a system, or rather, found expression in several systems. It does not matter what system one considers, for all of them make use of the magic word "projection."

Originally the projection theory was intended to solve certain problems regarding the visual perception of space. Thus understood, the projection theory is found already in Locke, Berkeley, Kepler, Donders, and others.[1] In a somewhat broader sense, projection means every more or less conscious attribution to another person or thing of what really belongs to the knowing subject. An innkeeper who is untrustworthy will "re-discover" his own untrustworthiness

---

[1] Cf. J. Fröbes, *Lehrbuch der experimentellen Psychologie,* Freiburg i. Br. 1917, vol. 2, pp. 263 f.

in his guests because he ascribes to others what is proper to himself.[2] Now in regard to God the projection theory says that the idea of God arises within the interior of the human psyche and that, after that, it is exteriorized as a reality by the same psychological factors. This idea is developed in two great but entirely different systems, namely, in the psychoanalysis of Freud and in the historical materialism of Marx. The system of Marx is the one to which we shall devote our attention here.

Atheism and Estrangement. If we wish to understand the atheism of Marx, we must study it within the framework of his theory of estrangement. According to Marx, Capitalism has divested man of his authentic humanity; it has made him lose what constitutes his true being-man, and one of the forms of estrangement is religion.

We do not mean to say that Marx's philosophy is primarily one of human estrangement. The doctrine of Marx is first of all a philosophy of man, conceived as history.[3] This is not always understood, for even the rulers of the Kremlin have imposed another obligatory interpretation of Marx's doctrine. Especially under the influence of Lenin, Marx's philosophy was interpreted as a total, all-embracing theory of reality. Reality is conceived as matter in motion, involved in an ascending evolution which reaches ever higher levels of development and in which a particular degree of quantitative complexity produces entirely new qualities through sudden transformations. Thus interpreted, Marx's doctrine is called "dialectical materialism" (*"Diamat"*). This interpretation of Marx is greatly regretted by those who can permit themselves to disregard the Kremlin when they wish to know what Marx actually taught, for they see that, because of the Kremlin's interpretation, Marx himself is not always acknowledged as a genuine philosopher. This is the more regrettable because there is thus a danger that what Marx was the first to "see" in reality may not be recognized sufficiently.

We do not have to occupy ourselves with exegetical questions, for it makes no difference in respect to our subject whether Marxism is interpreted as "historical materialism" or as "dialectical materialism." In both interpretations religion is considered to be a form of

---

[2]Cf. J. Grooten and G. Steenbergen, *Filosofisch lexicon,* Antwerpen, 1958, p. 231.

[3]"Communism ... is the solved riddle of history and shows itself as the solution." Karl Marx, *Zur Kritik der Nationalökonomie,* Berlin. 1955, p. 127.

estrangement. However, as much as possible, we shall let Marx and
Engels speak for themselves.[4]

1. HISTORICAL ANTECEDENTS OF THE ATHEISM OF MARX AND ENGELS

Marx received religious instruction during his studies at the
Gymnasium of Trier. His mental development toward atheism began
when he became a member of Berlin's so-called *Doktor-Klub,* a
group of Young Hegelians. He became a friend of Bruno Bauer. In
a supplement to his doctoral dissertation which he presented at the
University of Jena, Marx defended Epicurus' atheism against the
faith of Plutarch. But it was the influence of Feuerbach that gave
his atheism its definitive form.[5] Engels likewise received a religious
and pietistic education. In Bremen he became the apprentice of a
merchant and had the occasion to realize that the pharisaic virtue of
pietistic factory-owners did not prevent them from cruelly exploiting
their laborers. He read the historical criticisms of Strauss and they
undermined his pietistic faith. The influence of Schleiermacher still
preserved a kind of religiousness in him, but without a solid foundation. He then became acquainted with the philosophy of Hegel and
was easily led to accept the latter's idea of God. In Berlin he came
in contact with the Young Hegelians and his acquaintance with
Feuerbach made him definitively sever all relations with Christianity.[6]

Influence of the Young Hegelians

The *Doktor-Klub,* of which Marx and Engels had become members and which made them associates with Ruge, Bruno Bauer,
Strauss and others, opposed the ideas of the Old Hegelians who
conceived the Prussian State as the embodiment of the last phase in
the development of Spirit as perfectly sovereign, as the infallible
expression of what is right, as the realization of objective freedom

---

[4]We noted in passing that the official Soviet philosophy evokes no, or
hardly any, interest among genuine philosophers. Anyone who wants to convince himself on this point should read the lectures delivered by Georges
Politzer at the French Higher Institute of Labor in 1935-36. Their publisher
presents them as satisfying "the highest demands of scientific thought," and
regrets that "official educational institutions continue to disregard or misre-
present this philosophy." On comparing Marx and Politzer, one understands
the official disregard, but wonders who is misrepresenting Marx.

[5]Cf. P. Ehlen, *Der Atheismus im dialektischen Materialismus,* München, 1961,
pp. 13-23.

[6]Cf. Ehlen, *op. cit.,* pp. 24-36.

and therefore as mandatory for all. The Young Hegelians, on the contrary, tried to harmonize the doctrine of Hegel with the political liberalism and democratic development of Germany.

The Young Hegelians, in their fight against the Old Hegelians, rejected the Hegelian identification of religion and philosophy and considered these two irreconcilable. Prussia should become a "State of Reason" *(Vernunftstaat),* and abolish all divine and ecclesiastical laws. But since these rulers of Prussia constantly appealed to Christianity to defend themselves and their power, the Young Hegelians directed their attacks first of all against the Prussian State. The destruction of the State and of religion were considered the necessary conditions for the realization of the demands of Reason. The Old Hegelians were quite naturally considered to be reactionaries. Because of the great dangers involved in direct political action, the fight against the State was principally conducted by a roundabout fight against religion. The Young Hegelians tried to put history on the road of Reason by influencing the domain of religion.[7]

Bruno Bauer was one of the leading figures of the *Doktor-Klub.* Marx became his close friend and it is due to the influence of Bauer that the question about God's existence was in reality already settled in Marx's mind before he actually formulated it. Bauer did his best to show him that Hegel's philosophy of religion and his aesthetics were really atheistic. A god who absorbs man and nature and makes them meaningless for the sake of his own glorification is a pseudo-God. Bauer did not hesitate to identify this God with the God of Christianity. For, according to him, Holy Scripture knows only actions of God versus man's serfdom and misery. The affirmation of man's nothingness and rejection, in respect to God who operates everything in all things, robs man of the possibility to make history.[8]

After Bauer, it was Moses Hess who confirmed Marx in his atheism. Hess was an early advocate of a kind of communistic social order, which prerequired the abolition of private property. He thought, however, that a revolution that was carried out by believers in God would necessarily fail because they would accept one or other heavenly power or person outside themselves and subject themselves to it and thus renounce their own personality. Hence communism and religion, according to Hess, were irreconcilable.[9]

---

[7]Cf. Ehlen, *op. cit.,* pp. 37-40.
[8]Cf. Ehlen, *op. cit.,* pp. 42-50.
[9]Cf. Ehlen, *op. cit.,* pp. 50-51.

Feuerbach

Feuerbach likewise combined atheism with a criticism of Hegel. In spite of Hegel's sense of the concrete, Feuerbach blamed him for not considering man as he really is, a bodily being, bound to the world, and in dialogue with other men. And he also brought Hegel's philosophy of religion back to man. According to Feuerbach, everything religion imagines about God is only the dream of the individual who projects his own being in God.[10]

Immortality. Feuerbach's philosophy concerning God and religion is expressed in its definitive form in his book *The Essence of Christianity.* But his thought on this topic was presaged in *Thoughts concerning Death and Immortality.* In this work Feuerbach bases the belief in immortality on man's incapacity to think of the dead as dead. The dead are said to live but in reality they live the life of the dead—a nice way to express that they do not live but are dead. The belief in immortality rests on a "misunderstanding of human nature."

Man's true opinion concerning the dead can be learned from his lamentations about the dead, which signify that the dead have not passed on to a better life but are dead.[11] In fact, Feuerbach thinks, the so-called belief in another life is merely the belief in the *present* life. Man generally feels at home on earth and likes its kind of life. So he finds it impossible to recognize the reality of death and imagines that earthly life is prolonged in an imaginary hereafter.[12] For, "man does not want to relinquish what he has, is, and does; he wants to have, be, and do it forever. Eternity, then, is a subjectively necessary representation."[13]

The belief in immortality was always something vague and uncertain in antiquity. But Christianity committed the crime of eliminating the vagueness and uncertainty and proposing life in the hereafter as something definite and certain. It promised a better life, but the better is the greatest enemy of the good. In order to transform death into life, Christianity reduced life to death. It promised a better life in the hereafter but thereby let the evil in this life, which

---

[10]Cf. H. van Oyen, *Philosophia,* Utrecht 1949, Vol. I, pp. 250-253.

[11]Cf. Ludwig Feuerbach, *Gedanken über Tod und Unsterblichkeit, Sämtliche Werke,* neuherausgegeben von Wilhelm Bolin and Friedrich Jodl, Stuttgart, 1903, vol. I, pp. 98-99.

[12]*Op. cit.,* pp. 105-106.

[13]*Op. cit.,* p. 113.

man could remove, persist unopposed.[14] "Immortality is a desire of man's imagination and not of man's essence."[15]

The Idea of God. The same can be said about the idea of God; it too is a product of man's imagination. According to the theists, says Feuerbach, the belief in God is found among all peoples; they differ merely in their concepts and representations of Him. But these exegetes, who proclaim the universality of the belief in God, fail to see that the diverse names of God refer to different gods. He who takes away Zeus from the Greek, Odin from the German, Swantowit from the Slav, Yahweh from the Jew, and Christ from the Christian, does not take away from each his own representation or concept of God, but God Himself. God, therefore, originally is not a proper name but the name of a species; he is not a being but a property, not a subject but a predicate: dreadful, powerful, great, extraordinary, glorious, good, merciful. The subject is provided by Nature, and the predicate by man, for the predicate is but the expression of the human imagination and the feeling which man conceives toward Nature when it affects his sensibility and imagination and he characterizes Nature as powerful, terrible, or kind. There are numerous gods because there are so many different impressions which Nature makes on man. But this diversity arises once more from the diversity of men. So God is merely the impression that Nature makes on man.[16]

Man's Own Essence is the Object of Religion. Feuerbach develops these thoughts further in *The Essence of Christianity.*[17] In this work he maintains that "man's nature, as distinct from the brute, is not merely the basis but also the object of religion."[18] For, religion is the consciousness of the infinite. Hence it can be nothing but man's consciousness of his own unlimitedness and infinity. For, if man were really a finite being, he would not surmise in the least that there is an infinite being and still less be aware of it, for the limitation of a being is also the limitation of its consciousness. The consciousness of a caterpillar whose life and being is limited by re-

---

[14]*Op. cit.,* pp. 116-117.
[15]*Op. cit.,* p. 117.
[16]*Op. cit.,* pp. 107-108.
[17]Feuerbach, *Das Wesen des Christentums, Sämtliche Werke,* neuherausgegeben von Wilhelm Bolin and Friedrich Jodl, Stuttgart, 1903, vol. 6. English ed., *The Essence of Christianity* tr. by Marian Evans, London, 3rd ed., 1893.
[18]*Op. cit.,* p. 2 in the German edition. This sentence has been replaced by another in the English edition.

ference to a specific kind of plant, does not extend beyond that particular field. Hence it is not consciousness in the proper sense. But consciousness in the true sense and consciousness of the infinite are really identical. The finiteness of the "consciousness of the caterpillar is also the finiteness of its world, but the infinity of man's consciousness is also the infinite, and this is the object of religion."[19] Hence "the consciousness of the infinite is nothing else but the consciousness of the infinity of consciousness."[20]

Infinitude of Man's Essence. What is the essence of man of which he is conscious? What constitutes the being-human of man? It is reason, will, and the heart. Reason, will-power, and love are the highest powers, the absolute essence of man and the purpose of his existence. Man exists to know, to will, and to love. He knows in order to know, wills in order to will, and loves in order to love. And all this constitutes the essence of man. Now what is for its own sake is divine;[21] hence man's essence is for itself, is divine. "The divine trinity in man . . . is the unity of reason, love, and will."[22] And man necessarily experiences *infinite* joy when he is aware of that trinity.[23]

Individual men must, of course, feel and recognize themselves to be finite and limited. But this does not mean that man's essence is finite and limited. For the individual can feel his finiteness and limitations only because he has for his object the infinitude and unlimitedness of the species to which he belongs. But the individual deceives himself when he attributes his own limitations to the species. He is prompted to do so, however, because he feels humiliated and is ashamed when he must consider his limitations as exclusively his own. When the individual attributes his own limitations to the species to which he belongs, he thereby turns the humiliation away from himself. What I, for instance, fail to understand is also a mystery to others; hence why should I be ashamed? For it is not because of *my* mind that something is incomprehensible to me; the fault belongs to the mind of the species.

But, continues Feuerbach, this is a foolish and nonsensical way of conceiving things. Every being is self-sufficient; every being is infinite in and for himself; every being has its highest being, God, in

---

[19] *Op. cit.*, p. 2 (English edition).
[20] *Op. cit.*, pp. 2 f.
[21] *Op. cit.*, pp. 3 f.
[22] *Op. cit.*, p. 3.
[23] *Op. cit.*, pp. 6 f.

itself. Every limitation of a being exists only for another being. The life of butterflies is extremely short in comparison with the life of long-lived animals. But its short life is as long for the butterfly as the long life is for other animals. The leaf on which the caterpillar lives is for it an infinite space. If plants had eyes, taste, and the power of judgment, they would consider their own flowers the most beautiful of all.[24]

Religion is a Relationship of Man to His Own Essence. When there is question of sense-perceptible objects, consciousness of the object must be distinguished from self-consciousness. But the consciousness of the object of religion is fully identical with self-consciousness. The object of sense-perception lies outside man; the object of religion is within man.[25] Hence we can know man by knowing his God and can know God by knowing man. "God is the manifested inward nature, the *expressed* self of a man. Religion is the solemn unveiling of a man's hidden treasures."[26]

But, says Feuerbach, this does not mean that the religious man himself directly realizes that his consciousness about God is the self-consciousness of his own essence. Hence it is preferable to say that religion is the *first* consciousness of man. For at first man exteriorizes his own essence and only later does he find it in himself. "His own nature is in the first instance contemplated by him as that of another being."[27] Religion, therefore, is the childlike condition of humanity, for in childhood a man is an object for himself, under the form of another man.[28]

The historical development of religions thus consists in this, that what was accepted as objective in early religions was considered later to be subjective. What was first adored as God, was regarded later as something human. Every forward step of religion is therefore a forward step of man's self-knowledge. But every religion which looks down on its older sisters as worship of false gods cuts itself off from the general essence of religion. Such a religion is under the illusion that its content is superhuman because it has another object, another content, a content that is higher than that of earlier religions. The philosopher, however, discovers the true nature of religion

---

[24]*Op. cit.*, pp. 7-10.
[25]*Op. cit.*, pp. 12 f.
[26]*Op. cit.*, pp. 12 f.
[27]*Op. cit.*, p. 13.
[28]*Ibid.*

which is unknown to the particular religion itself, because religion, for him, is an object, whereas it is never an object of religion itself.[29]

Religion, therefore, "is the relation of man to himself, or more correctly to his own nature, but a relation to it, viewed as a nature apart from his own. The divine being is nothing else but the human being, or rather, the human nature purified, freed from the limits of the individual, real, bodily existing man, and made objective—i.e., contemplated and revered as another, a distinct being. All the attributes of the divine nature are, therefore, attributes of the human nature."[30]

It is readily conceded, says Feuerbach, that the attributes of the divine nature are merely attributes of man's nature, as long as there is question of the predicates of God, but not when the subject of those predicates is concerned. It is conceded that no predicate is perfectly fitting in its application to God, hence all predicates should be rejected. But, strange as it may seem, the rejection of the subject is called atheism, but not the rejection of the predicates. However, that which has no attributes cannot influence me, and that which cannot influence me is nothing for me. A being that has no attributes is one that is not an object, and a being that is not an object is a non-entity.[31]

But there exists also a rejection of the predicates that is more moderate than the direct rejection. It is then agreed that the predicates of the divine being are human predicates, but theists nevertheless refuse to reject them. Those predicates are defended because man cannot help making certain representations of God and, being man, he is incapable of constructing any non-human representations. Those attributes, it is said, are meaningless in respect to God, but God cannot appear to me in any other way than he actually appears, namely, as a human being or as a being similar to man.[32]

The Distinction Between God in Himself and God for Me. This view, however, presents the difficulty that there is no foundation for a distinction between God "in Himself" and God "for me."[33] It is

---

[29] *Ibid.*
[30] *Op. cit.,* p. 14.
[31] *Ibid.*
[32] *Op. cit.,* p. 15.
[33] "I cannot know whether God is something else in himself and for himself than he is for me; what he is to me, is to me all that he is. For me, there lies in these predicates under which he exists for me, what he is in himself, his very nature; he is for me what he can alone ever be for me." *Op. cit.,* p. 16.

absolutely impossible for me to know whether God "in Himself" is something other than He is "for me." The distinction between an object "in itself" and an object "for me" can only be made when an object can really appear to me differently from the way it does appear, but not when an object appears to me as it *has to* appear to me. But God *has to* appear to me as a human being or as a being resembling man.

Every religion considers the gods of other religions to be mere representations of God, whereas it considers its own representation to express God Himself, God as He is in Himself. But it is clear, says Feuerbach, that what man considers as the highest being is for him the divine being. How could he still ask what such an object is in itself? If God were an object for a bird, He would be a winged being for it, for the bird knows nothing higher or more blessed than to-be-winged. It would be ridiculous if such a bird made the judgment, "To me God appears as a bird, but what he is in himself I know not."[34] This is silly because God cannot appear otherwise to a bird than as a bird.

Man believes that love is a divine attribute because he himself has love. He calls God wise and good because he knows nothing better than wisdom and goodness—just as the bird knows nothing better than to-be-winged. Just as a Greek could not help being a Greek, so his gods were Greek gods.[35] The Greek was unable to doubt the existence of his Zeus because Zeus stood for the very reality of being a Greek.[36] For the same reason the gods of primitive people were themselves simple gods of nature. As soon, however, as man built houses, his gods began to live in temples. As soon as man became cultured, he began to distinguish between what was suitable or unsuitable to himself and he similarly began to distinguish between what was fitting for God or not. When courage in battle was considered a virtue, God was conceived as a god of war.[37]

"In the nature and the consciousness of religion there is nothing else except what lies in the nature of man and his consciousness of himself and of the world."[38] It is nonsensical, therefore, to make a distinction between God "in Himself" and God "for me," for this can be done only when an object can appear otherwise to me than it

---

[34] *Op. cit.*, p. 17.
[35] *Op. cit.*, p. 20.
[36] *Op. cit.*, pp. 20 f.
[37] *Op. cit.*, p. 21.
[38] *Op. cit.*, p. 22.

actually does. But God cannot appear otherwise to me than as having my own essence.

God Impoverishes Man. There is, moreover, another phenomenon, namely, that the distinction between God and man apparently becomes greater to the extent that God becomes more human. Theology, of course, denies the identity of God and man, and it tends to lower humanity as much as possible in order to establish that distinction. Because man lends the core of his being to a foreign being outside himself, there remain nothing else for himself except considerations that are inimical to man. In order to reach God, man must be poor and thus God will be all. Man doesn't need to be anything for himself, for whatever he takes away from himself will not be lost by giving it to God. Doesn't man have his essence in God? Why then should he have it also in himself? After all, he doesn't need to have his essence twice! Whatever man gives up and takes away from himself, he enjoys in an incomparably higher and richer measure in God.[39]

The Evolution of Religion. With these convictions in his mind, Feuerbach discusses everything he knows about Christianity. And the same thought reappears constantly: "Man . . . projects his being into objectivity, and then again makes himself an object to this projected image of himself converted into a subject; he thinks of himself as an object to himself, but as the object of an object, of another being than himself."[40] "God is the being who acts in me, with me, through me, upon me, for me, is the principle of my salvation, of my good dispositions and actions, consequently my own good principle and nature."[41] God is therefore a changeable being; He changes with the progress of history. "What yesterday was still religion is no longer such today, and what today is atheism tomorrow will be religion."[42]

This idea is more fully developed in Feuerbach's book *The Essence of Religion* than in *The Essence of Christianity.*[43] In it, he does not offer any new points of view, but he adds many historical considerations to his theory and emphasizes one of its aspects more than before, namely, the feeling of dependence. This feeling is the subjec-

---

[39]*Op. cit.,* p. 25.
[40]*Op. cit.,* p. 30.
[41]*Op. cit.,* p. 31.
[42]*Op. cit.,* p. 32.
[43]L. Feuerbach, *Das Wesen der Religion, Sämtliche Werke,* vol. VIII, 1908.

tive factor that is at work in the birth of religion.[44] The feeling of dependence on nature generates fear and anxiety and these give birth to the gods. But the feeling of dependence is also a source of joy and gratitude, because it frees man from fear and anxiety, and so joy and gratitude also produce gods, but always in virtue of the feeling of dependence. "All things come from God," we read in Ecclesiasticus, "happiness and misfortune, life and death, poverty and riches." "Idols may not be considered Gods," says Baruch, "for they cannot punish or help, they cannot curse or bless." In other words, they inspire neither anxiety nor fear, neither joy nor gratitude, and hence they are not true gods.[45]

From the Service of God to the Freedom of Citizens of the Earth. One might get the impression that Feuerbach has no other aim than the destruction of religion. But this is not so.[46] He wants, of course, to unmask and destroy religions but only as a necessary means to gain or regain for man his authentic character. The content and object of religion are human, theology is anthropology, the divine being is the human being. But religion does not acknowledge the human character of its content but rather combats what is human.

It is unavoidable, then, that there will be a turning point in history when it will be openly acknowledged that the awareness of God's existence is nothing else but man's awareness of himself as a species, and that man cannot accept any other being as absolute, as divine, than human nature itself.[47] For religion is man's first self-consciousness, and religions are sacred because they contain the traditions of this first self-consciousness. God, who according to religion is first, is in reality second, for man is first. Love for man, therefore, cannot be derived from something else.

This is the positive result of Feuerbach's critique. "If human nature is the highest nature to man then practically the highest and first law must be the love of man to man. *Homo homini Deus est.*" Moral attitudes are themselves religious attitudes. "Life as a whole

---

[44] "When we study either the religions of so-called 'Savages,' about which explorers tell us, or those of civilized peoples, when we gaze in our own bosom, which is immediately and inerrantly open to our inspection, we do not find any other relevant and encompassing psychological ground explaining religion than the feeling or consciousness of dependence." *Op. cit.,* pp. 31 f.

[45] *Op. cit.,* p. 39.

[46] "Our relation to religion is therefore not a merely negative but a critical one." *The Essence of Christianity,* p. 270.

[47] *Op. cit.,* p. 269.

is its essential, substantial relations, throughout of a divine nature."[48] That is why men, after being theologians, must become anthropologists; after being lovers of God they must become lovers of men; having been candidates for the hereafter they must become students of this our world; having been religious and political servants of heaven they must become self-conscious and free citizens of earth.[49]

Marx and Feuerbach

Feuerbach's teachings about God and religion made a deep impression on Marx and Engels. This is not surprising, for Marx and Engels shared Feuerbach's utter ignorance of God's transcendence. Even before Marx built his own philosophical system of historical materialism, he was already a convinced atheist—and it was evident that his teaching would be atheistic.

Marx completely agrees with Feuerbach, but he thinks nevertheless that Feuerbach's analysis does not go deep enough. Marx praises Feuerbach because he has replaced Hegel's idealism by materialism, but he criticizes him for casting out not only Hegel's idealism but also his dialectic method. Through this mistake Feuerbach neglected to consider history and paid no attention to the driving force of history, namely, labor and the socio-economic structures of society. Feuerbach, according to Marx, correctly realized that religion is merely a projection springing from man's interiority, but he did not explain why man wants to make such a projection.[50]

Old-style materialism got lost in the contemplation and interpretation of the material world. The same, according to Marx, is true of Feuerbach. For him the material world was still an object of contemplation[51] and he failed to realize that the original and most important relation of man to the world is not one of contemplation

---

[48]*Op. cit.*, p. 326.

[49]*Das Wesen der Religion*, pp. 28-29.

[50]"Feuerbach starts out from the fact of religious self-estrangement, of a duplication of the world into a religious and a secular one. His work consists in resolving the religious world into its secular basis. But that the secular basis raises itself above itself and establishes for itself an independent realm in the clouds can be explained only through the cleavage and self-contradictions within this secular basis. The latter must therefore in itself be both understood in its contradiction and revolutionized in practice." Karl Marx, "Thesen über Feuerbach," *Die deutsche Ideologie*, Berlin, 1953, p. 594. English ed., *The German Ideology*, New York, 1947, p. 197.

[51]*Op. cit.*, p. 593; English ed., p. 197.

but of *praxis*.[52] Feuerbach conceived the essence of religion as the essence of man but, because he failed to take note of the praxis, he also failed to see that man's essence is the product of the social attitudes that are conditioned by the praxis.[53] He speaks of man as an abstraction because he does not see that the religious man is simply a phenomenon of a specific type of society.[54]

Therefore, it was possible, so Marx thought, for Feuerbach to abolish religion and, on the other hand, to introduce a new religion, namely, that of man's love for man. If Feuerbach had realized the importance of the praxis, he would have seen that it is not love but work that brings men together and binds them together. Feuerbach substituted for the unity of work the unity of the human species, the inner and dumb universality which binds the many individuals together in a *natural* way.[55] But this unity is an abstraction, for real unity among men is the result of social life.[56]

Religion has its foundation in bourgeois society. Only a criticism of bourgeois society can deliver the fundamental critique of religion.

2. THE "PRIMITIVE FACT" OF MARX'S PHILOSOPHY[57]

Marx's criticism of Feuerbach reveals the trend of his own thought: he wants to transform Feuerbach's materialism into a philosophy of reality, applying to it Hegel's dialectic method.[58] Marx admired Hegel's view of man "as history," but he thought that Hegel made history "walk on its head" by reducing it to the history

---

[52]"Feuerbach, not satisfied with *abstract thought*, wants contemplation, but he does not understand our sensuous nature as *practical* human-sensuous activity." *Op. cit.*, p. 594, English ed., p. 198.

[53]"Feuerbach resolves the essence of religion into the essence of man. But the essence of man is no abstraction inherent in each separate individual. In its reality it is the *ensemble* (aggregate) of social religion." *Op. cit.*, pp. 594 f.; English ed., p. 198.

[54]*Op. cit.*, p. 595; English ed., p. 199.

[55]"Thus, the essence can be understood only as 'genus,' the inner dumb generality which naturally unites the many individuals." *Op. cit.*, p. 595; English ed., p. 199.

[56]All social life is essentially *practical.*" *Op. cit.*, p. 595, English ed., p. 199.

[57]In finding our way through the voluminous works of Marx and Engels, we have been guided by the following books: A. Etcheverry, *Le conflit actuel des humanismes*, Paris, 1955; P. Ehlen, *Der Atheismus im dialektischem Materialismus*, München, 1961; W. Banning, *Karl Marx, Leven, leer en betekenis*, Utrecht, 1960; R.C. Kwant, *De wijsbegeerte van Karl Marx*, Utrecht, 1961, and *Philosophy of Labor*, Pittsburgh, 1960; S.U. Zuidema, *Communisme in ontbinding*, Wageningen, n.d.; L. Dupré, *Het vertrekpunt der Marxistische wijsbegeerte: De kritick op Hegels staatsrecht*, Antwerpen, 1954.

[58]A. Etcheverry, *Le conflit actuel des humanismes*, p. 111.

of the Idea. Marx, on the contrary, sees the movement of thought as a reflection of the *real* movement which, in final analysis, is identical with the changes in the domain of the means of production.

But these ideas of Marx did not drop out of a blue sky. They were embedded in a vision of man as the subject of history. Man is the absolute, exclusive subject of history. This, to Marx's mind, is *a priori* certain. The question whether man and nature might not be creatures of God has no meaning for him because there is no standpoint from which such a question can be asked. He who asks whether man and nature were created must start by supposing a situation in which neither man nor nature existed. But in such a case both the questioner and the question are thought away and obviously in such a case no real question can be asked.[59] The whole history of the world, according to Marx, is nothing but man's self-creation and the development of nature for man, the question about a foreign being above man and nature is practically impossible to the mind that realizes this fact.[60]

Work as Self-Realization

The Distinction Between Man and Animal. Man realizes himself by turning to nature. By applying himself to nature, man makes it possible for himself to continue to live, for man is sustained by nature. This sense alone suffices to justify saying that nature is man's "body." But this expression acquires a much more profound meaning when man makes nature first the object and then the instrument of his activity. This is accomplished in and by human labor. In and by work nature becomes the "inorganic body" of man.[61] By this term Marx wants to indicate that there exists an interaction between man and nature. In labor man objectifies nature, conquers nature, distinguishes himself from it, liberates himself, and becomes true man. Hence man, who knows that he is needy in respect to nature, is more properly called rich, for the existence of man's need and want

---

[59]"When you ask about the creation of nature and of man, you make abstraction of man and nature. You posit them as *non-existent,* yet want me to prove them to you as *existing.* So, I tell you: 'Get rid of your abstraction and you'll also get rid of your question. Or if you want to retain your abstraction, be logical: when you conceive man and nature as *non-existing,* conceive yourself as non-existent, for you too are nature and man'." Marx, *Zur Kritik der Nationalökonomie, Ökonomisch-philosophische Manuskripte,* published in Marx-Engels, *Kleine ökonomische Schriften,* Berlin, 1955, p. 139.

[60]Marx, *op. cit.,* p. 139.

[61]Marx, *op. cit.,* p. 103.

is at the same time the existence of man's need for self-realization. Not only wealth but also poverty has human and social significance.[62]

Animals too are involved in nature, but in a way that differs totally from that of man. And this is the reason why the animal is not a man. An animal is entirely one with its activity and is not distinguished from it. The activity of the brute is taken up entirely by, and concerned with immediate bodily needs.[63] Man, on the contrary, can, as it were, keep at a distance from what he does; he makes his activity an object of his consciousness and willing; his activity is conscious and free. This ability enables man to improve his activity constantly and to raise it to an ever higher level, whereas the animal is and remains fixed and stagnant. Man began to distinguish himself from the brute as soon as he began to *produce* things. The first aim of this productive activity, was, of course, the food needed by man.[64]

This idea is valid, regardless of the form assumed by the society in which man lives. "Work is a process between man and nature, a process in which man initiates, regulates, and controls his metabolism with nature."[65] This metabolic process, first of all, presupposes the power of the human body. By means of it man acts on nature, introducing changes in it, but through these changes he changes also himself. He develops the powers and capacities that lie dormant in himself.[66]

Through Work Man Becomes Man. All this attains its full significance only when man uses the mechanical, physical and chemical properties of nature and makes them act as means to modify other things. This occurs when he makes instruments and tools by which

---

[62]"The *rich* man is at the same time the *needy* man, the man who needs a whole of expressions of human life; he is the man in whom his self-realization exists as an inner necessity, a *need*. Not only the wealth but also the poverty of man has equally a *human,* and consequently a social, value." *Op. cit.,* p. 137.

[63]*Op. cit.,* pp. 103-104.

[64]"Men can be distinguished from animals by consciousness, religion or anything else you like. They themselves begin to distinguish themselves from animals as soon as they begin to *produce* their means of subsistence; a step which is conditioned by their physical organization. By producing their means of subsistence men are indirectly producing their actual material life." Marx-Engels, *Die deutsche Ideologie,* Berlin, 1953, p. 17; English ed., p. 7.

[65]*Das Kapital, Kritik der politischen Ökonomie,* Hamburg, 1919, p. 140. English edition, *A Contribution to the Critique of Political Economy,* tr. by N.I. Stone, Chicago, 1904.

[66]"While through this motion he acts on nature outside himself and modifies it, he changes his own nature at the same time." *Op. cit.,* p. 140.

he adds a new dimension to his own body.[67] As soon as labor reaches a certain development, man feels the need of making use of instruments.[68] As a result, we are able to evaluate the perfection of the various types of social structures of the past according to the perfection of the means used by the workman, his tools and instruments. "Economic periods are distinguished not by what things are made but by the way they are made."[69]

Society and the Bond of History are Constituted by Work. Hence man is a being who realizes himself or, what according to Marx comes to the same thing, man is essentially a laborer. His work makes man be a man. But this is not all. For just as work is not truly productive until man makes tools, so it must be admitted that productive labor presupposes a division of labor. Work is truly productive when it is executed as a social project and task. The product, therefore, is always the product of social labor, and labor is a society-builder.[70] The division of labor actually means that men work for one another. Labor is truly mutual assistance, and this is most evident in modern industrial labor. Man would simply disappear if he did not work. But we express exactly the same thing when we say that man would disappear if men ceased to work for one another. Labor then not only makes man a man but also a fellow-man.[71]

Co-existence in work constitutes also the solidarity of man's *history*. The fact that each generation finds instruments of labor at its disposal which were produced by preceding generations signifies that everything man has is rooted in the past and dependent on it.[72] The present generation, in turn, will continue its life in the future by the fact that it leaves behind certain means of production, and these will serve as a starting point for the work of future generations. Man, then, is both source and product, the creator and creature of history,

---

[67]*Op. cit.,* p. 141.

[68]*Op. cit.,* p. 142.

[69]*Op. cit.,* p. 142.

[70]"The *object* as *being for man,* as the *objectified being of man* is at the same time the existence of man for *other men,* his human relation to other *men, the social relation of man to man.*" Marx-Engels, *Die heilige Familie,* Berlin, 1953, p. 146; English ed., translated by R. Dixon, *The Holy Family,* Moscow, 1956, p. 60.

[71]"Precisely in the work he does to modify the objective world, man reveals himself really as a being that is as a species (*Gattungswesen*). This making of products is his active way of being as a species." *Zur Kritik der Nationalökonomie,* p. 105.

[72]Cf. Marx's letter quoted by R. C. Kwant, *De wijsbegeerte van Karl Marx,* Utrecht, 1961, p. 25.

and it is labor that constitutes history's core. And because labor is at its heart, history is social history. Hence the bond between men is not secured by any "political and religious nonsense," but by the continuity of the means of production.[73]

These, then, are Marx's fundamental ideas: Man is not a static but a self-realizing being; and this self-realization is accomplished by means of his labor; the perfection of his work and hence the level of a particular phase of his history can be gauged by the perfection of the means of production; work brings man in contact with his fellow men, and the continuity of the means of production guarantees the bond of history.

All this, however, does not yet make work the "primitive fact," the "central reference point," of Marx's philosophy. For a "primitive fact" is an all-encompassing light, and human history shows other things than labor. Labor can be called the "primitive fact" of a philosophy only if whatever is not labor is viewed from the standpoint of labor. Marx tries to do this by means of his doctrine of the substructure and superstructure of society.

Substructure and Superstructure of Society

It is evident that he who wishes to speak about society and history does not cover the subject properly when he confines himself to a definition of labor. He must also take into consideration ownership, law, morals, the state, art, the sciences, philosophy and religion. All these are discussed by Marx, but always in relation to labor.

As we have seen, Marx considers man the "subject" of history. "Men make their own history, but," says Marx, "they do not make it just as they please; they do not make it under circumstances chosen by themselves, but under circumstances directly encountered as given and transmitted from the past."[74] What "circumstances" does he refer to?

---

[73]"Thus it is quite obvious from the start that there exists a materialistic connection of men with one another which is determined by their needs and their mode of production, and which is as old as men themselves. This connection is ever taking on new forms and thus presents a 'history' independently of the existence of any political or religious nonsense which would hold men together on its own." Marx-Engels, *Die deutsche Ideologie*, pp. 26 f.; English ed., p. 19.

[74]*Der achtzehnte Brumaire des Louis Bonaparte*, in Marx-Engels, *Ausgewählte Schreften in Zwei Bänden*, Berlin, 1952, vol. I, p. 226; English ed. in Marx-Engels, *Selected Works*, vol. I, Moscow 1962, p. 247.

Marx, throughout his massive writings, always presupposes the answer to that question and he defines it on many occasions. The "circumstances" which man finds while he is "making his history," are fundamentally the kind and level of the means of production and the corresponding relations of production. These means and relations together Marx calls the "substructure," the economic basis of society and its history. It is the substructure that determines all that a spiritualistic tradition has considered as the higher, spiritual aspects of man, of society and history, and which Marx calls the "superstructure."[75]

This idea, Marx believes, gives the death-blow to Hegel's concept of history. Hegel made history stand on its head, by reducing it to a movement of the idea. Marx puts history back on its feet by recognizing it as a movement of the means of production and the corresponding change in the relations of production.[76] This way of conceiving history, as opposed to Hegel's idealism, Marx calls "materialistic." Man's social character is not explained by man's consciousness, but man's consciousness is explained by his social character.[77] The ideological superstructure should be conceived as an echo, a reflection of the real process of life.[78] It will be necessary to explain this point in somewhat greater detail.

The Means of Production and the Relations of Production

We have already mentioned Marx's assertion that the mode of production, that is, the tools and the power of production, are clear indications of the level proper to a particular phase of history. In his famous Preface to the *Contribution to the Critique of Political Economy,* Marx asserts that the means of production determine the

---

[75]"The new facts made imperative a new examination of all past history. Then it was seen that *all* past history ... was the history of class struggles; that these warring classes of society are always the products of the modes of production and of exchange—in a word, of the *economic* conditions of their time; that the economic structure of society always furnishes the real basis, starting from which we can alone work out the ultimate explanation of the whole superstructure of juridical and political institutions as well as of the religious, philosophical, and other ideas of a given historical period." Engels, *Herrn Eugen Dürings Umwälzung der Wissenschaft,* Berlin, 1954, p. 30; English ed., *Anti-During,* Moscow, 1959, p. 41.

[76]Engels, *op. cit.,* p. 329; English ed., p. 461.

[77]Engels, *op. cit.,* p. 30; English ed., p. 41.

[78]Marx-Engels, *Die deutschte Ideologie,* pp. 22-23; English ed., p. 14.

relations of production.[79] The fact that a society uses specific means of production determines the special way producing men become related to one another. In a society that uses the spinning-wheel to produce wool, men do not have the same relations as in modern textile mills. Legally speaking, these relations of production are property relations.[80]

Property relations that are determined by the means of production create special social relations or classes in society, which correspond to a particular phase in the history of the means of production. It is possible for every individual to have his own spinning-wheel, but not everyone who is connected with the fabrication of textiles can have his own factory. The situation brought about by modern means of production creates the distinction of owners and non-owners. It implies that a particular phase of history shows society as composed of classes. A class is a "social group which, in virtue of its position in the process of production, has common economic, social, and political interests which are opposed to the economic, social, and political interests of other groups."[81] In regard to the phase of history in which Marx lived, only two classes were important: the bourgeois class of the capitalists and the class of the proletariat.

As we have said, Marx maintains that history is determined, in the last analysis, by the particular situation created by the means of production and the relations of production resulting from them. On the other hand, both Marx and Engels remark occasionally that history is the history of class struggle.[82] In reality the two expressions are identical in meaning. For at a definite level in the development of the means of production these means come in contradiction with the existing relations of production or property relations. A spinning wheel can without difficulty be privately owned, but this does not apply to a textile mill. Nevertheless, at a certain phase of history, the mill will be privately owned. There is then a contradiction, for a factory, or rather all modern means of production, are social by their

---

[79]"In the social production which men carry on they enter into definite relations that are indispensable and independent of their will; these relations of production correspond to a definite stage of development of their material powers of production The sum total of these relations of production constitute the economic structure of society." *A Contribution to the Critique of Political Economy*, p. 10.

[80]*Op. cit.*, p. 12.

[81]W. Banning, *Karl Marx, Leven, leer en betekenis*, Utrecht, 1960, p 109.

[82]"Then it was seen that all past history ... was the history of class struggles." Engels, *Herrn Eugen Dührings Umwälzung der Wissenschaft*, p. 30; English ed., p. 41.

very nature and can never be owned privately. Such circumstances breed revolutions which bring into play the power of the classes.[83] It is this factor that creates history.

The Juridical Order and the State

The legal order also should be understood from the standpoint of the actual situation governing production and ownership. For jurisprudence is but the will of the ruling, bourgeois class, raised to the dignity of law. The content of that will be determined by the material conditions of the ruling class.[84]

At a certain stage of society's development it becomes necessary to regulate the daily recurrent activities of production, distribution and exchange, to prevent the individual from going his own way in these matters. Such a rule is called a "law." As society makes further progress, the law becomes a more or less general system of legislation and man gradually forgets that the law is but an expression of the economic conditions of life. The legal order then begins to have a life of its own. Next, this order leads to the establishment of professional jurists and the science of law. The professional jurists compare the juridical systems of various peoples without realizing that they are expressions of economic relations; they think of them as independent self-supporting systems. "The comparison presupposes points in common, and these are found by the jurists compiling what is more or less common to all these legal systems and calling it *natural right*."[85] This natural right is the object of "justice." Once they have made this proclamation, the jurists conceive the development of law as the attempt to adjust the interhuman relations more perfectly to "eternal justice." But even this eternal justice remains the purely ideological and "heavenly" expression of economic relations.[86] The jurists imagine they are dealing

---

[83]"At a certain stage of their development, the material forces of production in society come in conflict with the existing relations of production, . . . with the property relations within which they had been at work before. From forms of development of the forces of production these forms turn into fetters. Then comes the period of social revolution." Marx, *Contribution to the Critique of Political Economy,* p. 12.

[84]Marx-Engels, "Manifest der Kommunistischen Partei," *Ausgewählte Schriften,* vol. I, p. 39; English ed., Marx-Engels, *Selected Works,* Moscow, 1962, vol. I, p. 49.

[85]Engels, "Zur Wohnungsfrage," *op. cit.,* vol. I, p. 592; English ed., "The Housing Question," *op. cit.,* vol. I, p. 624.

[86]Engels, *op. cit.,* vol. I, pp. 592 f.; English ed., vol. I, p. 624.

with *a priori* principles, whereas in reality they have to do with echoes and reflections of economic situations.[87]

Law in turn requires means to enforce it; it demands the State and State power. "The State is nothing but the organised collective power of the possessing classes, the landowners and the capitalists, as against the exploited classes, the peasants and the workers."[88] The State must continue to exist as long as society is made up of classes, for the ruling class has to make use of every means to keep the exploited class under control. The State calls itself the official representative of the whole community, the visible body politic of society, but in reality it only represents the economic interests of the ruling class.[89] Hence a worker really has no fatherland.

The State establishes a public power. This is not the armed power of the organized people, for the people are divided into classes. Slaves too are part of the people, but they are held in subjection by the State's public power. Justice is likewise class-justice. The State and public power are reflections of economic interests.[90]

Forms of Social Consciousness

We must now briefly consider man's ways of being-man, which Marx mostly calls "forms of social consciousness."[91] These too are determined by the particular economic foundation of society, although it happens mostly in an indirect manner and is not so immediately evident. What Marx has in mind here is mainly philosophy and religion.[92]

Philosophy. "The ideas of the ruling class are in every epoch the ruling ideas: i.e., the class, which is the ruling *material* force of

[87]Engels, "Brief an Schmidt," *op. cit.,* vol. I, p. 464; "Engels to C. Schmidt," *op. cit.,* vol. 2, p. 494.

[88]Engels, "Zur Wohnungsfrage," *op. cit.,* vol. I, p. 573; English ed., vol. I, p. 604.

[89]Engels, "Die Entwicklung des Sozialismus von der Utopie zur Wissenschaft," *op. cit.,* vol. 2, p. 139; "Socialism: Utopian and Scientific," *op. cit.,* vol. 2, p. 150.

[90]Engels, "Der Ursprung der Familie, des Privateigentums und des Staats," *op. cit.,* vol. 2, pp. 296 f.; English ed. "The Origin of Family, Private Property, and State," *op. cit.,* vol. 2, p. 263.

[91]"The sum total of these relations of production constitutes the economic structure of society—the real foundation on which rise legal and political superstructures and to which correspond definite forms of social consciousness." Marx, *Contribution to the Critique of Political Economy,* p. 11.

[92]"Religion, family, state, right, morality, science, art, etc. are merely *special* modes of production and fall under its general law." Marx, *Zur Kritik der Nationalökonomie,* Berlin, 1955, p. 128.

society, is at the same time its ruling intellectual force."[93] But these
predominant ideas are merely the spiritual expressions of the predominant material situation, i.e., of the conditions which give the
ruling class its power; they are therefore the ideas of its ruling
classes. Thus, in a country where the king, the aristocracy and the
bourgeoisie struggle for power, the theory of division of power becomes the dominant idea and it is proclaimed an "eternal law."
Within the ruling class the principle of the division of labor brings
about the division of spiritual and material work. A part of the
ruling class emerges as the thinkers of that class. They occupy themselves principally with elaborating the illusions of a class about itself.[94]

Next, the ideas of the ruling class are abstracted from the class
and acquire a form of universality. This implies that each class tries
to propose its own interest as the common interest of all the members of the particular society. Honor and fidelity, liberty and equality are spoken of as universal values, but in fact these ideas operate
only to the advantage of the ruling class.

Subsequently, a certain order, a mystic connection is introduced in
the ruling ideas; this is done by conceiving the dominant ideas as
"self-determinations of the idea."

Finally, an attempt is made to get away from the mystic appearance of this "self-determining idea"; it is then conceived as a
person—self-consciousness—or as a series of persons who represent
"the idea" in history. Philosophers are regarded as the makers of
history, but in this way the real foundation of history is simply
buried under a pile of verbiage.[95]

In reality such ideas about history are nothing but empty dreams
about history. In reality history is nothing else but the history of
the means of production. Philosophy is an echo of it. For instance,
Hobbes was the first modern materialist (in the sense given to that
term in the eighteenth century), but he was an absolutist when royal
absolutism flourished all over Europe and began to battle against the
people in England. The compromise between classes reached in
1688 produced Locke's religious and political ideas. The English
and French deists were the true philosophers of the bourgeoisie.

---

[93]Marx, *Die Deutsche Ideologie,* p. 44, English ed., p. 39.
[94]Marx, *op. cit.,* pp. 44-45, English ed., p. 39.
[95]Marx, *op cit.,* pp. 46-47; English ed., pp. 40 f.

The German burgher made his appearance in the German philosophy from Kant to Hegel.[96]

Religion. Religion also belongs to the superstructure of society that is determined by the substructure. "All religion is nothing but the fantastic reflection in men's mind of those external forces which control their daily life, a reflection in which terrestrial forces assume the form of supernatural forces."[97] At the beginning of history, this reflection was concerned with the natural powers, but later those powers produced an astonishing variety of personifications among various peoples. In regard to the Indo-European nations, comparative mythology is able to trace the process to its source in the Indian Vedas.[98]

At a later stage social forces began to operate alongside the powers of nature. At first man found them just as strange and incomprehensible as the forces of nature. He thought that the social forces ruled him with the same necessity as the powers of nature. The fancies first created by the imagination to represent natural forces later received social attributes and were thought of as historical powers. Still later, all the natural and social attributes of the many gods were transferred to a single almighty God. Religion could continue to live undisturbedly as long as man remained under the dominion of the forces of nature and of society.[99]

Accordingly, the life of religion is sustained by nebulous fancies of man's mind, and these fancies are nothing but the inevitable sublimation of his material process of life. Hence religion has no independent existence, no history of its own. It changes with the modifications occurring in the process of production and the relations of production; material life is not determined by the forms of consciousness, but these forms are produced by the material conditions of life.[100] All this receives added emphasis in the light of Marx's theory of "estrangement."

---

[96] Engels, "Brief an Schmidt," in *Ausgewählte Schriften,* vol. 2, p. 465; English ed., *Selected Works,* vol. 2, p. 495.

[97] Engels, *Herrn Eugen Dührings Umwälzung der Wissenschaft,* p. 393; English ed., p. 435.

[98] Engels, *op. cit.,* pp. 393-394; English ed., p. 435.

[99] Engels, *op cit.,* pp. 394-395; English ed., pp. 435 f.

[100] "Morality, religion, metaphysics, all the rest of ideology and corresponding forms of consciousness, thus no longer retain the semblance of independence. They have no history, no development; but men developing the material production and their material intercourse, alter, along with this their real existence, their thinking and the products of their thinking. Life is not determined by consciousness, but consciousness by life." Marx-Engels, *Die deutsche Ideologie,* p. 23; English ed., pp. 14 f.

3. THE THEORY OF ESTRANGEMENT

Marx borrowed the idea of "estrangement" from Hegel, but, as in the case of "history," he gave it an entirely different content. Hegel thought of history as the history of the idea, and he likewise thought of estrangement as taking place on the level of thought. Marx, on the contrary, reduces history to the history of labor and thus thinks of estrangement as taking place in the domain of labor.

The idea of "estrangement," as understood by Marx, can perhaps be best explained and clarified through the idea of "authenticity" that plays such an important role in modern existential phenomenology. According to this type of philosophy, man can be authentically or non-authentically whatever he is. He can be man authentically or inauthentically. When a man is inauthentically man, he disregards the "having to be" that characterizes man. For instance, according to Heidegger, being-man means being-in-the-world, but the authentic character of this being is abnegated when man does not experience it as dread. Whoever drives this existential dread out of his existence and submerges himself in the superficiality of anonymous being remains a man but he is not authentically a man. His existence is a sort of apostasy from his true being, an estranged existence. According to Marcel, being-in-the-world means "being destined for the other." He who refuses to acknowledge this and does not realize his existence as love, remains man but he is not authentically so, for he refuses to consider the "having to be" that characterizes his being. He apostatizes from his own essence and leads an estranged existence. Man, then, is estranged from his own being when he realizes himself in a way that is contrary to the "having to be" of his own essence. And when he goes so far as to explicitate his estrangement as his "having to be," he indulges in mystification.

Economic Estrangement

Similar ideas are found in Marx. He explicitates, or rather reduces man's being to being-a-worker. But man can be a worker authentically or inauthentically. Labor is what labor should be when the laborer can recognize and experience his own subjectivity in the product of his labor, since the subject expresses himself in his work. The subject puts himself into the object, into the product. Man becomes man by humanizing nature, for by humanizing nature he activates the powers and potentialities that lie dormant in him. Moreover, man realizes himself in his work as a fellowman, because labor becomes truly productive only from the time when man conceives and performs work as a social task. Hence labor that is authentically human is not a *means* for satisfying needs that are external to work, but it is itself the satisfaction of a need, namely, the need man has to realize himself as man. This, according to Marx, is what labor should be. However, it is far from being always what it should be.

Marx was occupied principally with the analysis of the conditions prevailing in his own time, during which capitalistic liberalism dominated society. In such a situation, Marx thought, labor is not what it should be. It is a kind of estrangement. The capitalist has made private property of the means of production which are social by their very nature, and the laborer, who has to live from the means of production, is forced to sell his labor to the capitalist. This itself is already something inhuman,[101] for labor is thus degraded to the level of merchandise and becomes a means for an external end,[102] whereas it should be performed as the means *par excellence* to man's self-realization. Labor is its own end.

Having to sell his labor, the laborer loses the fruits of his labor, for the products become the property of the capitalist. But the product is precisely that part of the world in which the worker expresses himself, in which he embodies his own subjectivity, and in which he recognizes and experiences his self-realization. Because the product of his work is appropriated by the capitalist, the laborer faces this product as an alien being.[103] Moreover, circumstances are such that the laborer becomes poorer in proportion to his producing more wealth. His self-realization is in reality a "de-realization" of self even unto death by starvation. His own work itself becomes an object which he can master only by using the

---

[101] Marx, "Arbeitslohn," *Kleine okonomische Schriften*, Berlin, 1955, p. 248; English ed., *Economic and Philosophic Manuscripts of 1844*, Moscow, 1961, pp. 21 f.

[102] "Life itself appears only as a means of life." Marx, *Zur Kritik der Nationalökonomie*, p. 104.

[103] "The object produced by labor, its product, faces labor as a *strange being*, as a power that is independent of the producer. The product of labor is labor as embodied in an object, as made into a thing, it is the objectification of labor. The realization of labor is its *objectification*. The realization of labor appears in the national economic situation as a "de-realization" of the laborer, the objectification as the *loss* and *slavery* of the object, the appropriation as *estrangement*, as alienation." Marx, *op. cit.*, p. 104.

greatest effort.[104] In this way labor becomes something that lies, as it were, outside the essence of the laborer. The laborer is no longer able to identify himself with his work. He feels that he is himself when he is not working, but in his work he feels, as it were, outside himself. He is "at home" when he does not work, but is not "at home" when he is at work.[105] Yet work is his genuine essence. Consequently, in a capitalistic regime the laborer is estranged from himself.

Connected with these considerations is Marx's conclusion that higher wages are not a solution to man's self-estrangement in the capitalistic system. For to labor for a wage is itself slavery. To give higher wages merely means to pay slaves better,[106] but slaves they remain. The radical evil lies in the fact that the means of production, which are by nature social, have fallen into the hands of private persons and that, consequently, the laborer is forced to sell his work to the capitalist. As long as this evil is not eliminated, no remedy can be found for the estrangement of man's labor.

Social Estrangement

The workman is estranged from his own being not only in his individual existence but also in his social existence. Work is authentically human, productive work when it is done in common with others. The modern means of production especially are essentially social and demand that men collaborate, for they can be used only when many work together. The laborer thus recognizes and experiences not only his personal self-realization and unfolding as man but also his co-existence with other laborers.[107] Labor, then, is also humanization in the intersubjective sense; in labor man becomes a fellow man.

This intersubjectivity too is lost in a capitalistic regime. For the product of his labor is taken away from the laborer; hence it is not only impossible for him to identify himself with his product, to consent to his being a worker, but he cannot even be a fellow man. When the products of labor are taken away from the worker, he is

---

104 *Op. cit.,* pp. 98 f.
105 *Op. cit.,* p. 101.
106 *Op. cit.,* p. 109.
107 "When man is placed in opposition to himself, the *other* also is in opposition to him. What is valid for the relationship of man to his work and to himself, applies also to the relationship of man to other men as well as to the work and the object of work of other men." *Op. cit.,* p. 106.

not able to experience either his own being-human or that of his fellow man. Or, to express it even better, co-existence in labor turns into its opposite, it becomes a source of conflict and struggle between man and his fellow man, between capitalist and worker, for the capitalist tries to appropriate as much of the laborer's product as possible, and in his turn the worker tries to keep as much as possible, because he needs it for his sustenance.

Private ownership and work for wages—which are fundamentally the same thing[108]—thus bring about the estrangement of co-existence.[109] This estrangement finds expression in class warfare, which is a necessary result of the capitalistic system. Higher wages are unable to save the worker from self-estrangement in his personal existence, and love cannot save man from the estrangement of co-existence. For this reason Marx opposes the humanism of Feuerbach. Feuerbach defended the mutual love between men as the highest moral demand. But, Marx thought, Feuerbach did not look deep enough. To talk about love is sentimentalism, for conflict, struggle, and hatred are incarnate in the actual system in which men live.

Ideological Estrangement

It goes without saying that the ruling class will use every means to perpetuate its power. And among these means are also so-called "ideologies." They are theories that try to camouflage, justify and mystify the fact that the estrangement exists. They consist principally of bourgeois theories about the State, philosophy and religion. It is necessary, therefore, to unmask those theories, for life in a bourgeois State, the pursuit of bourgeois philosophies, and submission to bourgeois religions are themselves modes of estranged existence. We shall say only a few words about the bourgeois theories concerning the State and philosophy, but speak at greater length about religion.

The State is the first ideological power controlling man.[110] In its own eyes, the State is the protector of the common interests of the citizens. It takes care of security within its own frontiers and protects the nation against attacks from outside. It formulates an order

---

[108]Marx, *op. cit.,* p. 109.

[109]"The *estrangement of man from man* is an immediate consequence of the fact that man is estranged from the product of his work, from the activity that is his life, from his specific essence." Marx, *op. cit.,* p. 106.

[110]Engels, *Ludwig Feuerbach and the Outcome of Classical German Philosophy,* New York, 1941, p. 54.

of law and safeguards it by the administration of justice. It preaches liberty, equality and fraternity. It considers itself the infallible expression of what is just and the realization of a state of liberty, and for this reason imposes itself as binding. In reality, however, this theory is one of the worst forms of mystification. The State is none of the things it proclaims to be. It is in reality a reflection of socio-economic relations, hence a sanction of injustice and inhumanity, it is *par excellence* the means used by the ruling class to perpetuate its economic power.[111]

Bourgeois philosophy, according to Marx, fulfills a similar role. He accuses it of busying itself all the time with "abstractions." This means for Marx that it is occupied with the products of uprooted thoughts which do not express reality. For how could a bourgeois philosopher be rooted in reality? He finds reality unacceptable and must, therefore, take refuge in "abstractions." Instead of speaking about *real* history, which is economic history, he expresses his dreams about history by conceiving it as the history of the Idea. Hegel is the typical example of that kind of philosophy. All this shows that philosophy is a form of estrangement.

Religious Estrangement

It was necessary for us to speak at length about the general philosophical theories of Marx in order to do justice to his ideas about religion, for the latter cannot be understood without the former.

We have already mentioned religion as being the echo of socio-economic life, that is as belonging to the superstructure of society. But, for Marx, religion is also a mode of estrangement and it is only when viewed from this standpoint that the anti-theism of Marx's atheism can be understood.

From Feuerbach he borrows the conviction that religion is merely the projection of man's own being into an alien being called "God." But Feuerbach, says Marx, restricts himself to stating it as a fact and fails to explain why man rejects his own essence and then worships it in an alien being.[112] Marx thinks that this can be explained only when we realize that man's true essence of man is a social product.[113] Hence a critique of religion is possible only by way of a critique of society.

111Engels, *ibid.*
112Marx "Theses on Feuerbach," in Engels, *op. cit.,* p. 83.
113Marx, *op. cit.,* p. 84.

Religion is a Mystification of Reality. Man feels the need to dream about a fantastic kingdom of heaven because he is not at home in his social life upon earth. The fact that the earthly foundation of human existence became separated from the earth and established itself as an independent kingdom in the clouds can be explained only by an internal division within that earthly foundation. That is why man needs the "consolation of religion." The existence of religion is simply "the existence of a distress."[114] It has absolutely no content that it can call its own, and it is not fed by heaven but by the earth. It is nonsensical to criticize religion as if it had a kind of independent existence, for it is only an epiphenomenon of social life.[115]

It is not religion that makes man but man makes religion. Man creates the "fantastic reality of heaven" as an echo of himself.[116] But man is not an abstract being; real man exists only in the world, in society, in the State. Here man meets real suffering, his real wretchedness. Here religion is born because man finds real life unbearable. But religion is nothing but opium. It is "the general theory of the world, its encyclopedic summary, its logic in a popular form, its 'point of honor,' its animation and moral sanction, its pompous complement, and its general source of consolation and justification." But all this means merely that "religion is the self-realization of man in the imagination, because man's *being* has no true reality in the realm of [earthly] reality."[117] Religion mystifies authentic reality, it makes it an illusion.

It is necessary to unmask this mystification. For this purpose it has to be shown that the sacred figure, which human self-estrangement assumes in religion, is unholy. But the unholy figure of man's self-estrangement is nothing else but his socio-economic estrangement. Hence the critique of heaven must be a critique of the earth; the critique of religion must be a critique of law; the critique of theology must be a critique of politics.[118]

The idea is clear: in real life man is unhappy and for this reason he imagines that he will be happy in heaven. In real life man has no rights; hence he imagines that he will obtain justice in the hereafter.

---

[114]Marx, "Zur Judenfrage," *Bücherei des Marxismus-Leninismus,* vol. 41, p. 34.
[115]Marx, *op. cit.,* p. 35.
[116]Marx, "Zur Kritik der Hegelschen Rechtsphilosophie," *Bücherei des Marxismus-Leninismus,* vol. 41, p. 11.
[117]Marx, *op cit.,* p. 11.
[118]Marx, *op. cit.,* p. 12.

In real life man does not feel at home; hence he dreams about a heavenly fatherland. Religion has spun a mysticism around man's real and unbearable life. It is evident that such a dream can never be eliminated unless the situation causing it is abolished. Hence the critique of heaven can be effective only when it is conceived as the critique of this valley of tears, which religion invests with an aureole.[119] The critique of religion ends with the insight that man should be the highest being for man, i.e., with the categorical imperative to overturn all the relations and situations in which man is a humiliated, enslaved, abandoned and despised being.[120] Man cannot base his selfhood on religion but solely on the ruins of religion.[121]

All Religion is Estrangement. Engels went to much trouble to show that the history of religions can be understood only through economic history.[122] As the substructure changes, so does the superstructure. But so long as the substructure preserves the divided character which has marked its entire history, man will feel the need of building fantastic kingdoms in the clouds. All religions, then, bring about man's estrangement from his own being because religion as such is a kind of estrangement.

It stands to reason that Marx and Engels aimed their critique of religion principally against Christianity. They accused it of justifying slavery in antiquity, of glorifying serfdom during the Middle Ages, of consenting to defend the oppression of the proletariat, albeit with a sorrowful face. The social principles of Christianity preach that it is necessary to have a ruling class and an oppressed class, and they merely express the pious wish that the former will practice charity. They postpone to heaven the punishment of all misdeeds and thereby justify the perpetuation of injustice on earth. They interpret the misery of the oppressed as a just punishment of original sin or of personal sins, or as a trial which the Lord in his infinite Wisdom sends to those who are saved. They preach cowardice, self-contempt, submission, humility, in short, all the characteris-

---

[119]"The abolition of religion as the people's illusory happiness is a condition of their *real* happiness. The requirement to eliminate their illusions about their condition is the *requirement to eliminate a condition which needs illusions.* Accordingly the critique of religion is *fundamentally* the *critique* of the valley of tears, of which religion is the *holy illusion.*" Marx, *op. cit.,* p. 12.

[120]Marx, *op. cit.,* p. 20.

[121]Marx, "Critique of the Hegelian Dialectic and Philosophy as a Whole," *Economic and Philosophic Manuscripts of 1844,* Moscow, 1961, p. 161.

[122]Engels, *Ludwig Feuerbach and the Outcome of Classical German Philosophy,* passim.

tics of the riff-raff. This is pure hypocrisy, for in this way the oppressed are not handed over to God but to their exploiters.[123] And these will, of course, defend religion.

There is no need to add anything, for the above-mentioned ideas express the essence of Marx's teaching regarding religion. A brief consideration could be attached about Marx's assertion that religion is doomed to disappear, but this point will be more fittingly treated in the general Marxist theory of the future.

4. Eschatology, Phophecy, and Messianism

As a philosophy of history, the doctrine of Marx and Engels does not confine itself to a consideration of the past and the present; it also envisages the future; it is an "eschatology."

The one great evil afflicting society consists, according to Marx, in the fact that the means of production which by their very nature are social, have been appropriated by private owners. This evil therefore is the center of one great conflict. "And this conflict between productive forces and modes of production is not a conflict engendered in the mind of man, like that between original sin and divine justice. It exists, in fact, objectively, outside us, independently of the will and actions even of the men who have brought it on."[124] It is this conflict that will have to be ended first of all in the future. Marx, however, does not expect its elimination to come about as the result of any particular initiative by which a definite plan or an ensemble of aims is fulfilled; it will be eliminated by virtue of the objective process of history. History tends *of necessity* to a state of affairs in which the proletariat will take over the ownership of the means of production.

This point brings us to the difficult problem of "determinism," of the necessitating force which, Marx believes, must be accepted in the development of history. Marx definitely needs that idea in order to speak of the future as he does. The future, as he conceives it, is determined, of necessity pre-established in the actual situation and is independent of "intentions."

Some commentators of Marxism have expressed surprise at the constant attention Marx gave to the history of economics. On that

---

[123] See texts quoted by Ehlen, *Der Atheismus im dialektischen Materialismus,* pp. 203-204.

[124] Engels "Die Entwicklung des Sozialismus von der Utopie zur Wissenschaft," *Ausgewählte Schriften,* vol. 2, p. 127; English ed., vol. 2, p. 137.

account he was sometimes considered to be principally an economist and certainly not primarily a philosopher. Today the situation is different. It is now generally recognized that Marx is primarily a philosopher, but it is also noted that it was necessary for him to deal with dry and monotonous economic questions which repel and annoy the reader, because he wanted his philosophy to be a philosophy of history. As a philosopher of history, Marx had to create a perspective of the future. And since history was fundamentally the history of economics, he had to start from the present and past conditions of the economy in order to be able to open a vision of the future.

It stands to reason that the study of present and past economic conditions does not allow us to speak about the future as absolutely and definitively as Marx does, unless the future is already fixed and determined in the present and the past. This, precisely, is Marx's opinion, and he was not the only one in his era to maintain it. For at that time not only Hegelianism but also positivism was the vogue and there existed an unshakeable faith in the positive sciences, a faith that had degenerated into absolutism. It was firmly believed that the only reason why the future could not yet be infallibly foretold was the fact that the past and the present had not yet been sufficiently analyzed by science. This defect, however, constituted no problem for the positivists, because they believed in the existence of an all-embracing and necessary causal interconnection which, *in principle,* made it possible to foretell the future with scientific certainty.[125]

The Economics of Marx

Marx also shared that faith. For reasons we have mentioned above Marx's positivism took the form of economics. Marx thought that he was able to foretell the future by means of the iron-clad, necessary laws of economics. This determinism gave Marx's socialism a "scientific" character in contrast to the utopian socialism of Proudhon. Marx viewed Proudhon's socialism with contempt, for, although Proudhon criticized the capitalistic relationships of production, he was unable to explain them scientifically and, consequently, did not know how to handle them.[126] As a consequence, he was unable also to say anything with certainty about the future and

---

125 S.U. Zuidema, *Het communisme in ontbinding,* Wageningen, n.d., pp. 25-35.

126 Engels, "Die Entwicklung...," *op. cit.,* vol. 2, p. 125. English ed., vol. 2, pp. 127 f.

could merely utter prophecies and pious wishes. Proudhon, to Marx's mind, still belonged to the founders of the many sects that sprang up everywhere at the time when the proletarian movement was in its infancy.[127]

It is not necessary for our purpose to explain in detail Marx's thoughts regarding the economic laws which are destined to destroy capitalism. Marx has formulated them as the law of the constantly decreasing surplus value of labor, the law of concentration and centralization, the law of recurrent economic crises and the law of progressive pauperization.[128] Basing himself upon those economic laws, Marx felt certain that, in view of the capitalist system of private property and labor for wages, a situation must necessarily arise in which a very small number of capitalists will be confronted with an immense army of proletarians, driven to extreme misery. Having nothing to lose except their chains, the proletarians will revolt against the ruling powers and overthrow them by taking over the means of production.[129] The laws that govern the capitalist economy clearly indicate, says Marx, that capitalism "produces its own gravediggers. Its fall and the victory of the proletariat are equally inevitable."[130]

Accordingly, the positivism of Marx is a kind of economism. The economy *proves* with scientific infallibility what Marx foresees about the future. There is, he believes, no escape from this. The very nature of the capitalist system, considered objectively and independently of the capitalists' intentions, contains in germ its own destruction. "Private property, too, drives itself in its economic movement towards its own dissolution, only, however, through a development which does not depend on it, of which it is unconscious and which takes place against its will, through the very nature of things; only inasmuch as it produces the proletariat as proletariat."[131]

The communist future lies in the objective reality of the proletariat, and is independent of the "intentions" of this proletariat. "The question is not what this or that proletarian, or even the whole of

[127]Engels "Zur Wohnungsfrage," *op. cit.*, vol. 2, p. 602; English ed., vol. 1, p. 634.
[128]Zuidema, *op. cit.*, pp. 65-73.
[129]Marx, "Geschlichtliche Tendenz der kapitalistischen Akkumulation," *Ausgewählte Schriften*, vol. 1, p. 434; English ed., "Historical Tendency of Capitalist Accumulation," *Selected Works*, vol. 1, p. 460.
[130]Marx-Engels, "Manifest der Kommunistischen Partei," *op. cit.*, vol. I, p. 35; English ed., vol. I, p. 45.
[131]*Die heilige Familie*, p. 137; English ed., p. 52.

the proletariat, at the moment *considers* as its aim. The question is *what the proletariat is,* and what, consequent on that *being,* it will be compelled to do. Its aim and historical action is irrevocably and obviously demonstrated in its own life-situation as well as in the whole organization of bourgeois society today."[132]

Capitalist private ownership is the first negation of individual private ownership, which is based upon the individual's own labor. But the capitalist system contains the seed of its own destruction, that is, it brings about its own negation. History is thus advancing toward the negation of the negation "with the necessity of a natural process."[133] The development of the means of production and the relations of production will reach a stage when the tension between the proletariat and the capitalist framework becomes unbearable. This framework will then be torn asunder and the dispossessors will be dispossessed.[134]

Abolition of Private Ownership

The abolition of private property will be first on the agenda after the Revolution because the one great evil and source of all others lies in the fact that the social means of production are privately owned.[135] Man's estrangement will cease with the abolition of private ownership; then he will regain the kingdom of freedom, or rather the pre-history of man will come to an end and be replaced by the history of man as a definitively free being. Labor will lose its burdensome character and be merely the free exercise of man's energy and the unfolding of his powers. Labor will no longer be a means, to which level it had been degraded in the capitalist system, but a self-realization of man and therefore an end in itself. Marx goes even so far as to hold that, when private property is abolished, "man will come into possession of his 'all-sided' essence in an 'all-sided way,' i.e., he will be totally and integrally man."[136] Only after private ownership has been abolished will man's human relations with the world—his sight, hearing, taste, smell, feeling, thought, experience, will, activity and love—be authentically human.[137] We could sum up

---

[132]Marx-Engels, *op. cit.,* p. 138; English ed., p. 53.
[133]Marx, "Geschichtliche Tendenz der kapitalisticschen Akkumulation," *Ausgewählte Schriften,* vol. I, p. 434; English ed., *Selected Works,* vol. I, p. 460.
[134]*Ibid.*
[135]Marx-Engels, "Manifest der Kommunistischen Partei," *op. cit.,* vol. I, p. 36; English ed., vol. I, pp. 46 f.
[136]Marx, *Zur Kritik der Nationalökonomie,* p. 131.
[137]Marx, *op. cit.,* pp. 131-132.

Marx's thought by saying that man will be perfectly man after the proletarian revolution.

Brotherhood and Peace

Every form of estrangement will disappear when its principal form is removed. Social estrangement will also vanish. Communism will not only abolish the split between man and nature but it will abolish the division between men, or to put it concretely, between classes. Classes will disappear and only brotherhood and peace will reign among men. The proletariat as a class will also cease to exist: it will abolish itself as a class. For, "if the proletariat during its contest with the bourgeoisie is compelled, by force of circumstances, to organize itself as a class, if, by means of a revolution, it makes itself the ruling class, and, as such, sweeps away by force the old conditions of production, then, it will, along with these conditions, have swept away the conditions for the existence of class antagonisms and of classes generally, and will thereby have abolished its own supremacy as a class."[138]

Brotherhood and peace are foreshadowed and potential in the objective reality of the proletariat, because the proletariat possesses a "universal character through its universal suffering."[139] All particular categories of life have lost their meaning for proletarians. Particular categories are meaningful for the capitalist: he can be the father of a family, a Frenchman, or a German, a lover of art, a member of societies, or against cruelty to animals. All this no longer exists for the proletarian. It has lost its meaning for him since the inhuman character of the capitalist system has reduced his existence to mere labor, to pure emptiness.

However, in this condition of pure emptiness the proletarian is also *pure* solidarity with his fellow-worker, for whom, likewise, particular categories are meaningless; hence their solidarity cannot be threatened by conflicts arising in particular categories of life. Here then is the "universal character" of the proletariat, the fellowship in brother-

---

[138]Marx-Engels, "Manifest der Kommunistischen Partei," *Ausgewählte Schriften,* vol. I, p. 43; English ed., vol. I, p. 54.

[139]". . . an estate which is the abolition of all estates, a sphere which possesses a universal character through its universal suffering and does not take any *particular* right into consideration because it is the victim not of any *particular* injustice but of injustice without any qualification." Marx, "Zur Kritik der Hegelschen Rechtsphilosophie," *Bücherei des Marxismus-Leninismus,* vol. 41, p. 26.

hood and peace. Unfortunately, this brotherhood exists as yet only negatively, namely, in the suffering of having to work in estrangement. After the Revolution, however, that negativity will be transformed into positivity. The Revolution will give birth to the integral man, the one who is man in the subjective and intersubjective sense.

Disappearance of the State

It stands to reason that the elimination of man's social estrangement will be accompanied by the disappearance of his political estrangement. For the State is the product of the class struggle. By means of the legal order and its sanctions the State defends and perpetuates the ways of production and the corresponding relations of production which the exploiting class has created. But when the means of production have become the common property of society there will no longer be any class of exploited. And since the State consists essentially of the oppression of the exploited class, it will lose its very nature as soon as there are no more classes. Thus, there is no need to abolish the State, for it will simply wither away.[140] Its place will be taken by an "Association" in which the free development of every individual is the condition for the free development of all.[141]

The collapse of the substructure of necessity brings about the collapse of the entire superstructure. The elimination of man's fundamental estrangement leads to the disappearance of the ideological alienation. The abolition of private property means the *total* return from all estrangement and alienation. Hence the "forms of consciousness," especially philosophy and religion, will also change. Bourgeois philosophy will disappear, i.e., the illusion that the domination of the ruling class is the predominance of certain ideas will vanish. As soon as there is no longer any ruling class, no class will feel it necessary to present a particular interest as the common interest of man.[142] Now this is what bourgeois philosophy has always done. It will, therefore, disappear.

Disappearance of Religion

Finally religion, too, will cease to exist. Man will have no longer any reason to lose himself in religious estrangement. For the reli-

---

[140]Engels, "Die Entwicklung des Sozialismus von der Utopie zur Wissenschaft," *Ausgewöhlte Schriften,* vol. 2, p. 139; *Selected Works,* vol. 2, p. 150.
[141]Marx-Engels, "Manifest der Kommunistischen Partei," op. cit., vol. I, p. 43; English ed., vol. I, p. 54.
[142]Marx-Engels, *Die Deutsche Ideologie,* p. 46; English ed., p. 41.

gious alienation has its source in the economic estrangement, and this estrangement will disappear when society seizes the means of production. Man will no longer feel the need of dreaming about happiness after he has found his *true* happiness. He will no longer need consolation when he has no more *true* sorrow. Religion is the reflection and echo of economic misery, but it will vanish when economic wretchedness is gone, for it will no longer have anything to reflect or echo.[143]

Hence the religious narrow-mindedness and its hold on men do not have to be combated with positive weapons. All that is necessary is to take away economic estrangement, and religion will wither away. According to Marx, history has always been "dissolved" in superstition. Henceforth, however, superstition will be dissolved in history.[144]

Accordingly, in a communist society not only religion, but also atheism, will no longer exist. Atheism will no longer have any meaning, for it has meaning only as the negation of God which permits man to affirm himself. In communism the affirmation of man comes both first and last, as principle and terminus; hence there is no longer any need to have recourse to the denial of God. Once man is *really* affirmed, God is no longer talked about.[145]

These are the fundamental outlines of Marx's eschatology. History is on the road toward its final stage, viz., the communist society. The road is prefigured in the actual condition of society, and history will of necessity follow this road. Communism, then, is not an "ideal," a goal for which men strive, but expresses the *real* movement of history.[146] "Communism *is* the solution of the riddle of history and it also *knows* that it is the solution."[147]

5. CRITICAL CONSIDERATIONS

Objections Against Our Procedure. We can imagine that some of our readers have objections against the way we have presented the teaching of Marx. They might remark that we have disregarded the

---

[143]"When therefore man no longer merely proposes but also disposes—only then will the last alien force which is still reflected in religion vanish and with it will also vanish the religious reflection itself, for the simple reason that there will be nothing left to reflect." Engels, *Herrn Eugen Dührings Umwälzung der Wissenschaft,* p. 395; English ed. p. 437.

[144]Marx "Zur Judenfrage," *Bücherei des Marxismus-Leninismus,* vol. 41, p. 32.

[145]Marx, *Zur Kritik der Nationalökonomie,* p. 139.

[146]Marx-Engels, *Die deutsche Ideologie,* p. 32; English ed., p. 26.

[147]Marx, *Zur Kritik der Nationalökonomie,* p. 127.

so-called "Diamat," or official Soviet philosophy, which also appeals to Marx, that we do not consider the Soviet interpretation as something that has to be taken seriously. This objection is rather frequently made by those who consider the official Soviet philosophy pure nonsense without philosophical importance and, for reasons which we can understand but not justify, wish to transfer the same "lack of importance" to Marx himself.

It could also be objected that we have not confronted the quotations from Marx with other texts which would have shown clearly that his work is full of contradictions. It could be said that we have avoided revealing those contradictions by referring principally to his early writings and have thus failed to give a faithful description of Marx's doctrine. These objections are not groundless; hence we owe an explanation to the reader as to why we have disregarded those points.

Reply to These Objectons. It is true that we have approached the philosophy of Marx with a special "attitude," namely, that of a contemporary philosopher who wants to express the meaning of reality in a relatively independent way. In order to do this, he needs the past and especially the great philosophers presented to us by the history of philosophy. The contemporary philosopher starts from the idea that the history of philosophy should not be viewed as the record of the errors made by thinking humanity or as that of ideas which people held at one time and which we hold no longer. For otherwise one virtually reduces the great philosophers to nonentities and rejects their opinions as having no more value than an ordinary cancelled stamp. Their opinions would then have value for those alone who, like stamp collectors, are interested in things only after they have been "cancelled" and withdrawn from circulation. But what the great philosophers have said still retains value for us, even though this value should be appraised in the proper way. Let us illustrate the matter with an example.

Undoubtedly, one is justified in saying that it is nonsense to hold that the soul once lived in a world of abstract and universal ideas, that it was banished from that world because of some fault, incarcerated in a body, and therefore involved in a world that has no true reality—as Plato affirmed. When looked at from that standpoint, Platonism is indeed like a cancelled stamp. And yet Plato still lives in the thought of today, and no philosopher can refuse to be *also* a Platonist. This, however, means neither more nor less than that the philosopher of today must hold as valuable what Plato actually "saw," but exaggerated and expressed in a formula whose very brevity appears nonsensical. In other words, the modern philosopher succeeds in giving Plato his due only if he understands him better than Plato understood himself.

Something similar must be said about Marx. The philosophy of Marx is not valueless like an ordinary cancelled postage stamp; on the contrary, it belongs permanently to the classics of philosophy.[148] But the contemporary philosopher who wishes to realize the reason why Marx's ideas remain valuable must free himself from the nonsensical formulation to which Marx's system can be reduced—as, after all, can be done with any great system by reducing it to a summary statement.

The official Soviet philosophy has committed this fault;[149] worse still, it imposes its own summary of Marx as the highest and absolute wisdom. On that account it is Marx, and not the official Marxists, who attracts the attention of earnest philosophers. Marx "saw" something. But every serious philosopher, who does not conceive the history of philosophy as a collection of cancelled stamps, knows that an original thinker, a genius, who tries to survey the whole of reality in the light of a new primitive fact or central reference point, seldom if ever succeeds in finding a proper balance. Geniuses are especially liable to fall into contradictions. No one should take offense at that. It can scarcely be avoided and, after all, the new system cannot be simply "learned," as one learns how to operate a machine. There always remains something to be "thought." But that which a genius like Marx "really" has seen can no longer be dismissed as something not worth a thought. Now the ideas of Marx that belong to perennial philosophy are found principally in his early writings. For this reason we have quoted principally from them and not from his later works.

General Critical Considerations

As is well known, it is especially existential phenomenology that has shown sufficient openness toward the ideas of Marx to integrate the elements of perennial value in this thought into a more balanced

---

[148] Cf. Kwant, *De wijsbegeerte van Karl Marx*, Utrecht, 1961, pp. 96-97.
[149] W. Banning, *Karl Marx, leven, leer en betekenis*, Utrecht, 1960, pp. 175-176.

way of thinking, and to avoid the naive absolutism which Marx's thought certainly contained in germ and in which he personally fell repeatedly. It may be useful to mention here the most important of Marx's valuable insights.

Man's Existence as Being-"at"-the-World. It cannot be denied that man *is* existence, that is, that man is a subject who is involved in the world. Both Marx and the phenomenologist find it absolutely impossible to think of man in the Cartesian way, that is, to isolate the subject, man, from the world. The subject is an authentic subject only *in* and *"at"* the world.[149a] The addition of *at* means that we should not conceive being-in-the-world as a static reality, for then it would be no longer possible to understand that the subject-in-the-world has, and even *is,* a history. The existence of man is a being-"at"-the-world; through his *activity* in relation to the world man achieves his authenticity. Man is a self-realizing and history-making being. Marx rightly accentuates in this way the *central* significance of labor. Man becomes authentically man only when he "sets to work." And in his work it is the perfection of the means of production that is, evidently, decisive; for work leads to authenticity only when man becomes truly productive, that is, when he forces nature to yield a surplus—and this does happen when man uses only his hands.

Moreover, productive labor is a builder of society, for man can be productive only through division of labor and cooperation in labor. By labor existence realizes itself as co-existence in the authentic sense of the term.

Finally, it is obvious that the demand for the productivity of labor can be satisfied only by introducing *modern* means of production, which enable work to become technological labor. For, the modern means force nature to yield a surplus and at the same time oblige man to undertake labor as a community pursuit, which is the second requisite for making labor productive.

The Gestalt Character of Man's Being. One of the fundamental insights of the phenomenologist is to the effect that everything in man refers to everything else in him. The being of man is a Gestalt;

[149a]We use "at" the world rather than "to" the world, to express the idea that man's existence is a dynamic, active way of being in the world. "At," therefore has here the same value as in the expression: "He is at it again." Cf. Luijpen *Existential Phenomenology,* 3rd impr., Pittsburgh 1963, pp. 39 f. (Tr.)

the ways of being-man which we distinguish cannot be separated from one another like so many separate elements or atoms. The human dimensions which we distinguish from one another are what they are only in the unity of reciprocal implication with other dimensions and with the totality. It stands to reason that a particular facticity of existence and co-existence on the economic level is also significant for, and is found again on the level of, an existence and co-existence that is not identical with the economic level. This also was seen by Marx, and he may have been one of the first to take notice of it. What takes place on the economic level finds an echo in the social, juridical, ethical, family, political, philosophical and religious levels of co-existence.

Authenticity and Inauthenticity. Finally, no sensible man will deny that on any level of man's being a distinction must be made between authenticity and non-authenticity. Man *is* not man as rain is wet or a willow-tree is gnarled. Some phenomenologists express this insight by stating that man is not, but *has-to be*. Of course, any man can refuse to acknowledge or realize what he has-to be, and when he does this he can camouflage his refusal to realize what he has-to be by specious theories. He then presents what he has not to be as what he has to be. Expressed in Marxist terms, man can alienate his own being and then mystify his alienation. Since everything in man refers to everything else in him, it is not surprising to find that the estrangement on the economic level has its counterpart on other levels of existence and co-existence, and that one type of mystification causes other mystifications.

Objectionable Aspects of Marx's Philosophy

We find it difficult to imagine that a modern philosopher whose task it is to express the ultimate meaning of reality in a relatively independent way would neglect those insights of Marx. In this sense every authentic philosopher should be *also* a Marxist, just as he must be *also* a Platonist, a Thomist and a Cartesian. This does not mean that his philosophy should be a kind of patchwork containing theses of Plato, Thomas, Descartes and Marx. It means rather that his "vision" should be co-inspired by the "vision" of those geniuses. What is "seen" is undeniably something of everlasting value.

Lack of Equilibrium. A philosophy does not fail in what it states, but by what it discards. Differently expressed, a philosophy fails through "absolutism," by making absolute what has only a relative truth value, for in this way it is led to deny *other* truths that likewise possess a relative value. It is quite certain that Marx's philosophy sins by absolutism. He let himself be carried away by his genial vision to such an extent that he was no longer capable of viewing his ideas "from a distance." For Marx, a man is *nothing else* except a being-"at"-the-world and this way of being is practically nothing else but labor. Man is exclusively a social being, and labor alone builds society. Man is pure historicity, and necessity *alone* governs history. The driving power of history is *nothing else* but the situation in the realm of the means of production, and the estrangement of man is *solely* of an economic nature.

From the summary, presented above, of the essential elements pertaining to Marx's philosophy, we realize how difficult it must be for a philosopher to preserve the necessary but precarious balance when he starts to embody his insights into a connected whole of details. This statement applies particularly to a time like that of Marx when the battle between spiritualism and materialism was still in full swing. It was, practically speaking, not yet possible to attain such an equilibrium, not even for a man of Marx's stature. That is why his work is full of contradictions. They would cause little worry except for the fact that some people have seized his philosophy in an unphilosophical fashion and have made it almost impossible to examine it in a calm and peaceful way.

Disregard of Man as Subject. In Marx's philosophy we find both a materialistic and a spiritualistic inspiration. When he speaks about labor, he rightly appeals to man as the human subject in order to contrast labor as *human* labor with the activity of the brute animal. Man is not a brute animal, because man *alone* works.

What he means is that man's activity springs from man as a subject, that it is a conscious and free activity—which cannot be said about any animal activity. And yet Engels attributes to labor the evolution of man-as-subject from the ape.[150] Here we have an evident contradiction. And is it not sufficient to reply that this is only a contradiction between Marx and Engels, for Engel's opinion is perfectly in line with the thought of Marx himself. The latter constantly fosters Engel's opinion when he says that man is nothing but a "part of nature."[151]

---

[150]Engels, "Anteil der Arbeit an der Menschwerdung des Affen," *Ausgewählte Schriften,* vol. II, pp. 70-82; "The Part Played by Labour in the Transition from Ape to Man," *Selected Works,* vol. 2, pp. 80-92.

[151]Cf. Ehlen, *Der Atheismus in dialektischen Materialismus,* pp. 133-138.

According to Marx, labor presupposes man as subject, but man emerges as subject from the evolution of the cosmos by labor.[152] This is like saying that, when a man is sinking in a swamp, he can save himself from his precarious situation by pulling himself up by the hairs of his head. When Marx tries to explain man's origin, he has already forgotten that man is a subject. Thus, it is to be expected that later also he will frequently lose sight of man as a subject.

This happens, in fact, when Marx declares without any qualification that being determines consciousness. He expresses the same thought also in other words, but the intention remains the same. He wants to emphasize the fact that, ultimately, the "life of the mind" and the "spiritual process of life," the superstructure of society and the "forms of consciousness," are *determined* by the situation in regard to the means of production. One who asserts this as apodictically as Marx thereby eliminates the value of the subject as co-origin of what Marx calls "being." "Being" here means for him the "means of production," and these means evidently are not what they are without the inspiration and initiatives of the subject, that is, without the "forms of consciousness," as Marx calls them. For how could one think of and express the "being" of the modern means of production without naming also "consciousness" as it exists in modern physical science? And if this is so, it is not possible to assert that "consciousness" is determined exclusively by the means of production, for the means of production presuppose "consciousness."[153]

Marx's contentions in this respect merely repeat on a higher level the tenet that labor is human by the fact that it is the labor of a subject, but that man-as-subject has evolved from the ape through the instrumentality of labor. But the "being" that Marx conceives as matter, is "human matter" (Merleau-Ponty); hence man cannot be fully explained by "being" alone.

Disregard of the Subject's Ethical Inspiration. The levels of being-man, which Marx discusses, become increasingly complex and, as a consequence, the original contradiction also becomes more and more complicated. Fundamentally, however, it remains unchanged. Everything Marx speaks of presupposes the subject, but the way he speaks about everything eliminates the subject. The thesis that the substructure determines the superstructure implies for Marx, e.g.,

---

[152]Cf. Ehlen, *op. cit.*, p. 133.
[153]Cf. Kwant, *De wijsbegeerte van Karl Marx,* pp. 9-36.

that the situation in regard to the means of production and the relations of production *determines* the juridical order. Likewise, moral consciousness which tells man, e.g., that he *ought* to respect the juridical order is merely a mirror-like effect of *actual* relations.

It stands to reason that, in such a view of the subject, the subjective inspiration and the personal attitude of one who is, or desires to be, just become meaningless. And this inevitably leads to difficulties. For if the subject and the moral inspiration of the subject are meaningless, it becomes impossible to judge at any time whether certain actually existing relations and attitudes are not what they "ought to be." And yet Marx has made such a judgment. On what ground, we may ask. Could he do it on the basis of the "mirror-like effect of the actual relations"? The reply is negative, for such a mirroring of what *de facto* is yields nothing but the image of what *de facto* is. Surely the possession of an image of what *de facto* exists is something other than the conviction that this existing situation is not what it *ought* to be. Such a condemnation is possible only on the basis of a subjective inspiration.

In other words, Marx can protest against actual relations and attitudes only because "the mirroring of what *de facto* is" contradicts the "sense" of justice in Marx's consciousness. All those who oppose Marx agree that the "sense" for justice was his driving force. His sense for justice was more keen, clearsighted and demanding than that of many of his contemporaries who chattered incessantly about it. Yet, strange to say, that which animated and propelled Marx did not appear, nor could it appear, in his doctrine. For, in Marx's view, consciousness is *determined* by "being."

It is not surprising, therefore, that Marx here also falls into evident contradictions. The subjective, ethical inspiration supposedly does not count; yet Marx accuses the capitalist of greed.[154] What can be the meaning of such an *accusation* when it may not be conceived in relation to the subject's attitude? Can one "accuse" an earthquake of cruelly ruining the countryside? But, according to Marx, the capitalist system is included in being "with the necessity of a natural process."

Disregard of Circular Causality. On rare occasions Marx admits what no one can deny, and affirms the mutual influence, the circular

---

[154]"The only wheels which the national-economist puts into motion are *greed* and the *wars of the greedy,* competition." Marx, *Zur Kritik der National-ökonomie,* p. 97.

causality, of mutual implication proper to the substructure and the superstructure, to being and consciousness, to material conditions of life and spiritual processes of life.[155] Now he who earnestly holds this conviction can no longer profess that a unilateral, determining causality is exercised by the economic basis of society on the other levels of coexistence.

In a letter addressed to Bloch, Engels likewise speaks about circular causality as if it were the most natural thing in the world. He holds that we should not picture the application of his theories as being even more simple than the "solution of an equation of the first degree"; yet one would commit this fault if one were to proclaim that the economic basis of society is the "only determining factor" in history.[156] The movement of history is not determined solely by the economic basis. The subject also must be taken into account, with his attitudes, convictions, inspirations, insights and intentions. And yet the basis of this mutual influence is "ultimately again economic necessity";[157] in other words, in the last analysis, the course of history is still deterministic.

It would have been unthinkable, indeed, if Marx had not repeatedly become the victim of that idea. For, if the course of history is not *determined,* there is also no guaranteed future. But Marx was committed to such a future and, had he abandoned his eschatology, he would have had to drop also the communist future. But Marx could not even allow any doubt about that kind of future. The communist future, he held, is clearly and irrevocably prefigured in the objective organization of bourgeois society; it is implied in the objective reality of the proletariat, independently of the latter's "intentions."

The determining factor, then, is not the aim "proposed" and "pursued" by the proletarian; it is solely what the proletariat *is* and what it is *forced* to do in virtue of its historic *being.* The subject and his "forms of consciousness" do not count. To take account of them in his theory would have made it impossible for Marx to guarantee the future. Consequently, the disappearance of capitalism

---

[155]"Political, juridical, philosophical, religious, literary, artistic, etc. development is based on economic development. But all these react upon one another and also upon the economic base. It is not that the economic position is the *cause and alone active,* while everything else only has a passive effect. There is rather interaction." Engels to H. Starkenburg, Marx-Engels, *Selected Correspondence,* New York, 1942, p. 517.
[156]Engels to J. Bloch, *op. cit.,* p. 475.
[157]Engels to H. Starkenburg, *op. cit.,* p. 518.

would likewise have been uncertain, for the subject could then have molded and reformed capitalism. But this *has* to be impossible, for otherwise Marx's theory would lose its prophetic and messianic character. Only by retaining the theory of determinism in history can its messianic and prophetic role be preserved.

Contradiction in the Theory of Progressive Pauperism. Neither does Marx want to countenance efforts gradually to improve the conditions of the workers. For, according to the theory of progressive pauperism, the wretchedness of the workers must reach such a depth that the proletarian class will be ripe for revolution. The theory of pauperism is precisely for the purpose of showing that the Revolution is *bound* to come. Since misery has *of necessity* to reach its greatest depth, consequently, all "initiatives" which strive to better the conditions of the worker are evil because they retard the coming of the Revolution. We get the impression that Marx wants to say: the inspiration, the intention and the attitude of the *subject ought* to be such that they fit the theory that the communistic future has to come of necessity. But this implies that the subject can also assume an attitude which does not fit in with the theory about the future. In other words, here is another contradiction. Revisionism has seen that contradiction and drawn conclusions from it. And history has shown that the revisionists were right. Everyone has acknowledged this, except the "official" Marxists.[158]

Disregard of the Subject in the Final Period of History. Finally, Marx eliminates the significance of the subject in the situation that will exist after the Revolution, that is, during the final period of history, which will be a state of brotherhood and peace. The whole world will be a gigantic community of workers, characterized by the recognition of man by man. According to Marx it *cannot* be otherwise. For even now the "objective" reality, the "being" of the proletariat, already is the realization of the universal, intersubjective, solidary man, though it is still in its negative phase. But this universality, intersubjectivity, and solidarity will *of necessity* be transformed into positive reality after the Revolution. Marx, of course, can say this only if the subject and his attitude do not count. But if the subject is a factor, it is evident that the gigantic community of workers can also be an unmitigated hell—namely, if its members hate one another. Universal coexistence of men in labor does not *of itself* bring brotherhood and peace.

---

[158]Cf. W. Banning, *Karl Marx, leven, leer en betekenis,* pp. 134-139.

Mystification by the Official Soviet Philosophers

The philosophers and politicians of Soviet Russia took hold of one horn of the Marxist contradiction, namely, the determinism of history. The proletariat is the bearer of the future universal man; the proletariat is represented by the party; the party is represented by its Secretary; the latter therefore *of necessity* represents the future universal man! One who opposes his directives opposes the future universal man. One who sees the demands of history differently from the leader has the wrong view of things. One who complains about his directives bewails the coming of the universal man. One who wants to "argue" with him can only wish to postpone the coming of the universal man; he is therefore necessarily wrong and must be eliminated.[159] This, of course, means terrorism, but it should not be called that since it fosters the coming of the universal man.

But who does not realize that the Secretary of the Party is a subject? Did not Khrushchev accuse Stalin of being a subject? Who does not see that the Secretary of the Party follows a subjective attitude, inspiration and aim, just as any other subject? Khrushchev blamed Stalin for doing it. Who does not see that a subjective attitude can mean murder and terrorism? But, from the Marxist viewpoint, one who sees this is already on the wrong side, for the subject does not count. There is nothing else but the objective course of history and it will *necessarily* produce the universal man. The Secretary of the Party represents the future of mankind by his thought and action. Hence his murders and deeds of terror are neither murder nor terrorism. Anyone who does not see this is on the wrong side! Nevertheless, Khrushchev has accused Stalin of murder and called him a terrorist. Was Khrushchev then on the

---

[159]Kwant has taken this line in his discussion with the Marxist Gerards concerning the possibility of a dialogue with Marxism. Gerards' reply was: "Such a one-sided view really surprises me." One, however, who understands Marx's doctrine will not be surprised by Kwant's line of thinking. Gerards referred him to the works of Varga, Lukacks, Bloch and Kolakowski, to indicate that thought has progressed since Marx. While this is undoubtedly true, it does not take away the dilemma that only one of the following two possibilities can be true: either these thinkers have dropped the determinism of history or they have continued to affirm it. If they have dropped it, the absolutism of the Marxist expectation of the future has lost its foundation; hence it would be possible that non-Marxists prepare better for the coming of the universal man than the Marxists. And if these thinkers continue to affirm the determinism of history, they continue to believe in the absolute future of communism; hence it follows that the non-Marxists are of *necessity* in the wrong and therefore have to be eliminated. Cf. *Ter Elfder Ure*, vol. VIII (1961), pp. 228-314.

wrong side? If he had expressed his opinion during Stalin's life, he would, of course, have been on the wrong side, for the Secretary represents the future of mankind and Stalin then was Secretary. But when Khrushchev spoke he himself was the Secretary of the Party. He spoke therefore as the representative of the future universal man. So anyone who does not agree with him is necessarily on the wrong side.

Under those circumstances, it is surprising that those who "are on the wrong side" arm themselves to the teeth and prefer to risk the destruction of the world and to end history, in order to escape from the "coming universal man"? Never before in the history of the world has *reality* been so entangled and imprisoned in mystification as is done by communism.

6. God and Religion

What Marx says about God and religion is, in a certain sense, evident. In a certain sense it is quite natural for Marx to conceive the affirmation of God as a projection springing from an "unhappy consciousness," and his explanation of the unhappiness of consciousness was certainly not less intelligent than that which Freud was to give at a later time. And yet it is necessary to add "in a certain sense." For it is only when one accepts one of Marx's presuppositions that the affirmation of God is "obviously" a projection; namely, when one starts from the presupposition that God does not really exist and cannot exist. If God does not exist, Heaven can be nothing else but a fantastic dream; if God does not exist, the consolation of religion can be nothing but opium; if God does not exist, adherence to God is necessarily man's self-estrangement. And if God does not exist, Marx is right and one must then admit that Marx has actually penetrated into the depths of religion when he explains the phenomenon of religiousness.

But everything becomes entirely different if God really exists. In that case all that Marx has said about religion does not thereby become totally meaningless, but would rather be applicable only to a vulgar kind of pseudo-religiousness. In that case one could say at most that what passes for the affirmation of God is not infrequently mixed up with the affirmation of pseudo-gods, of projections. In that case also there is a need for purifying the authentic affirmation of God and removing whatever falsity is mingled with it.

Marx, of course, never applied himself to such a task, which presupposes that one takes God's real existence seriously. But Marx "solved" that question without having taken the trouble to ask it. For it cannot be said that that question is considered seriously by one who, like Marx, limits himself to a quick rejection of the ontological proof. Nor can it be said that one has deeply examined the implications of finality in nature when, with Engels, he holds that this finality must of necessity be explained by physical and chemical forces, since otherwise we would have to admit the existence of a purposeful Creator and God.[160]

For Marx and Engels it is *a priori* settled that God does not exist. In that case it becomes very simple and almost self-evident that religion should be reduced to conditions affecting the economic basis of human existence. Then the affirmation of God has no reality of its own because God has none. God and religion must therefore be understood as forms of another reality. This entire reduction to another reality, of course, would collapse as a theory to explain the affirmation of God, if God had a reality of His own, if God did actually exist. But God *may* not be accepted, for otherwise it would be impossible to maintain the theory of estrangement as *the* explanation of religion; at most it could be used to explain some forms of pseudo-religiousness.

Marx and Engels never asked themselves seriously whether or not God existed, but rejected His existence. To them in particular is applicable what we have already asserted regarding the denial of God by all atheists: they deny only a God who is affirmed by others; their denials are possible only in virtue of the affirmation of God by others, or *of what passes for such an affirmation.* The words in italics are of capital importance and make the denials of Marx and Engels particularly impressive. What is the idea of God which they borrowed from others? What exactly do they deny when they think they reject and have to reject God?

No New Perspectives

Lenin. Let us first observe that no really new viewpoints concerning God and religion appear in later Marxism. Lenin continues to hold that the powerlessness of the exploited class in its struggle against the exploiters just as inevitably produces faith in a hereafter as the impotence of the savage in his struggle against nature

---

[160]Cf. P. Ehlen, *Der Atheismus im dialektischen Materialismus,* pp. 165-169.

makes him believe in gods, devils and miracles. "Fear gave birth to the gods."[161] First came the fear of the dominion of the blind forces of nature; later it was the fear of the blindly ruling powers of capital. The populace was unable to foresee the workings of the capitalist forces; these might at any time bring about their "sudden," "unexpected," and "accidental" ruin; they could reduce them to beggary, pauperism, prostitution, and starvation.

The fear of all these things, says Lenin, is the root and source of religion.[162] To the man who labors and suffers all his life, religion teaches meekness and patience, and it comforts him with the hope of a heavenly reward.[163] But to those who live from the product of other people's labor, religion teaches to be charitable on earth; in this way it offers them an inexpensive way of making up for the injustice they perpetrate in exploiting others and at the same time gives them tickets of admission to heavenly salvation at a cheap rate. "Religion is the opium of the people."[164] "All religions, churches and religious organizations are viewed by Marxism as organs of bourgeois reaction; they protect the exploitation of the working class and envelop it in a mist."[165] Even the most refined and best-intentioned defense of the idea of God is nothing but an attempt to justify the bourgeois reaction.[166]

Verret. In our own day we still find the same ideas, for example, in Michel Verret. God is almighty, for He is the sum of all the powers that oppress man. God is universal, for as soon as powerlessness appears anywhere God is there also, and as long as there is impotence everywhere God is omnipresent. God is mysterious, for to Him are attributed all the secrets which man has not yet been able to snatch from nature. God is a hidden God for He represents what is still unknown and uncontrolled, that is, what is *still* hidden.[167] "God's power lies in the fact that man is weak in the presence of nature and in his social relations."[168] This explains why the gods of idealistic religions loathe to renounce their bodies. They are

---

161Lenin, "Über das Verhältnis der Arbeiterpartei zur Religion," *Über die Religion,* Berlin, 1960, p. 23.
162Lenin, *op. cit.,* pp. 23-24.
163Lenin, "Sozialismus und Religion," *Über die Religion,* p. 6.
164Lenin, *op. cit.,* p. 7.
165Lenin, "Über das Verhältnis der Arbeiterpartei zur Religion," *op. cit.,* p. 20.
166Lenin, "An A.M. Gorki," *Über die Religion,* p. 50.
167M. Verret, *Les Marxistes et la religion, Essai sur l'athéisme moderne,* Paris [1961], pp. 15-16.
168*Op. cit.,* p. 7.

always ready for reincarnation and return to earth, for, after all, they were born on earth.[169]

At the same time God is "the best safeguard for the continuance of the established order," for "He is the great preserver of all taboos."[170] His almighty power and omniscience are a welcome complement for the human system of police which, of course, always has limitations. If an all-seeing Eye observes all souls and all sins, we may count on it that all crimes against the established order will be punished. God is the supreme policeman (*"le gendarme en soi"*).[171] On that account there takes place in the exploited class a process of "interiorization" similar to what takes place in the child in respect to the commands and prohibitions of adults. The exploited man fights against his own needs and desires; he makes his interior struggle take the place of the social war; he prefers to change himself rather than modify the established order.[172] Then self-denial becomes a task imposed on him by God.[173] And being sanctified, it inspires its victims to the slavish virtues of obedience and resignation.[174] Yet the victim is not without hope; the heavenly fatherland awaits him.[175] From this standpoint poverty is a divine grace, and the exploiters are only too happy to accept such a teaching.[176]

We see that the content of religion, according to Michel Verret, is merely a "class content." God is never above the classes. As soon as classes appear, God necessarily serves one of them. If we want to find out the kind of god people have, we have only to see what moral sanctions the Almighty is expected to administer, that is, what attitudes the particular religion teaches regarding property, the state, the family and so forth. The religious morality could be one that protects the established order; God is then the servant of the ruling class. He is conservative and, with the progress of time, becomes reactionary. Or God turns against the actual condition of things. Then a new God arises against the ancient God, a new God, whose moral program is the expression of the aspirations of the progressive social forces that are destined to overthrow the former order.

---

[169] *Op. cit.*, p. 23.
[170] Verret, *op cit.*, p. 47.
[171] *Op. cit.*, p. 48.
[172] *Op. cit.*, p 51.
[173] *Op. cit.*, p. 52.
[174] *Op. cit.*, p. 54.
[175] *Op. cit.*, pp. 55-56.
[176] *Op. cit.*, pp. 54.

It is evident, therefore, that the gods have a historical relativity. Each one serves as the standard bearer of some particular social force whose fortunes He shares. The god of the conquered dies with them. But the victorious god dies also in due time.[177] "History is a vast cemetery of classes. The dead gods are their funeral memorials."[178]

We have considered it necessary to give many quotations because we wanted to show that the Marxist theory about God and religion is something permanently frozen and petrified. Even the most dogmatic religions do not have to hold dogmas as rigidly fixed as those of Marxism. One who now—Verret's book appeared in 1961—is given a dish of such indigestible morsels can hardly be blamed for declining to eat. He is not even imprudent if he refuses to determine whether Verret's ideas contain anything digestible. Verret serves the crudest kind of dogmatism, but is not aware of it. Neither does he realize how foolish his assertions sound, for example, in today's affluent society. Its people would not even know what he is talking about.

On the other hand, it must also be said religion has learned much from Marx's criticism. His ideas, like those of many others, have been the occasion for a purification of theology and theodicy, of which the new book of Dondeyne is a brilliant example.[179] Michel Verret insults believers in God by refusing to see anything else in religion besides what he says and by affirming (in 1961!) that religion is the concern of asses, obscurantists and swindlers.

There was also a time when believers described Marxists as people who wished to create a society of men "whose god is their belly." That time is gone, as should be the time for hurling any kind of insult. Or does dialogue *have* to be rendered impossible?

For the critical considerations that follow it is necessary to make a sharp distinction between the various aspects of the Marxist denial of God. For it should be evident that this negation has different aspects, which therefore cannot be treated alike.

Prometheus and God

It is an established fact that the question whether God really exists has never been asked in Marxism. As early as in his doctoral

---

[177] *Op. cit.*, pp. 60-61.
[178] *Op. cit.*, p. 61.
[179] Albert Dondeyne, *Faith and the World*, Pittsburgh, 1963.

thesis, Marx put himself on the side of Prometheus. According to Marx, not the man who despises the gods of the masses is an atheist, but he who adheres to the idea of the gods as the masses conceive them. "I hate all gods," says Marx, and he makes the reply of Prometheus to Hermes, the messenger of Zeus, his own: " 'I will never exchange my miserable lot for slavery. I prefer to be chained to a rock rather than be the slave of Zeus.' Prometheus takes first place among the saints and martyrs in the calendar of philosophy."[180]

Prometheus wished to make man equal to the gods. He stole from them the fire which enabled man to save himself, for fire makes technological work possible. But Zeus took revenge by chaining Prometheus naked to a rock. It is not difficult to see that Marx is mistaken when he thinks that, by rejecting Zeus, he has also discarded the God of Christianity. Marx discards a god who, as in Greek mythology, is thought of as competing with man, as a being who has to share the earth with man and thus loses ground when man develops his power. For Marx the dilemma is either Prometheus or Zeus. He chooses Prometheus, and he is right. But he is mistaken when he imagines that the problem of God presents itself to every man in the form of this dilemma.

The Christian chooses both Prometheus and God, but he rejects Zeus. This the Christian can do because his God is a transcendent God, who does not need the earth, who does not rule the earth in the way man wants to rule it, who does not have to pull back when man conquers the earth, and who does not feel the need for vengeance when man is successful in his endeavors.[181] In other words, Marx rejects another God than the one who is affirmed by the Christians, but he is not aware of the difference. Because the God of Christianity is a transcendent God, man's conquest of the world can never be a challenge to God. In the light of authentic Christian thought, we must even call man's conquest of the world a divine project. Hence the affirmation of God's existence does not, in principle, make man lose his authentic being. Neither does such a belief constitute *per se* a sort of estrangement. And if man, as Christianity teaches, must be conceived as a being that is oriented to God, then the recognition of a transcendent God belongs to the authenticity of man's being.

---

[180]Cf. J.Y. Calvez, *La pensée de Karl Marx,* Paris, 1956, pp. 56-58.
[181]Cf. Dondeyne, *Faith and the World,* Ch. IV.

The Sciences and Religion

From what we have seen it follows that, if the affirmation of God as conceived in Marxism does not refer to a transcendent God, then Marxism is forced to speak about religion as something archaic, obscurantist and backward, as the concern of *"Dunkelmänner"* (opinionated obscurantists), as Lenin calls them.

Such a concept of religion is the necessary accompaniment of the failure to recognize God's transcendence. In primitive times the obscurity and mystery of nature were looked upon as the presence of God. Modern sciences have dissipated that obscurity and mystery and, as a consequence, says Marxism, God has lost ground.[182] God was eliminated from nature, and his departure made it increasingly clear that man could easily dispense with that superfluous hypothesis. The religions continue to make desperate attempts to stop the elimination of the mystery, but it is no longer possible to prevent the progress of the sciences.[183]

Although admiration for the sciences is praiseworthy in itself, in Marxism it degenerates into scientism. Even in the most recent Marxist literature scientism is potently present. In this respect Marxism lags far behind the newest developments in human thought. The Marxist acknowledges no other objectivity than that which can be conceived in the same fashion as physical science.[184] He recognizes no other "true" knowledge than that of physical science.

It is not necessary for us to develop this point further since we have fully dealt with the matter in the second chapter. The contentions of scientism were already refuted by Kant, and any up-to-date philosophy does not hesitate to draw the necessary conclusions. It is evident in any case that the proof of God's existence cannot be based on any argument drawn from physical science; nor can any argument supplied by physical science prove His non-existence, for the simple reason that the God of Christianity is a transcendent God. The objects of the natural sciences are, in the last analysis, quantitative measurements; as such, they are clearly inapplicable to

---

182Cf. Verret, *op. cit.*, p. 81.

183Cf Verret, *op. cit.*, pp. 92-93.

184"Modern science implies a *radical critique* of traditional philosophy, of ideology in all its forms. Science requires philosophy to submit, like science, to experience and practical verification, in a word, to conquer conscientiously and methodically an objectivity comparable to that of science." Verret, *op. cit.*, pp. 82 f.

the transcendent God of Christianity. Consequently also, it is not God, but a legion of pseudo-gods, that is eliminated by physical science. The affirmation of God is not based on the absence of lightning rods, of penicillin, or radar, and if men were to base their affirmation on such an absence, they would affirm pseudo-gods.

Marx's atheism was not a *consequence* of his anti-capitalist attitude, for he had already accepted it before he developed his anthropology and his philosophy of history.[185] He even considered "the critique of religion as a *condition* for every critique."[186] Only later did he describe religion, in function of his anthropology and philosophy, as a phenomenon of estrangement, as a reflection, an echo, a mirroring of man's economic estrangement. He then viewed religion as a powerful weapon in the hands of the exploiters and as the opium for their victims. These two aspects of Marx's conception of religion must now be considered more in detail.

Religion as an Instrument of Power

Stahl's Christian State. At early age, Marx became acquainted with religion as an instrument of power over men. At the time when he felt drawn to the ideas and aims of the Young Hegelians and associated with them, the Prussian State was a constant object of their discussions. This State called itself Christian and sought to defend itself by means of Christianity.

In those days the principal theorist of the Christian State was Julius von Stahl, who sought his inspiration in Lutheran theology. He was concerned with the answer to the question of how God's will, which is the necessary basis of morality and justice, can be interpreted with certainty. For Stahl no other solution appeared possible than an appeal to an authority that is above reason and the natural law. This authority, he says, is the State, since the State is guaranteed by God the supreme Lawgiver.[187] Stahl appears to have been driven to this extreme view because, accepting the Lutheran teaching about man's radical sinfulness and corruption, he found it impossible to have any confidence in reason and the natural law. They cannot guarantee justice and peace. It is the task of the State to provide this guarantee; hence the State represents God on earth

---

[185]Cf. Calvez, *Op. cit.*, pp. 57 f.
[186]K. Marx, "Zur Kritik der Hegelschen Rechtsphilosophie," *Die heilige Familie*, p. 11.
[187]We follow here the explanations of Calvez, *La pensée de Karl Marx*, pp. 55-78.

and interprets His will. This concept had led the Prussian State to exercise a rigorous censorship of the press.[188]

Marx's Critique of the Christian State. Marx combated Stahl's ideas about the State in his articles in the *Rheinische Zeitung* and defended the autonomy of politics. In his opinion those ideas meant the estrangement of man as a political being and the mystification of all real politics. For there is nothing specifically Christian in the actual conduct of the Christian State and the citizens. On the contrary, in actual politics, it is reason and philosophy that serve as guides, and they do not need the help of Christian dogmas.

The actual State and actual politics are the function of reason and philosophy. But in the Prussian State that which is nothing but the work of reason and of philosophy is provided with divine guarantees. Moreover, it is evident to Marx that the actual Prussian State, in spite of its divine guarantees, does not even follow the dictates of reason and philosophy in its actual politics; for instance, it refuses to contribute to the emancipation of the Jews. What is in accord with reason in the Christian State has nothing to do with Christianity and, on the other hand, Christianity does not pertain to the essence of the State. Why, then, does the State persist in calling itself Christian? What can be the meaning of the statement that the State rests on religion as on a foundation?

For Marx, there is only one possible answer: a State which presupposes and needs religion, is not yet a *real* State. There is something defective in such a State, and religion is a sign of this defect.[189] It is necessary therefore to emancipate the State, and a prerequisite of this emancipation is the elimination of religion. However, it is not enough to criticize religion; the State itself has to be made an object of critique. Here we see already Marx's trend toward "reduction," which finally led him to explain religion as a phenomenon of estrangement caused by man's economic alienation.

Having reached the stage in which religious wretchedness is described as an echo, a mirroring and reflection of man's real or economic misery, Marx turns once more against religion because, in the hands of the exploiters, it has become a means to keep the proletarians in their state of slavery. The same ideas are found in Lenin and later Marxists. The capitalist exploiters base the existence of the

---

[188]Cf. Calvez, *op. cit.,* pp. 59-61.
[189]Cf. Calvez, *op. cit.,* p. 67.

established order upon God's will and providence, and teach the oppressed that they have the moral obligation of submitting to God that is, to the established order, as the expression of God's holy will. In this way religion, by way of its morality, becomes power wielded by the exploiters.

Past Abuses. The Marxist concept of religion gave Christians food for serious thought and its criticism is still so impressive that it cannot be simply disregarded. For we have to admit that, in the past, many Christians appealed to God in a very illegitimate way in order to safeguard and preserve social and political conditions that were certainly unjustifiable, and to protect their own social and political activities against any kind of criticism. *"Dieu le veut!"* (God wills it) has far too often been a slogan covering the most flagrant disregard of justice. In other cases the perpetuation of inhuman conditions was certainly not the intended result of hypocritical appeals to God's holy will and Divine Providence. Nevertheless, the fact that God's will was brought to bear on the problems meant that criticism of, and opposition to, the existing abuses did not get the chance of success they deserved; as a consequence, inhuman conditions were not eliminated with all possible dispatch.

Fortunately the worst forms of that misuse of God's will are a thing of the past, but they did exist in Marx's time. Perhaps we might be permitted to say that, from the psychological standpoint, Marx had to be an "atheist" in order to be able to see reality as he actually has seen it. We have, on purpose, put the word "atheist" within quotation marks, for the god whom Marx rejected was evidently a pseudo-god. Did Marx, we may ask, actually have any chance to learn the distinction between God and pseudo-gods? Is not the tact that he never seriously asked himself the question about the real existence of God to be explained by the absence of this chance? Whatever may be the reason why Marx did not have this opportunity, today no one has to become an "atheist" in order to see the demands of humanity which Marx perceived. Hence no one is justified now in calling a religion *as such* a power of oppression placed in the hands of oppressors and exploiters.

Present Day Examples of Abuse. And yet it is not easy to overcome the temptation to proceed unjustifiably in the name of God. We have merely to recall the "dirty" war of France against Algerian nationalism. How frequently, for instance, it was alleged that in

Algeria France was defending "Christian" culture! *Dieu le veut!* God wills it, so who has the right to oppose us? The enemy goes against the will of God!

Portuguese Catholics in Goa made pilgrimages to the grave of St. Francis Xavier when India threatened to engulf the small colony. Why? Perhaps to make God side with the colonists through St. Francis' intercession? Apparently they did not understand that only pseudo-gods can be used that way.

American television some time ago presented a discussion between a Marxist of Angola and a Portuguese Catholic. The Marxist defended the elimination of the present "order" of things in order to secure a more human situation. The Portuguese rejected the Marxist's plea alleging that a Marxist is an atheist and God must, after all, come before everything else. But who is that god, who in order to come before everything else has to accept the inhumanity of the Portuguese regime in Angola? He is only a pseudo-god!

The Spanish Falange attacked the Catholic Church and the bishops because these gave their support to justified strikers although strikes are unlawful in Spain. They wanted to teach the Spanish bishops a lesson and preached to them that "civil obedience is a *moral* obligation."

In South Africa, the need of maintaining the existing regime of terror and the lawfulness of the inhumanity that is practiced by the whites in regard to the colored are defended as *theological conclusions* from the Protestant-Christian belief in God, and those who refuse to accept those conclusions are expelled from their churches. In the name of God? But who is that God who rejects man, when he recognizes, accepts and loves his fellow man? He is, of course, a pseudo-god!

Authentically Human Activities and Atheism. The economic, social and political activities of the Christian are *autonomous* activities of man as a being-in-the-world. This means that they are inspired by a specific *cogito* and *volo* (I think and I will) that is proper to man as a subject-in-the-world. Expressed negatively, it comes down to this that the appropriateness of the Christian's economic, social and political activity—just like that of the non-Christian—depends not on his piety but on his competence in those particular realms.[190] A Christian *as* a Christian does not know more

---

[190]Cf. Dondeyne, *Faith and the World*, p. 246.

about economics, sociology, and politics than others, just as, in his capacity as a Christian, he does not know more about mathematics and physics, is not a better poet, a superior chess player, or a better swimmer.

However, man's economic, social and political activity can be human or inhuman. It can benefit or harm the realm of subjectivity and freedom, i.e., that which makes man truly man. The authentically human character of the economic, social and political organization of the world and of society is for the Christian a demand of God's will, for he views the commandment of loving one's neighbor as a divine commandment.[191] But this does not mean in the least that *therefore* the Christian's concrete economic, social and political thinking and doing are guaranteed by God or are *per se* the concrete expression of God's will.[192] Belief in love of our neighbor as a divine precept does not justify any concrete choice or measure. Every concrete choice or measure that is taken implies the danger that it might result in harm to man and be inhuman, even though the Christian believes in the obligation of charity. The Christian should remember that he, too, can cause calamities in human history and he must not think that what he does is necessarily good because he thinks that faith dictates those actions.[193]

This many Christians have forgotten and, as a consequence, many atheists, even those who are not Marxists, claim that, in order to be authentically human, man must be an atheist.[194] For he who endows his concrete thought and activity with divine guarantees, thereby denies the fallibility of human thought and conduct, that is, he fails to recognize their human side. But can anyone who fails to recognize the *human* character of his thinking and doing still take a serious view of his thought and action themselves? For, after all, there is no other thinking or doing in the economic, social, and political realms than *human* thinking and doing; and what remains after their *human* aspect has been taken away? And if anything remains, is it

[191]Cf. Dondeyne, *op. cit.*, pp. 244 f

[192]"We will not find before us values or orders which will make our conduct legitimate. Thus, we do not have, either before us or behind us, justifications or excuses in the luminous domain of values. We are alone, without any excuses." Sartre, *L'existentialisme est un humanisme,* Paris, 1954, p. 37.

[193]Cf. Jeanson, "Les caractères existentialistes de la conduite humaine selon Jean Paul Sartre," *Morale chrétienne et requêtes contemporaines,* Paris, 1954, p. 181.

[194]Cf. E. Schillebeeckx, "De betekenis van het niet-godsdienstige humanisme voor het hedendaagse katholicisme," *Modern niet-godsdienstig humanisme.* Nijmegen, 1961, pp. 78-79, 84-84.

still to be taken seriously? Hence, in order to become man once more, man should reject God, for this is the only way to get rid of divine guarantees.

No Concrete Acts are a Priori Guaranteed by God. This conclusion, however, goes a little too far. It would be legitimate if Christianity or any other faith in God required man to bolster up his thought and action with divine guarantees. But this is not so. Only pseudo-gods can lower themselves to this level and that is why they must be rejected.

No one can appeal to God's will as a justification for his own *concrete* behavior, nor can he invoke it to prevent criticism of, and opposition to, his *concrete* activity. There exists no *a priori* guarantee for the authentically human character of any *concrete* action. He who thinks he can maintain that he is the executor of God's will is guilty of mystification of his conduct. He thereby exposes himself to the danger of conservatism, intolerance and tyranny. He who considers his own thinking and doing as characterized by the absoluteness of God's will, can no longer accept anything else, anything new, anything better, for what can be better than God's will? Whoever does not agree with him is automatically in disagreement with God's will. But, we must ask, where in heaven does anyone find such a divine sanction for his own way of thinking and acting? It is horrible to contemplate the terrible injustices that have been perpetrated in the past and the terrorism that has been practiced *in God's name*! Kings ruled by the "grace" of God and frequently imagined that whatever they thought or did was a heaven-sent grace for everybody.

Marxist Mystification. Marxism has efficaciously unmasked that sort of mystification. But, unfortunately, the mystification reappears in Marxism in an even more baneful form. Now, it is no longer God who guarantees the humanity of man's conduct but the proletariat which is represented by the party, which is represented by the party's secretary. The party-secretary incarnates mankind, the coming of the universal, economic, social, and political man. Anyone who criticizes or offers opposition by that very fact is wrong. Now what is this but a mystification of reality?

Religion as Opium for the People

Religion, according to Marxism, is therefore an immobilizing, petrifying, and breaking force; in a word, a reactionary force with respect to the movement of history, because it acts as instrument of power in the hands of a class that is by definition reactionary. But the same applies to the religion of the oppressed class, for it operates there as an opium which prevents man from recognizing and seeking a cure for his real wretchedness.

"The Consolation of Religion." Here we meet religion as "consolation." And in this respect also things are not as simple as all Marxists and many Christians imagine. It is necessary to make prudent distinctions if we wish to avoid misunderstandings and failure to recognize what is the heart of the matter.

It stands to reason that health, food and drink, clothes, education, housing, freedom and prosperity are the proper "consolation" needed by those who are sick, hungry, thirsty, naked, uneducated, homeless, oppressed, and poor. The Christian who, in dealing with such people, contents himself with "offering God alone to them," even by pointing to a happy hereafter when all tears will be wiped away and all pains will cease for all eternity, merely adds insults to their woes. Man, to be authentically human needs earthly "consolation." And it is to the credit of Marxism's past and present that it has so greatly stressed the need for that kind of "consolation" if man is to be authentically human. This idea is a precious gain against a conception of Christianity that is too one-sidedly spiritual. The Marxists are right also when they want to introduce into the world and society the kind of objective structures that will give man, in a humanized society, values which are within the reach of all, instead of giving him "consolation" in the form of a condescending "charity."

But the Marxists are mistaken when they think that the "consolation" of which Christianity speaks, is none other than a substitute for earthly values that are absent from an inhuman world. And they are also mistaken when they imagine that the proletarians are really like opium-addicts when they refuse to give up the "consolation" of religion.

It is impossible, or at least most difficult, to explain this point to Marxists. For, in order to accept our explanation, they would have to admit that Christians are not deceivers and swindlers when they maintain that their God is transcendent and that on that account no earthly value is comparable to Him, and that man in his deepest being is directed toward God just as truly as he is directed to the world. They would have to admit, therefore, that man, in the existential "want" which he himself *is,* cannot be "consoled" by earthly values alone; in other words, that man will never find and realize himself when he is offered nothing but the earth and its social life. But who can make the Marxist see this point, so long as the latter continues to look upon religion as the opium of the people and refuses to consider even the question about the existence of a transcendent God?

It has always angered Marxists that even among their disciples there are people who refuse to accept atheism and especially that many of whose who belong to the exploited class absolutely refuse to become Marxists *because* of Marxist atheism. We shall not attempt to discover "the" reasons for these phenomena, for in all probability we have here to do with a complex of reasons and motives. In any case there are many who have subscribed to the economic, social, and political intentions of Marxism, and yet did not want to join Marxism because they would then miss the "consolation that is given by religion." Yet these people did not conceive that consolation as a substitute for what they were unable to find in the world, but as that which enabled them to realize their most profound dimension, even if, in other respects, they would be handicapped in this world. They realized that man can be crippled in more than one way, and in given circumstances they had to make their choice between different handicaps. Marxists, however, are not particularly clearsighted on that point. In this matter they are not attentive to the proletariat as it *really* is, but are occupied with their *idea* of it.

Belief in God and Consolation. Those for whom the idea of a transcendent God is meaningful can see also that, from a certain standpoint, religion brings consolation to man in his earthly misery without becoming a substitute for earthly values of which a man is deprived through the inhumanity of others. For earthly wretchedness means something different when it is borne in union *with* God instead of being undergone *without* Him by man alone—just as illness does not have the same meaning for the solitary sufferer and the one who has to bear it in union with a loving and beloved fellowman.

We realize that our statement is dangerous and can easily be misunderstood. It appeals to the value of the subject. Now those who, in their philosophy, refuse to grant any value to the subject and attribute all value to the objective structures of co-existence might interpret our assertion as equivalent to the statement that a slave in his chains is as free as a king on his throne, and that therefore the need for a revolution is cleverly buried in verbiage. This would be true if the meaning of the world were constituted totally by the subject. But this is not so and is not implied in our statement.

The Believer and the Revolution. However, the Marxist might object that, if earthly misery can be borne differently and more patiently by the man who suffers in union with God than by one who rejects God, the Christian is thereby less ready for the Revolution, for he is less disturbed by the objective situation and hence less inclined to destroy the established economic, social and political order. Religion would therefore still act like opium.

Here especially we must make careful distinctions. First of all, let us note that the Marxists do not direct their accusation to this or that Christian but to Christianity and religion *as such.* If the objection held only for some Christians, it would not carry much weight. It would then be possible to reply that those Christians are wrong.

Secondly, it must be admitted that the Christian who has the consolation of his religion in his economic, social and political misery is indeed less violently inclined to destroy the established order. But what does this mean? This less violent readiness means that for the Christian it is possible to do justice to the demands of morality, that is, to the demands of *man's own being;* that lesser inclination toward revolution implies that *humanity* remains the aim of his revolutionary activity. For the revolution itself can be either human or inhuman, but what is at stake in it is man and a human way of being.

Inhumanity and Revolution. We stated above that no one has the right to appeal to God's will to justify his concrete activity; there exists no *a priori* guarantee that anyone's concrete deeds will be as befits a man. He who thinks he can deduce such guarantees from God's will commits the mistake of mystifying his conduct. In a similar way, he who bases his claim to such a guarantee upon the Revolution is just as guilty of the same mystification. He raises himself above and beyond the criticisms and opposition that are aimed, not at the Revolution, but at inhumanity.

That the *Revolution* itself can be inhuman should be evident. Marx *demanded* and required that the proletariat should sink into utter misery, and opposed anyone who advocated a gradual improvement of the workers' lot. Today's Marxists also want to promote chaos. There has to be as much wretchedness as possible and where it does not exist, a Marxist endeavors to *cause* it for the sake of the Revolution. For non-Marxists, this means that the Marxist prepares the Revolution *by means of* inhumanity *for the sake of* the Revolution. Such a procedure goes against the demands of ethics. The same applies to the means which the Marxist must use after the Revolution, namely, dictatorship and terrorism. But to sacrifice whole generations in order to establish a new world in the shortest possible time is inhuman and dangerous, for terrorism generates terrorism and lowers man to the level of the brute. Thus there is danger that, in the long run, the eagerly awaited new world will be worse than the old one.[195] In this context, Merleau-Ponty was right when he said that no revolution can fully count upon the Catholic.[196] In other words, for the Catholic, the final end and purpose of his revolutionary activity is not the Revolution but *humanity*.

Conclusion

A philosophy does not fail by what it *says* but by what, in speaking, it silently eliminates. We do not mean that such a philosophy cannot be imposing. Marxism is a great philosophy, for it made man grasp reality through a central reference point or primitive fact that had not been used before, and managed to throw light upon some aspects of reality that had not been clearly seen until then. But, on the other hand, Marxism also eliminated certain aspects of reality that are very important. Some of these we have considered elsewhere,[197] but here, in connection with the theme of this book, we want to limit ourselves to the attitude of Marxism toward religion.

The Marxist elimination of God from reality flows directly and necessarily from the way it absolutizes the primitive fact around which the system is constructed—namely, man's being-in-the-world as laborer. The philosophy of the past had little or no awareness of the fact that the human subject is an "involved" subject, that is, a subject who brings himself to authenticity in and "at" the world. Marx rightly placed great emphasis on this view of man.

The way, however, in which a philosophy starts is decisive for what can be attained or not attained by its future development. For this reason the very fact that a philosophy takes as its central point of reference that man is *nothing else* but a being-in-and-"at"-the-

---

[195]Cf. Dondeyne, *Faith and the World*, p. 222.

[196]"In the social question one can never fully count on them." *Sens et Nonsens*, Paris, 1948, p. 352.

[197]Cf. Remy C. Kwant, *De wijsbegeerte van Karl Marx*, pp. 95-132

world suffices to make it an atheistic philosophy. Obviously, it is no longer possible to add in a final chapter that man is also directed to God if the first chapter defines man as a being that is *solely* directed to the world. The decision in such a case has already been made at the start. For what could be the meaning of such an assertion that man is directed to God when it was stated from the start that being-man is *encompassed* by being-in-the-world"? The subsequent affirmation of God cannot be anything else but the affirmation of a god who is not essentially different from the world, in other words, of a pseudo-god. The philosopher has the right and the duty critically to investigate what element of truth is contained in any accepted convictions. He has the right and the duty critically to examine what is valid in such a general conviction as that regarding God's existence. But he has no right to make decisions about the outcome of the critique prior to an examination. Yet this is precisely what Marx has done by his decree that man is *nothing else* but the project of his world.

That is why there is an unbridgeable chasm between Marxism and Christianity with respect to metaphysics. And in this matter Christianity has definitely nothing to learn from Marxism. Christianity would have the duty of taking note if it were challenged by a strong Marxist metaphysics.[198] But there is nothing! Nothing except the uncritical dogma that God does not exist and that man is *nothing else* but the project of his world.

However, it would be a mistake to think that Marxism, as an economic, social and political movement, is the antithesis of Christianity. The antithesis is found in capitalist liberalism, not in Christianity.[199] Christianity is not an economic, social and political theory of development. And there are also no specific Christian economics, sociology and politics which the Christian can derive from the Revelation he believes in, or for which his faith gives him a divine

---

[198]Marxists, such as Michel Verret, have tried to fill the gap at least to a certain extent. His ideas, however, concerning the requirements of serious metaphysical thinking are astonishingly primitive. It is impossible for God to create a world, he argues, because God is a pure spirit and therefore has no hands to make anything with. "The metaphysical God is a workman without hands. [On the other hand,] He could not create matter in the fashion of a magic operation. For what essential difference would there be between a sorcerer who thinks that he produces rain by using a magic formula and a God who creates by his word?" *Op. cit.*, p. 41.

[199]A. Dondeyne, *Faith and the World*, p. 219.

guarantee.[200] Marxism and Christianity are not *the* antagonists in the economic, political and social realms.[201]

And yet Marxists constantly point to the opposition between Marxism and Christianity, even regarding the economic, social and political activities which man is obliged to pursue. And it is precisely for the sake of these activities that they demand atheism, as we have mentioned when we spoke of religion as a means of exercising power and as opium. Christianity can, indeed, learn something from that "atheism" or rather from that rejection of pseudo-gods, even though the "metaphysical" atheism of Marxism has nothing to offer that is philosophically worthwhile.

Christianity should learn from Marxism, among other things, that today special demands are made upon its ethics. Love for the neighbor is one of its most fundamental and central commands. Love must be defined as: accepting, willing, supporting and fostering[202] the subjectivity, the selfhood, and the freedom of "the others."[203] The subject however who the other is, is an "existing" subject, a subject involved in the world, a subject who has to reach his authenticity in and "at" the world. But the world in which the subject is involved is not merely the world of "nature" but the whole of the economic, social, and political structures which human history has developed.[204]

Since man is a subject-in-the-world, the Christian's love for his neighbor would be meaningless, if it did not find expression in making the world accessible to his neighbor. This opening-up of the world takes place nowhere else than in the realms of economic, social and political activities. To the extent that the established economic, social and political structures make the world inaccessible to man, the Christian's love for his neighbor imposes on him the obligation to reform those structures. For when an established

---

200"The only thing faith demands is that whatever economic policy a country may choose, it must respect man and recognize the inalienable rights and values of the human person." Dondeyne, *op. cit.*, p. 219.

201We say emphatically *the* antagonists, for, to the extent that Marxism does not recognize man and the inalienable rights and values of the human person, Christian ethics is an antagonist of Marxism. But in this respect there is no question of an economical, social and political theory or movement *as such.*

202"Love is the will to promote. The I who loves wants above all the existence of the you, and this I wants, in addition, the autonomous self-development of the you." M. Nédoncelle, *Vers une philosophie de l'amour*, Paris, 1946, p. 11.

203"To love is to will the other as subject." G. Madinier, *Conscience et amour*, Paris, 1947, p. 95.

204Cf. Dondeyne, *op. cit,* p 11.

system makes it impossible for particular subjects to attain self-real-ization, the very existence of such a system is an objective violation of man's freedom and to permit it to go on is its subjective viola-tion. Both are contrary to Christian charity. All too often man's free-dom itself has to be freed before this freedom can have any real meaning. This love of one's neighbor has to assume the form of economic, social, and political activities.[205]

Fortunately nowadays we witness that this is being done more and more and that "humanity" is increasingly more embodied in objective social structures. Of course, one result of it is that an ever-growing number of tasks devolves upon the government. But it is sad to have to record that there are still Christians who complain that in this way "true" charity, "Christian" charity, is eliminated. "There are," they say "institutions for all sorts of services and the State assumes responsibility for all." We ask ourselves what these people mean when they speak of "true" and "Christian" charity in that connection. Is it the "charity" of people who condescendingly and "lovingly" stoop over the victims of an inhuman system which they themselves help or allow to remain? But those who want to use the bent backs of their own victims as stepping stones to Heaven are certainly not authentic Christians.

The foregoing considerations are particularly important in connec-tion with the global world situation. For when we take a global view of things, as is now possible, we realize that, at present, seventeen per cent of mankind is in possession of eighty percent of the wealth of the world. In fact, this means that two thirds of mankind are prematurely eliminated from the world. And there is also that added horrible dilemma that in communities that lack everything, the soc-iety itself has to decide who the victims shall be. This decision, of course, is not made "officially" but it is really made neverthe-less—namely, by the decisions that are made regarding the manner in which the economic system will work. Such societies in a certain sense "choose" their victims.

An economic situation in which seventeen per cent of mankind disposes of eighty per cent of the world's wealth is from an objective standpoint equivalent to "government" by violence and murder. Kill-ing and murder are imbedded in the objective economic system of the world. But, unlike the consequences of an earthquake or typhoon, this situation is not the result of a blind process of nature;

---

[205]"Modern love either is political or does not exist." Verret, *op. cit.,* p. 153.

much less is it possible to base it on the action of Divine Providence. The situation has been created by man himself.

It is perfectly clear, of course, that *we* ourselves did not create it, but this alibi does not express what is most important. For we live in and by that situation! I am able to write this book because I belong to the seventeen per cent who have eighty per cent of the world's wealth at their disposal. Others like me plan international congresses, build theatres and churches, promote longer vacations and better educational systems. But all this we can do because we belong to the seventeen per cent. Whatever we gratefully receive from our culture and civilization is stained by an objective sinfulness, from which no sacramental absolution can absolve us. On the other hand, it is also impossible to "withdraw our hands" and stay idle in order not to soil them.[206] He who withdraws his hands makes them dirty, for he commits a sin of omission; he leaves everything as it is—inhuman. There is but one way out, and that is reform on a world-wide scale.

Does the West still have an ideal that is sufficiently lofty to take the lead in that task? If not, the West will be put to the axe, and those who handle it will do more than make martyrs. They will liquidate people with "clean principles" but "dirty hands." The necessary great idea, however, is still with us. It is love of our fellowman. Although this love is Christian by birth, it is now at the disposal of everyone who has become authentically man. But this idea of love will appear to be great enough only when it is interpreted in a realistic way, that is, as a way of existing, of being-effectively-in-the-world.

---

[206]"By the very fact that I continue to exist in this world, I give up the right to claim that I *absolutely* do not want murder. For murder is already in this world, for I live from this murder-of-fellow-men committed in an indefinite way by a social organization with which I remain solidary in various ways. I do not even need to lift a finger to be an accomplice, but it is enough that I abstain" from preventing it. Jeanson, "Les caractères existentialistes de la conduite humaine selon Jean-Paul Sartre," *Morale chrétienne et requêtes contemporaines,* Paris, 1954, p. 182.

CHAPTER FOUR

EXISTENTIAL PHENOMENOLOGY AND ATHEISM

As is generally known, the terms *phenomenology, existentialism,* and *existential phenomenology* refer today to one and the same sphere of thought which, as a kind of unifying movement, has become the predominant trend in the philosophical thought of continental Europe. It is only in relatively recent years that it has been possible to define that unifying movement. Although previously there were already phenomenologists and existentialists, no one seemed able to explain what made their thought phenomenological and existential. This is not surprising, for philosophizing is primarily a way of life. And as of any other way of human life, it can be said of philosophizing that man knows what he is doing when he lives it, but also that he does *not* know.

A distinction was made formerly between a left and a right wing, an atheistic and a theistic trend, in existentialism. Sartre, however, thought it justified to identify existentialism with atheism, or, more exactly, he thought he could define existentialism by atheism.[1] For this reason some were induced to designate right wing existentialism by the term "existential philosophy."[2] Gabriel Marcel completely rejected the term "existentialism" as a characterization of his philosophy because its acceptance would have put his own philosophy under the same heading as that of Sartre.[3] Marcel prefers to call his own philosophy "Neo-Socratism."[4] Nevertheless, the impression remained that there was really a kind of unified movement of thought; hence the question arose whether or not that unified movement is *essentially* atheistic.

---

[1] Sartre makes a distinction between two existentialist schools of thought, but in practice this distinction remains unimportant. For him existentialism and atheism are *de facto* identical. Cf. Jean-Paul Sartre, *Existentialism and Humanism*, London, 1948, p. 26.

[2] Cf. R. Verneaux, *Leçons sur l'existentialisme et ses formes principales*, Paris, n.d., pp. 19-20.

[3] Cf. B. Delfgaauw, *Wat is existentialisme?*, Amsterdam, 1952, pp. 107-118.

[4] Marcel, *L'Homme problématique*, Paris, 1955, p. 72.

161

1. Existential Phenomenology as a Unified Movement

In the present work we make no distinction between existentialism and phenomenology; hence we shall speak of "existential phenomenology." It may be useful, however, to sketch in a few words the course of development toward unity before we explain the fundamental ideas of existential phenomenology.

A Short History

Kierkegaard, the founder of existentialism, could hardly be called a phenomenologist. Husserl, the philosopher who launched phenomenology, was not an existentialist. This means that there was a time when it was necessary to make a distinction between existentialism and phenomenology. We must, therefore, see how these two differ and how there arose a unified existential-phenomenological movement.

In spite of the differences characterizing the thought of Kierkegaard and that of Husserl, there is in them a certain agreement in their modes of thinking. This agreement perhaps expresses itself most strongly in their common opposition to atomistic or elementaristic ways of thinking about man and everything human. Man is not something like an atom. But the manner in which Kierkegaard and Husserl oppose atomistic thought about man is different. Kierkegaard speaks about *man,* whereas Husserl practically confines himself to *consciousness* or *knowledge.*

Soren Kierkegaard. Kierkegaard conceived man as "subject in relationship to God." Man is not a self-sufficient spiritual atom, but he is, as a subject, authentically himself only in his relation to the God of Revelation. Existence, however, in Kierkegaard's conception, is absolutely original, irrepeatable, radically personal and unique. This view has important consequences. Kierkegaard's insistence on the uniqueness and irrepeatability of existence jeopardizes the universal character of knowledge to which all science aspires when reflection about man is concerned.

If one stresses *exclusively* the unique and irrepeatable character of existence, he is forced to accept the consequence that, in principle, what a thinker expresses about existence is in reality not applicable to any other existence than that of the thinker himself, and that, in principle, its validity does not extend beyond the thinker himself.

Kierkegaard's thought is consciously and wilfully anti-scientific.[5] In principle, it cannot aim beyond the monologue, the "solitary meditation."[6]

There is, undoubtedly, something seductive in this view of philosophy. And when, in the past, existentialism was accused of not being (in the classical sense) a science and even of being incapable of becoming one, those who sought their inspiration in Kierkegaard simply replied that existentialism could not permit itself to be a science. Usually this rejection of the term "scientific" was based upon an aversion to a *particular* conception of what makes reflection on man scientific. In the philosophy of Hegel, who figures as the black sheep in Kierkegaard's work, as well as in positivism, the "scientific" way of speaking about man was such that the original, irrepeatable, unique and exceptional character of human subjectivity was simply buried under verbiage.[7] Yet it was this kind of talk that was considered eminently "scientific"! It is understandable, therefore, that the reaction against Hegel and positivism was averse to being called "scientific."

This remark, however, does not solve the difficulty. For, when one rejects a particular view about the nature of scientific thought regarding man, it is by no means evident that philosophizing about man can or should in no sense be scientific. One who philosophizes about man can hardly avoid philosophizing about man in general. He uses universal and necessary judgments to express universal and necessary structures of being-man; hence, he speaks "scientifically." This idea has led some to the opinion that one should perhaps choose between authentic existence and existentialism.[8] In this view he who speaks about existentialism should be resigned to speak about the general structures of being-man as such, but he who opts for authentic existence would have to renounce existentialism as the *general* theory about man as such.[9]

---

[5] Cf A. de Waelhens, "Kierkegaard en de hedendaagse existentialisten," *Tijdschrift voor Philosophie,* vol. 1 (1939), pp. 827-851.

[6] "We *speak* of the philosophy of existence;...we are concerned with questions which, strictly speaking, belong to solitary meditation and cannot be subjects of discourse." Jean Wahl, *A Short History of Existentialism,* New York, 1949, p. 2

[7] J. Peters, "Hedendaagse visies op den mens," *Gesprekken op Drakenburgh,* Heerlen, n.d., pp. 228-230.

[8] "Is it, perhaps, necessary to choose between existentialism and existence?" Wahl, *op. cit.,* p. 33.

[9] "One may ask further if the search for Existentials and for Being is compatible with affirmations of existence." Wahl, *op. cit.,* p. 21.

Edmund Husserl. The difficulties we have just mentioned scarcely exist for one who is guided exclusively by Husserl's thought. Husserl was originally a mathematician and a physicist and, like Descartes, he was disturbed by the diversity of opinions and the confusion of terms prevailing in the realm of philosophy. For this reason he launched his phenomenology as an attempt to make philosophy a *rigorous science.* It is hardly surprising, therefore, that he conceived philosophical thought as a way of thinking which should, likewise, be characterized by the subjective and objective *universality* of its statements.

In order to realize his intentions with respect to philosophy, Husserl examined the nature of human consciousness or knowledge. He conceived consciousness or knowledge as "intentionality," as being directed to that which is not consciousness or knowledge. His way of conceiving consciousness and knowledge as intentionality showed an unmistakable resemblance to Kierkegaard's concept of man as existence. Both opposed the closed, atomistic concept of man and human consciousness. But Husserl was principally interested in theoretical problems of knowledge, whereas Kierkegaard emphasized questions of a theological-anthropological nature. In this way existentialism and phenomenology were distinct.

The Merger. This situation did not last very long. In Heidegger's *Being and Time,* Kierkegaard's existentialism and Husserl's phenomenology merge, as it were, to become the basis of the philosophy which now is rather generally called "existential phenomenology." Heidegger presents us with a *scientific* (*wissenschaftlich*) philosophy of man which does not sink into the illusions of idealism and positivism. (The term "scientific" is used here again in its classical sense and not in the narrow modern sense which identifies science with physics and mathematics.) Under the influence of the phenomenological theory of knowledge and the phenomenological ideal of science, existentialism renounced its antiscientific stand; on the other hand, phenomenology, as a theory of knowledge, became enriched by borrowing numerous things from Kierkegaard's existentialism; and in this way it developed into a philosophy of man as such.[10] And so there arose a unified movement of existential phenomenologi-

---

[10]It is, of course, not our intention to affirm that Heidegger's intervention did not do more than remove this antiscientific character. To be specific, we may say that precisely through Heidegger phenomenology found the road to metaphysics.

cal thinking of which, alongside Heidegger and (in a more restricted sense) Sartre, Merleau-Ponty and the School of Louvain are the principal exponents.

The antiscientific attitude of existentialism, however, was maintained in the thought of Karl Jaspers and Gabriel Marcel.[11] For this reason these thinkers put themselves more or less outside the unified movement of existential phenomenology, although there remain numerous points of contact.

We could now begin to explain the fundamental ideas of existential phenomenology and after that direct our attention to the question whether or not these fundamental ideas include atheism. However, there are several points on which the author has to defend his own position precisely in connection with the question about the possibility of affirming God's existence within the existential-phenomenological trend of thinking.[12] For this reason we shall take the liberty to present first a brief introductory description of the two great currents of thought about man, namely, materialism and spiritualism. We do this reluctantly because we already spoke about that in our work *Existential Phenomenology*.[13] But since a clear explanation of these two currents will, we hope, serve as a basis for answering some criticisms levelled at existential phenomenology, we shall try to give an improved description of it, even though this description will necessitate repeating certain pages of our previous book.

2. MATERIALISTIC AND SPIRITUALISTIC MONISM

He who tries to penetrate into the history of thought realizes that the attempt to express what man is involves the search for an arduous equilibrium between extremes. Materialistic systems on the one side, and exaggerated spiritualistic systems on the other, bear witness to the difficulty man's mind encounters when there is question of stating what man is. Both types of systems are the result of a certain lack of balance in thinking. Nevertheless, they are not useless, for there is no philosophy that is wrong in every respect and, consequently, concerned with nothing. Yet moments of equilibrium are rather rare in the history of philosophy.

---

[11]Marcel, *Du refus à l'invocation,* Paris, 1940, p. 193.
[12]Cf. D.M. De Petter, "Een geamendeerde phenomenologie," *Tijdschrift voor Philosophie,* Vol. XXII (1960), pp. 286-306.
[13]Pittsburgh, 3rd impr., 1963.

Existential phenomenology provides such a moment of equilibrium. Avoiding the onesidedness of materialism and of exaggerated spiritualism, it appreciates, at its true value, the reality which the proponents of these systems have seen and attempted to express.[14] Existential phenomenology uses the term "existence" to express one of the most fundamental and essential characteristics of being-man, and in this way tries to fix, as it were, the equilibrium of its vision of man.[15]

Materialism

All materialistic systems agree in looking upon man as a product of forces and processes just as is the case of any other thing. Hence a materialist would agree that man's being should be called a being-in-the-world, but for him it would mean that man is, like any other thing, a thing amidst other earthly things, a particle of nature, a moment in the endless evolution of the cosmos.[16]

This idea is not so foolish that one can dismiss it as being destitute of meaning. It expresses, on the contrary, a valuable vision, takes account of a reality that should never be lost sight of, and takes seriously the undeniable fact that whatever man is, he is only "on the basis of materiality."[17] Sooner or later every philosopher has to face the temptation to agree with materialism if he does not want to disregard the importance of matter. For there is not much distance between the idea that man is whatever he is only on a material basis[18] and the conviction that man is nothing else but a fragment of matter or a passing phase in the endless evolution of the

---

[14]This point is treated more extensively in nearly every book *about* the philosophy of existence. For a clear summary of the critique which existential philosophers make of materialists and spiritualists, see Dondeyne "Beschouwingen bij het atheistisch existentialisme," *Tijdschrift voor Philosophie,* vol. XIII (1951), pp. 1-41.

[15]Merleau-Ponty, *Sens et non-sens,* Paris, 1948, pp. 142 f.

[16]"There are...two classical views. One consists in considering man as the result of physical, physiological and sociological influences which would determine him from without and make him a thing among things." Merleau-Ponty, *op. cit.,* p. 142.

[17]A. Dondeyne, "Dieu et le matérialisme contemporain," *Essai sur Dieu, l'homme et l'univers,* ed. by Jacques de Bivort de la Saudée, Paris, 1957, p. 24.

[18]"Our scientific experience has not yet shown us any forces that lack a material basis, any 'spiritual world,' which would be outside and beyond nature." Ernst Haeckel, *Die Wellrätset,* Leipzig, 10th ed., p. 99. English title, *The Riddle of the World.*

cosmos.[19] For there is no spiritual or intellectual knowledge without sense-perceptible objects, without brains, physiological processes, sensible images and words. There is no spiritual love without sensible love. There is no personal conscience without biological structures and no artistic act without expression in matter. That is why a biologist, for instance, can speak about knowledge, love and conscience, and what he says about them is concerned with reality.

This example shows that a certain way of thinking can be materialistic even though the thinker does not explicitly state that man is a "thing." Materialism is often camouflaged. It presents itself most frequently as scientism, as an exaggerated esteem for physical sciences which deal *ex professo* with "things" and use categories and models that are applicable only to "things." The pursuit of the sciences changes into scientism when one asserts that there are no other realities than those that are revealed by the physical sciences.

Since man is whatever he is only on a material basis, the physical sciences *also* are able to say something about what man is. But there is then also a strong temptation to take the fatal step of declaring that nothing can be added to what the physicist has said. The philosopher should know that temptation in order to avoid minimizing the power and significance of materialism. That fatal step, however, makes the sciences degenerate into scientism. Scientism is a materialistic theory, for it holds that whatever is not dealt with by science (in the narrow sense) is not worth mentioning.

In regard to man, materialism is a "detotalization" of reality (Le Senne).[20] Materialism fails in its attempt to explain man, that is, to express what it is to be man, to account for the totality of man, because it pays attention to only one, albeit essential, aspect of this totality. Materialism is a kind of monism which accepts only one type of being in the totality of reality, namely, the material thing. And so man is likewise a "thing" and his life a mere chain of processes. If one claimed merely that man *also* is thing-like and that his life *also* has process-like aspects, he would express a truth. But materialistic monism neglects an essential aspect of being human, because the assertion that man is a thing does not take into account the fact that man exists for himself and that things exist for man.

---

[19]"We human beings also are merely passing phases in the development of the eternal substance, individual forms in which matter and energy appear; we realize the triviality of these forms when we view them from the standpoint of endless space and eternal time." Haeckel, *op. cit.,* p. 259.

[20]Quoted by A. Dondeyne, *art. cit.* (footnote 17), pp. 24-25.

Strictly speaking, the view, "man is a thing," cannot explain that this statement itself can be made, for every materialist would agree that layers of rock or rain-showers, in other words, *things* cannot make such a statement.

It can be said in general that a philosophy does not fail so much by what it says as by what it omits to say or eliminates from reality. This assertion is definitely and clearly applicable to materialism. The materialist fails to pay attention to the fact that man exists for himself *as* man: that is, to be man has value and meaning for man and that things likewise have value and meaning for man, whereas things have no meaning for themselves or for other things. If nothing existed except things, then nothing would have any meaning or value. Accordingly, materialism disregards the fundamental fact that it is only *with and through* man that things and processes can be spoken of. However thing-like man may be, it is never possible to maintain that "man is a *thing*," for if this assertion were true, it would be impossible to assert it, at least if we agree with all materialists that layers of rock and rain-showers are incapable of making assertions. If man is capable of asserting that man is a thing, he must be able to transcend his thing-like condition at least to the extent of being able to make assertions.[21] This point alone suffices to show that the being of man cannot be like the being of a thing.

Accordingly, what the materialist denies is man's subjectivity.[22] The being of man, on the proper level of his being man, is a being-conscious by which man exists *for* himself[23] and is able to give himself a name. Man calls himself "I." Through the "light" of the *ego*, of the subject, the conscious *I* which man is, man exists *for* himself and there is "light" in the world of things, so that things appear to man as having value and meaning. Differently expressed, through this light things are for man.

Materialism, thus, fails to recognize an essential aspect of man's being, for, in the last analysis, it does not acknowledge that man's

---

[21]Cf. Sartre, *Existentialism and humanism*, p. 45.

[22]"I am not the outcome or the meeting-point of numerous causal agencies which determine my bodily or psychological make-up. I cannot conceive myself as nothing but a bit of the world, a mere object of biological, psychological or sociological investigation. I cannot shut myself up in the universe of science. All my knowledge of the world, even my scientific knowledge, is gained from my own particular point of view, or from some experience of the world without which the symbols of science would be meaningless." Merleau-Ponty, *Phenomenology of Perception,* tr. by Colin Smith, London (Routledge and Kegan Paul), 1962, p. VIII.

[23]"In no case can my consciousness be a thing, for its mode of being in itself is precisely a being for me." Sartre, *L'Imagination,* Paris, 1948, p. 1.

being is a *being-conscious*. The materialist cannot defend himself by saying that man's acts of consciousness can be reduced to a play of atoms and molecules like all other processes in the realm of material things. For he has to admit, in that case, that there are certain "atoms" which are distinct from other atoms by the fact that they exist *for* themselves as atoms and by the fact that other atoms exist *for* them as atoms, and that they can philosophize about themselves and the other atoms. Now such atoms we call "men."

Materialism, then, subsists by virtue of a hidden contradiction.[24] For, it is absolutely impossible for the materialist to justify his own existence as a materialist philosopher if he maintains that there is only one type of being, namely, that of a thing. The contradiction consists in this that a materialist philosopher admits, on the one hand, that layers of rocks and rain-showers, plants and brutes, cannot create a philosophy, not even one that is materialistic, whereas, on the other hand, he wishes to explain his own being, as a materialistic philosopher, by means of the same categories he uses to express the being of layers of rocks and rain-showers, plants, and brutes.[25] Materialism contains not only the material world, but also the materialistic philosopher,[26] and the latter's existence remains unexplained by it.

Spiritualism

The fact that things and processes have a meaning for man as a conscious subject justifies the recognition that subjectivity has a certain priority over things. He who eliminates the subject which

---

[24]"Scientific points of view, according to which my existence is a moment of the world's, are always both naive and at the same time dishonest, because they take for granted, without explicitly mentioning it, the other point of view, namely that of consciousness, through which from the outset a world forms itself round me and begins to exist for me." Merleau-Ponty, *Op. cit.*, p. IX.

[25]Merleau-Ponty, *Sens et Non-Sens*, p. 143.

[26]"One cannot refute through *a priori* concepts the materialism which wants to reduce the totality of being to an interplay of moving particles of matter, susceptible only of causal explanation. This materialism is not a contradiction *in terms* but it is a contradiction '*in actu exercito*,' i.e., it contains, alongside the material system of the world with its causal laws, also the affirmation and the conscious pursuit of the causal explanation; and these two are acts of consciousness which, viewed in their essential structure, transcend causal determinism." Dondeyne, "Belang voor de Metaphysica van een accurate bestaansbeschrijving van de mens als kennend wezen," *Kenleer en Metaphysick (Verslag van de twaalfde algemene vergadering der Vereniging voor Thomistische Wijsbegeerte en van de derde studiedagen van het Wijsgerig Gezelschap te Leuven)*, Nijmegen, 1947, p. 39.

man is thereby eliminates all meaning; hence the term "to be" like-wise loses all meaning. For how can the term "to be" have any meaning if "to be" is not affirmed by a subject? What human mean-ings and values in the world of things can still be acceptable as real, if, in the absence of any subjects, "to be" can be called only "to be for no one"? Moreover, I can make the supposition that there are no subjects, only because and to the extent that I *do not really* make that supposition. In other words, only a purely verbal formulation of that supposition is possible. The subject, therefore, is wholly undeni-able and exhibits a certain priority, a certain primacy in regard to the world of things.

We can also make this priority explicit in the following way. The world of things always manifests itself necessarily as the *not-I*. *To-be-not-I* belongs to the reality of the world of things. Things which are not distinct from the *I* and do not reveal themselves as the *not-I*, are not *real* things. Hence he who wishes to express the reality of things is always forced to affirm implicitly the thing's non-identity with the subject. Now this includes the impossibility of denying or elimin-ating the *I* from the discussion of the *reality* of things, for in that case the world of things could no longer be expressed as *not-I*. But *to-be-not-I* belongs to the *reality* of things.

It is necessary, then, to admit a certain priority of the *I* and for this reason it is impossible to consider the *I* as the product of cosmic processes and forces. For without the *I* those forces and processes in the cosmos are not what they *really* are, namely, *not-I*. Now could that which, without the *I*, is not what it really is make the *I* be? To affirm that this is possible, is similar to saying that a man who is sinking in quicksand can pull himself out of it by his hairs.

These few remarks indicate the direction that will be taken by thinkers who want to exploit the weak point of materialism. For the materialist the conscious subject is not a reality worth mentioning. For the spiritualists, however, thought about reality begins with the affirmation of the subject.

It is definitely necessary to feel the power of materialistic thought in order to understand the crude expression: man is a thing. But the same must be said of spiritualistic monism. As soon as we really see the priority of the subject, we run the danger of exaggerating the significance of the subject. Without the *I* it is impossible to speak about the world of things, and the term "to be" loses all meaning. Slight exaggeration again is sufficient to make one consider things as products of a kind of creative activity of the subject, or as the contents of the subject's consciousness.

When spiritualistic monism thus absolutizes the value of the subject, it reduces the being of material things to the being of the subject; hence its "detotalization of reality" takes exactly the opposite direction from that taken by materialism. Whereas materialism simply discards the value of subjectivity, or at least considers it not "worth mentioning," spiritualistic monism reduces the density of material things to vacant contents of consciousness.[27]

Hence spiritualistic monism pays due regard to what materialism neglects, namely, "the being out of itself" (*aus-sich-sein*) of subjectivity. Since the subject cannot be produced "out of" material processes, he is "out of himself." Exaggerating this easily leads to the temptation of changing the subject's "out of himself" into an "of himself" (*a se; durch sich*); we then absolutize and finally divinize subjectivity.[28]

It stands to reason that spiritualists did not simply identify the divinized *I* with the "little," finite *I* which I and the others are. In monistic spiritualism the "little," finite *I's* lose their identity, their selfhood, their distinction and consistency because they are thought of as functions and particularizations of the all-embracing *Ego*, or as moments in the development of the absolute Mind.[29] For, the characteristics attributed to the subject through exaggeration of its priority were so fantastic that such a subject could not possibly be identified with the "little," insignificant *I* that any particular *I* is.

He who realizes the force of spiritualistic thought, understands that it has never been completely overcome in the history of philosophy. And it must not ever be totally overcome, in the sense that nothing of the original inspiration from which it arose is preserved in present thinking. On the other hand, one who reflects upon the final achievement of spiritualism cannot fail to realize that it retains very little of the original inspiration which gave rise to materialism. In an irresponsible fashion monistic spiritualism disregards that man is whatever he is only on a material basis.

---

[27] "Transcendental idealism too 'reduces' the world since, insofar as it guarantees the world, it does so by regarding it as thought or consciousness of the world, and as the mere correlative of our knowledge, with the result that it becomes immanent in consciousness and the aseity of things is thereby done away with." Merleau-Ponty, *Phenomenology of Perception*, pp. XV f.

[28] Cf. J. Ortega y Gasset, *Man and People*, New York 1957.

[29] Cf. Dondeyne, "Beschouwingen bij het atheistisch existentialisme," *Tijdschrift voor Philosophie*, vol. XIII (1951), pp. 27-28.

3. Existential Phenomenology

The struggle between materialism and spiritualism shows good reason for trying to find a midway position which takes into account the valuable insights of both without falling into the extremisms defended by them. As we have already said, existential phenomenology endeavors to undertake this task.

A. *The Existent Subject as "Cogito"*

We have seen that existential phenomenology rightly emphasizes man's being a subject. He who refuses to recognize the subject can no longer say anything meaningful, for by eliminating the subject he also eliminates all meaning from the world. If there is no subject, it is no longer possible to affirm any being, for affirmation presupposes an affirming subject. Even the denial of the subject is a contradiction, for any denial presupposes a denying subject. He who denies the subject likewise is incapable of denying meaning, for any denial contains an implicitly affirmed meaning. It is thus impossible to deny the subject and, therefore, meaning also is undeniable. The subject as *Cogito* is the implicit, pre-predicative affirmation of meaning, and this assertion is affirmed even in a denial—it even is a condition presupposed by denial.

All this could still be understood in a purely Cartesian way. He who, like Descartes, divorces the subject from the world, nonetheless accepts the subject. And he who, like Descartes, places meaning within the subject as *Cogito,* nonetheless accepts meaning. But he misjudges both subject and meaning as they are *in reality.* For meaning does not appear to man as a volatile content of the subject as *Cogito,* but as the worldly thing itself, facing the subject, in its own autonomy of being.[30] Meaning reveals itself as the other than the subject, as the *not-I.* The autonomy of being, facing the subject, the being-not-I, constitutes the real being of the meaning.

The affirmation of meaning, which is the subject itself as *Cogito,* is the recognition of the meaning's autonomy of being with respect to the subject; it is the recognition of the meaning in its "bodily"

---

[30]"Truth does not 'inhabit' only 'the inner man', or more accurately, there is no inner man, man is in the world, and only in the world does he know himself. When I return to myself from an excursion into the realm of dogmatic common sense or of science, I find, not a source of intrinsic truth, but a subject destined to be in the world." Merleau-Ponty, *op. cit.,* p. XI.

presence.[31] That is why the subject is *bound* and cannot proceed arbitrarily when he explicitates, conceptualizes, and expresses the meaning. For that which is *is* and must be acknowledged as such in man's speech. In speaking we take up the implicit affirmation of the subject as *Cogito,* and this implicit affirmation *is* the recognition of the meaning in its own independence of being with respect to the subject. Hence the meaning is not a content of the subject as *Cogito.*

Just as meaning is not a content of the subject as *Cogito* so neither is the subject isolated from the meaning. The subject, as he *really* is, is an intentional, an existent subject.[32] He is not divorced from the worldly meaning or shut up within himself. The subject as *Cogito* is directedness to the meaning. This directedness is expressed by the term "intentionality." The term "existence" emphasizes the same idea. The subject "exists" that is, puts himself outside himself (*ex-sistit*) in the world,[33] or, as Heidegger expresses it, he is *Dasein* ("being there"). The prefix *Da* showing the "ec-centric" character of the subject.[34] The subject, as intentionality, as existence, *is* the immediate presence to a present reality, which is meaning.[35] The subject as *Cogito* is a mysterious self-affirmation with which the affirmation of the world is inseparably intertwined. It is the affirmation of the world, which affirmation is equiprimordial with the self-affirmation of the subject.[36]

Functioning Intentionality and Explicit Act of Intentionality

Subject and Meaning. When we say that the subject as *Cogito* should be described as self-affirmation inseparably intertwined with the affirmation of the world, the term "affirmation" should not, of course, be understood as an explicit cognitive act formulated in a judgment. It is rather that which is presupposed by, and makes pos-

---

[31]"The spatial thing which we see is, despite its transcendence, a 'perceived,' a conscious 'given' in its 'bodily reality.' No image or sign is given in its place. One should not substitute a sign-consciousness or an image-consciousness for perceiving." Husserl, *Ideen,* I, pp. 98 f.

[32]"The primary truth is indeed 'I think' but only provided that we understand thereby 'I belong to myself' while belonging to the world." Merleau-Ponty, *op. cit.,* p. 407.

[33]*Sein und Zeit,* p. 53; English ed., p. 78.

[34]*Sein und Zeit,* p. 11; English ed., pp. 32 f.

[35]"If the subject *is* in a situation ... this is because he forces his ipseity into reality only by actually being a body, and entering the world through that body." Merleau-Ponty, *op. cit.,* p. 408.

[36]"In saying 'I', *Dasein* expresses itself as being-in-the-world." Heidegger *Sein und Zeit,* p. 321; English ed., p. 368.

sible, every explicit act of cognition. Every explicit act of cognition
in which a judgment is made about meaning, presupposes the meaningfulness of that which is judged. But this meaningfulness of what
is expressed in the judgment presupposes the existence, the presence
of the subject as *Cogito,* for there can be no question of meaning
without such a presence. The explicit cognitive act of judgment expresses that the meaning has autonomy of being. But this presupposes that the subject as *Cogito* has already recognized this autonomy of being. The subject as *Cogito* is itself the recognition of the
meaning's autonomy of being.

Judgment and Existence. This idea can be expressed in another
way, namely, from the standpoint of the explicitly formulated judgment. A judgment taken in itself, that is, purely as the union of the
predicate and the subject of a judgment, has no foundation in itself;
if nothing more is offered than such a union, no one knows what the
judgment is about; no one can agree or disagree; the judgment
hangs in the air. A judgment requires a basis if it really is to say
something. Now it really says something only when the subject of
the judgment points to a meaning that is present and about which
something is said by means of the predicate. But the presence of
meaning presupposes the existence, the presence of the subject as
Cogito, the "affirmation" of meaning. What the subject as *Cogito*
itself *is,* as well as the predicates, which in a plurality of judgments
are affirmed of the meaning, are only explicitations of that "affirmation." In this sense Plato is right when he declares that judgmental
knowledge is, strictly speaking, a remembering. Every judgment
ultimately goes back to existence and it is there that it has its
ground and foundation.

Experience. The term "experience" may be used to designate the
presence of the subject as *Cogito* to the meaning, but this procedure
is not without dangers. First of all, the term "experience" has
generally being understood as a mirroring of reality. Secondly, an
almost indestructible tradition ties the term so intimately to physical science that one can hardly avoid thinking about experience in
terms of physical science as the only trustworthy form of experience,
even though such a dogmatic exclusivism is untenable. Thirdly, he
who maintains that experience, the foundation of any judgment
whatsoever, must be conceived exclusively as viewed in physical science, loses sight of the fact that he thereby removes the truly incon-

testable foundation from *all* judgments, for the simple reason that this scientific experience also needs a foundation.

In this perspective it is evident that a judgment of physical science rests on a scientific experience, understood here as the presence of the subject as *Cogito* to nature viewed from the standpoint of physical science. But it is also evident that he who, by means of such scientific experiences, appropriates what the judgments of physical science express, ultimately does not yet know what he speaks about.[37] His judgments lack an *ultimate* foundation, because scientific experience is not our first and original experience in the order of knowledge. Let us illustrate this by an example.

How do I learn the real meaning of landscapes, rivers, and seas? I could consult a geography book and thus learn from the *experiences* of geographers. But I would then realize that I would not know the meaning of all those experiences if I didn't know that, after all, the book speaks about landscapes, rivers, and seas, known to me from my own experience gathered in my travels before I began to study. If I refuse to accept that the landscapes, rivers, and seas which I enjoyed during my travels are the *real* landscapes, seas, and rivers, no one will ever be able to tell me what real landscapes, rivers, and seas are. As should be evident to anyone, the original experience of the world in which we live is much richer than the experience of the geographer's world. It is obvious also that the latter experience is rooted in the former.[38]

I could define speech, as is done by the behaviorists, saying that it is "a series of certain laryngal movements with their corresponding sound-waves," but I know only what this definition means because I've had the experience of simply speaking with someone. This simple experience is more original, more fundamental and richer than the experience of speech in terms of physical science, for the latter is only a "second order expression."[39]

Subject as Cogito and World of Life. The scientific experience is only a derived and abstract mode of the subject-as-*Cogito's* exist-

---

[37]"Classical science is a form of perception which loses sight of its origins and believes itself complete." Merleau-Ponty, *op. cit.,* p. 57.

[38]"To return to things themselves is to return to that world which precedes knowledge, of which knowledge always *speaks,* and in relation to which every scientific schematization is an abstract and derivative sign-language, as is geography in relation to the country-side in which we have learnt beforehand what a forest, a prairie or a river is." Merleau-Ponty, *op. cit.,* p. IX.

[39]Merleau-Ponty, *op. cit.,* p. VIII.

ence, which mode is contained in a more comprehensive *Cogito*.
The scientific experience is only an experience obtained by the subject assuming a very special standpoint in reference to a very special
whole of meanings of the world. First in the order of "knowledge" is
the subject as *Cogito*, who is involved in the everyday world of life
according to a Gestalt of attitudes. This *Cogito* is not an act in the
usual sense of the term, but is the very being of man as existence.[40]
It is the "natural light,"[41] the "light" which constitutes the "nature"
of the subject, a "light" for the subject himself and also a "light" in
the world, by means of which the world manifests meaning, appears
to be meaningful.

Husserl designates this most radical form of intentionality by the
expressions "functioning intentionally" (*fungierende Intentionalität*)
or "world-experiencing life" (*Welterfahrendes Leben*) and he distinguishes it from the intentionality of explicit acts of cognition,
which he calls "explicit act of intentionality" (*Aktintentionalität*).[42]
Husserl undertook his phenomenology in an attempt to find a basis and
foundation for every kind of judgment. Now, that foundation can be
found only by a return to "the things themselves," by a revaluation of
the "lived world."[43] But this world of life refers to the subject as
Cogito, the first and original "affirmation" of meaning, the integral
experience,[44] which is nothing else but man as existence. In experience conceived in this way, philosophy attains the "radicalism of
foundation" (*Radikalismus der Begrundung*) which always remained
Husserl's goal.

---

[40]"The relation of the subject and the object is not that *cognitive* relationship, spoken of by classical idealism, in which the object always appears as
constructed by the subject, but a *relationship of being* through which the
subject, paradoxically, is his body, his world and his situation, and somehow
interchanges with them." Merleau-Ponty, *Sens et Non-sens*, pp. 143 f.

[41]Heidegger, *op. cit.*, p. 133; English ed., p. 171.

[42]"Alongside this 'explicit intentionality,' which it accepts also, existential
phenomenology, taking up Husserl's later 'functioning intentionality,' admits a
more fundamental form of intentionality. This basic type of intentionality expresses not merely that man in his cognitive activity is of necessity directed to
something else, but primarily intends to indicate that being-man itself implies
an essential reference to the world and that this intentional relationship of
being is the proper and ultimate root of all meaning." Joseph A. Kockelmans,
Phaenomenologie en natuurwetenschap, Haarlem, 1962, p. 41.

[43]Merleau-Ponty, *Phenomenology of Perception*, p. VIII.

[44]Phenomenology "endeavors to conceive philosophy as the explicitation of
integral human experience." Alphonse de Waelhens, "Signification de la phénoménologie," *Diogène*, 1954, no. 5, p. 60.

Existence as "Being-in"

By viewing man as existence, we draw away from both materialism and spiritualism.[45] Existential phenomenology defines man as subject, but this subject is involved in material things. Worldly things thus co-constitute what man is, so that one who thinks away the world inevitably also thinks away the whole of man. On the other hand, material things, as meanings, point to the subject, so that all meaning and man also are thought away when we think away the subject.

The *being-in* which man himself is, therefore, is a very special way of *being-in*. It cannot be compared with anything else because man's *being-in* is that of a *subject*. That is why prudence is needed in the use of the term "being in the world." The materialist could also use that term, but for him it would mean that man is a portion of matter in a material world, or a passing phase in an endless cosmic evolution. Secondly, *being-in* which defines the being of man is not like the being of a pen *in* a drawer or a cigar *in* a box.[46] These two cases do not express that we are dealing with the *being-in* of a *subject,* as is essential when man's being is described as a *being-in.* For this reason it will be necessary to use such terms as "to dwell," "to associate with," "to be present to," "to find oneself," and "to be on intimate terms with," which expressions clearly presuppose a subject.

Positivity and Negativity in Existence as Cogito

He who sees that the existent subject as *Cogito* is the ontological recognition of the meaning's autonomy of being with respect to the subject will also understand that there is a moment of negativity in existence. Precisely because the thinking subject recognizes the meaning's autonomy of being, he also sees that he is not identical with the meaning but distinct from it. This distinction could not be

---

[45]"The merit of the new philosophy is precisely that it seeks the means to think [the human condition] in the notion of existence. Existence, in the modern sense, is the movement by which man is to the world, enters into a physical and social situation which becomes his standpoint with respect to the world." Merleau-Ponty, *Sens et non-Sens,* p. 143.

[46]"Das In-sein meint so wenig ein räumliches 'Ineinander' Vorhandener, als 'in' ursprünglich gar nicht eine räumliche Beziehung der genannten Art bedeutet; 'in' stammt von innanwohnen, habitare, sich aufhalten; 'an' bedeutet: ich bin gewohnt, vertraut mit, ich pflege etwas; es hat die Bedeutung von colo im Sinne von habito und diligo." Heidegger, *Sein und Zeit,* p. 54; English translation, p. 80. We prefer to leave this passage untranslated because the words on which it hinges cannot be rendered adequately. Tr.

maintained within the Cartesian perspective. For Descartes, that of which the subject is conscious is not something which the *Cogito* is *not*, but it is precisely the content of the *Cogito*. For the existential phenomenologist, on the contrary, the subject is an intentional, existent subject; he is directedness to what is not the subject himself. Inherent in the recognition of the autonomy of being proper to meaning is the recognition of the non-identity of the meaning and the subject. The subject "nihilates" the meaning, we may even say, he is this "nihilation" itself.[47]

It stands to reason that this "nihilation" must not be viewed as an *explicit* denial, but rather as a moment of the functioning intentionality which makes all explicit denials possible and is presupposed by, and embodied in, all explicit denials.[48] Just as the affirmation of meaning, the negation in question is an attitude of being, a moment of human existence itself. Sartre has enormously exaggerated the significance of this moment of existence and made it absolute, so that he finally conceived the subject as pure Nothingness.[49] This is going too far but, on the other hand, we should not neglect the negative moment in the existence of the subject-as-*Cogito*.

B. *The Existent Subject as "Volo" (I Will)*

It is impossible to conceive man as a thing because man is a subject. Thus far we have spoken of the existent subject only as a *Cogito*, that is, we have considered the cognitive level of existence. That consideration threw light on the fact that man exists for himself and that the world appears as meaning—a fact which every kind of materialism buries under verbiage. To be man is to be *conscious* in the world.

There are phenomenologists who use somewhat strange expressions to express this idea that to be man is to be conscious. Sartre

---

[47]"The for-itself is a being such that in its being, its being is in question in so far as this being is essentially a certain way of *not being* a being which it posits simultaneously as other than itself." Sartre, *Being and Nothingness*, tr. by Hazel E. Barnes, London (Methuen and Co.), 1957, p. 174.

[48]Nothingness "founds the negation as an *act* because it is the negation as *being*. Nothingness can be nothingness only by nihilating itself expressly as nothingness of the world; that is, in its nihilation it must direct itself expressly toward this world in order to contribute itself as refusal of the world. Nothingness carries being in its heart." Sartre, *op. cit.*, p. 18.

[49]"The Being by which Nothingness arrives in the world is a being such that in its being the Nothingness of its Being is in question. *The being by which Nothingness comes to the world, must be its own Nothingness.*" Sartre, *op. cit.*, p. 23.

calls man a be-ing for whom its being is in question in its being.[50] Heidegger uses almost the same expression when he says that man is the be-ing who in his being is concerned with his being.[51] He means by this that man has a relation to his own being and this relation is an "understanding of being."[52]

When we realize that man is distinguished from a thing because man is concerned with his being, we note also that this concern does not exist on the cognitive level alone. When I feel bored, am joyful, sad or anxious, "I am also concerned about my being," but the meaning is quite different from when I am merely conscious of myself. This shows that "concern with my own being" does not occur exclusively on the cognitive level; as the examples have shown, it is present also on the affective or volitive level. That I am concerned with my being on this level presupposes—as is true of the cognitive level—that I am a subject. Hence the subject which man is exists not only as *Cogito* (I think) but also as *Volo* (I will).

We are trying to make clear distinctions, for phenomenologists have sometimes been accused of professing a "monism of existence" because they failed to make the necessary distinctions.[53] Man is defined as existence and some authors do not always keep in mind that existence is realized on many different levels. Although the subject is always identical with himself, he realizes his existence on many levels.

He who fails to recognize the subject as *Cogito* can no longer make any meaningful statement, for, by rejecting the subject, he has eliminated all meaning from the world. We can say something similar about the subject as *Volo*. One who rejects the latter can no longer recognize any meaning, i.e., any value. But the meaning reveals itself clearly as value, as object of a certain "affirmation" by the existent subject. This "affirmation," however, is not on the level of cognition; it is not merely a recognition of the meaning's au-

---

[50] *Op. cit.*, p. 174.
[51] *Sein und Zeit*, p. 12; English translation, p. 32.
[52] *Op. cit.*, pp. 12 ff; English translation, pp. 32 ff.
[53] "If in every problem one goes straight to the 'existential project,' the 'existential movement' which any authentically human conduct entails, there is a danger of not paying attention to the specific character of the problems, of seeing the outlines of the various functions as a kind of undifferentiated existential monism, which ultimately leads one to repeat the same exegesis of 'existence' in reference to the imagination, emotion, laughter, gesture, sexuality, speech, and so on." Paul Ricoeur, "Méthodes et tâches d'une phénoménologie de la volonté." *Problèmes actuels de la phénoménologie,* ed. by Herman Leo Van Breda, Paris, 1952, pp. 115 f.

tonomy of being, but it is an "agreeing with," a kind of "I love" (*diligo*),[54] an affective and volitive "Yes" to the meaning, and this "Yes" is the existent subject as *Volo* himself. Here again it is not an explicit act of the will, nor an explicit desire; it is rather something presupposed and the condition which makes all explicit desires, strivings, volitions, and emotional acts possible. It is the existing subject himself, as realizing himself on the affective and volitional level, an aspect, therefore, of the functioning intentionality which man himself is.

We could use Heidegger's expression *Befindlichkeit* to designate that aspect of human existence.[55] *Befindlichkeit* indicates the affective tonality of "finding oneself in the world," of existence. It is not a "feeling" in the sense in which the term is used in the psychology of consciousness to express a kind of interior commentary on external events. All so-called "internal commentaries" presuppose the primordial being-tuned which existence is; they presuppose the primordial evaluation, in virtue of which man already "knows" what his being-in-the-world is worth. The *Befindlichkeit* is the affective tone of the *Da* of *Dasein,* that is, of the existent subject, of man himself.[56]

Positivity and Negativity in Existence as *Volo*

The existent subject as *Volo* reveals itself in positivity and negativity. The subject as *Cogito* is the affirmation and recognition of the worldly meaning in its autonomy of being which is intertwined with a mysterious self-affirmation. So also is the subject as *Volo* a consent to the worldly meaning, with which a consent to oneself is intertwined. The subject is a certain "Yes" addressed to the world, and on the basis of that "Yes" there is a certain "Yes" to oneself. This consent implies a certain fullness of being, a certain fulfillment and satisfaction, a certain rest and peace, which may be called an existential happiness.

---

[54]Heidegger, *Sein und Zeit,* p. 54; English ed., p. 80.

[55]*Op. cit.,* pp. 134-140; English ed., pp. 172-179.

[56]"Being-attuned is not related to the psychical in the first instance, it is not itself an interior state which then in an enigmatic fashion reaches forth and gives 'color' to things and persons. It is in this that the second essential characteristic of *Befindlichkeit* manifests itself. The world, *Dasein* with, and existence are equi-originally disclosed; *Befindlichkeit* is a basic existential species of this disclosedness because existence itself is essentially being-in-the-world." Heidegger, *op. cit.,* p. 137; English ed., p. 176.

Negativity, however, is equally undeniable. The "Yes" to the world, which is the subject himself, is immediately affected by a "No" to the world, with which a "No" of the subject to himself is intertwined.[57] That is why all fullness of being is permeated with emptiness, all fulfillment and satisfaction is affected by unfulfillment and dissatisfaction, and all rest and peace is disturbed by unrest and lack of peace: existential happiness is equiprimordial with unhappiness. All this makes a man what he is as a subject in the world.

"Finding onself in the world" is therefore a "finding oneself well" in the world; hence we must say that man is "at home" in the world. At the same time it is "not finding oneself well" in the world; therefore man is also "not at home" in it. For my existent subjectivity as *Volo* the world is my home, but at the same time, while in it, I am longing for a better "home."

C. *The Existent Subject "as Ago" (I act)*

Man's being as existence reveals itself not only as a being in the world, but equi-primordially as a being "at" the world. Being man is something dynamic, and this dynamism we call "history."

It is evident, of course, that there is also a static moment in being man. The facticity, the determination, the "already" of existence, which we express by grammatical qualifiers, signify a certain "fixation" of the subject. For instance, we use expressions like "stupid," "fat," "Bostonian," "boxer," and "inactive." Nevertheless there is no facticity which does not include a certain potentiality of being, and every "already" opens toward a certain "not yet."[58] And this is not an accidental characteristic of facticity, but the potentiality of being *co*-constitutes the *reality* of the facticity.

On the other hand, there is no *real* potentiality of being that is not rooted in a particular facticity. Existence, therefore, is the oppositional unity, the unity in opposition, of *de facto* being and the potentiality of being. Heidegger calls this unity "project."[59] Sartre, somewhat enigmatically but correctly, defines this characteristic of existence by saying that man "is not what he is, and is what he is

---

[57]"Something massive and fleshy is lacking in his assent." Merleau-Ponty, *Eloge de la philosophie,* Paris, 12th ed., 1953, p. 81.

[58]"Dasein is always already 'beyond itself,' not as a way of acting toward other beings which it is not, but as being toward the potentiality for being which it itself is. This structure of being pertaining to the essential 'it is concerned with' we will call the Dasein's 'being-ahead-of-itself.'" Heidegger, *op. cit.,* p. 192; English ed., p. 236.

[59]*Op. cit.,* p. 145; English ed., pp. 181 f.

not."[60] For man is not exclusively facticity; he is also ability-to-be, albeit not *de facto*. Here we must keep in mind, however, that both the *de facto* being and the potentiality of being are the being *of the subject*. Man is not factually stout just as a dead elephant is massive; he is not factually chaste just as a lily is white, not hunchbacked just as a willow tree is gnarled, or bald just as a billiard ball is shiny. Likewise man's potentiality of being is not like the potentiality of a thing with which "something can come to pass."[61] The project which man is is a *self-project*. Man is master of his situation and holds his possibilities in his *own* hands.

Here again let us keep in mind that man's "project of existence" must not be conceived as a plan which man makes and which he can discard.[62] Man himself is a project; to be a project has an ontological significance. His being a project is the ground on which the possibility of every concrete plan is based. Every concrete plan is conceived as a possibility to be realized on the basis of a particular facticity. Such a plan, therefore, explicitly takes up what existence itself as project *is*.

But man is not only a self-project. He is also, and *per se,* the execution of the self-project which he is;[63] he acts. In acting, the subject reaches beyond his facticity to the fulfillment of one of the as yet unfulfilled potentialities of his existence. The result of the action, after it has been realized, remains in the existence as facticity, which in its turns opens up certain new possibilities. The subject as *Ago* constantly transcends its facticity. And man cannot refuse to do this. For even if man refuses to realize himself, he will nonetheless realize himself, be it only as a loafer, a quietist, a good-for-nothing and a dullard. Here too we find that existence is given a certain meaning, the source of which lies in the subject as *Ago*. If man were to refuse to construct a human world he would nevertheless construct a world, albeit an inhuman world. To will nothing is also to will something, and to do nothing is also to do something. The constantly self-transcending movement[64] which the existent subject as *Ago* itself is, ceases only when man ceases to be man. Man's being *in* the world is equiprimordial with his being "at" the world.[65]

---

[60]*Being and Nothingness*, p. 79.
[61]Heidegger, *op. cit.*, p. 143; English ed., p. 183.
[62]Heidegger, *op. cit.*, p. 145; English ed., p. 185.
[63]"The essence of *Dasein* lies in its existence." Heidegger, *op. cit.*, p. 42; English ed., p. 67.
[64]Merleau-Ponty, *Phenomenology of Perception*, p. 430.
[65]Merleau-Ponty, *op. cit.*, pp. 434-456.

We have taken the liberty to explain the main lines of existential phenomenology in such a way that certain points are emphasized and others neglected. The justification of this procedure lies in the purpose of this chapter, viz., to consider whether or not the existence of God can be affirmed within the framework of existential-phenomenological thought. But the immediate preparation for the answer to that question has still to be made. It is concerned with the examination of the ontological status of the world. It will be useful to preface this examination with a very short exposition of the significance of the human body as a transition from the subject to the world.

D. *The Human Body as Transition from Subject to World*

One who wishes to speak about the human body must first take the necessary precautions to make sure that he will truly speak about the *human* body. For he could easily be led to speak about the human body as *a* body, as belonging to the large family of "bodies"[66] which we have in mind, for instance, when we say: "A body that is wholly or partially immersed in a liquid loses a weight that is exactly equal to . . ." One who speaks about the human body in this fashion entirely loses sight of the *human* aspect of man's body. The human body is *human,* because it is "mine," "yours," "hers," and "his," that is, because it is the body of a subject. A human body participates in human subjectivity: the subject permeates the body. My grasping hands are "I who grasp," my feet are "I who walk," my eyes are "I who see," my ears are "I who hear." Hence my body is not a thing among other things.[67] My hands do not lie in the graspable world; my feet do not belong to the world on which one can walk; my eyes do not lie in the visible world; my ears do not belong to the world of sound. The *human* body lies on the side of the subject. From this point of view we must say that man *is* his body.[68]

The human body is not what biology, physiology and anatomy say about it.[69] The *human* body does not appear in books of biology,

---

[66]Sartre, *Being and Nothingness,* pp. 223 f.
[67]"My body as it is *for me* does not appear to me in the midst of the world." Sartre, *op. cit.,* p. 303.
[68]Gabriel Marcel, *Metaphysical Journal,* London, 1952, p. 243.
[69]"As far as the body is concerned, even the body of another, we must learn to distinguish it from the objective body as set forth in works on physiology." Merleau-Ponty, *op. cit.,* p. 351.

physiology, or anatomy because "I", "you," "he," and "she" do not appear in those books. This does not mean, of course, that those sciences in no way speak about the body, but they say nothing about the human character of the human body.[70] Moreover, those sciences do not know what they are speaking about if they neglect the original "knowing about the body," which the subject as embodied *Cogito* himself is.

If we understand this properly we also see that "my" body signifies the transition from "me" to my world, that "my" body is the place where I appropriate my world,[71] that it grafts me on things, that it gives me a solid or a slippery foothold in the world. The fact that my hand has five fingers contributes to making the world graspable in a particular way, different from the way it would be graspable if I had only one finger. The fact that I have feet contributes to make the world something that can be walked on in a special way, different from the situation in which I should have wings or fins. I have ears and these contribute to make the world before me a world of sound. I have eyes, and these contribute to make for me a field of vision. From the standpoint of my body I call the mountain peak Pilatus "high" and the sidewalk "low," Sirius "far away" and my desk "near,"[72] fire "hot" and ice "cold." Anything in the world that is called hard, soft, angular, sharp, clammy, red, yellow, roomy, light, heavy, sweet, nourishing, digestible, smelly, small and so forth, refers to the human body. A bicycle implies some reference to a position and movements of the human body; similarly a football, a bed, a house, a door, a room, in a word, all cultural objects have reference to the body.

We see, then, that my body lies on the side of the subject that I am; at the same time it involves me in the world of things. My body opens me up to the world, or rather it opens me in the direction of the world and signifies my standpoint in it.[73] "It keeps the visible spectacle constantly alive, and it breathes life into it and sustains it inwardly."[74] When my body disintegrates, my world also

---

[70]"In other words, ... the objective today is not the true version of the phenomenal body, that is, the true version of the body that we live by; it is indeed no more than the latter's impoverished image, so that the problem of the relation of soul to body has nothing to do with the objective body, which exists only conceptually, but with the phenomenal body." Merleau-Ponty, *op. cit.*, pp. 431 f.

[71]Merleau-Ponty, *op. cit.*, p. 154.

[72]Merleau-Ponty, *op. cit.*, p. 440.

[73]Merleau-Ponty, *op. cit.*, p. 166.

[74]Merleau-Ponty, *op. cit.*, p. 203.

collapses; the complete dissolution of my body means a break with my world and at the same time death, the end of my being as being conscious in the world, the end of my being man.[75]

Accordingly, when we reflect upon the human body we meet the subject that is immersed in the body and is involved in the world by way of the body. We encounter the world which, as a totality of meaning, is attached to the body and which as human refers to the subject. We meet man as existence.

Pact Between Body and World

For some one who conceives the human body as a thing among things, as just another one of the great mass of bodies, all these remarks about the human body are wholly unintelligible. The same thing is true for one who is somewhat more circumspect but still thinks that the human body, as *human,* can be the object of the "sciences." So long as one speaks about the human body after the manner that is customary in the sciences, it remains absolutely incomprehensible that the world has a meaning which clings to the body as incarnation of the subject, a meaning which is already "known" and "affirmed" by the body. But then he also keeps in the dark the fact that all the positive sciences which speak about the body presuppose a more fundamental and original "knowledge," namely, that "knowing" in which my hands and my feet are unconcealed from me when I use tools and walk around in a world.[76] One who takes a scientistic view of the sciences forgets or refuses to recognize the source from which those sciences themselves spring.

It might be worthwhile to reflect for a moment on that mysterious "knowing" which the human body itself is. Our body is human because it is the body of a subject. The subject permeates the body and the body participates in the subject. We have described the subject as *Cogito,* as *Volo* and as *Ago,* as "I think," "I will," and

---

[75]"Now if the world is atomized or dislocated, this is because one's own body has ceased to be a knowing body, and has ceased to draw together all objects in its one grip." Merleau-Ponty, *op. cit.,* pp. 282 f.

[76]"We have relearned to feel our body; we have found underneath the objective and detached knowledge of the body that other knowledge which we have of it in virtue of its always being with us and of the fact that we are our body. In the same way we shall need to reawaken our experience of the world as it appears to us in so far as we are in the world through our body, and in so far as we perceive the world with our body. By thus remaking contact with the body and with the world, we shall also rediscover ourself, since, perceiving as we do with the body, the body is a natural self and, as it were, the subject of perception." Merleau-Ponty, *op. cit.,* p. 206.

"I act." But if the body participates in the subject, it must also be called a kind of *Cogito, Volo* and *Ago* in the world. And this evidently is the case. Before making any intellectual judgment about space, I have already orientated myself in space; this is the same as saying that "I have eyes," or that "I am able to see." If I wish to make a scientific study of colors, I must presuppose that my eyes already "know" colors and can "distinguish" them. My body "knows" better than I do what is meant by hard, soft, sharp, sticky, cold, warm, fragrant and tasty.[77] Joe DiMaggio's arms and legs "know" the baseball bat and diamond much better than he himself does when he thinks about them. My feet "know" the steps of the staircase I daily use much better than I personally do, and my body is much more "capable" of playing tennis than I myself can. One who leads a large congregation in prayer will run less risk of getting "stuck" if he can trust that his lips know the prayers better than he does. The human body, as sexually differentiated, signifies a corporeal *Cogito* and *Volo* with respect to the opposite sex on which any personal sexual initiative is based.

Hence a pre-personal subject is at work beneath the *personal* subject.[78] Every personal *Cogito, Volo* and *Ago* presupposes that pre-person subject and takes up the latter's "pre-history" into its own personal *Cogito, Volo* and *Ago* in the world.[79] Now, that pre-personal subject—one could almost say that "anonymous" subject is the human body.[80] The latter has already made a pact with the world before the personal subject makes its history,[81] and this pact is never made superfluous by any personal history.[82] This pact, however, is made in semi-darkness; it becomes entirely incomprehensible when it is replaced—as is done in the sciences—by "purely

---

[77]Merleau-Ponty, *op. cit.,* p. 238.

[78]"There is, therefore, another subject beneath me, for whom a world exists before I am here and who marks out my place in it. This captive or natural spirit is my body, not that momentary body which is the instrument of my personal choices and which fastens upon this or that world, but the system of anonymous 'functions' which draws every particular focus into a general project." Merleau-Ponty, *op. cit.,* p. 254.

[79]Merleau-Ponty, *op. cit.,* p. 253.

[80]"Perception is always in the mode of the impersonal 'One'. It is not a personal act enabling me to give a fresh significance to my life." Merleau-Ponty, *op. cit.,* p. 240.

[81]"My first perception and my first hold upon the world must appear to me as action in accordance with an earlier agreement reached between X and the world in general." Merleau-Ponty, *op. cit.,* p. 254.

[82]Cf. also R.C. Kwant, "De geslotenheid van Merleau-Ponty's wijsbegeerte," *Tijdschrift voor Philosophie,* vol. XIX (1957), pp. 217-272.

corporeal processes." This is the profound truth contained in psychoanalysis, although Freud himself perhaps failed to see it clearly.[83]

The pact between the body and the world is also the "place" where many psychic disturbances occur.[84] These are not caused by unilateral, deterministic processes that have their source in stimuli coming from the "outside world." Nor can they be understood as an externalization of the "inner world's" disorganization. They are rather a break between the body and the world, usually on the level of affectivity, and the rupture cannot be healed by personal intellectual effort or a personal decision of the will. To heal this rupture it is necessary that the body, aided by psycho-therapeutic means, opens itself once more to the world and to the other.[85]

E. *The Ontological Status of the Worldly Meaning*

Far-reaching consequences are attached to existential thought with reference to the status of being proper to wordly things. If it is true that man is existence, that he is a subject in the world, that man[86] clings to the world, it follows that the world also clings to man. Then it is no longer possible to ask what the world is without man, nor can it be said any more that there is a world without man. We realize, of course, that such expressions need to be explained lest phenomenology be accused of fostering most silly notions. The following pages are intended to offer these explanations.

When Husserl defined the subject as intentionality, he at the same time "put between brackets" the actual existence of the worldly meaning to which the intentional subject is directed. This is the first sense in which Husserl uses the term "reduction": being is placed between brackets (*Einklammerung des Seins*), i.e., we sus-

---

[83]"Whatever the theoretical declarations of Freud may have been psychoanalytical research has in fact led to an explanation of man, not in terms of his sexual substructure, but to a discovery in sexuality of relations and attitudes which had previously been held to reside *in consciousness*. Thus the significance of psychoanalysis is less to make psychology biological than to discover a dialectical process in functions thought of as 'purely bodily', and to reintegrate sexuality into the human being." Merleau-Ponty, *op. cit.*, pp. 157 f.

[84]Merleau-Ponty, *op. cit.*, pp. 154-173.

[85]Merleau-Ponty, *op. cit.*, p. 163.

[86]We follow here the accepted way of saying that "man clings to the world," although strictly speaking, the expression is not correct. For it is not *man* who clings to the world but the *subject*. Man is the unity of reciprocal implication of subject and world. Because the world is part of what constitutes being-man, it is, strictly speaking, not correct to say that *man* clings to the world.

pend our judgment regarding the reality of that to which the subject is directed. What prompted Husserl to suspend this judgment?

According to De Waelhens, Husserl was motivated by the nineteenth century philosophies which were still struggling with the "critical problem," with the question whether an external reality corresponds to the contents, the representations and concepts of the self-encompassed, isolated and closed *Cogito*. For idealism, meaning was a content of the *Cogito* and, therefore, the being of meaning should not really be distinguished from the *Cogito*. For realism, on the other hand, meaning was entirely separate from the *Cogito* and its being was totally foreign to the *Cogito*.

Husserl did not wish to get involved in the controversy between realists and idealists, for he was afraid he might get hopelessly stuck in it. He was afraid that his phenomenological plan would never bear fruit if he were to get involved in the conflict. On the other hand, he believed that his phenomenology would succeed, even though he refused to take sides with any of the two antagonists. Husserl himself did not realize that his own idea of intentionality makes it impossible to "place between brackets" the factual existence of meaning. He did not see that suspending judgment about the actual existence of meaning is possible only for one who starts from a closed *Cogito*—a condition which he himself most emphatically rejected.

If the *Cogito* is intentionality, it is no longer possible to ask whether the meaning to which the *Cogito* is directed really exists.[87] On the contrary, we must then immediately recognize that the really existing wordly meaning is a co-constituent of what the *Cogito* is, and that the *Cogito* is not what it is—namely, intentionality— without the really existing worldly meaning.[88] Unsurprisingly, therefore, a phenomenological reduction in the sense of placing being between brackets no longer occurs in the works of Heidegger.[89]

Representative Realism

The world about which phenomenology speaks is the real world. This may sound trivial, but we must remember that there is a

---

[87]"From this point of view we can see how the problem of the existence of the external world strictly speaking has no meaning at all." Marcel, *Metaphysical Journal*, p. 25.

[88]"So far as I am concerned, I'd say that Heidegger has shown in a probably definitive way that it is absurd to isolate the existent subject and to ask one self on the basis of such a subject whether or not the world exists. For *de facto* this existent subject is an existent subject only in his relation to the world." Marcel, *L'homme problématique*. Paris, 1955, pp. 141 f.

[89]Cf. Joseph A. Kockelmans, *Martin Heidegger*, Tielt, 1962, p. 21.

kind of spiritualistic monism or idealism which reduces the reality of worldly things and of the world itself to etherial contents of the subject as *Cogito*. Now it is precisely this that phenomenology rejects when it says that worldly things and the world are *real*. These things are not contents of the *Cogito*: they are the hard, immovable massiveness and density of reality, of "givenness in the flesh" (Husserl). This, of course, does not mean that I can no longer make mistakes when I speak about the world, or that I do not have dreams and hallucinations, fears and desires, that are not real meanings. However, the very fact that I can distinguish a dream world, or a world of hallucinations, from the real world shows that I already have "distinguished" between those worlds prior to any reflection upon them; I already "know" that, when I am dreaming or have hallucinations, I am not dealing with the *real* world facing my subjectivity as *Cogito*.[90]

Thus it follows that there is no "critical problem" in the sense in which it has been traditionally formulated.[91] The elimination of this problem should not be a reason to reject phenomenology. For, if there exists a critical problem—and there is one indeed, though not in the traditional sense—the terms in which it is formulated will have to be borrowed from the *Cogito*, as this *Cogito* is in reality.[92] The scandal of philosophy is not that it has never been able to offer a valid proof for the existence of the "external world," but rather that such proofs are still expected and attempted.[93]

Shall we have to say, then, that the reality of earthly things and of the world is perhaps the crude, inhuman reality defended by the realism of the British empiricists under the leadership of Locke and Hume and by many Thomists? Is the real world a world in itself *(monde-en-soi),* a collection of things in themselves *(Dinge-an-sich),* a world totally divorced from man? Let us try to realize what that means. According to realism, the subject and the world appear as totally separate, isolated and divorced from each other, as shut up and foreign to each other. As a consequence, knowledge is conceived as a representation or mirroring of crude reality in the looking glass

---

[90]Merleau-Ponty, *op. cit.,* p. XVI.
[91]Heidegger, *op. cit.,* p. 61; English ed., p. 88.
[92]"What court of appeal is to decide whether and in what sense there is to be a problem of knowledge other than that of the phenomenon of knowing itself and the mode of being proper to the knower?" Heidegger, *op. cit.,* p. 61; English ed., p. 88.
[93]Heidegger, *op. cit.,* p. 205; English ed., p. 249.

of a passive *Cogito*. The meanings of the world which, after all, manifest themselves only in existence as encounter with the world are cut loose from that encounter and viewed as "in themselves."[94] Thus knowledge is no longer conceived as an encounter, as an immediate presence of the subject as *Cogito* to the present reality, but as a mirrored reflection of that which is "in itself"; and the *Cogito* is described as concerned with its own immanent contents or mirrored images.[95]

Hume was thus led to defend complete skepticism. For, in that interpretation of the world's reality, the world appears as divorced from the subject as *Cogito,* as divorced from the *Cogito* as "affirmation" and as "knowledge"; hence it appears as neither affirmed nor known. Also truth, as the agreement of knowledge with reality, becomes a mere figment of the mind, for in that interpretation reality would mean "not known reality," and truth would be the agreement of the known reality with the not known reality. But how would anyone be able to make such a comparison? Yet this comparison is necessary to determine if there is *agreement* between the two.

The "in itself" of representative realism is the "real" as existing outside the *Cogito,* as that which is foreign to the *Cogito.* "It is evident that such an 'in itself' becomes nonsense as soon as it is affirmed. It is outside of thought in the strictest sense and as such is indeed unthinkable. It is reality 'as it is when I do not know it,' and with Kant we must say that this reality is by definition unknowable."[96]

Phenomenological Realism

When phenomenology defends the *reality* of the world, it rejects, on the one hand, the view that the world is a content of the *Cogito* and, on the other, the view that the world is a world in itself in the sense given to that term by representative realism.[97] But the re-

---

94"The return to perceptual experience, in so far it is a consequential and radical reform, puts out of court all forms of realism, that is to say, all philosophies which leave consciousness and take as their datum one of its results." Merleau-Ponty, *op. cit.,* p. 47.

95Merleau-Ponty, *La structure du comportement,* Paris, 4th ed., 1960, p. 205.

96D. M. De Petter, "Een geamendeerde phaenomenologie," *Tijdschrift voor Philosophie,* vol. XXII (1960), p. 291.

97"The thing is inseparable from a person perceiving it, and can never be actually *in itself* because its articulations are those of our very existence, and because it stands at the other end of our gaze or at the terminus of a sensory exploration which invests it with humanity." Merleau-Ponty, *op. cit.,* p. 320.

jection of representative realism does not mean that phenomenology denies *every* form of realism. The choice does not lie between either idealism or representative realism as the only possibilities, for there is also phenomenological realism in which the reality of the world is conceived as the *appearing* reality for the subject as *Cogito,* as "phenomenon." "Phenomenon" here does not mean "appearance,"[98] as that behind which the reality "in itself" is hidden, but it means "that which shows itself, the self-revealing, the manifest, in other words, the appearing-being-itself.[99] Phenomenologists used the term in-itself-for-us or "being-for-us" to distinguish that "in itself" from the "in itself" of representative realism,[100] and to express the automony of being which the worldly meaning has in reference to the subject.

Phenomenology conceives knowledge as the *encounter* of the subject as *Cogito* with the worldly meaning. The meaning is the appearing being itself, which manifests itself through the re-vealing activity of the subject.[101] The meaning is the unconcealed, which in the act of knowing as encounter imposes itself upon the subject.[102] It is *the real* itself.

Representative realism, on the contrary, *first* accepts all meanings of the world that impose themselves in knowledge as encounter and then makes them "real," that is, places them ouside the encounter,[103] It considers them as "given" before and outside the encounter, as beings in themselves, and then reconstructs knowledge by means of those "data." Hence representative realism considers itself capable of going outside the encounter which knowledge itself is, for it affirms as beings the things in themselves, that is, as outside the encounter. But this is a contradiction, for what is a real affirmation if not an encounter?

It should be evident now why phenomenology conceives the *real* world as radically *human.* For the world, in its proper autonomy of

---

[98]Heidegger, *op. cit.,* p. 222; English ed., p. 265.
[99]Heidegger, *op. cit.,* p. 28; English ed., p. 51.
[100]Merleau-Ponty, *op. cit.,* p. IX.
[101]Heidegger, *op. cit.,* p. 219; English ed., p. 262.
[102]"Asserting is a [mode of] being toward the thing itself that is. And what does the perception of it show? Nothing else than that it [the thing] is the being itself which was intended by the assertion.... The being itself intended [by the assertion] shows itself just as it is in itself, i.e., [it shows] that it, in its selfsameness, is just as it is pointed out, disclosed, as being in the assertion." Heidegger, *op. cit.,* p. 218; English ed., p. 261.
[103]"For the first time the philosopher's thinking is sufficiently conscious not to anticipate itself and endow its own results with reified form in the world." Merleau-Ponty, *op. cit.,* p. XX.

being in reference to the subject, is a *term of encounter,* and as such, is inseparable from the subject. The being of the world is a being for man, a being for us.[104] When phenomenology rejects the term "in itself," it is *only* for the purposes of discarding a being that is *not* a term of encounter. The emphasis on "for us," therefore, puts the accent on the meaning as a term of encounter.[105] Phenomenology, by affirming the radical "humanness" of the world, passes beyond the choice between either representative realism or idealism.[106]   To be man is to dwell in the human world, to vibrate with its meaning, and this meaning is inseparable from human subjectivity.[107]

The Subject as "Speaking Word"

From all this it follows clearly that we must affirm that there is no world without man. Heidegger has said so explicitly.[108]   When he said that, he was not giving evidence of mental decrepitude; he was merely drawing the last conclusions from the idea of intentionality. And, in fact, there is no world without man, for what can be meant by such a "world"? Is it the world in itself of representational realism? But then it means by definition the not-known, the not-affirmed world.[109] But whoever says that the world is *affirms* this world. He thus affirms a world that by definition is a not-affirmed world—which is nonsense. Or does "world" mean the world for us of phenomenological realism, that is, the human world? If so, it is evident that this human world is not without man. Since "to be" means nothing else except "to be for man," the assertion, that without man there is no world, merely states that without man there is no world for man.

Affirmation and "to Be." It is crucial, of course, to keep in mind that the term "to be," has no meaning except when the one who uses the term really wishes to *affirm* something. He who says that

---

[104]Merleau-Ponty, *Sens et non-sens,* p. 187.

[105]"The phenomenological world is not the bringing to explicit expression of a pre-existing being, but the laying down of being. Philosophy is not the reflection of a pre-existing truth, but, like art, the act of bringing truth into being." Merleau-Ponty, *Phenomenology of Perception,* p. XX.

[106]Merleau-Ponty, *op. cit.,* p. 430.

[107]"The world is inseparable from the subject,... And the subject is inseparable from the world, but from a world which it projects itself." Merleau-Ponty, *op. cit.,* p. 430.

[108]"If no *Dasein* exists, no world is 'there' either." Heidegger, *op. cit.,* p. 365; English ed., p. 417.

[109]De Petter, *art. cit.,* p. 291.

something *is* and at the same refuses to *affirm* the being of that about which he says that it is *says* nothing. The term "to be" is, therefore, used as "speaking word,"[110] as word expressing reality. Of course, the term can also be used as "spoken word."[111]   The spoken word is the congealed, sedimented speech, the speaking that can be severed from the speaking word, a speaking that does not *really* say anything because it does not express any *reality;* it is then nothing more than the manipulation of words as so many empty shells. When Husserl called for a "return to things themselves" he meant at the same time a return to the "speaking word," to the living affirmation of reality which the existent subject as *Cogito* himself is, and which is taken up in every explicit statement.[112] Only he who uses the term "to be" as "speaking word" *really* says something; he expresses *reality*. But he who affirms that to be cannot bypass the affirmation as an encounter with what he affirms to be. The affirmation *itself* is an encounter with a human world, with a being for man. In this sense the term "to be" never means anything else but "to be for man." It is therefore necessary to say that without man there is no world (for man). By saying this, phenomenology does not go one step further than its criticism of representational realism. For there are two approaches leading to the rejection of what by definition is the non-affirmed world of representational realism. One shows that there is nothing that can be thought of as intelligible if one constructs a non-affirmed *world*. The other shows that if one thinks away the *affirmation* there is nothing left that can still be understood.

Objections. There are many who do not understand the meaning of the "speaking word." For this reason the phenomenologist is often forced to defend himself against the most inane objections when he claims that without man there is no world. Generally opponents of phenomenology concede that it is not possible to speak about a world in itself and that this world cannot be affirmed, "but," the

---

[110]Merleau-Ponty, *Signes,* Paris, 1961, pp. 111-115.

[111]Merleau-Ponty, *Phenomenology of Perception*, p. 229.

[112]"Speech can be either an original and authentic speaking in which what is signified by it is itself present or a non-original speaking in which what is signified is present only as an empty shell, i.e., the signified itself is not visible there before our eyes. To examine experience with respect to its originality, therefore, means in the first instance to take the meanings of expressions of language, to take that which they are designed to convey, and to inquire from that standpoint about the experiences which have given these expressions their meaning." Cf. Ludwig Landgrebe, *Philosophie der Gegenwart,* Bonn, 1952, p. 33.

objectors add, "after all that world *is!*" And, in proof of this assertion, they refer to the world that existed before Adam, to Laplace's
primitive nebula, geological strata that are much older than man,
heavenly bodies that have not yet been discovered by man, the world
that existed before I was born and which will continue to exist after
my death. Are these not worlds without man, worlds having a meaning in themselves? *Are* they not without man?

Almost despairing of being understood, the phenomenologist replies with the question: "Do you think you have affirmed all those
worlds outside your own affirmation?" An affirmative reply, of
course, cannot be maintained. He who *really* says that all those
worlds *are,* that is, he who uses the term "to be" also for those
worlds as a "speaking word," presupposes his own subjectivity as
"speaking word"; and the worlds which he thus affirms solidly
cling as human worlds to his affirmation. They are not "in themselves" but "in themselves for us."

Then the final objection is couched in these terms: "So, all phenomenology claims is that no one can speak about anything except
by speaking about it? But this is surely a most trivial statement and,
if that is all that phenomenology means, it surely has nothing special
to offer."

Such objections and remarks are made by people who seem to
forget that representational realism has existed, that it has permeated
English empiricism completely, that nearly all Thomists have defended and still continue to defend that interpretation of realism.
The objectors seem to forget that all the sciences, until recently,
shamelessly presupposed that kind of realism and they argue as if
everybody has accepted phenomenology! If that were true, it would
be foolish, of course, for the phenomenologist to defend phenomenology with such ardor! Phenomenology is indeed nothing special,
but let us not forget that even the most common things are sometimes talked out of existence by philosophers.

4. Existential Phenomenology and Atheism

The reader may ask himself what relation there is between the
philosophy we have explained above and atheism. Yet there are
critics who connect the two. They think that the above-mentioned
ideas go too far and even believe that these ideas make it in principle impossible to affirm God. Hence existential phenomenology,
they claim, is *per se* atheistic, despite the theism of its defenders. It

often happens, and it is not even surprising, that philosophers fail to suspect to what their thoughts lead if they are developed to their ultimate conclusions. In the case of existential phenomenology, these critics argue, it means that this philosophy is *ultimately* atheistic, in the sense that the affirmation of God is no longer *possible*. Hence this proclaimed "philosophy of openness" contains a dangerous "closedness," by which the faith in God is undermined in its very roots. Because interest in existential phenomenology is rapidly gaining ground in the English-speaking world it will not be superfluous to examine this critique somewhat more closely. In this way we may forestall the rise of the same controversy among the readers of this book.

A Typical "Realistic" Critique

The typical "realistic" critique argues in the following way: "The roads that can lead us to the affirmation of God are open for us exclusively in the world in which we ourselves are with our fellowmen. And whether or not those roads will be open for us depends entirely on the meaning which man himself gives to the world, on whether man sees the world as an authentic reality, which then can point to God, or as a world for and of man, which then can point only to man."[113] But in existential phenomenology the world is not seen as *authentic* reality. Therefore, . . .

Everything in that argument depends, of course, on what is meant by "authentic reality" and the conditions that have to be met if one is to be permitted to speak about it. Authentic reality, the critique argues, is not the "in itself," the reality of representational realism which by definition is non-affirmed. "It is evident that such an 'in itself' becomes nonsense as soon as it is affirmed by consciousness."[114] Authentic reality, nevertheless, is an "in itself" although not in the sense of representational realism. It is "reality itself in its own autonomy of being in reference to our subjectivity."[115]

It is somewhat surprising to read those words, for they express precisely the view of phenomenology. The latter discards the "in itself" of representational realism, but also refuses to reduce meaning to the content of the subject as *Cogito*. Meaning, authentic reality, is

[113]De Petter, *art. cit.,* pp. 303-304.
[114]*Art. cit.,* p. 291.
[115]*Art. cit.,* p. 302.

therefore an "in itself" in a certain sense; it is automony of being. In order to emphasize the difference between phenomenology and idealism, phenomenology retains the term "in itself" of traditional realism. But, on the other hand, in order to exclude "representationism" and in order to indicate that there is question of autonomy of being in reference to *the subject,* phenomenology uses the term "in itself for us" to express authentic reality. Where our critics speak of "in reference to our subjectivity," phenomenology speaks of "for us." There is therefore no real difference between the two expressions.

Nevertheless, our opponents accuse phenomenology of not recognizing the "authentic reality" of the world. They accept the phenomenologist's criticism of representational realism, but believe that phenomenology makes an improper use of it by surreptitiously going further and attacking the world's autonomy of being. "The intention," they say, "is evident: the phenomenologist is not satisfied with asserting that the world without man cannot be *affirmed;* he adds that the world without man *is* not, not merely that it is not for man, but that it *is not,* without any qualifications."[116]

We have explained above how such expressions must be understood, and we have shown that, in using those expressions, phenomenology does *not* go *one step beyond* its critique of representational realism. In order to realize this, it is absolutely necessary to grasp the distinction between the "spoken word" and the "speaking word." But our critics do not seem to have noticed phenomenology's use of that distinction. The expression "back to the things themselves" is identical with the return to the "speaking word"; the expression "back" to authentic reality "in reference to the subject" is identical with "back" to the authentic subject as the living affirmation of the autonomy of being in relation to the subject, that is, as "in itself for us," as being for man. The term "to be" means nothing when the subject does not affirm anything. And when the subject really affirms, he does not affirm anything *separately* from that affirmation, he does not affirm anything outside the affirmation as encounter; hence he always affirms "being for man." This shows that it is pointless to accuse phenomenology of not being satisfied with asserting that without man there is no world for man and for wanting to go beyond that and claim unqualifiedly that without man there *is* no world. For both expressions signify *exactly the same.*

---

[116]*Art. cit.,* p. 292.

As we have said, those who claim that existential phenomenology is *per se* atheistic do not seem to grasp the distinction made by phenomenology between the "speaking word" and the "spoken word." Moreover, they accuse phenomenology of stealthily going beyond what is justified by its critique of representational realism. These two facts give us good reason for suspecting that, despite their explicit and repeated identification of authentic reality with autonomy of being in reference to *the subject,* they have something else in mind when they speak of authentic reality. As we already remarked above, the criticism of representational realism can be made in two ways. One can show that nothing intelligible can be thought of in the attempt to construct a non-affirmed *world,* or one can show that nothing intelligible remains when the *affirmation* is thought away. Our opponents agree with phenomenology when it follows the first way. But when it makes use of the second way *also,* they think that the world's autonomy of being in reference to the subject is placed in jeopardy. Yet the second way simply makes explicit that which is contained in the words "in reference to the subject." For this reason we suspect that their criticism fails to assign due weight to the words "in reference to the subject," and that therefore we have here a return to representational realism. In that case the "objectivity" of the world's autonomy of being in reference to the subject would not be sufficiently objective according to their thinking. Let us examine this suspicion.

The Return to Representational Realism

Undifferentiated Examples. Our critics observe that phenomenology in speaking about the world for man usually gives examples borrowed from the cultural world, whereas its statement that the world is radically human applies also to the world of nature. They admit that the cultural world evidently clings to man.[117] The same is true of the various "relational meanings" that cling to the subject's various points of view.[118] "For that viewpoint is not defined solely by the place from which I look at things from this or that side. It is defined and specified by everything in my world that constitutes my standpoint regarding things and men, for example, the fact that I was born at a definite time, in a particular country, in a community that has a particular degree of culture; the fact that I

117*Art. cit.,* p. 290.
118*Art. cit.,* p. 289.

am healthy or not healthy in body, that I have a particular character, particular abilities; the fact that I have had or not had the opportunity to study, that I exercise a certain function in the community and have a particular job; the fact that I have made some particular irreversible decisions in life, and so on. Hence, to a certain extent one can truthfully say that there are as many worlds as there are possible attitudes, as many worlds or at least as many views of the world."[119] In other words, the critics agree with phenomenology in admitting that man is included in those worlds; but the question is: "How precisely must we understand that inclusion of man in his world? How exactly must we conceive the existential character itself of human consciousness?"[120]

The reproach addressed to phenomenology is that it neglects properly to differentiate the illustrative value of the examples it uses in its argumentation.[121] Both "being for man" and the existential character of man have to be presented with greater care. In other words, *the manner in which man is included in his world* has to be clarified. The phenomenologist answers that man is *always* included in his world and phenomenology is not as careless in appending the necessary nuances as is implied by its critics.

The Correlation Man—World. When the critics then introduce the desired "nuances," they refuse to admit that being man is totally encompassed by the correlation man—world. For, man's consciousness contains an unmistakable transcending of that correlation. "Our knowledge of reality is always limited by the particular standpoint that is ours in the world, but from this standpoint we know reality itself in its own independence of being in reference to our subjectivity."[122]

The phenomenologist is agreeably surprised to note this statement, for it coincides with his own view. If the recognition of the world's own independence of being with respect to the subject is the meaning of the expression "transcending the correlation subject—world," phenomenology is quite willing to admit there is a moment in consciousness when the correlation subject—world is transcended. Our critics consider it wholly excluded that "a consciousness that is locked up in the correlation man—world can be a consciousness of

---

[119]*Ibid.*
[120]*Art. cit.,* p. 290.
[121]*Art. cit.,* p. 295.
[122]*Art. cit.,* p. 302 .

reality in the authentic sense of the word."[123] The phenomenologist however, answers: the recognition of the world's autonomy of being in reference to the subject suffices, so it is said, to justify the claims that the correlation man—world is transcended and that one defends a consciousness of reality in the authentic sense of the word; but in that case phenomenology also transcends the correlation man—world and defends a consciousness of reality in the authentic sense of the term, for phenomenology recognizes the world's autonomy in reference to the subject.

Nevertheless, phenomenology dislikes the expression *"transcending the correlation man—world."* For even when one recognizes the world's autonomy of existence in reference to the subject, one cannot avoid affirming anew the correlation "autonomous world—subject" because he speaks of *autonomy of being* in reference to the *subject.* The so-called "transcending of the correlation man—world" can at most signify that there are different correlations in different cases. But this does not mean that the correlation is ever *really* "transcended."

World for Man and World Without Man. This, however, our critics refuse to accept. According to them, one who defends a consciousness that remains locked up in the correlation man—world, does not accept any consciousness of reality in the authentic sense of the terms, but buries the world's autonomy of being under verbiage. Here again the phenomenologist suspects that the terms "authentic reality" and "autonomy of being" have a very special meaning for his opponents, and he suspects also that they unwittingly discard the qualification "in reference to the *subject.*" Perhaps, then, they still are in favor of representational realism.

Our suspicion grows stronger when they go into details in their efforts to introduce the necessary nuances and analyze our example[124] regarding the meanings of water. They say: "True, water has constantly new meanings *in its relations* to the swimmer, the fireman, the fisherman and so on. But in all those meanings, *water itself* has for our original experience a proper and unique meaning, namely, that of being simply water. And this one, and let us say, absolute meaning is for our original experience just as definite as the various relational meanings."[125]

---

[123]*Art. cit.*, p. 304.
[124]Cf. *Existential Phenomenology*, p. 32.
[125]*Art. cit.*, p. 296; his italics.

They are mistaken if they think that phenomenology does not recognize that "one" meaning of water. But this is not the question that concerns us. Our question is whether or not that "one" meaning is a "relational meaning." The phenomenologist answers without hesitation in the affirmative, although the "one" meaning stands in a different relation to the subject from those meanings which they call "relational." But for our critics that "one" meaning stands as an "absolute" in contrast to the meanings which they call "relational meanings." We are almost forced to conclude that for them that "one" meaning is *not* a "relational meaning." Thus they come dangerously close to accepting the "in itself" of representational realism. Or must we say that they have already accepted it?

The following quotation will not leave any doubt about the affirmative reply to this question: "If it is granted . . . that man is totally involved in the world, it follows indeed that man is unable to say anything about the world in such a way that he himself does not enter into the picture, it follows that the world is really human *for man,*[126] and that *for man* there is no world without man. But all this says nothing about the being of the world itself."[127]

Here, then, their mind stands clearly revealed: the world *for man* stands in evident opposition to the world *itself*. We are told: When it has been established that there is no world for man without man, nothing has yet been said about the world *itself,* that is, in *contrast* to the world for man, about the world without man. The implication is that it is still possible to say something about that world without man, that is, about the world that is by definition not known and not affirmed. Now this is exactly what representional realism wants: the consciousness of the representationist is the "authentic consciousness of reality" and the representational world is the world of "autonomous being." The qualification "in reference to the subject" evidently is no longer important.

Skeptical Consequences. The same situation was the immediate occasion which led Hume to skepticism. Do our critics go in the same direction? One may judge this question from what they say next: "Of course, regarding this being of the world. . . ." We interrupt the quotation on purpose to point out that there is question here of being, that is, they say that the world *is,* in other words, that it is *affirmed*. To resume the quotation, "Of course,

[126]His italics.
[127]*Art. cit.,* p. 295.

regarding this being of the world itself, we cannot then affirm anything, but for the same reason neither can we deny it."[128] Let us try to explain what this means. There is question here about the being of the world, that is, it said that the world *is;* hence the world is *affirmed.* Next, we are told that that world cannot be affirmed nor denied. Was Hume therefore wrong when he became a skeptic? And are our critics also skeptics? It would be foolish to maintain that, but we may ask: What then is the meaning of the above-quoted statements? When those critics on their own analyze consciousness in the world, they are clearly phenomenologists, for they admit that the dialogue between the subject and the world "takes up the whole man, with his being, his thought, his feeling, his moral conduct and activity."[129] But when they undertake to criticize phenomenology, they consider the objectivity of phenomenology no longer sufficiently objective. Phenomenological realism for them is neither sufficiently objective nor sufficiently real. And when one investigates what kind of realism satisfies their requirement, he finds that it is objectivistic, representational realism.

Existential Phenomenology is Not an Atheism

There is no need to add much about the so-called atheism of phenomenology. The accusation is based on the alleged phenomenological rejection of the world's "authentic reality." The "authentic reality" of which the accusation speaks reveals itself to be identical with the "in itself" of representational realism. Thus, the accusation collapses, for the accusers themselves also view representational realism as philosophically untenable. Its collapse implies, of course, also the collapse of the assertion that the perspective of phenomenology does not permit us to ask the question whether there is a Creator-God.

According to our accusers, such a question is meaningless in phenomenology since phenomenology declares that man himself is the foundation of beings. They add that in consequence phenomenology attributes a creative value to the subject himself,[130] for all being

---

[128]*Ibid.*

[129]D. De Petter, *Metaphysiek en phenomenologie, schets voor de besprekingen op de vergadering van de Vereniging voor Thomistische Wijsbegeerte van 20 november 1960,* p. 6.

[130]"Now this independence of being, as such, in reference to consciousness, is also a necessary presupposition of the proof of God's existence, for the affirmation of God would somehow become superfluous if consciousness itself could be the foundation of being." De Petter, "Le caractère métaphysique de la preuve de l'existence, de Dieu et la pensée contemporaine," *L'existence de Dieu,* Cahiers de l'actualité religieuse, 1961, p. 174.

is being for man. But phenomenology does not mean that at all. The expression "being for man" is used solely to reject representational realism. However, those who think that existential phenomenology is *per se* atheistic appear unable to see this and therefore think that the human subject creates meaning as being for man. Now there is not a single phenomenologist who maintains that. One could point to Sartre as an exception, but this reference is worthless, for precisely in this point Sartre is not a phenomenologist.

If that is the situation, should not the accusation of atheism be withdrawn? Otherwise we give to atheists the impression that, to be a theist and find a way to God in the world, one has first to consider himself capable of affirming a non-affirmed world, or of affirming something outside the affirmation.

In regard to the affirmation of God, phenomenology, with due changes, holds exactly the same theses as with respect to the world. Without man there is for the phenomenologist no God for man; God is a God for man.[131] Here again "to be" means nothing else but "to be for man," for here also man cannot affirm anything outside his affirmation.[132] God's Absolute, Transcendent Autonomy of Being and man's absolute dependence of being are recognized *within* human knowledge and not outside it. We said "with due changes," for the affirmation of God is essentially different from the affirmation of the world. However, this point does not concern us at present.

5. PHENOMENOLOGY AND RELIGIOUS PROJECTION

For reasons that will appear later, it might be well to say a word here about Sierksma's ideas concerning religious projection.[133] They are directly connected with phenomenology because of the way

---

[131]"A God who has nothing to do with existing men is by definition a non-God." E. Schillebeeckx, "De betekenis van het niet-godsdienstige humanisme voor het hedendaagse katholicisme," *Modern niet-godsdienstig humanisme,* Nijmegen, 1961, p. 75.

[132]"We will say that it is absolutely certain that one must not look for any other kind of being than being-for me. This follows from the fact that no other kind of being is possible. A being or a kind of being which would not be for-me would by definition be radically outside of, and foreign to any apprehension and any knowledge. From this viewpoint God, if He is, is of necessity for-me; He somehow enters the field of my experience and on this basis, He of necessity assumes its form." R. Jolivet, "Le problème de l'absolu dans la philosophie de M. Merleau-Ponty," *Tijdschrift voor Philosophie,* vol. XIX (1957), p. 59.

[133]F. Sierksma, *De religieuze projectie,* Delft, 2nd ed., 1957. Similar ideas are said to be expressed in Bertrand Russell's work, *Why I am Not a Christian.* Tr.

Sierksma conceives projection in general and religious projection in particular. He expresses his concepts within an evidently philosophical context.

The opinion that religion is merely a projection is very old. The arguments that are invoked to prove it are mostly of a *purely* psychological nature; this makes it impossible for the philosopher to discuss them with the psychologist. For the psychologist who maintains that religion *as such* is a projection, starts from the assumption that God does not exist and then begins to search for an explanation of the fact that there are still so many people who believe in God. And psychology can, he says, give such an explanation.

The philosopher, however, begins by asking whether God exists. He knows that he has no right to start with an unexamined conviction that there is no God. And he knows also that no psychologist has such a right. The philosopher is highly interested in everything the psychologist tells him about religious projection, but he never feels fully convinced when he is told that religion *as such* is nothing but a projection. For the one crucial question remains unanswered, and the philosopher asks himself what remains of everything that the psychologist has told him, *if God is an objectively existing reality*. For, through psychology, one can never prove that there is no God, and if any kind of psychology makes the opposite claim or simply asserts that there is no God, it reveals itself thereby as a philosophy, be it a bad one. It is not possible to reject the objective reality of God's existence without philosophy. What is noteworthy in Sierksma's approach is the fact that he tries to conceive his doctrine of projection within the frame of a theory about objectivity in general, which, according to Sierksma, presupposes a certain anthropology. That is why he is unable to avoid phenomenology; and this is the reason for our discussion of Sierksma's ideas in this chapter. On the other hand, it would be unwise wholly to neglect the views of those for whom religion, as such, is a projection, and who use only psychological proofs to defend their doctrine. That is why we want to start with a few words about Freud, for the latter's approach is the classical example of a psychologistic philosophy of religion.

A. *The Projection Theory of Freud*

According to Freud, his criticism of religion is new only insofar as he provides a psychological foundation for the ancient views of religion as projection.[134] And, as was to be expected, he borrows his arguments from the principles of psychoanalysis.

For Freud, religion is merely a psychical scheme by which man defends himself against the overpowering forces of nature. The first step consists in humanizing nature. The impersonal forces of nature in whose presence man feels powerless are then human beings of an extraordinary form. Those forces thereby lose some of their fearfulness, for man can use the very means he exploits in society, namely, he can try to plead with them, pacify and bribe them.[135] This is nothing new for man, for when he was a child he was in exactly the same situation with respect to his father. He feared his father, and yet he expected protection from him. In the same way man attributes a fatherly character to the forces of nature and makes gods of them. His attitude toward the gods is characterized by the same ambivalence as that toward his father.[136]

In the next stage of culture man discovers nature's own laws, and in this way nature loses its human characteristics. But man continues to feel powerless. The gods now have the function of making up for the defects and disadvantages of man's culture; they must lighten the burden of suffering and watch over the moral prescriptions which are imposed by the culture. In this way man's need and helplessness result in all sorts of religious representations. These are finally united in one God. The father image, which lies hidden in every image of a god, is then made explicit and put in the foreground, so that man's childlike attitude toward God can attain its full development.[137]

Totemism and the Father Image. Is it possible to delve deeper into the father image that lies hidden behind every image of a god? According to Freud, this can be done by a study of totemism. For totemism was the first form of religion, and the other religions have developed from it.[138] In totemism the totemistic meal plays a very important role. On solemn occasions the totem animal is killed in a

---

[134]Freud, *Die Zukunft einer Illusion, Gesammelte Werke chronologisch geordnet,* Imago Publishing Co., London, Band XIV, p. 358; English ed., *The Future of an Illusion,* tr. by W. D. Robson-Scott, London (Hogarth Press), 1949, p. 62.
[135]Freud, *op. cit.,* pp. 337 f.; English tr., pp. 28 ff.
[136]Freud, *op. cit.,* pp. 338 f.; English tr., pp. 29 f.
[137]Freud, *op. cit.,* pp. 339-342; English tr., pp. 30 f.
[138]Freud, *Totem und Tabu, Gesammelte Werke,* Band IX, p. 177; English tr. in *The Basic Writings* of *Sigmund Freud,* tr. by Dr. A. A. Brill, New York (The Modern Library), 1938, p. 920.

cruel fashion by all the members of the tribe acting together. They tear it to pieces and devour them raw. The tribesmen have an idea that they are doing something that no individual person would be allowed to do, but that is justified when done by all together. After the deed, tears are shed and the animal is mourned. Apparently those who have participated in the act try to get rid of responsibility for it. The mourning is followed by wild festivities.[139]

But what is the meaning of the killing of the totem animal, and the subsequent mourning and joy? According to Freud, the totem animal takes the place of the father. Since the feelings toward the father are always ambivalent, consisting, namely, of love and hatred, it is easy to understand that the death of the father symbol brings with it mourning as well as joy.[140] If one joins the data of psychoanalysis with the Darwinian hypothesis of the primitive horde, two distinct series of phenomena form an unsuspected unity.

The Primitive Hordes and Taboos. In the hypotheses of the primitive horde, a violent, jealous father kept all females for himself, oppressed and cast out his adolescent sons. But on a certain day the brothers came together, killed the father, and devoured him. Together they dared to execute a deed which each of them separately would have liked to perform but was unable to do. In the act of eating their father they identified themselves with him and appropriated his power. The totem meal is the repetition of that criminal scene and signals the beginning of social organizations, moral restrictions and religion.[141] This is explained as follows.

The brothers hate their father because he prevents them from fulfilling their sexual cravings and yet they also love him. Their hatred dies after they have murdered him, but their tender feelings have been violated. That is why they show contrition and atone for the murder by forbidding the killing of the totem animal, which is the symbol of the father, by renouncing relations with the women who are now free, by proclaiming the prohibition against incest and imposing the law of exogamy on themselves.

In this way were born the two fundamental taboos of totemism, corresponding to the components of the Oedipus-

---

[139]Freud, *op. cit.,* pp. 169 f.; English tr., pp. 914 f.

[140]Freud, *op. cit.,* pp. 170 f.; English tr., p. 915.

[141]"The totem feast, which is perhaps mankind's first celebration, would be a repetition and commemoration of this memorable, criminal act with which so many things began, social organization, moral restriction and religion." Freud, *Totem und Tabu, op. cit.,* p. 172; English tr., p. 916.

complex, with which morality began.   Moreover, the prohibition of incest was necessary also because the brothers became competitors for women after they had eliminated their all-powerful father. It was only by such a prohibition that their social organization could be saved.

The other taboo clearly shows the tendency toward a religion. The prohibition against killing the totem animal is, as it were, a contract with the father by which the sons oblige themselves to spare his life, and the father binds himself to protect and safeguard his sons. These, according to Freud, are henceforth characteristic of all religions. All religions are attempts to solve the problem of guilt arising from the murder of the arch-father.[142]   We can draw the provisional conclusion, according to Freud, that society is founded upon a common guilt resulting from a common crime; religion is based upon guilt-consciousness and contrition, and morality is based partly upon social necessity and partly upon the atonement demanded by the consciousness of guilt.[143]

Deification of the Father Image. The next stage in the development of religion, according to Freud, is as follows. The ancient totemistic meal reappears in the primitive sacrifice. But there is an entirely new element, namely the presence of the tribal god. Now according to psychoanalysis, God is merely a sublimated father-image. But in that case we have to admit that the father is twice present in the primitive sacrifice, namely, as God and as the totem sacrificial animal. How is that possible?[144]

According to Freud, the totem was the first father-surrogate, and God is a father-surrogate of later date. This addition was possible because the attitude toward the father underwent a fundamental change in the course of time. The murder of the arch-father must have created a most powerful desire for the father. But none of the brothers who had killed the father in a common crime found it possible to fulfill that desire, for there was none among them who could become equal to the father. As a result their bitterness against their father subsided, while their longing for him increased, giving birth to the father ideal. The father was raised to the dignity of God

---

[142]*Op. cit.*, pp. 173-176; English tr., pp. 916-919.

[143]"Society is now based on complicity in the common crime, religion on the sense of guilt and the consequent remorse, while morality is based partly on the necessities of society and partly on the expiation which this sense of guilt demands." *Op. cit.*, p. 176; English tr., p. 919.

[144]*Op. cit.*, pp. 177 f.; English tr., pp. 919 f.

and this divinization of the murdered father was a much more powerful means of reconciliation than the contract with the totem. At the same time it became possible for the fatherless society gradually to change into a patriarchal society. Here fathers reappeared, but their powers were limited, so that the distance between them and the arch-father was sufficiently great to insure the permanence of the unsatisfied longing for the father, in other words, for the preservation of religious cravings.[145]

We see, then, why the father is indeed twice present in the sacrifice and clearly note the ambivalent attitude toward the father. The father attains his highest triumph in the sacrifice in which the victory over the father is celebrated. On the other hand, the same sacrificial act in which the father is given reparation and satisfaction, serves to keep alive the memory of the original crime.[146]

Further Development of Religion. In a following stage the animal loses its sacredness, and the sacrifice its connection with the totemistic feast. The sacrifice now becomes exclusively an offering of gifts to the divinity. God Himself is now so high above men that He can be approached only through the intermediary of priests. The sons have now even greater facility to free themselves from their guilt-consciousness. The sacrifice lies beyond their own responsibility; God Himself has desired and instituted it. This means that we have here the ultimate renunciation of the original crime.[147] However, we should not imagine that the anti-father sentiments disappeared at the time when the authority of "the" father was on the increase. The yearly offering of a god seems to have been characteristic of the Semitic religions. And in most diverse places on earth men seem to have been sacrificed as representing the divinity. Thus it appears that the memory of the first great sacrifice could not be erased.[148]

But, according to Freud, we note an ever clearer striving of the son to put himself in the place of the father-god. What Christianity calls original sin is an offense against the father-god. Christ offers Himself to accomplish the reconciliation; hence the crime against the

---

[145]*Op. cit.*, pp. 178-180; English tr., pp. 920 f.
[146]"The meaning which sacrifice has quite generally acquired is found in the fact that in the very same action which continues the memory of this misdeed it offers satisfaction to the father for the ignominy put upon him." *Op. cit.*, pp. 180 f.; English tr., p. 921.
[147]*Op. cit.*, p. 181; English tr., p. 922.
[148]*Op. cit.*, pp. 181 f.; English tr., p. 923.

father was murder. But the son also achieves his ambition in respect to the father by means of the same act in which he offers himself. He becomes God in his turn in place of the father. As a sign of that exchange the ancient totem meal is revived as communion, in which the brothers no longer devour the father but eat the flesh and drink the blood of the son.[149]

Freud later described in even greater details the development of religion in the direction of Jewish monotheism and Christianity.[150] We shall not go into those details, for they are not necessary to understand Freud's ideas regarding the intrinsic value of religious concepts.

Religion as an Illusion. According to Freud religious ideas have no objective significance. We have merely to subject them to the same critical examination and evaluation as are used in other matters to see that religious ideas do not have any objective counterpart.[151]

Religious ideas, then, are mere illusions. They are the illusory fulfillment of "the oldest, strangest, and most insistent wishes of mankind."[152] Childlike helplessness arouses the need for protection, and this is given by the father. The persistence of this need throughout life creates the illusion of a father who is much more powerful—namely, God. According to Freud, an illusion is a belief that is based on a "wish-fulfillment." When a belief is in contradiction with reality, it becomes superstition. Freud considers religion to be wholly illusion and partly superstition.[153] He expresses his astonishment because mankind has been and continues to be so uncritical in the matter of religion. There is no department of life in which man is so naive as in the religious realm. There is no other way, he argues, to reach objectivity than that of science.[154]

Should the Illusion Be Unmasked? At this stage Freud asks himself whether it is permitted to unmask religion and to show that it is an illusion, for, after all, everything that is valuable in culture is founded on religion. Would the unmasking of religion not mean a

---

[149]*Op. cit.*, pp. 183, 185; English tr., pp. 924 f.
[150]Freud, *Der Mann Moses und die monotheistische Religion, Gesammelte Werke*, Band XVI, pp. 210-246.
[151]S. Freud, *Die Zukunft einer Illusion*, pp. 346-352; English tr., pp. 36 ff.
[152]Freud, *op. cit.*, p. 352; English tr., p. 52.
[153]Freud, *op. cit.*, pp. 352-354; English tr., pp. 52 ff.
[154]Freud, *op. cit.*, pp. 354-356; English tr., pp. 55 f.

return to chaos? Doesn't culture demand that we act toward religion at least "as if," for, after all, science has not taught us very much?[155]

Freud replies to the effect that others before him have said what he says, but without giving a psychological foundation to it; again, those who believe will not shed their beliefs because of what psychology might say; lastly, the preservation of religion in the long run is more harmful to culture than its unmasking.[156] For, though it is true that religion has made great contributions to culture, especially toward the control of unsocial passions, it has not done enough. It has not given happiness to the majority of men, it has not given them the consolation they desire or made them bearers of culture. They view culture and the control of the passions as a yoke and threaten to shed that yoke. As soon as men realize that religion is an illusion, chaos will follow. Yet that discovery is unavoidable, for the progress of the sciences will necessarily undermine the faith. But in that case culture and morality must be provided with a non-religious foundation; they will need to be anchored in reason and science. Only in that way can the predicted chaos be avoided.[157]

A culture's moral commands and prohibitions possess a special lustre so long as they are backed up by the absoluteness of religion. But when religion disappears, culture can be saved only by basing morality on reason. Moreover, the progress of culture will no longer be impeded when new and better adapted norms have been introduced. As long as religion sanctions morality, no progress is impossible. Hence to reject religion is to promote culture and morality.[158]

But, one may object how can Freud plead for a rational foundation of morality, if morality is based on the irrational foundation of totemism's taboos? Freud answers that the plea is possible. But, to understand this requires one to realize that, like the individual child, mankind as a whole passes through periods that resemble neuroses. Every child has its periods of neurosis, because the passions are so violent that they cannot be managed in a fully rational way and have to be repressed. However, those neuroses are overcome spontaneously in the course of development; if not, psychoanalysis is able to cure them through proper treatment. The same thing happens with mankind as a whole. So long as the passions cannot be handled rationally, they

---

[155]Freud, *op. cit.*, pp. 356-358; English tr., pp. 59 ff.
[156]Freud, *op. cit.*, pp. 358-360; English tr., pp. 62 ff.
[157]Freud, *op. cit.*, pp. 360-363; English tr., pp. 66 ff.
[158]Freud, *op. cit.*, pp. 363-365; English tr., pp. 70 ff.

have to be repressed. This causes the collective neurosis of religion. This idea is in harmony with the fact that devout believers are to a great extent properly protected against the dangers of neurosis. Having accepted the collective neurosis of religion, they are freed from the task of nourishing a personal neurosis. However, in the normal course of affairs mankind will spontaneously overcome the religious neurosis that was present in its early development. According to Freud, mankind is now in that period of transition.[159]

Freud's Scientism. No one will expect us to present here a critique of Freud's *psychology* of religion, for that task belongs to psychologists, not to philosophers. Philosophers, nevertheless, have the right to point to the weak spot in Freud's *philosophy* of religion. For Freud's theory is *also* a philosophy. Freud does not only discuss the purely psychological implications of the religious attitude; he also defines religion as such. No philosopher can object to Freud's remark that "the personal attitude of man toward God depends on his attitude toward his human father and that it changes and evolves accordingly."[160] This is a psychological fact, and the philosopher does not want to contradict it, just as he does not protest when the psychologist records any other fact that he has discovered. The philosopher is not dealing with such matters. But it is the philosopher's business to examine the statement that God "is nothing but a sublimated father-image,"[161] and that religion as such is nothing but a remnant of an Oedipus-complex that was not liquidated in time. When such assertions are added in one breath to the recording of a psychological fact, psychology degenerates at once into psychologism, which is a form of scientism. As such, it becomes subject to all the philosophical objections that can be made to every form of scientism. Scientism is a degeneration of one or other science. It is the rejection of philosophy but is at the same time itself a philosophy, though it does not even understand itself as a philosophy. Freud was evidently guilty of scientism in the form of psychologism. For him there is no other way to reality than that of "scientific work.[162] If religions speak of God as a Being about whom science is unable to say anything, they are, of course, beyond the reach of scientific cri-

---

[159]Freud, *op. cit.,* pp. 366 f., English tr., p. 75 f.

[160]Freud, *Totem und Tabu, Gesammelte Werke,* Bd. IX, p. 177; English tr. in *The Basic Writings of Sigmund Freud,* tr. by A. A. Brill, New York (The Modern Library), 1938, p. 919.

[161]Freud, *ibid.*

[162]Freud, *Die Zukunft einer Illusion,* p. 354; English tr., p. 55.

tique. But in that case, says Freud, no one will be any longer interested in God.[163] It is obvious that such remarks are not statements of psychology but of philosophy, a bad kind of philosophy.

When psychology degenerates into psychologism it must expect that it will have to defend itself against the weapons which it itself has fashioned. When one psychologist uses psychoanalysis to reduce religion to a component of the Oedipus-complex, it is to be expected that another psychologist will unmask his colleague's atheism by a similar psychoanalysis. Such a psychoanalysis of atheism is possible. It has been made by Zilboorg, who analyzed the anti-religious attitude of Freud and came to the conclusion that it was traceable to his pessimism, which is itself explained by the feeling of affective frustration that Freud suffered when he was about three years old.[164] The philosopher is ready to accept this statement of the psychologist, but he will add that it does not tell him anything about atheism as such and that it does not bring him one step closer to a philosophical reply to the question regarding the essence of religion and the problem of God's existence.

B. *The Projection Theory of Sierksma*

We have already mentioned that Sierksma's projection theory[165] has direct connections with existential phenomenology because it is based on a philosophy of objectivity. Sierksma is surprised because so many psychologists of religion seem to attach so little importance to the idea of "projection," and because those who show interest, "immediately start analyzing the problem of truth, in other words, they simply skip psychology."[166] Thus the job is left to the experimental psychologists, but they speak exclusively about projection in general and likewise neglect the religious projection. Sierksma wishes to discuss religious projection within a general frame—namely, the frame of the psychology of perception.[167]

The author mentions Xenophanes, Euripides, Feuerbach and Nietzsche who, without narrowing the idea of projection, revealed that they were aware of the human components of religious repre-

---

[163] Freud, *op. cit.*, p. 378; English tr., p. 94.
[164] J. Latil, "Athéisme et psychologie de la profondeur." *Lumière et vie*, vol. 13 (1954), p. 64. (Gregory Zilboorg, *Freud and Religion*, Westminster, 1958. Tr.)
[165] F. Sierksma, *De religieuze projectie*, Delft, 2nd ed., 1957.
[166] *Op. cit.*, p. 3.
[167] *Op. cit.*, pp. 6 f.

sentations. Their criticism has often, but incorrectly, been understood as negativism "According to those four thinkers, as well as others who are not named but for whom projection was and still is a problem, it is *the will to truth that leads to a separation between objective reality and subjective illusion.* This is an anthropological fact of primary importance. It is fundamental. *Man is the being who is able to distinguish, or at least thinks he can distinguish, between real and unreal, true and untrue, objective and subjective.*"[168]

After reading this profession of the fundamental possibility to distinguish the true from the false and reality from illusion, we ask ourselves whether the few psychologists of religion who pay attention to the problem of projection are, after all, not justified in "immediately starting to analyze the problem of truth." We would expect that Sierksma also would take the trouble to distinguish between the true and the false, reality and illusion, authentic religiousness and pseudo-religiousness. Does he not tell us that this is fundamental? Yet the author does not go into this question and we may ask ourselves what the reason might be. The answer can be found in Sierksma's approach, the general psychological frame in which he tries to grasp the religious projection, namely, his theory of perception. For the author defends a psychology of perception that becomes the source of endless confusion and makes it impossible, in principle, to distinguish between reality and illusion, not only in the realm of religion, but in every field of human existence.

Perception as Projection

In his attempt to discover the unity within the diversity of phenomena ordinarily designated by the term projection, Sierksma makes up a list, in which he mentions the following:

1. The seeing of images in the outside world which nonetheless are perceived as differing from the outside world (hallucinations).

2. Directing love or hatred to another than the one who is the original object of love or hate.

3. Attributing one's own characteristics, tendencies and structures to another; those who do ill, for instance, think ill.

4. The "coloring" of nature and of men according to one's own moods and feelings.

---

[168]*Op. cit.,* p. 3.

5. Concretizing in images psychic archetypes which are present in the unconscious only as potential structures but become concrete in the projection.

6. *Our normal perception, which—as is well known—does not give man the world "in itself".*[169]

Difficulties already begin at this stage. While it is well known that perception does not give the world in itself to man, it is, however, not so well known, or rather it is not known at all, that *on that account* it is necessary to call perception a form of projection. In fact we are given here the central thought of Sierksma's entire work together with what he believes to be the original light and general frame required for the understanding of projection in general. Projection is "the subjective change of the objective world,"[170] and perception is its archetype. "The unity in diversity of the projection phenomena consists in the fact that man knows that his own perceptions, as well as those of other living beings, create a world which does not always correspond with the world as it is apart from those perceptions."[171] Hence the "objective" world, which is changed by the projection, is the world "in itself," the "world apart from perception."

Man and Animal

Wishing to get a solid idea of the typical aspects proper to *human* projection, Sierksma begins by studying how projection works on the non-human level. For that purpose he describes the behavior of the animal in its *"Merkwelt"* (Plessner).[172] What is most important in that behavior is the undeniable fact that the animal with its limited, sensitive organization is encompassed by the *Merkwelt*, locked up in it, unable to place itself at a distance from it, and living wholly in the immediacy of its *Merkwelt*. It is precisely on this point that man differs from the beast. Man places himself at a distance from the world, so as to be able to see it according to its own merits and as it is in itself. Man objectifies the world in order to be able to cultivate it, through tools and words, through technology and lan-

---

[169]*Op. cit.,* p. 4-5. Our italics.
[170]*Op. cit.,* p. 7.
[171]*Ibid.*
[172]*Op. cit.,* pp. 8-21. The term "Merkwelt" indicates the sensory-behavioral environment as this environment occurs to the animal. Tr.

guage.[173] This standing at a distance, this splitting into subject and object (*Subject-Object-Spaltung*), can be expressed in one term: consciousness.

It is true that we cannot deny every form of consciousness to the animal, but its consciousness is different from that of man. For man's consciousness is self-consciousness. This means that man, as it were, places himself at a distance, not only from the world, but even from himself.[174] Man remains bound to his world but is not wholly encompassed by it. He is a being who stands in objectivity. That is why he is able to take up a critical position toward his world of perception. That is why he is able to "speak of projection, implying by it that he knows that the world is really different from the one given him in perception."[175] Finally, that is why he *can* also take back his projections. This is the paradox of the "projecting man" (*homo projiciens*), the paradox of the objectivating and subjectivating being, who lives by reality and by appearance.[176] A beast can only project, but man can take back his projection in favor of objectivity.

All this, says Sierksma, must not be understood as if man, on the one hand, has received the capacity for objective critique while, on the other hand, he retains unchanged his "animal" projective capacities. This not the case. For by the fact that man has the human capacity for being objectively critical of himself and the world, his projective behavior has been greatly modified, it has become different from that of the animal. For man is also a self-conscious being and therefore projects also the *contents of his self-consciousness*. An animal is not a self-conscious being and therefore is not able to project *itself*. Man not only projects his *sensible limitedness* but also *himself*.[177]

It seems to us that the thesis, presented by way of introduction, namely, that perception itself is the archetype of projection, has somewhat been lost in the background in Sierkma's explanation of the principles and the anthropological foundation underlying his projection theory. The thing which Sierksma has made us see clearly until now is that the attribute which characterizes man in contrast to the animal must be viewed as "standing in objectivity." The reader

---

[173]*Op. cit.,* pp. 21-22.
[174]*Op. cit.,* p. 22.
[175]*Op. cit.,* p. 26.
[176]*Ibid.*
[177]*Op. cit.,* pp. 26-29.

is inclined to interpret this standing in objectivity as a "seeing" (in its widest sense) of the "real," the "objective," in contrast to acts of phantasy, hallucinations, dreaming, and projecting what is not real and not objective. This "seeing" of what is objective could also be called "perceiving," but then perception is precisely *not* projection. For projection is "the subjective *changing* of the objective world."[178]

Standing in Objectivity as Projection

Yet Sierksma occasionally uses expressions which make the phenomenologist raise his eyebrows. He says "that the world is really different from the one that is given him in perception,"[179] and that man, in contrast to the beast, can stand critically facing his "world of perception." The question that arises at once is: How does man know that the world is different from the world given in perception? For, after all, he can know this only on the basis of . . . a perception! Without perception man knows nothing about the world, not even that the world is different from what subsequently appeared to be a *seeming* perception or a projection. Consequently, it is meaningless to require man to take a critical stand against his "world of perception," or that he should doubt the objectivity of what he *thinks* he sees and *thinks* he perceives, for it often happens that what he accepts as perception is in fact a hallucination, a product of the imagination, a dream, a projection, that is, *not* an actual perception at all.

We might think that we have here nothing but an unfortunate use of terms, were it not that Sierksma at once explains what in his view is not a projection. He tells us that in only one case man would not "project," namely, if he could be "absolutely objective," if he could "absolutize into unqualified objectivity" the distance at which he has placed himself from himself and from the world.[180] Precisely the fact that man is not capable of attaining "complete objectivity" makes him the projecting being he is. In other words, the "standing in objectivity" with respect to both himself and the world *is itself a projection*; because this objectivity is never "absolute objectivity," it can never be "unqualified objectivity." "The paradoxical structure of 'ec-centricity' implies that man has to project whether he likes it or not. Absolute objectivity would be tantamount to sawing off the branch on which he is sitting, to losing contact with his world."[181]

---

[178]*Op. cit.*, p. 7.
[179]*Op. cit.*, p. 26.
[180]*Op. cit.*, p. 29.
[181]*Op. cit.*, p. 110.

We see clearly that we meet here what the introduction made us expect: if we could perceive the world apart from perception, if we could attain the world in itself, if we could have contact with the world without having contact with it, if we could attain "absolute objectivity," that is, an objectivity that is not objective *for a subject*, then we could say that we do not project. But this is evidently impossible. Therefore, "standing in objectivity," objective "seeing," in its widest sense, is also a projection.

The confusion reaches its apex when we recall that, according to Sierksma, "the will to truth leads to a separation between objective reality and subjective illusion."[182] We are asked to understand the term "objective reality" as "objectivity without a subject." And for man, who is essentially a subject, this objectivity is unattainable. Yet that "objective reality" is opposed to "subjective illusion"; hence the impossibility of reaching absolute objectivity implies "standing in illusion." Therefore the "standing in objectivity"—which distinguishes man from the brute—is nothing else but "to project." The confusion here is extreme, especially because in such a situation "withdrawing the projection" also becomes meaningless. For "withdrawing projections" would mean to take a position-in-objectivity. But now even this taking of a position in objectivity is a projection for Sierksma, for man *necessarily* projects, because absolute objectivity is impossible: man would saw off the branch on which he is sitting and lose contact with his world if he did not project.[183]

Within the context of Sierksma's own theory it is no longer clear whether his theory is a projection or not. Sierksma analyzes man as a projecting being. Now, according to Sierksma's own ideas, it is never possible to attain man as a projecting being in himself, in his "absolute objectivity." Therefore Sierksma *projects*, and if he does not project, he is sawing off the branch upon which, speaking of projection, he is sitting. So we may ask: does Sierksma attain the "reality" or only the "illusion" of man as a projecting being?

The general framework within which Sierksma tries to grasp projection is seen to be particularly misleading. This is not surprising, for Sierksma ventures into a field that is not his own. His whole "psychological" discourse needs to be based on a philosophical theory of knowledge and a philosophical anthropology. Phenomenology could help supply this foundation, but Sierksma refuses that

---

[182]*Op. cit.*, p. 3.
[183]*Op. cit.*, p. 110.

help because he is full of rancor toward psychologists who seek their inspiration in Merleau-Ponty.

Objectivity and Objectivism

Yet Sierksma's view contains ideas that could serve as connecting links with phenomenology. In the chapter which compares man and animal, his ideas about man certainly are not very distant from the definition of man as existence, that is, as subject in the world. A more thorough development of this idea would have shown that it is absolutely meaningless to conceive the world as an "in itself," as a "reality" apart from man. The world clings to the subject, and it is on the basis of that clinging to the subject that we must seek the possibility to speak about "objectivity" and reality. Such a possibility, however, does exist. For by the very fact that man can distinguish between "seeing," "perceiving," and "experiencing," on the one hand, and "dreaming," "having hallucinations," and "projecting," on the other, he shows that, prior to any explicit distinction, he already knows that he is in a real, objective world when he "sees," and that he is in an unreal, non-objective world when he "projects." Man, of course, can *think* that he is seeing when, in reality, he is projecting things. Hence he must constantly ask himself whether or not he really *sees*. But he cannot ask himself whether or not what he *does see* is objective and real.[184]

In this way, it is no longer possible to conceive the real and objective as "in itself," as a reality which man can look at "apart from himself,"[185] for the "looking at," of which Sierksma speaks, is an involvement of the knowing subject in the world; hence the world can never be considered "apart from man." It follows that, when Sierksma speaks of objectivity, he understands the term in an objectivistic sense. When he contrasts man with the animal, he stresses man's standing in objectivity, *in virtue of which man can withdraw his projections.* But when Sierksma stipulates what is required for

---

[184]"We must not, therefore, wonder whether we really perceive a world, we *must* instead say: the world is what we perceive. In more general terms, we must not wonder whether our self-evident truths are real truths or whether, through some perversity inherent in our mind, that which is self-evident for us might not be illusory in relation to some truth in itself. For insofar as we talk about illusion, it is because we have identified illusions, and done so solely in the light of some perception which at the same time gave assurance of its own truth. It follows that doubt, or the fear of being mistaken, testifies as soon as it arises to our power of unmasking error, and that it could never finally tear us away from truth." Merleau-Ponty, *Phenomenology of Perception,* p. XVI.

[185]Sierksma, *op. cit.,* p. 35.

objectivity, he emphasizes that it is impossible to fulfill those requirements, and concludes that man *always projects*, that he *has to
project, whether he likes it or not.*[186] Once more the confusion is
extreme, for we were told before that man "stands in illusion"
as long as he projects.[187] So we may ask, Does Sierksma want to
introduce his readers to the illusion of the "projecting man" (*homo
projiciens*)?

Objectivity, however, should not be understood in an objectivistic
sense. For this reason we can distinguish between "seeing" and
"projecting," between reality and illusion. The knowing subject,
while "seeing," dwells in objectivity for the subject and stands in
truth as unconcealed.[188] When he is projecting he dwells in illusion,[189] and his existence is uprooted.[190] It is useless to object that
man makes frequent mistakes, for the very fact that he *can* notice
them implies that man has already made a distinction between
"standing in objectivity" and "standing in illusion," that is, between
seeing on the one hand, and imagining, having dreams, hallucinations
and projections on the other. The realization of having made a mistake means that man retracts an assertion which, evidently, is not
in conformity with the "things themselves, with what manifests itself, with beings in the 'how' of their unconcealedness."[191] This is
evident when man *really* "sees" and does *not* project.[192]

Needless to say, the terms "seeing" and "objective" may not be
understood in a univocal fashion. Phenomenology acknowledges that
grass is *objectively* green, that H_2O is an *objective* meaning of
water, that all beings *objectively* agree in being beings, that justice
objectively demands that things, which by their very nature are
social means of production, should not be absolutely the private
property of anyone, and that a particular phase of history has an
objective character. Phenomenology acknowledges all this because
such things are "seen" and are therefore undeniable.

---

[186]Sierksma, *op. cit.*, p. 110.
[187]Sierksma, *op. cit.*, p. 26.
[188]"To *logos* belongs unconcealedness—*a-letheia.*" Heidegger, *Sein und Zeit*,
p. 219; English ed., p. 262.
[189]"Beings are not wholly concealed; they are precisely the 'uncovered' but
at the same time 'disguised'; they show themselves but in the mode of semblance (*Schein*)." Heidegger, *op. cit.*, p. 222; English ed., p. 264.
[190]*Dasein's* "being toward beings is not extinguished but uprooted." Heidegger, *op. cit.*, p. 222; English ed., p. 264.
[191]Heidegger, *op. cit.*, p. 219; English ed., p. 262.
[192]We cannot enter into the question that arises here of what guarantees
truth.

These examples show that the term "seeing" must not be understood in only one sense. "To see" is the subject's immediate presence to a present reality, but that "being present" varies, for the subject can take different attitudes. But the "objective" always clings to the subject, to the "seeing," and it is nonsense to require that the objective be divorced from the subject, in order to deserve to be called really objective. To the extent that all objectivity is objective for the subject, we may say with Heidegger that all objectivity is "subjective." But this does not mean that all objectivity is abandoned to the caprice of the subject,[193] or that it is ultimately a projected pseudo-objectivity. It merely means that objectivity should not be understood in an objectivistic sense.[194]

The Religious Projection

When one realizes the serious objections that must be made against the general framework and the original light in which Sierksma wants to speak about projection, he sees no longer any need for dealing explicitly with this religious projection.[195] For in view of that general framework we already know what the conclusion will be: religiousness is *always* a form of projection regardless of whether it is based on objective knowledge or on projection, for standing in objectivity itself is a form of projection and in fact the most fundamental form. And since projection is a form of standing in illusion, the same must also be said of religiousness. However, we want to add just one remark because there are other objections against Sierksma's ideas.

In a section in which Sierksma deals with human equilibrium,[196] he says that there are many things that cause man to loose his equilibrium. Both man's equilibrium between himself and the outside world and that between himself and his inner world are precarious. But man can live only in a known, stable and closed world. For this

---

[193]"All truth is relative to the being of *Dasein* because the way of being that is essential to truth has the character of *Dasein*. Does this relativity mean that all truth is 'subjective'? If one interprets 'subjective' as 'left to the preference of the subject,' then it certainly does not. For uncovering, in its most proper sense, withdraws asserting from 'subjective' preference and places the uncovering *Dasein* face to face with the beings themselves." Heidegger, *op. cit.*, p. 227; English ed., p. 270.

[194]"If the 'subject' is ontologically conceived as existent *Dasein* whose being is grounded in temporality, then one must say: the world is 'subjective.' But in that case this 'subjective' world, as temporally transcendent, is 'more objective' than any possible 'object'." Heidegger, *op. cit.*, p. 366; English ed., p. 418.

[195]H. Fortmann, "Het probleem der religieuze projectie," *Annalen van het Thijmgenootschap*, vol. 49 (1961), p. 115.

[196]F. Sierksma, *op. cit.*, pp. 51-64.

reason he puts the mechanism of projection to work, i.e., "when the equilibrium is broken, subjective factors are *added* to the subjective factors that are already contained in every perception . . . How much subjectivity man 'puts' into his perception depends on the question of how much or how little his objectivating 'ec-centric' distance shrinks when the equilibrium is broken."[197] "It is preferable for man to have the quasi-stabilized world of projection than to live in a vacuum in which he is unable to orientate himself, loses his foothold, and falls into Nothingness. Projection is the *means of perception* that enables him to create this uneasy equilibrium and, if necessary, to restore it."[198] Hence the fundamental characteristic of projection consists in this, "that to perception is 'superadded' an extra dose of subjectivity, for the sake of preserving or restoring the threatened equilibrium."[199]

Contradictions

We cannot get rid of the impression that the author once more gets entangled in contradictions. We were already told in the first pages that perception *itself* is a form of projection.[200] The reason given for it is that objectivity can never be divorced from the knowing subject and that the subject can never be eliminated from objectivity. But when Sierksma speaks of human equilibrium, he says that the *fundamental characteristic* of projection consists in this that *an extra dose of subjectivity is superadded to perception*. Now this can hardly mean anything else except that, when *no* extra dose of subjectivity is added, we are not dealing with projection but simply with perception alone. Yet a little further Sierksma once more calls projection the "subjective factor of *perception*."[201]

Amidst such confusion the reader cannot be blamed if he gets the impression that the author himself does not know in what direction he is going. Sierksma's attempt to penetrate profoundly into projection reveals itself as an impediment obstructing any genuine understanding. His great light manifests itself as a criteriological and anthropological misconception.

Religiousness as Loss of Equilibrium

Starting from those premises, Sierksma deals with religious projection. The foundation for that discussion is found in the section

---

[197]*Op. cit.,* p. 61.
[198]*Op. cit.,* p. 63. Our italics.
[199]*Op. cit.,* p. 88.
[200]*Op. cit.,* p. 5.
[201]*Op. cit.,* p. 107.

which describes man's equilibrium and its loss. Religion, according to Sierksma is "the awareness that there is 'something' . . . behind, in, or with things, 'something' behind, in, or above the world, that plays hide and seek with man."[202] Man "seeks for the truth behind phenomena, but behind every truth other enigmas constantly arise. Truth is like the horizon: the closer one gets to it the more it recedes. When we think we have overtaken truth, we discover that something else lies behind that also. No matter how much man gets to know the world, another world of the 'unknown' always looms up and beckons him. Now it is precisely in regard to this *'hidden something'* existing behind things, the world and man, that religious experience arises. Here lies the ultimate meaning of the term 'hidden god' (*deus absconditus*), spoken of not only by the Christian but also, for instance, by the Maori in respect to *his* god 'Io'."[203]

But this "something" is not enough to make man become religious. A process of learning is required, which every child goes through, and by which it acquires a number of interpretations of the hidden "plus" of the world: a father-god, the spirits of ancestors, a half personal, half impersonal "power." The visible and invisible are thus synthesized in one world view in which stability reigns and man is able to live.[204]

The institution of a religion is almost always based on some revelation. This revelation is "a break of the psychical equilibrium, by which man becomes aware of his insufficiency, his helplessness and unfinished character."[205] Man loses control and the world slips from his grasp. This happens in a variety of circumstances: in a storm, at the sight of a dead person, a rock on the road, a mountain, a snowstorm, the dawn, of when he sees unseen things in a dream, travels beyond suns and stars in an ecstasy, or is devoured by remorse of conscience.[206]

A revelation is a disturbance of the human equilibrium. And man cannot bear this. He must give a meaning to the unknown, "so that it loses part of its mystery and can be absorbed by the world of experience as a marginal phenomenon. Man subjectifies the unknown—which he is unable to control by objectifying it and which threatens to upset the balance—into a part of his world, so that he

---

[202] *Op. cit.*, p. 136.
[203] *Op. cit.*, pp. 136 f.
[204] *Op. cit.*, p. 137.
[205] *Op. cit.*, p. 139.
[206] *Op. cit.*, pp. 139 f.

recovers his balance in a stable world of perception in which he is able to orientate himself and to act, even with respect to those marginal religious phenomena. The unknown becomes known, and both realms are integrated into an animated synthesis by means of religious projection."[207]

The phenomena man calls religious are all related to the fact that man is aware of his insufficiency, so that he can create or restore stability only by means of subjectification. Perception and religion have this function in common, that both serve to restore man's lost equilibrium.[208] The "purpose" of religion is to achieve the coherence or animated synthesis. Every religion tries to make the "totally other" look less strange.[209] It does so "by adding an extra dose of subjectivity."

Pseudo-Religiousness

The objections that come to mind in regard to Sierksma's manner of conceiving religion are partly the same as those which are provoked by his general theory of projection. Here also when he describes the world of religion, he conceives the projected meanings as meanings of the world of *perception*. Now this is inadmissible for the reasons we have mentioned above.

But there is more than that. In spite of the fact that Sierksma considers perception as the archetype of projection, he has tried to preserve a kind of "objectivity." But this attempt was bound to fail because he thought that "objectivity" could be understood only in an objectivistic sense. Nevertheless, Sierksma did make the attempt, and therefore was convinced of the need for making such an attempt. As soon, however, as there is question of God and religion, Sierksma no longer seems to feel any need to find out in what sense there could perhaps still be question here of objectivity. In this matter the meaning of the term "objective" differs, of course, completely from the one it has in *all* other cases in which we speak of something as being "objective," but that does not mean that the term does become entirely meaningless.

Can God be an "objective" God? Can God "really" exist? Is there a God who is not a projection? Those questions are truly pressing, because Christians consider Sierksma's entire dissertation about "gods" to be applicable to pseudo-gods, and his entire dis-

---

[207] *Op. cit.,* p. 142.
[208] *Op. cit.,* p. 143.
[209] *Op. cit.,* p. 157.

sertation about religiousness to be applicable to pseudo-religiousness. That this is so is evident to Christians, because Sierksma's work does not give the slightest hint that he has any notion of a Transcendent God. He speaks about the "hidden other side of the world," about a "strange rock on the road," about the "inexplicable absences of seals" where the Eskimos expect to find them. He speaks about the accompanying loss of psychical equilibrium, and honestly thinks that this loss is a religious experience. All this betrays great naiveness.

Sierksma, however, has foreseen this objection and endeavored to forestall it. He begins by complaining that the few psychologists of religion who are interested in the problem of projection "immediately tackle the problem of truth, that is, they neglect psychology."[210] The same idea recurs later when he observes that those "who in their critique of alleged psychologism always emphasize the 'objective' character of religion, usually have a secret apologetic intention. They are not interested in a psychological discussion but wish to safeguard the so-called 'problem of truth'."[211] We could therefore sum up Sierksma's answer to our objection as follows: *As a psychologist, I am not interested in the question whether or not a Transcendent God exists, for I pursue only the psychology of religion.*

This apparently simple reply, however, is very deceptive. We fully agree that a psychologist, *as* psychologist, is not able to determine whether or not a Transcendent God exists, for this is not a psychological question. But if a psychologist nonetheless asks such a question, he goes beyond the realm of psychology, just as the attempt to answer this question through any physical science implies a transgression of its boundaries. But for the same reason the psychologist, *as* psychologist, may not maintain that religion *as such* is a projection and that God is nothing but the result of the "superadding of an extra dose of subjectivity."

Sierksma's statement that religion as such is a projection, we may retort, results likewise from a "secret, apologetic intention." It lies just as much beyond the frontiers of psychology as the thesis that there is a Transcendent God. Whatever Sierksma says about religious projection, is indeed concerned with religious projection, that is, with pseudo-religiousness. Pseudo-religiousness really is an epiphenomenon of all forms of authentic religiousness, and this explains why Sierksma is able to find it everywhere. But Sierksma does not stick to psychol-

---

[210] *Op. cit.,* p. 3.
[211] *Op. cit.,* p. 141.

ogy when he asserts that religion, as *such,* is a projection. Moreover, the proclamation that religion, as such, is a projection is at the same time an answer—a negative answer—to the question whether there is a Transcendent God. And this answer likewise goes beyond psychology.[212]

Of course, we can imagine that Sierksma objects when Christians accuse him of never even mentioning *authentic* religiousness in his book. We can agree with him on that point. But our own objections remain exactly the same even if we admit that Sierksma never speaks about what Christians mean by the adoration of a Transcendent God and their experience of this adoration.[213]

Hence the "truth problem," the question concerning the "objective" existence of a Transcendent God, cannot be avoided. It is not a psychological question, not even a question of religious psychology. But this suggests that religious psychology alone cannot cope with it. For how could psychology itself make a distinction between authentic and inauthentic religiousness? How could it know what its own object is? In fact no positive science, *as such,* knows what its own formal object is and what the formal character of its own activity is. In this respect the position of psychology is similar to that of physical science. A physical science does not know what a "thing of nature" is, i.e., the thing whose empirically verifiable laws it investigates, and still less does the physicist, *as physicist,* know what physical science really is. Only a philosophy of science can solve such questions. The same applies also to psychology in general and to religious psychology in particular. One who forgets this point will not be disturbed at all when a religious psychologist omits religion entirely and limits himself to being a psychologist of pseudo-religiousness.

---

[212]Fortmann, *art. cit.,* pp. 115-117.

[213]Frequently Christians express themselves very badly. When, e.g., Sierksma claims that the depth of faith merely proves how deep the projection is, Fortmann replies: "That is all too often true" (*art. cit.,* p. 117). Fortmann does not exactly express here what he wants to say. Not the depth of *faith* but the depth of *pseudo-faith* proves how deep the projection is. The same applies to what Fortmann says about the Eskimos' "religiousness." Their helplessness when the seals fail to appear he wants to interpret as a kind of awareness of God's presence and a vague inkling of a pointer to God (*art. cit.,* p. 116). This, too, is an unfortunate expression. For *this* awareness of man's "helplessness" is concerned with his being-in-the-world as such and *not* with his "helplessness" as orientation to the Transcendent. The pseudo-god of the seals' absence is unmasked by the progress of oceanography, but not the Transcendent God, whom man encounters in an entirely different dimension of his "helplessness."

CHAPTER FIVE

EXISTENTIALISTIC ATHEISM

1. INTRODUCTION

We have emphasized repeatedly that those who call themselves existentialists or phenomenologists, or those who, while not calling themselves such, are nonetheless so designated by others, are not unjustly considered to be followers of a unified movement of thought indicated by the term "existential phenomenology." This common denominator does not mean that there are no differences of opinion among those philosophers or that those differences are not important. Nevertheless, it implies that there is a fundamental agreement among them in spite of those differences.

We have shown elsewhere in a general way that the "primitive fact" of existential phenomenology definitely does not *per se* imply the impossibility of a theistic attitude,[1] and in the preceding pages we have refuted the contention that such an impossibility is implied in it. Everyone, however, knows that there are atheists among the followers of existential phenomenology. In some milieus this is even the only thing that is known about existentialism, and it is then easy to proclaim the identity of existentialism and atheism. However, this identification is not always purely the product of ignorance, for Sartre himself has defined existentialism by atheism. According to him, existentialism is the only philosophy which draws the ultimate conclusions from a consistent atheistic attitude.[2] Sartre does not deny that there are several forms of atheism, but to his mind they are insignificant because they do not dare or wish to draw the ultimate conclusions and apply them to the whole of life. Existentialism alone, according to him, draws the consequences that are demanded by a consistent atheistic attitude.

It is possible to see that Sartre's definition of existentialism is unjust because it is possible to understand existential phenom-

---

[1] W. Luijpen, *De fenomenologie is een humanisme,* Amsterdam, 1961.

[2] "Existentialism is nothing else but an effort to draw all the consequences from a coherent atheistic position." Sartre, *L'existentialisme est un humanisme,* Paris, 1954, p. 94.

enology as a unified movement of thought. But the fact remains that
Sartre is an atheist and that several others make a similar profession
of atheism. So the question must be asked whence this atheism
originates.

If existential phenomenology is not *per se* atheistic, it might be
that atheism is a consequence of the fact that certain atheists have
accepted certain fundamental ideas of existential phenomenology and
yet, on the other hand, also deny these ideas. It is also possible that
some fundamental ideas of existential phenomenology were originally
conceived in a proper way, but were developed later in the direction
of atheism. In that case the question arises whether such a development is *per se* necessary. Lastly, it is possible that some particular
doctrine, looked at from the outside, seems atheistic, but that it is
not so when it is critically examined. For, a philosopher may think
that he rejects God when what he discards is only a pseudo-god;
just as also he may think that he affirms God when in reality he
merely affirms a pseudo-god.

Keeping in mind that all those possibilities could happen simultaneously either in whole or in part, that they can appear explicitly
or be present only implicitly, but especially that pseudo-gods can be
discarded as well as a Transcendent God, we see clearly that
prudence is needed. The fact that Kant was rejected before his doctrine was given a thorough examination should serve as a warning
to modern philosophers.

In the title of this chapter we spoke of *existentialistic* atheism.
We do not wish to insinuate by this that the philosophers whom we
are going to deal with *do not* belong to the unified movement of
existential phenomenologists of which we have spoken. We merely
wish to designate a definite group of philosophers in whose work
atheism is *de facto* found, namely, the group of which Sartre and
Merleau-Ponty are the chief representatives.

First Orientation

Reading the works of the French existentialists who profess atheism, one notices very soon that one and the same motive recurs in
them on which they base their rejection of God. This motive is not
borrowed from the traditional interpretation of Kant and still less
from considerations traceable to the scientism of Comte. The considerations that lead to the denial of God are more anthropological
than criteriological in nature. The anthropological considerations

could perhaps be summed up in the propositions: If man exists, there can be no God. But it is undeniable that man exists. Therefore, there is no God.

The works of those French existentialists, whether they are philosophers or literateurs, enrich that summary argument with a description of man's essence; next, they confront this essence implicitly or explicitly with some particular notions about God, and then they conclude that man and God are incompatible. What is said about the essence of man they view as beyond dispute; hence the rejection of God becomes inevitable. Their line of thought proceeds more or less along the pattern that is followed in the Prometheus myth.

In the Promethean myth man is described as a being who realizes himself by means of science and work. This concept of man is then confronted with a particular concept about God; in the case of the Prometheus myth God is conceived as a competitor with man's self-realization. After that, man's claim that he has an undeniable right to realize himself in the world is emphasized. This finally leads to the conclusion that to be faithful to himself man has to reject God.

Being man can, of course, be considered in many ways, and consequently the confrontation with God's existence can take place on many levels. As a matter of fact, this is what actually happens. More important however, is to stress at once that the confrontation of man with God is, and cannot be anything else but a confrontation of a particular *conception* of man with a particular *conception* of God.

We intend to give a detailed description of these views about man. The fact that these views are explicitly taught by the philosophers whose doctrine we want to examine makes it possible to do so. In any case, however, the views these philosophers have regarding God remain implicit and are contained in their rejection of God. This is not surprising, for they precisely reject God and, therefore, have no concept about God that is their *own*. In other words, they reject God as he is conceived by *others*.

Accordingly, we must ask ourselves against whom and against whose ideas of God atheistic existentialists battle. Which God do they reject? Certainly they do not aim their criticisms at the gods of Eskimos, Maoris or Papuans. Nor do they solely deny the God of Hegel, though they reject Him *also*. The God who is principally rejected by them is the God of Christianity. Most French atheists know Christianity because they were at one time members of a

Christian Church. They continued to be confronted with it because they could not completely disregard men like Maritain, De Lubac, Mounier, Daniélou, Lacroix, Lepp, and Marcel. For this reason the dispute is very important. If they had rejected the God of Christians together with the gods of Eskimos, Maoris and Papuans, they would have oversimplified the issue. But that kind of naiveté could hardly be expected on the part of French existentialists.

A Brief History of the Problem

The problem about the coexistence of God and man is not new. In French existentialism it reaches its climax in the question of how it is possible to conceive man as a contingent and free subject in the presence of God conceived as the Necessary Being. This question is then developed into problems concerning the essential characteristics of man as subject, as tending to truth and goodness, in confrontation with the Absolute Truth and the Absolute Goodness of God. Is it possible under such conditions to safeguard man as subject and to preserve his tendency to truth and goodness which realizes itself in the contingency of history, if he is confronted with God as the Absolute and Necessary Being, as Absolute Truth and Goodness? Or does the affirmation of God as affirmation of *the* Being *per se* demand the negation of mere be-ings?

All this merely indicates the terms to be used in the discussion of those questions. Hardly any *real* question has yet been asked, for everything depends on the way a particular philosopher or a particular school of philosophers gives content to those terms. However, from the way in which the questions are formulated we readily see that we have here age-old problems, the most difficult problems that a philosopher can face. As a matter of fact, contemporary thought takes up questions which have remained unsettled since the Golden Age of Scholasticism.

Whatever may be our opinion of the solution, or rather the examination of these problems by Golden-Age Scholasticism, it seems undeniable to us that those scholastic thinkers always began with the conviction that creatures have their *own* being, their *own* causality, and their *own goodness,* in spite of the fact that God is Being Itself, the First Cause and the Supreme Good. In its attempt to shed some light on the relationship between God and creatures, Scholasticism, at least in its Golden Age never proposed the rather easy solution of denying that creatures have their *own* being, their

own causality, and their *own* goodness. These were never reduced to pure appearances.[3] Even in regard to the most difficult
point, namely, that of the relation between the freedom of man's
action and the necessity of God's will, man's freedom was *never*
reduced to a mere appearance, although the temptation to do so was
readily present in the rather predominant role physical causality played
in the thinking of that age.

This situation, however, did not last. Already in Late Scholasticism a breach was made in the conviction that creatures have their
own being, their *own* causality and their *own* goodness. William
of Ockham, was the first and most influential thinker who went in
that new direction. It found its clearest expression in his concept of
the moral law. According to Ockham, the moral law is not anchored in the essence of the creature, but reveals itself solely as the
purely positive will of God. God could have willed and decreed the
opposite of the existing moral law. That is good according to
Ockham, which agrees with God's arbitrary will.[4] All this evidently
puts into jeopardy that which is proper to the creature *itself*. The
Reformation went even much farther in that direction. Luther
denied man's rational power of free choice, and Calvin did away with
man's *own* decisions through his doctrine of predestination. Adam
had to betray Our Lord.

Those ideas were completely secularized by the Occasionalists. In
Geulincx and Malebranche we find, with some variations and nuances, the conviction that God is the *sole* Cause of all that happens,
and creatures are merely occasions for God's intervention. Spinoza
drew the ultimate conclusions from those ideas. God is the only and
absolute substance and the things of the world are only *modes* of that
substance. So nothing remained of the fundamental starting point of
Golden-Age Scholasticism expressed in the question whether God's
existence can be reconciled with the *proper* being, the *proper* causality, and the *proper* goodness of creatures.[5]

There was, of course, also a counter current of ideas. Descartes'
Cogito ergo sum implied a clear protest against Ockham, a revaluation
of what belongs to man as his *own*. The *Cogito* is, for Descartes, the
very first, and this *Cogito* belongs to man; we say it *is* man himself.
Even if an evil spirit causes man to be convinced that he "is" when he

---

[3] H. Pfeil, *Der atheistische Humanismus der Gegenwart,* Aschaffenburg,
1961, pp. 88 f.
[4] H. Pfeil, *op. cit.,* pp. 89 f.
[5] H. Pfeil, *op. cit.,* pp. 90 f.

"thinks," that spirit would not be able to make man not be, as long as man "thinks" that he is. Catholic theology has always opposed the Reformation's devaluation of man, and Molinism emphatically rejected the Calvinistic doctrine of predestination. Deism also should be viewed as an extreme protest against the devaluation of what is *proper* to the creature.[6]

Accordingly, the problem faced by the existentialistic atheists is already very old and has a long history. We do not claim, however, that the French atheists explicitly seek contact with the history of the problem. But the fact remains that they again take up a question that has a long history.

We have already mentioned that human existence as freedom is the basis on which some French existentialists establish their atheism. That is why we will first propose in our own way the phenomenology of freedom, for it will give us the necessary framework for the ideas that serve as a basis for atheism.

2. To Be a Subject Is to Be Free

Everyone who meaningfully uses the term "freedom" expresses negatively that there is a certain absence of determination, and, positively that there is a certain autonomy. These are actually two aspects of one and the same reality, namely, man.[7]

It is also in this same twofold sense that existential phenomenology speaks of freedom. It was led to do so by the way various human sciences used to think about man. They conceived man as the "result" of certain forces—the ones considered in this or that particular science. There was a time when practically all the human sciences absolutized their own specific way of asking questions as the only legitimate approach, and were blind to anything that could not be seized by their own scientific apparatus.[8]

As a result of that attitude man was considered to be merely the "result" of economic and social forces when studied in economics and sociology. In biology man was the "result" of all kinds of biological processes. In orthodox psychoanalysis he was the product of various drives dwelling deep down in the *Id*. Man was conceived

---

[6]H. Pfeil, *op. cit.*, p. 91 ff.

[7]Cf. Albert Dondeyne, "Truth and Freedom," *Truth and Freedom* by Louis de Raeymaeker and others, Pittsburgh, 2nd impression, 1955, p. 29.

[8]Cf. Stephan Strasser, *Phenomenology and the Human Sciences*, Pittsburgh, 1963, pp. 193 ff.

in all kinds of ways, but always as the "result" of processes and forces. And these forces were, of course, interpreted in a unilateral and deterministic way because of the prestige enjoyed by physical science. Man was thus looked upon as if he *too* were a thing, for a thing, in the strict sense of the term, is the result of processes and forces.

All existentialists and phenomenologists have always opposed such a view. If man is *nothing but* a "result" of forces, he *himself* is nothing. But this is inadmissible.

The Being of a Thing. A *thing* can be completely explained by its antecedents. A thing is nothing but the result of processes and forces; the being of a thing is encompassed by being a result. If we know all the processes and forces that have causally influenced the thing, we know everything about it. A thing is only a point in the endless evolution of the cosmos; it is nothing new in reference to the processes and powers that have brought it about.[9] A thing, then, is essentially relative; it is merely a part of the material cosmos; it is not *itself* something transcending its antecedents.[10] The being of a thing is nothing but its belonging to the material cosmos.

To say that the being of a thing is totally encompassed by being a result is the same as saying that the being of a thing is nothing but being necessitated, because determinism rules the world of things. The cosmic forces act with necessity and give to the processes the constancy which the physicist expresses in his laws. If some individual events are not explained by those laws, he knows that there are other forces acting of necessity which interfere with the laws he has already discovered.

The deterministic forces of the cosmos work "blindly." They do not know themselves as forces, or their results as results. The world of things is stricken with "blindness." Things lie, as it were, crushed in themselves; they are not for themselves or for other things. In short, the being of a thing is being a blindly determined result.

But how is it possible to *say* this? It is not possible to say that things do not exist for themselves or for other things, that things

---

[9]Cf. A. De Waelhens, "Linéaments d'une interprétation phénoménologique de la liberté," *Liberté, Actes du IVe Congrès des Sociétés de Philosophie de langue française,* Neûchatel, 1949, p. 82.

[10]Cf. D. M. De Petter, "Personne et Personnalisation," *Divus Thomas* (Piac), 1949, p. 164.

have no meaning for themselves or for other things, unless we admit that the totality of reality is not identical with the totality of things. If there were nothing but "things," processes and forces, there would be no sense, no meaning. But there is meaning. To express it paradoxically, if there were nothing but things, processes and forces, then there would *be* nothing, in the only sense the term "to be" can have, namely, "to be for man." But something *is*! There *are* things, processes and forces.

Man Is Not Merely a Thing. Once this is understood, it becomes absolutely impossible to hold that the totality of being man, *all that man is,* can be reduced to being the blindly determined result of processes and forces. If man were such a determined being, he would be a thing, and in that case—using the same paradoxical expression—there would, strictly speaking, *be* nothing. But something is, namely, by the fact that man exists. Hence the being of man cannot be reduced to being totally a result. The being of man is *itself* something. Therefore his being cannot be called totally a thing, purely a part of the material cosmos. Although man is *also* a result, *also* determined, *also* part of the cosmos, he cannot be totally result, totally determined, totally part of the material cosmos, for then there would be nothing.

Now what is it in the reality of man that makes him rise above being a blindly determined result of processes and forces? The answer is: his subjectivity.

With the appearance of subjectivity in the endless evolution of the cosmos the darkness is pierced. Man as subject is the "natural light," the light by which something *is* in the only possible meaning of the term.[11] Hence it is through man's being as subject that it is possible to transcend being a result, being merely a part, being necessitated—all of which *also* have to be affirmed of man.

One who uses the term "freedom" meaningfully expresses negatively a certain absence of determination. Hence it is clear that being a subject is the same as being free, for man's subjectivity transcends his being a thing, his being a blindly determined result. No matter in how many respects man must be called a necessary result of processes and forces, it is not possible to maintain that this constitutes the totality of his being man; for we must admit that it is only

---

[11]Cf. Heidegger, *"On the Essence of Truth,"* in *Existence and Being,* London, 1949, pp. 332 ff.

because of man's subjectivity that there are necessity, results, processes and forces.[12] If man were nothing but the deterministic result of processes and forces, he would be a *thing* and would be stricken with the "blindness" that affects all *things*. And then nothing would be for man. But something *is*. There are things, processes and forces. The being of man as subject is being free as the "letting be" of the cosmos.[13]

Freedom of Man's Being. It is clear that we are not speaking here about freedom as a quality attached to an action or a faculty. The freedom we speak of concerns the *being* of man on the specific level of his being man. To be man as subject is to be free. It is only when we keep this in mind that we can understand the freedom of human action and the many other meanings which are expressed by the term "freedom" in modern philosophical literature.[14]

When we consider being free from the positive standpoint, it expresses a certain autonomy of man as subject.[15] Not everything in man is the result of processes and forces; man's being as subject is a being-*himself*. It is impossible to explain man fully by his antecedents; the being of man as subject is a "being *out of* himself" *(aus-sich-sein)*. The being of man is not purely being a part of the cosmos; it is not exclusively a belonging to the cosmos; as subject, man subsists and belongs to himself.[16]

But what is man *himself?* The answer permits no hesitation. Man's "self", is an "I," a person.[17] Man's being free as subject must

---

[12]"If it is proper to man to discover and establish meanings, then the idea that determinism could apply to him becomes in truth simply absurd." De Waelhens, *art. cit.,* p. 83.

[13]"The freedom to reveal something overt lets whatever 'is' at the moment *be* what it is. Freedom reveals itself as the 'letting-be' of what-is." Heidegger, *op cit.,* p. 333.

[14]"The affirmation that ontologically man is free by definition and that freedom is for him the condition of truth because a non-free being could not say that things are, does not, of course, solve all the problems that could be raised by the existence of freedom. Neither is it equivalent to the denial that freedom in reference to man can be understood in many ways. Nevertheless, the affirmation of this principle, it is thought, alone permits us to understand the exact bearing of those further difficulties and the meaning which the idea of freedom must have when it is considered in the various domains of philosophy and especially on the psychological moral, social, and religious levels." De Waelhens, *op. cit.,* p. 83.

[15]In general, man's autonomy of being as a subject is approached by way of the autonomy of his human actions. By virtue of the principle, "action follows being," man's *self-action* leads to the conclusion that he himself is. Cf. De Petter, *art. cit.,* p. 170.

[16]Cf. H.D. Robert, "Phénoménologie existentielle et Morale thomiste," in *Morale chrétienne et Requêtes contemporaines,* Tournai-Paris 1954, pp. 208 f.

[17]Cf. De Petter, *art. cit.,* pp. 170 f.

be understood positively as a certain autonomy of being, as a certain independence of being, as a belonging to himself on the basis of his *own* being *(esse proprium),* and therefore also as "non-generated" *(ingeneratum),*[18] for it is *not* the result of processes and forces. Scholasticism reserved the term "subsistence" for that autonomy of being of man.[19] Man "subsists" as "I," as subject, as person.[20]

To Be Free Is to Be Rational

Man's superiority of being as subject equiprimordially constitutes his rationality. This is very clearly expressed in Boethius' definition of the person as an "individual substance of a rational nature."[21] The being of man as "I" signifies a certain superiority of being in respect to the things of the cosmos. But this "I", as superiority of being, is the natural light, the light by which man is for himself and the world is for man. It is the light through which there is objective meaning. It is traditionally called "the light of reason." But it is necessary to eliminate all rationalistic and scientific prejudices if we wish to see human reason in its original form. Human reason is both the place where objective meaning appears and the power which lets this meaning appear. This place and power are evidently the existent subject himself. Whence man is traditionally defined as rational animal. To be subject means to be free, and it means equiprimordially to be rational.[22]

However, it also and inevitably seems that man's freedom is not without bounds. The subject reveals himself as freedom, and freedom manifests itself as reason, hence as the power that lets meaning appear. But meaning is an *objective* meaning, and the light of subjectivity is an "objective" light; consequently, meaning is not left to the caprice of the subject. The subject, as "natural light," is the

---

[18]Cf. De Petter, *art. cit.,* p. 171.

[19]Cf. Louis de Raeymaeker, *The Philosophy of Being,* St. Louis, 1954, p. 241.

[20]Cf. De Petter O.P., "Het Persoon-zijn onder thomistisch-metaphysische belichting," *De Persoon, Verslag van de dertiende algemene vergadering der Vereniging voor Thomistische Wijsbegeerte en van de vierde studiedagen van het Wijsgerig Gezelschap te Leuven,* Nijmegen, 1948, pp. 45 f.

[21]*De duabus naturis,* c. III.

[22]"It is important to note most explicitly that in the case of the person the concept 'rational nature' is not related to the concept 'subsistence' or 'supposit' as an extrinsic difference. Rationality means a higher perfection of subsistence itself. Moreover, in the strict and proper sense, it is only in the case of a rational nature that there can be question of subsistence." De Petter, *art. cit.,* (footnote 20), pp. 45 f.

"letting be" of reality.[23] As such it is *bound* to objectivity.[24] The existent freedom is equiprimordially existent "being bound."

All this remains unintelligible for anyone who is not willing to understand freedom and objectivity in their most fundamental sense. We are not concerned here with the capacity for doing *this* or *that* in accordance with an arbitrary decision.[25] Nor are we speaking of objectivity as a property of the judgment.[26] What we have in mind here is rather that which makes every choice of *this* or *that* possible and is the basis giving rise to the possibility of objective judgment. It is man as *subject*.

To Be Free is to Be Ethical

It is rather easy to understand that man's freedom in his human activity is based on his being free as subject. But we should note that we speak here about man on the *proper* level of his being man. There are also "actions" of man which he does not perform on the authentically human level and in reference to which we cannot speak of freedom. This will become clearer as we proceed.

Man's activity is not a "process." Whereas the being of a thing must be called being a result of processes and forces, there is a dimension in human existence in which man transcends being a result of processes and forces. As subject man is an *I*, which *itself* possesses a certain autonomy of being as distinct from the processes and forces that affect him.

That autonomy of being manifests itself also in human activity. For man is *himself* the source of his action to the extent that his action is human. The *I* from which the action springs means that the chain of deterministic processes is broken. The result of the action is a meaning which is "new" in reference to the forces that influence man. The local movement of billiard ball *B* is not new in respect to the force with which ball *A* strikes ball *B*. But when John knocks down his friend Peter, the meaning of Peter's fall cannot be evaluated by measuring the force with which John floored Peter. Peter's

---

[23]"The freedom to reveal something overt lets whatever 'is' at the moment be what it is. Freedom reveals itself as the 'letting-be' of what-is." Heidegger, *op. cit.*, p. 333.

[24]"Participation in the revealed nature of what-is does not stop there, it develops into a retirement before it so that what-is may reveal itself as *what* and *how* it is, and the approximation which represents it in the statement may take it for criterion." Heidegger, *op. cit.*, p. 334.

[25]Heidegger, *op. cit.*, p. 334.

[26]Heidegger, *op. cit.*, p. 336.

position in space is "new" in reference to that force, in virtue of the attitude that Peter *himself* assumes in that regard. Because man *himself* acts, his action is not a process; to the extent that man's activity is not a process, man is free.

It may be preferable, however, to state explicitly that human action always "*co*-proceeds" from man *himself*. For there is a danger that otherwise the *I*, the *self-hood* of man, will be conceived again as isolated, as divorced from the facticity of the situation. Subjectivity is not what it is, it is not a *human* subjectivity, if it is not involved in facticity.[27] The subject "exists." Hence, when I say that I *myself* execute a certain action, my statement rules out the possibility that the action is exclusively the result of a deterministic influence of facticity; but it also implies that the action would not be what it is without facticity.[28]

The consequences of this insight are far-reaching. There is no personal philosophizing without the settled philosophies, no personal justice without a juridical order, no personal religiousness without institutions, no personal love without sensibility,[29] no personal morality without biological and sociological conscience, and so forth. Hence the significance of asceticism in man's life can never consist in "killing" his facticity, for without facticity a person cannot do anything.

The facticity of the situation speaks, as it were, to the knowing subject in a specific way, but that facticity does not exercise a causal influence in such a way that the subject's action is a mere reaction.[30] On the specific level of being man there is not a single situation which determines the human action. A most painful economic situation does not determine me to act in a revolutionary way.[31] The only thing that happens is that a particular facticity "speaks to me" in such a way that a particular decision is likely to be made.[32]

---

[27] Merleau-Ponty, *Phenomenology of Perception*, p. 408.

[28] "There is, therefore, never determinism and never absolute choice, I am never a thing and never bare consciousness." Merleau-Ponty, *op. cit.*, p. 453.

[29] Humanus, "Zinnelijkheid en liefde," *Kultuurleven*, vol. XXIV (1957), pp. 485-497.

[30] "The choice would seem to lie between scientism's conception of causality, which is incompatible with the consciousness we have of ourselves, and the assertion of an absolute freedom divorced from the outside." Merleau-Ponty, *op. cit.*, p. 435.

[31] Merleau-Ponty, *op. cit.*, p. 442.

[32] "Our freedom does not destroy our situation but gears itself to it: as long as we are alive, our situation is open, which implies both that it calls up specially favored modes of resolution and also that it is powerless to bring one into being of itself." Merleau-Ponty, *ibid.*

The way that facticity speaks to me *co*-motivates my decision. But the motive has no meaning in itself; it derives its meaning *also* from my subjectivity as a definite project.

I *take* the motive as a motive. My poverty does not necessarily propel me to a revolutionary party in the way a storm drives a ship to the rocks. Poverty does indeed "speak to me" in a definite way which readily inclines me to join a revolutionary party, but I take and make the motive a motive, I take it in function of a definite purpose, namely, a more prosperous life. The situation would have a totally different meaning if I had another end in view, for instance, the acceptance of a life of poverty. Hence we cannot speak of a unilateral, deterministic influence of facticity, for subjectivity always co-originates the new meaning.

When we spoke about the fundamental ideas of existential phenomenology we described existence as a being "at" the world. It described the being of man as action, his existence as *Ago* (I act), whose freedom we have just now explicitated. We have also described man's being "at" the world as the execution of the project which human existence is. We are now permitted to call that execution a *free*, human self-realization. This self-realization of man is the realization of his essence by man *himself* because, and to the extent that, the meaning created by human activity has its co-source in the subject and therefore is new in reference to the results of any kind of cosmic process or forces. Man's life is not a process, but a history.[33]

We have already stressed also that man's self-realization is never complete. One becomes aware of this when he understands that the affective No of the subject as *Volo,* in respect to any newly created meaning whatsoever, is undeniable and permanent. The subject as *Volo* is evidently a certain Yes to the meaning which, as object of this Yes, is called "value." Every Yes, however, is affected by a No, and every value manifests itself as a non-value in respect to possible new actions and new values. For this reason man cannot come to a standstill in any "factical" situation; goaded by the negativity that is inherent in his being a subject, man must constantly go forward. Hence man "is" not, as a thing *is*; the being of man is a "having to

---

[33]"One explains nothing by man, for he is not a strength but a weakness in the heart of being; [he is not] a cosmological factor, but the place where cosmological factors, through a never-finished mutation, change meaning and become history." Merleau-Ponty, *Eloge de la philosophie*, p. 61.

be," an *avoir à être*,[34] a *zu sein*.[35] Man is a task, a task in the world. Hence he is never "finished." A task that is "finished" is no longer a task. A man who is "finished" is no longer a man. Man can, of course, disregard the task-like character of his being in the world, but in that case he disregards his being man. He then gives himself the being of a thing, for a thing "is not concerned with what it is"; being is not a project for a thing because a thing is not a subject, it is not free.

Accordingly, being a subject is the foundation of "having to be," because the subject as *Volo* includes an invincible negativity. This same subject as *Cogito* is a light for himself and for the world. This is an objective light and as such it is tied to the objectivity of existence. Man is the being who is concerned with his being, with the *objectivity* of his being; man is the being who is characterized by "understanding of being."[36] This "understanding" is a pre-predicative awareness of the reality of existence.

There are, in that pre-predicative awareness, moments when man truly "understands," that is, moments of insight into the essence of existence. The fact that man understands himself as existence is already a proof of such an insight. To exist belongs to man's essence. Now that in virtue of which man is precisely man, and not a thing or a God, is his *existence,* his being a subject in the world. It is possible to make objective, universal statements about man on the basis of that "understanding." On a deeper level of reflection existence manifests itself also as essentially destined for other existences, and man executes that destiny in love.[37]

There are, of course, many other essential characteristics of being man that can be explained in this fashion. We may say that whatever is explicitated by philosophical anthropology is already known implicitly in the original light of the "understanding of being."

When we now say that the subject as *Ago* realizes himself in the world, it stands to reason that man's activity is accompanied by his awareness of being bound to the objectivity of his own essence. For man is *himself* that awareness, because he exists as *Cogito*. The awareness of being bound to the objectivity of his essence forbids man to say about his existence what his whims dictate, or what a

---

[34]Sartre, *Being and Nothingness,* p. LXV.
[35]Heidegger, *Sein und Zeit,* p. 12; English ed., p. 33.
[36]Heidegger, *op. cit.,* pp. 12-15; English ed., pp. 32-35.
[37]Cf. Luijpen, *Existential Phenomenology,* pp. 240-259.

particular government or a particular tradition wants him to acknowledge as "truth."

Here we encounter the ethos of truth that has animated and prompted so many authentic thinkers. No threats, no attempts to break their careers, no violence was able to turn them away from their purpose: To acknowledge and express what man *is*. This awareness of being bound to the objectivity of his own essence plays a role when man acts, that is when he realizes the unfulfilled possibilities of his existence as project. Not only when he speaks, but also, and perhaps most of all, when he acts, man is able to acknowledge or deny his own essence. When man acts he is accompanied by the awareness of being bound to the objectivity of his own essence, and this awareness, this companion, he himself is. Driven by that awareness, men who lived authentically have preferred to sacrifice their lives rather than renounce or betray the essence of man in their actions.

Let us state once more that the subject as *Volo* is the basis of man's "having to be" and that the subject as *Cogito* includes his being bound to the objectivity of his essence. When we realize that we are dealing here with one same object, we are obliged to assert that the being of the existent subject is a "having to be" which is bound to the objectivity of his essence. Hence, if it is true that the subject as existence includes essentially a being destined for other subjects as existences, it follows that we must admit that man owes it to the objectivity of his own being man to prevent himself from ever destroying the subjectivity of others.[38] Men who lived authentically have given their lives for that idea; they have preferred to die rather than to renounce the objectivity of their own essence in their conduct. Such an authentic man is traditionally called "the ethical man." The "understanding of being," which can be considered in a broader perspective, reveals itself here in this perspective as what is traditionally called "conscience." And since man himself is this understanding of being, the *being* of man must be called a "conscientious being."

Since the time when man began to philosophize authentically, philosophers have tried to explicitate and conceptualize the being of man, including his being ethical. Of course, it was not the philos-

---

[38]This example should not be understood as if the "ethical man"—as we shall call him hereafter—is fully described by the expression "destined for the other." The essence of existence evidently contains far more than this.

ophers' intention to give the individual man a recipe for what he ought to do or not do in individual circumstances. Such an attempt could only have been a deception. They were concerned with unfolding and expressing the moments of man's being as a "having to be" which is bound to the objectivity of his essence. This endeavor, precisely as the explicitation of essential moments, yielded objective universal laws and norms—laws therefore that are not written in heaven,[39] but "in the hearts of men."[40] The fact that those laws and norms, once they have been stated and formulated, can begin to lead a kind of isolated life, divorced from their origin, may become an occasion leading to the most foolish ideas regarding the ethical man as well as provoke the most foolish reactions against those concepts.[41] However, this point does not concern us here.

What we have said thus far can serve as a frame within which one can place the ideas of some atheistic existentialists. For they try to base their rejection of God on definite ideas regarding man as freedom and as ethical being. These ideas contain either the rejection or the exaggeration of what we have stated above.

The French atheists are not the first to defend atheism on anthropological grounds. For in Nietzsche we already meet atheism as a postulate, that is, atheism as a demand based on certain concepts about man as a free and ethical being. For this reason we shall first explain Nietzsche's ideas, for they have exercised an unmistakable influence on atheistic existentialism.

3. The Atheism of Nietzsche

In his childhood and youth Nietzsche was very devout. The poems he wrote as a young man reveal an authentic Protestant-Christian religiousness. He explicitly acknowledged God's almighty

---

[39]"The existentialist finds it extremely embarrassing that God does not exist, for there disappears with him all possibility of finding values in an intelligible heaven. There can no longer be any good *a priori,* since there is no infinite and perfect consciousness to think it. It is nowhere written that 'the good' exists, that one must be honest or must not lie, since we are now precisely on the plane where there are only men." Sartre, *Existentialism and Humanism,* p. 33.

[40]"The heart and the root of moral choice contains a constant and immutable design of value, which we have not to invent or create in its entirety but to accept and make our own. This design is the acknowledgment of the eminent dignity proper to the human person and of the values constituting man's personality." Dondeyne, "Les problèmes soulevés par l'athéisme existentialiste," *Sapientia Aquinatis, Communicationes IV Congressus Thomistici Internationalis,* Roma, 1955, p. 468.

[41]Luijpen, *op. cit.,* pp. 318-320.

Will and the goodness of His Providence. He conceived his relation to God as that of a child to his father and was firmly determined to consecrate himself entirely to the service of God. He had the intention of becoming a minister and prayed for divine guidance in that respect. By becoming a preacher of the Gospel he would have continued a respectable family tradition, for both his father and grandfather had chosen that vocation and so had many more remote forebears.

Until his seventeenth year Nietzsche had not the least doubts about his faith and still less did he have any uncertainty about his future. He remembered for a long time his official reception into the Lutheran church as one of the important, solemn and happiest days of his youth. But from his seventeenth to his twentieth year he went through a period of serious difficulties and doubts. Those difficulties were apparently gone when, at the age of twenty, he passed his final examination at the Gymnasium "Schulporta" near Naumburg, and he experienced a strong revival of his religiousness.

Nevertheless, the difficulties and doubts which Nietzsche thought he had overcome were in reality the beginning of the end insofar as his religiousness was concerned. Going to Bonn, he became acquainted with the then current critique of the Gospels and the examination of the sources of the New Testament. He read and reread Strauss' *Life of Jesus* and was caught in the net of its denials that the Gospels contain divine Revelation and that Christ is God. In regard to philosophy, Nietzsche encountered insuperable difficulties in the relationship of the creature to God. He was unable to see anything else in medieval philosophy but disparagement and vilification of the earth and of man, and thought that this infamy reached its limit in that most scandalous doctrine of predestination professed by the Reformers: "Grandiose but barbarian."

When Nietzsche went to Leipzig to continue his studies, he was already an atheist. In a letter of April 17, 1866 addressed to Carl von Gersdorff, he wrote that, if Christianity is supposed to refer to a historical event and a historical person, he no longer wants to have anything to do with it. Only to the extent that Christianity coincides with the fundamental ideas of Schopenhauer does he consider it to have any merit.[42]

---

[42]Because we are not writing a book about Nietzsche, we allow ourselves to be guided in the presentation of Nietzsche's ideas by the "systematization" made by H. Pfeil in his work, *Friedrich Nietzsche und die Religion*, Regensburg, 1949.

Nietzsche's View of Man

It would be useless to look for a systematic study of man's essence in Nietzsche's works. He is too much the visionary and the prophet to be capable of philosophizing in a way that resembles, for example, that of Kant. Nietzsche speaks about man in a thousand ways, but he nowhere gives us a "treatise" on man. But this does not mean that he does not present us with a view of man's essence, for he does offer such a vision. His philosophy may not have been proposed in a scholastic way, but it is not right to say that his philosophy is a "tale told by an idiot." His philosophy, too, has its coherence, a coherence of its own because it is animated by its own primitive fact.

Nietzsche calls upon man to be *himself*. "Will a Self and you'll become a Self."[43] But this call should not be interpreted in a modern personalistic sense. For man's selfhood, according to Nietzsche, must be understood primarily in a bodily sense. Nietzsche is particularly strong in his statement that man is "body entirely and nothing more and the soul is only a name for something in the body."[44] He is driven to use those extreme expressions because many philosophers neglect or despise the body. For him man is primarily body, and if we wish to speak of personalism it should—paradoxically—be called a biological personalism.

Since man is primarily body, there are, properly speaking, only two classes of men, namely, the healthy and the sick, the strong and the weak. Both types of men *suffer in life* but for very different reasons. The sick and weak man suffers because of the misery of life and would like to abolish all suffering. Since this is impossible, he takes a negative attitude toward life and the world and becomes more and more decadent. He is increasingly less a Self and increasingly more a slave.[45] The healthy and strong man, on the contrary, suffers from a superabundance of life. He knows that all that is great and noble issues from suffering. That is why he does not blame life for anything, because it invites him to become a Self and to rise to greater power and dominion by his "Yes" to life.[46]

---

[43]Nietzsche, *Menschliches, Allzumenschliches*, p. 154. References to Nietzsche's German works will be made according to the edition of the Kroner Verlag, Stuttgart.
[44]*Thus Spake Zarathustra*, in *The Philosophy of Nietzsche*, Modern Library, New York, *ibid.*, p. 32.
[45]Nietzsche, *Die fröhliche Wissenschaft*, p. 284.
[46]"The tension of soul in misfortune which communicates to it its energy, its shuddering in view of rack and ruin, its inventiveness and bravery in under-

In Nietzsche, biological personalism takes the form of a biological heroism. Only the healthy and strong man has the right to exist, according to him, but this right is based on his "Yes" to the world, on his doing violence to and overcoming himself, on being a source of pain and sorrow for himself and for others, on rising to ever increasing greatness, power, force and dominion. But for this a "new health" is needed, of which the weak, the slaves, have not the least idea.[47] But there is no other way of being faithful to the earth. That is the message which Zarathustra brings to the world.[48]

What we have said already shows what constitutes the "primitive fact" of Nietzsche's philosophy and which we could sum up in the words: "Life is Will to Power."[49] This is particularly true of man, but the will to power is seen by Nietzsche as animating everything. It is the will to power and nothing else that is at work in the higher forms of conscious life, in the striving for truth and values, in religion, in the primitive forms of affectivity, in remembrance and forgetfulness, in organic life and in the processes described by chemistry.[50]

The will to power is, as it were, a primordial cosmic will. It has, of course, no goal outside itself; the will "to" power is therefore rather the will "as" power. The cosmic primordial will, as power, strives for itself, namely, in appropriating and conquering, in exploiting and absorbing what is foreign and weak. It is from this standpoint that Nietzsche attempts to make the totality of reality intelligible: the will as power functions as the primitive fact of his philosophy.

Nietzsche strongly battles against every form of eudaemonism; against any striving for happiness as the definition and purpose of

---

going, enduring, interpreting, and exploiting misfortune, and whatever depth, mystery, disguise, spirit, artifice, or greatness has been bestowed on the soul—has it not been bestowed through suffering, through the discipline of great suffering?" *Beyond Good and Evil* in *The Philosophy of Nietzsche*, p. 530.

[47] *Die fröhliche Wissenschaft*, p. 301.

[48] "I conjure you, my brethren, *remain true to the earth,* and believe not those who speak unto you of superearthly hopes! Poisoners are they, whether they know it or not." *Thus Spake Zarathustra*, in *The Philosophy of Nietzsche*, pp. 6 f.

[49] *The Will to Power,* vol. 1, p. 213.

[50] "Would you have a name for my world? A *solution* of all your riddles? Do ye also want a light, ye most concealed, strongest and most undaunted men of the blackest midnight? *This world is the will to power*—and nothing else! And even ye yourselves are this will to power—and nothing besides." *The Will to Power,* vol. 2, p. 432.

life. He is particularly hard on the eudaemonism of Bentham. According to Nietzsche, plants, animals and men are not on the road to happiness but on the road to power. Every living organism wills an "increase of power" (*Plus von Macht*). Happiness is the road to decadence. Only living dangerously is human and this implies suffering, being abandoned, distrusted, mistreated and despised.[51]

In this perspective the question whether or not the human will is free has no meaning at all for Nietzsche. The important point is not whether the will is free or not free, but whether the will is strong or weak.[52] The strong will alone is capable of fighting, conquering and ruling.

The Superman

The "Yes" to the world of the man who lives authentically is identical with his will to power. This doctrine logically leads Nietzsche to his views regarding man as Superman. For, Nietzsche thinks that neither the man of the past nor the man of the present is authentically man. "Verily, my friends, I walk among men as among the fragments and limbs of human beings....The present and the bygone upon earth—ah my friends—that is *my* most unbearable trouble and I should not know how to live if I were not a seer of what is to come."[53]

The future man, the Superman, is still far distant from the human beings that he sees around him. The European has not renounced his striving for greatness, but he has in fact sunk into an ever more flimsy, mediocre, Christian existence. For Nietzsche the European culture is only the result of the sickness of the European man. The European has philosophized, prompted by his misery and poverty, hoping to find in it rest, cure, progress and salvation. It does not matter whether a culture is true or false, good or bad, for no sensible word can be said about it. All that matters is whether it is hunger or affluence that becomes creative.[54] In European culture it was hunger, poverty, decadence, and these have again produced decadence and slavery.

---

[51] H. Pfeil, *op. cit.*, pp. 55-58.
[52] *Beyond Good and Evil*, in *The Philosophy of Nietzsche*, pp. 403 f.
[53] *Thus Spake Zarathustra, op. cit.*, p. 152.
[54] *Die fröhliche Wissenschaft*, p. 285.

All this, according to Nietzsche, is the result of the fact that the European has renounced the will to power. Hence a new man can arise only when man decides to say "Yes" to the will to power and acts accordingly. For man holds his own being man in his hands. But as such he is also a being who must be overcome.[55] What can be loved in man is that he is transition and passage; he is a bridge and not a goal, a cord linking animal and Superman.[56] But it will take a long time before the Superman can be generated. However, man can always transform himself into a father and forebearer of the Superman and in this transformation is the best of his creating.[57]

Nietzsche apparently first conceived the Superman as a superior kind of living being who was actually distinct from man. At that rate there has never yet been an example of that new kind of being.[58] The Superman will surpass man in power and might as man surpasses the animal. His advent will be terrible to the petty people who are lords and masters and who preach surrender, humility, reasonableness and diligence. These virtues do not constitute the power from which will rise the Superman. What is required is wickedness: "The vilest is necessary for the Superman's best."[59] The cry that comes from men's wickedness is still much too small. However, greater dragons will appear on earth. But first much hot sunlight will have to glow on the most virgin forest. Tigers must first evolve from wild cats, and crocodiles from poison-toads. The "good and the just" will view all that with fear and trembling. They will call the Superman "the devil." Nietzsche wishes to sit among them in disguise "that I may mistake you and myself: for that is my last manly prudence."[60]

At a later time, Nietzsche changed his views about Superman.[61] The latter is no longer essentially different from man, but is the highest type in the human species. Napoleon was an example of a Superman in the past. In the future not all men will belong to that higher type, but only a few. They will be the lords. But the others will also have a right to exist, for they will serve the lords as slaves

---

[55]"I teach you the Superman. Man is something that is to be surpassed." *Thus Spake Zarathustra, op. cit.,* p. 6.

[56]*Op. cit.,* pp. 8 f.

[57]*Op. cit.,* p. 90.

[58]"Never yet has there been a Superman. . . . Verily, even the greatest found I—all too human !" *op. cit.,* p. 99.

[59]*Op. cit.,* p 322.

[60]*Op. cit.,* pp. 158 f.

[61]Cf. Pfeil, *Op. cit.,* pp. 149-153.

and be their tools. The lords will be hard on themselves; they will delight in suffering, will bear the heaviest responsibility without flinching; they will be so strong that they do not need virtues. They will be beyond and above all morals, and all crimes will be permissible to them except the crime of weakness. They will be the glory and the justification of life.[62] "God hath died: now do we desire the Superman to live."[63]

"God is Dead"

Nietzsche's struggle for the advent of the Superman is at the same time his battle against the negation of the world and against the slavery of man which have their source in weakness. Since man must become lord and master by his "Yes" to the world, everything that stands in the way of his dominion must be destroyed. The principal obstacle is belief in God and especially Christianity.

Nietzsche's rejection of God passed though various stages. But one thought was dominant throughout: no God *can be permitted* to exist, for if God exists man cannot fulfill his vocation: he cannot become Superman. The belief in God has always stifled that hope in his future. That is why the Superman will also be victor over God and the Antichrist.[64]

The Superman will give new hope to mankind. But the time when this will come about is still far off, for, though God is dead, there will be thousands of years during which there will still be caves in which the shadow of God will be shown. But the man of the future will have to overcome even that shadow.[65] This is the task of the healthy and the strong. They alone know the meaning of the will to power and that is why they are ready to clear away all the obstacles that stand in the way of their dominion.

Psychological Explanation for the Origin of Religion. Nietzsche has a psychological explanation for the origin of religion. When man is suddenly overwhelmed by a feeling of power—and this is the case whenever he is deeply affected—man has doubts about his own person.

---

[62]Cf. Pfeil, *op. cit.,* p. 151.

[63]*Op cit.,* p. 320.

[64]*The Genealogy of Morals,* in *The Philosophy of Nietzsche,* p. 716.

[65]"After Buddha had died, they continued for centuries to show his shadow in a cave—a frightfully horrible shadow. God is dead, but, man being what he is, there will perhaps continue to be for thousands of years caves in which they will show his shadow. And we—we must overcome also his shadow." *Die fröhliche Wissenschaft,* p. 126.

He does not dare to look upon himself as the origin of that emotion of astonishment and attributes it to a person who is stronger than himself, namely God. The origin of religion therefore must be sought in *man's* feeling of power. This feeling of power appears strange and overwhelming to him. He feels like a sick person who, experiencing a heaviness or strangeness in one of his limbs, comes to the conclusion that another human being lies in top of it. In a similar fashion does the naive religious man explain himself as a plurality of persons. Religion is a product of man's doubt about the unity of his person. Man separates his weak and wretched part from that which is strong and startling; the first he calls "man" and the second "God." Hence the concept of God represents man's loathing for life. Nietzsche analyzes this idea in its various dimensions.

First, God stands in the way of the will to power, for all kinds of moral precepts are connected with the idea of God. These forbid the strong to develop their power; they combat the instinct of life and are therefore inimical to real life. "The holy man who pleases God is the ideal castrate. . . . Life ends where 'God's Kingdom' begins."[66]

Morality is the greatest obstacle retarding the advent of the Superman. The belief in God has a paralyzing effect on man's urge to create. God is an idea that makes straight all that is crooked and causes everything that is static to move. All doctrines about the One, the Full, the Unmoved, the Self-sufficient, and the Imperishable are evil and inimical to man. If there were gods, the man of the future would not be able to stand his not being a god. *"Therefore,* there are no gods."[67]

Secondly, connected with the idea of God is that of the equality of all men. This is the invention of the populace,[68] their way of revenging themselves upon the strong. The weak and worthless "are glad in their inmost heart that there is a standard according to which those who are over-endowed with intellectual goods and privileges, are equal to them; they contend for the 'equality of all before God'. . . .It is among them that the most powerful antagonists of atheism are found,"[69] for, if God does not exist, no one will continue to hold that the weak are equal to the strong.

---

[66]Nietzsche, *Götzen-Dämmerung*, p. 105.
[67]*Thus Spake Zarathustra, op. cit.,* p. 91.
[68]*Op. cit.,* p. 320.
[69]*Beyond Good and Evil,* in *The Philosophy of Nietzsche,* p. 522.

That situation, however, is the deathblow to the will-to-power, for the equalization of the weak and the strong impedes the ascent of the strong. The latter eventually get the idea that there are still virtues among the populace and they are tempted to judge themselves according to the standard of virtue of the rabble. They find themselves proud and thus judge that all their higher characteristics and qualities are to be rejected. The result of all this is a lower type of human being. This kind still controls the fate of Europe and acts according to the principle that all men are equal before God.[70] But now God, the greatest danger to the Superman, is dead! Let the Superman live![71]

Thirdly, faith in Divine Providence robs man of the motive for striving for the new future of human power, greatness and dominion. For, according to Nietzsche, the belief in Providence gives us the idea that man does not matter and it does not depend on him to determine what the shape of the future will be, God determines the course of things. He cares for us in every situation, He knows every hair on our heads. He cures our colds, acts as our servant and messenger, and directs all that happens to us to our good. But in such a case man can leave everything to God and should expect everything from Him alone. This, then, prompts man to refrain from energetic activity; he who believes in Divine Providence lets his hands rest in his lap.[72] There is no longer anything to be done for those who believe in Divine Providence.

Lastly, it is necessary to reject God in order to restore and recognize the original "innocence" of man and his world. This is necessary in order that man may unreservedly express and realize his "Yes" to the world, by which he executes his will to power. For Nietzsche the world is neither good nor bad, neither meaningful nor meaningless, neither valuable nor worthless, for no standard exists by which one can make such an evaluation. The world in itself is "innocent."[73] The same is true of human actions; there are no moral or immoral actions. Man's conduct is likewise "innocent" in itself. Hence morality is immoral when it says that certain actions are good and others evil. Sin, therefore, is not something immoral.

---

[70]*Op. cit.*, p. 49.
[71]*Thus Spake Zarathustra, op. cit.*, p. 32.
[72]Cf. Pfeil, *op. cit.*, pp. 70-72.
[73]"Verily, it is a blessing and not a blasphemy when I teach that 'above all things there standeth the heaven of chance, the heaven of innocence, the heaven of hazard, the heaven of wantonness'." *Thus Spake Zarathustra, op. cit.*, p. 183.

The value of man and the world is man's own creation.[74] That is good, meaningful, and has value which is from power; that which is born from weakness is evil, meaningless, and worthless. According to Nietzsche, faith in God has hidden and falsified all that. Faith in God speaks about "another" world, an ideal world, it rejects and despises the real world. Faith in God attributes to God the highest moral qualities and thereby denies the moral value of man's creative power. Instead of honoring the original innocence of man's creative power, faith in God has lowered man and reduced him to slavery.

Faith in God has established God as a witness to human ugliness. But that God must die; a God who sees all things must die; a God whose compassion seriously penetrates into the filthiest corners of man's being must die. Man must wreak vengeance upon such a witness, for "man cannot endure it that such a witness should live."[75]

Nietzsche and Christianity

What Nietzsche says about faith in God in general he applies to Christianity in particular. He batters down Christianity with the same violence with which he defends the Superman, because he is convinced that no religion so greatly lowers man and reduces him to slavery as Christianity. He can understand that men accepted to be Christians in earlier days, but to be a Christian in our own time is simply indecent. For, says Nietzsche, anyone is bound to know that theologians, priests and popes are not merely mistaken in every thing they utter, but that they are liars.[76] This conviction, and especially his firm belief in the salvation of mankind that shall come about with the Superman, prompts Nietzsche to make use of such coarse language that even today the reader can hardly believe his eyes. We shall not present an anthology of it, for it would not contribute anything to philosophy.

Nietzsche knows what he is doing. He is aware of the fact that terrible memories will be attached to his name. He knows it and says about himself: "I am not a man, I am dynamite."[77] When he speaks about Christianity, it is as if he brings himself to explosion. He wants to make Christianity despicable, for in his eyes Christianity is *the* great blasphemy, *the* great internal corruption, *the* in-

---

[74]Nietzsche, *op. cit.,* p. 61.
[75]*Op. cit.,* p. 297.
[76]*Umwertung aller Werte,* p. 235.
[77]Nietzsche, *Ecce homo,* in *The Philosophy of Nietzsche,* p. 923.

stinct for revenge which considers no means too poisonous, too insidious, too cunning, too low; Christianity is *the* immortal stain of shame on mankind.[78]

The Decadence of Christianity. The reasons why Nietzsche rejects God return in an even more concrete fashion when he endeavors to destroy Christianity. It is especially Christianity that appeals to God in order to defend a morality which enslaves man. Nietzsche calls the Christian virtue of justice the most poisonous poison that it is possible to conceive, for it attacks the distance separating man and man. Christianity has transformed the resentment of the rabble into a doctrine of justice that is a weapon against all that is excellent, noble, healthy and powerful on earth.[79] An ethics of the herd. . . . This ethics has also penetrated into politics and has produced socialism and democracy. One herd and one shepherd, one sheep like every other sheep. . . . Christian justice spells the death of the will to power, it kills the possible coming of the Superman. The coming of the Superman demands that unequals should never be made equal.[80] Men are not equal. There should be an ever-increasing inequality and struggle so that the Superman may triumph.

Virtues also, such as goodness, charity, helpfulness and love, lead only to decadence. He who practices them loses power.[81] They interfere with the law of selection. The health of the species requires the elimination of misfits and weaklings. Yet it is precisely to these that Christianity addresses itself. And that is called love! According to Nietzsche, man must learn to love himself with a love that is healthy and wholesome. Man must learn to endure being with himself and not go roving about among others. This wandering and roving about among others has been called "brotherly love." Armed with this word, men have practiced hypocrisy and deceit and done harm to mankind.[82] This love is immoral and a crime against authentic life. Christianity preserves and multiplies decadence.[83]

If we keep in mind what Nietzsche teaches about the Superman, we readily understand why he so vehemently attacks the Christian

---

[78]"Der Antichrist," *Umwertung aller Werte*, p. 283.
[79]*Umwertung aller Werte*, p. 244.
[80]*Götzen-Dämmerung*, p. 172.
[81]"Power is lost when one has compassion. Compassion increases and multiplies the loss of power which suffering as such itself inflicts on life." *Umwertung aller Werte*, p. 195.
[82]*Thus Spake Zarathustra, op. cit.*, p. 214.
[83]*Umwertung aller Werte*, p. 196.

virtues of humility, temperance, self-renunciation, and the evangelical counsels of poverty, chastity and obedience. He looks upon humility, temperance and self-renunciation as upon so many means by which man withdraws from the world and refuses to be actively involved in it. He sees them as a kind of "will to nothing" and a loathing for life. The purpose and goal of Christian life is not success but failure. What an emasculated ideal! It is *the* calamity in the history of health![84] "And all this was believed in as *morality! Ecrasez l'infâme.*"[85]

Christianity, then, is a "No" to the world, a flight from reality. In Christianity man tries to freeze himself in the contemplation of a hereafter. What slavery! Against that, Nietzsche proposes fidelity to the earth, fidelity to the will to power, fidelity to the man of the future.

The "No" of Christianity in reference to the world and life is also implicit in the rejection of the original "innocence" of the world and man.[86] This, according to Nietzsche, is most evident in the Christian attitude toward the body. In Christianity there is contempt for the body, and hygiene is rejected as sensuality. Procreation also, woman and marriage, have been degraded by Christianity. It has caused sex to be looked upon as something unclean and has cast dirt upon the beginning of life. Moreover, it has attached the danger of eternal damnation to sex, so that Christians can bring children into this world only with a bad conscience.[87]

Finally, Christianity has met all joy with mistrust; it has soiled and cast suspicion upon all that is beautiful, glorious, rich and proud, and has removed good conscience from the whole of culture. Priests, as underground leeches, have invented sin in order to block science and culture and prevent everything tht would raise and ennoble man. Christianity tries to strangle real life and for that reason it must itself be strangled.[88] This is the task of the strong. We can forgive the weak who calumniate the world and adhere to Christianity. For, they are misfits and failures of reality, who, no doubt, get a certain satisfaction and exhilaration from heaping insults upon

---

[84] Cf. Pfeil, *op. cit.*, pp. 105 f.

[85] *Ecce homo*, in *The Philosophy of Nietzsche*, p. 933.

[86] "All concepts of the Church are recognized for what they are: the most malicious forgery that exists for the purpose of debasing nature, the values of nature." *Umwertung aller Werte*, p. 236.

[87] Cf. Pfeil, *op. cit.*, p. 111.

[88] Cf. Pfeil, *op cit.*, p. 112.

the world. "No one is free to become a Christian; no one is 'converted' to Christianity; one has to be sick enough for it."[89]

According to Nietzsche, no culture has ever soiled and degraded mankind as much as Christianity. And all this was done in God's name. The Christian concept of God is the canonization of the "will to nothing," an insult to the human world and a lie regarding the hereafter. "The Christian concept of God—God as God of the sick, God as [preying] spider, God as Spirit is one of the most corrupt ideas that was ever invented on earth."[90] That is why it has to be rejected with all the strength residing in healthy man.

Hatred of Priests. Nietzsche's torrent of abuse is inexhaustible when he pours out his hatred toward priests, for they are the bearers of Christianity. They are the ones whom the strong have been unable to overcome until now, because priests use weapons against which there is no defense. The priests have presented themselves as representatives of the slaves and by their slave-ethics have inverted the natural course of events. That which is harmful to life they have called "true"; that which fosters and justifies life and causes its triumph they have called "false." He who seeks a criterion for truth has merely to go to the theologians and turn their value judgments upside down.[91] The priests have learned their insidious and sly way of acting from the Jewish priests whose role they prolong. Judaism is fundamentally a religion of rancor. According to Nietzsche, Judaism was born from a resentment against the spirit of classical paganism, and Christianity inherited that resentment. The greatest crime committed by Judaism is that it spawned Christianity, for the latter released and brought about the full development of the slaves' hidden feelings of vengeance against life. Even the Germanic races were unable to resist Christianity. In fact, the German emperors made Christianity a world-empire during the Middle Ages. And when Christianity was in its death throes, it was once more a German, Luther, who revived it.

Nietzsche was firmly convinced that Christianity was nearing its end and that he had a vision of its ruin. He was also fully convinced that he would play the chief role in that debacle, that he would split the history of mankind in two.[92] Men's lives would be dated as

---

[89]*Umwertung aller Werte*, p. 258.
[90]*Op. cit.*, p. 208.
[91]*Op. cit.*, p. 198.
[92]*Ecce homo*, in *The Philosophy of Nietzsche*, p. 931.

before or after that event. Christianity's demise would be followed by a new morality since, before its ruin, so-called "truth" was nothing but the most rude and subversive form of a lie. The priests, says Nietzsche, will then appear as the lowest and most indecent men that ever lived. But there must be no martyrs! The best way to refute Christianity is carefully and respectfully "to freeze it."[93] Nietzsche describes his meeting with the last pope as one who is "out of service."[94]

The Death of God and the Tragedy of Man

Nietzsche would not be a prophet if he had not tried to figure out what the consequences of the murder of God would be for the future of man. He wrote about the present and the past, but also about the future. The future, he says, will be a time without God. It is already possible, he argues, to write the history of the future, for necessity itself is at work in bringing it about. The future is already proclaimed by a hundred omens and announces itself everywhere. The whole of European culture "has long been writhing in an agony of suspense which increases from decade to decade as if in expectation of a catastrophe, ... like a torrent that *will reach its* bourne and refuses to reflect—yea, that even dreads reflection." Nietzsche thinks he has the prophetic vocation to write the "history of the next two centuries" and to describe "what must necessarily happen: The triumph of Nihilism."[95]

The fantastic fact that God is dead and that belief in the God of Christianity has become unbelievable, says Nietzsche, already begins to cast its first shadows over Europe. Shadows? That term should not be taken to mean that the death of God will not bring light, happiness, relief and the dawn.[96] The contrary is true; but these are only the immediate results. For the philosopher the death of God means liberation and for man a new innocence. But there are also more remote consequences.

For the few whose eyes are sufficiently strong to see, the death of God means that a sun has gone down and that an ancient and deep trust has been turned into doubt. The fact that God is dead is too

---

[93]"To refute something one respectfully 'freezes' it—and in this way also one refutes theologians." *Umwertung aller Werte*, p. 263.
[94]*Thus Spake Zarathustra*, in *The Philosophy of Nietzsche*, p. 286.
[95]*The Will to Power*, Vol. I, Preface, p. 1.
[96]*Die fröhliche Wissenschaft*, p. 236.

great and too distant to be grasped by most men, so that it is not yet possible to say that they have received the message. Most men have not the least inkling about the coming collapse of all that was built on the belief in God, of an eclipse the like of which, in all probability, has never been witnessed on earth.[97]

Because God is dead, man can no longer pray, no longer worship or find rest in infinite confidence. Man can no longer rely on an ultimate Truth, and ultimate Goodness, and an ultimate Power. In his loneliness he has no longer a Friend. He lives without hope on a mountain whose summit is covered with snow and whose heart is afire. There is no longer an ultimate Rewarder nor one who turns everything into good. There is no longer any reason or love in anything that occurs. There is no longer any place of rest for the heart, no place where one can find and need not to seek any further. All this man must renounce. But who has the energy for such an ordeal? "No one as yet has the strength to face this."[98]

The Future of Man. Nietzsche has felt, with an incredible visionary power, what the death of God would mean for the future European.

First, there will be no more striving for the moral good, for morality is most intimately connected with the existence of God. Nietzsche ridicules the superficial atheists who preceded him and thought that they could abolish religion but preserve morality. "What guilelessness! As if morality could remain when the sanctioning deity is no longer present!"[99] The future European must prepare himself for the fact that, if there is no God, the will to destroy shall be just as essential to life as the will to create. The existence of God has been disproved but not the existence of the devil.[100]

Secondly, in the future there will be no striving for truth. In the past, science in its search for truth always secretly lived in virtue of religion. But when there is no Eternal Truth, there is no longer any truth in things. The scientists sought for truth and did not wish to receive. But why not? Because morality forbade them to do so. Without being aware of it they clung to morality, that is to religion, there-

---

[97]*Op. cit.,* p. 235.
[98]*Op. cit.,* p. 188.
[99]*The Will to Power,* Vol. I, p. 212.
[100]Pfeil, *op. cit.,* p. 128.

fore to God.[101] But God is dead! The future European must expect that deceit will be a part of life. He must realize that life in the future will consist of confessing and deceiving.[102]

Thirdly, because the will to truth and goodness does not exist, man will be equal to the animal. As long as God exists, man can be the crown of creation, even a child of God. But God is dead! So now the ape stands at the beginning of the road travelled by man, and at the end of this road there is the urn containing the ashes of the last man and gravedigger.[103]

If there is no God, it is ridiculous to assign a special place to man in the cosmos. He is merely a kind of animal which differs from other animals only by the fact that he is a "sick animal,"[104] —sick because his mental life has led him away from his instincts. Animals look upon man as a being like them, but one that has dangerously lost the healthy animal mind. They look upon man as the foolish animal, the laughing animal, the crying animal, and the most unhappy animal.[105] Nothing would be lost if man disappeared. Many species of animals have already vanished! On the contrary, the disappearance of man would be a sort of cure and purification of the earth. Mankind is a skin disease of the earth.[106]

Finally, because of God's death, man's life becomes a senseless martyrdom. The man of the future will be his own torturer and executioner. "O eternal 'in vain'!" Without God, the world in which man lives is no organism and has neither form nor beauty. That is what they used to say in the olden times of faith. If there is no God, the world is chaos, a gap between two nothings, an event without plan, reason, or will. Nothing remains to man except his "No" to all things, a "No" in judgment and deed: Nihilism! Nothing in the future will be able to stop the advent of nihilism. "Nothing has any purpose."[107] All values are nothing but bait through which life's comedy endeavors to prolong itself without ever coming

---

[101]*Die fröhliche Wissenschaft,* p. 239.
[102]Pfeil, *op. cit.,* pp. 128-130.
[103]"The road travelled by mankind is supposed to serve as a proof of its glory and relationship to God. Alas! It too is no good. At the end of this road stands the funeral urn of the last man and digger of graves (with the inscription: *Nihil humani a me alienum puto*)." Nietzsche, *Morgenröte,* p. 46.
[104]"The Genealogy of Morality," *Beyond Good and Evil, op. cit.,* p. 746.
[105]Nietzsche, *Die fröhliche Wissenschaft,* p. 169.
[106]"The earth, said he, has a skin; and this skin has diseases. One of these diseases, for example, is called 'man'." *Thus Spake Zarathustra, op. cit.,* p. 143.
[107]*The Will to Power,* vol. I, p. 6.

nearer to a solution. Everything is "in vain!" However, "nihilism is not only a meditating over the 'in vain!'—not only the belief that everything deserves to perish, but one actually puts one's shoulder to the plough; one destroys." Strong minds are not content with saying "No" in a judgment; they follow it up with the "No" of the deed. "Annihilation by the reasoning faculty seconds annihilation by the hand."[108]

Pascal was of the opinion that without the Christian belief man would become a monster and nature chaos. Nietzsche agrees: "We fulfilled this prophecy."[109]

Nietzsche's Personal Suffering from God's Death.   Nietzsche personally suffered much at the thought of God's demise. This is perfectly clear from several passages in his letters and posthumous works. He felt an inexpressible loneliness, knowing that God was dead. He has had to bear alone the vision of the future European nihilism. A classic passage in *Die fröhliche Wissenschaft* dramatically expresses this lonely suffering:

> Have you heard about the fool who on a bright sunny day lit a lantern and, running into the square, kept on repeating, "I am looking for God! I am seeking God!" It just happened that there were many men standing together, all atheists, and seeing and hearing the fool they had a great laugh. "Has He gone astray?" cried one. "Has He taken the wrong road like a child?" said another. "Or is He trying to hide?" "Is he afraid of us?" "Has He taken a boat and emigrated?"

> So they shouted and laughed among themselves. The madman sprang in their midst and pierced them with his eyes. "Where has God gone to?" he cried, "I will tell you! We have killed Him—you and I! We are all His murderers!"

> "But how did we do it? How were we able to drink the ocean dry? Who gave us the sponge to wipe away the whole horizon? What did we do when we unhooked the earth from the sun? Where is the earth going now? Whither are we going? Away from all suns? Aren't we constantly on the run? Backwards, sideways, forwards, in all directions? Is there still an

---

[108]Nietzsche, *op. cit.,* vol. I, p. 22.
[109]*Op. cit.,* vol. I, p. 69.

above and a below? Aren't we wandering through an endless Nothing? Does not the void gape at us? Hasn't it become colder? Isn't the night constantly darker? Don't we have to light lanterns by day? Aren't we already hearing the racket of the gravediggers who are burying God? Don't we yet smell the corruption of God?—for gods also are subject to corruption! God is dead! God remains dead! And we have killed Him! How do we, murders above all murderers, console ourselves? The holiest and mightiest that the world possessed until now has bled to death under our daggers—who will wash away the blood that clings to us? With what water can we purify ourselves? Is the greatness of the deed not too great for us? . . . Never was a greater deed accomplished!". . .

The madman then stopped speaking; he looked once more at his hearers; they too were silent and strangely looked at him. Finally he threw his lantern on the ground, breaking it to pieces and extinguishing its flame. "I have come too soon," said he, "my time has not yet arrived. This horrible event is still on its way. . . . This deed is still farther away from them than the most distant star. Yet they have done the deed!"

People add that the madman entered several churches that same day and there intoned his "eternal rest to god" (*requiem aeternam deo*). When he was led outside and had recovered his composure, he could reply only this: "But what else are those churches now than graves and tombstones of God?"[110]

In his infinite loneliness, Nietzsche realizes that man has murdered God in order to free himself . . . for nothingness. Formerly men were offered in sacrifice to God and frequently those who were most cherished became the victims. Later men offered to God the strongest instincts they possessed, and the festal joy resulting from that kind of sacrifice shines in the cruel glances of the ascetic. What else remained to be offered? Was it not necessary in the end to sacrifice all that is consoling, holy, healing, all hope, all faith in a hidden harmony a future salvation and justice? Was it not necessary to offer God Himself, and, out of cruelty to oneself, to worship the Nothing? To offer God for Nothingness! This "mystery of ultimate cruelty has

---

[110]*Die fröhliche Wissenschaft,* pp. 140 f.

been reserved for the rising generation; we all know something thereof already."[111] In the future, life will drag as in a sepulcher.

> And I saw a great sadness come over mankind. The best turned weary of their works.
>
> A doctrine appeared, a faith ran beside it: "All is empty, all is alike, all hath been!"
>
> And from all the hills there re-echo: "All is empty, all is alike, all hath been!"
>
> To be sure, we have harvested: but why have all our fruits become rotten and brown? What was it fell last night from the evil moon?
>
> In vain was all our labour, poison has our wine become, the evil eye hath singed yellow our fields and hearts.
>
> Arid have we all become; and fire falling upon us, then do we turn dust like ashes:—yea, the fire itself have we made aweary.
>
> All our fountains have dried up, even the sea has receded. All the ground trieth to gape but the depth will not swallow.
>
> "Alas, where is there still a sea in which one could be drowned?" So soundeth our plaint across shallow swamps.
>
> Verily, even for dying we come too weary; now do we keep awake and live on—in sepulchres.[112]

This desire for a prolongation of life is absolutely senseless: since God is dead, man no longer has any purpose or haven.

> Ah, where have gone all my goodness and all my shame and all my belief in the good! Ah, where is the lying innocence which I once possessed, the innocence of the good and of their noble lies!
>
> Too much hath become clear unto me: Now it does not concern me anymore. Nothing liveth any longer that I love—how should I still love myself?
>
> "To live as I incline, or not to live at all": So do I wish; so wisheth also the holiest. But alas! How have *I* still—inclination?
>
> Have *I*—still a goal? A haven towards which *my* sail is set?
>
> A good wind? Ah, he only who knoweth *whither* he saileth, knoweth what wind is good and a fair wind for him.

---

[111]*Beyond Good and Evil*, in *The Philosophy of Nietzsche*, p. 440.
[112]*Thus Spake Zarathustra, op. cit.*, pp. 146 f.

What still remaineth to me? A heart weary and flippant; an
unstable will; fluttering wings, a broken backbone.

This seeking for my *home,* O Zarathustra doest thou know
that this seeking hath been *my* home-sickening? It eateth me up.

"Where is—my home?" For it do I ask and seek, and have
sought but have not found it. O eternal everywhere, O eternal
nowhere, O eternal—useless![113]

In his extreme loneliness Nietzsche finally called God back:

Nay! Thou back!
With all of thy great tortures!
To me the last of lonesome ones,
Oh come thou back!
All my hot tears in streamlets trickle
Their course to thee!
And all my final hearty fervour
Up-glow'th to *thee!*
Oh come thou back,
Mine unfamiliar God! My pain!
My final bliss![114]

Nevertheless, Nietzsche remained convinced that God was dead.
And he was equally convinced that the murder of God would thrust
Europe into nihilism. He knew that he stood alone with his frightful knowledge. In a letter of 1885 addressed to Overbeck he wrote:
"My life is now only a wish that all things may be different from the
way I understand them and that some one will make my 'truths' incredible."[115]

Nietzsche in Retrospect

At present anyone who, with an open mind, examines the work of
Nietzsche becomes the prey of a strange mixture of reactions. On
the one hand, Nietzsche succeeds in provoking his readers most
thoroughly by the evident pride of his words. He says of himself
that his whole existence is an exceptional form of pride and godless-
ness, even when measured by ancient Greek standards. Pride is his

---

[113]*Op. cit.,* p. 306.
[114]*Op cit.,* pp. 283 f.
[115]Cf. Pfeil, *op. cit.,* p. 140.

attitude toward nature; pride in his attitude toward God; pride, his attitude toward himself, for he experiments with himself. "What do I care about the salvation of the soul?"

That pride looks with haughtiness on the tortures of its own hell and with contempt on the congenial, nebulous world of others. He contemptuously recalls the most noble and beloved illusions with which he played in the past, and takes pleasure in calling forth that contempt from the very bottom of Hell.[116]

This is why he angers his readers, for they realize that they would become themselves object of his contempt if they dared to oppose the prophet in the least. Speaking about his *Zarathustra,* Nietzsche says that it is the greatest present mankind ever received: "This book, whose voice resounds across the ages, is not only the loftiest book in the world . . ., but it is also the deepest book, born of the inmost fullness of truth, an inexhaustible well into which no pitcher descends without rising again laden with gold and goodness."[117] What is a critical reader to think when he sees such lines especially if he realizes that it is Nietzsche's intention "to philosophize with the hammer"?[118]

On the other hand, Nietzsche the man comes very close to his readers provided they keep an open mind, not to his doctrine, but to his message. It is possible, of course, to summarize Nietzsche in a set of theses, and he who wants to do this, especially when he makes use of Nietzsche's own extreme terminology, can easily present a ridiculous caricature. We may even say that every "reproduction" of Nietzsche's doctrine does an injustice to Nietzsche as a philosopher, even if no injustice is intended. The same, however, is true for every "reproduction" of any great philosophy. Yet it is impossible to escape from making a reproduction when one wants to speak about a philosopher. It is particularly easy to make the "reproduction" of Nietzsche a caricature. This is all the more regrettable when one keeps in mind that up to 1950 about two thousand books and twelve thousand articles had been written about the philosophy of Nietzsche. This flood of studies should suffice to show that he who reduces Nietzsche to a caricature makes himself ridiculous.

The Insufficiency of Psychological Explanations. It is equally unreasonable to try to explain Nietzsche's philosophy by means of psy-

---

[116]Cf. G. Siegmund, *Der Kampf um Gott,* Berlin, 1957, pp. 183 f.
[117]*Ecce homo,* in *The Philosophy of Nietzsche,* p. 813.
[118]*Op. cit.,* p. 816.

chology or psychiatry, although the tragic life of this god-seeker offers a ready opportunity for doing so. But it would be an injustice against the philosopher and his thought. Nietzsche had the occasion to object to such an approach, for that method was applied to his doctrine even in his own lifetime. Referring to it, he says: "In relation to my critics, I often had the impression that I was dealing with scoundrels. What alone seems to interest them is not what is said, but that it is I who say it, and how I may have come to say it. . . . In practice, the only reply to them is a kick. I am judged so that they do not have to examine my work. They explain the origin of my work and think that this is enough to dispose of the work itself."[119]

Nietzsche is perfectly right in objecting against such a procedure. Even if psychology would succeed in fully explaining the genesis of a philosophy, nothing worthwhile has yet been said for the philosopher. For the thing that is philosophically important is whether and to what extent a philosophy is *true* or *false*. Nothing has been said yet about that philosophical question when the psychologist has fully solved the genesis of a philosophy. He who confuses the psychological genesis with the truth content of a doctrine and defends a psychologistic concept of truth undermines his own doctrines, for he is forced to allow others an equal right to explain his psychologism on psychological grounds.

What Did Nietzsche "See"? Nietzsche wants his critics to examine his work. This examination does not mean that the contemporary philosopher should accept or reject a series of theses formulated by Nietzsche. Today's philosopher is willing to examine Nietzsche's work when, reading what this philosopher and prophet has said, he tries to be sensitive to what Nietzsche has "seen." For one thing is certain: If Nietzsche belongs to the classics, we cannot say that he has "not seen anything." He did see something. The modern philosopher, then, is not asked to accept Nietzsche's theses, but it is expected of him that, in his attempt to express the meaning of reality in his own way, he personally assigns due value to what Nietzsche has seen.

He who takes this attitude does not have to hold a debate with Nietzsche. The manner of thinking of this philosopher does not lend itself to such a method. His extremism makes a calm exchange of ideas impossible. If Nietzsche were still able to reply in a debate, he

---

[119]Nietzsche, *Die Unschuld des Werdens,* *Nachlass,* Vol. 1, p. 383.

would relapse into extremes of wholly different shapes and forms. These new extreme views would again offer food for thought to one who, while remaining faithful to reality, tries to obtain a better understanding of it.

What did Nietzsche actually see? This question is the one possible topic of discussion, when we recall his extremisms, insults, mordant mockeries, contempt, pride, hatred, immorality, and blasphemies against God. "Morality is immoral" Nietzsche once said, and this is only one example. Christians are tempted to reject that "thesis." But that is not the question. What did Nietzsche have in mind when he made that statement? Is it not true that a morality that generates anxiety and fear and educates men in those dispositions is immoral? "That is a bad morality indeed, but it has nothing to do with authentic Christianity," Christians are ready to reply. We agree, but Nietzsche was not speaking about that! What he has in mind is the fact that there are types of morality that generate anxiety and make men live in fear and that all this is done *in the name of God*.

It is a *fact* that such a morality oppresses man in the name of God. Such a morality must be destroyed and the god who sponsors it must be rejected. One who tries to "see" what Nietzsche saw does not subscribe to his "theses," but is strongly influenced by him when he endeavors to express reality and life in his own personal way.

Liberty and Morality as a Foundation for Atheism

We have spoken of Nietzsche by way of an introduction to the sphere of thought that is proper to existential atheism. We are not concerned with the possibility of establishing that this kind of existentialism is directly dependent on Nietzsche. What we are concerned with is the "attitude" of certain contemporary philosophers. This attitude is such that it implies atheism as a postulate. The atheism in question is not based so much on the rejection of a proof for the existence of God, or on a particular form of agnosticism, but rather on the conviction that the recognition of what is essentially implied by being man *demands* the rejection of God. According to existential atheism, it is not possible to acknowledge the authentic being of man and his essential dignity if one accepts God. It is this conviction that existential atheism has borrowed from Nietzsche.

It is easy to see, from what we have said, that "postulatory" atheism can assume many forms. It is a question of saving and preserving man's being and his essential dignity. But all kinds of interpretations are possible. It is particularly a matter of saving and preserving human freedom and authentic ethical action. And this again can have many meanings.

Nietzsche has his own ideas about that. And these have not been taken over bodily by existential atheism. Sartre is perhaps closest to Nietzsche when freedom and morality are concerned. Merleau-Ponty is clearly opposed to Sartre on these points, and yet he too rejects God on the basis of freedom and morality. With respect to Jeanson and Camus the situation is different again. All this shows that we may not try to simplify things.

CHAPTER SIX

THE EXISTENTIALISTIC ATHEISM OF SARTRE AND MERLEAU-PONTY

1. THE ATHEISM OF SARTRE

Jean-Paul Sartre is most helpful to those who want to discover the foundation of his atheism. He indicates that foundation very clearly and without any ambiguity. God cannot exist because the freedom which is traditionally attributed to God really belongs to man.[1] A certain view of man's freedom makes it impossible to affirm both God and man. Now, according to Sartre, man's existence as freedom is undeniable. Therefore, God does not exist.

A. *Sartre's View Regarding Descartes' Concept of Freedom*

In an article in which Sartre follows Descartes step by step in his concept of freedom, Sartre comes to the conclusion that this philosopher had a very strange idea about freedom. On the one hand, he says, Descartes considers freedom as a kind of autonomy which, however, he makes consist merely in the will's refusal to agree with error or ideas that are not "clear and distinct"; in other words, that autonomy of freedom is somehow "negative." Yet, on the other hand, he also understands it as something "positive," as a positive agreement of the will, but one through which the will loses its autonomy because the clear and distinct ideas permeate and determine it.[2]

"What a strange liberty!" Sartre exclaims. And he adds that it is useless to follow Descartes step by step in his explanations, for they do not bring one to a true understanding of what such an independent, proud and individualistic man like Descartes really wanted when he wrote about freedom. Sartre thinks that the *man* Descartes

---

[1] Sartre, *Situations,* Vol. I, Paris, 1947, pp. 314 f.

[2] "Strange freedom! Finally, it is resolved into two phases. In the first, freedom is negative and it then is an autonomy; but it is reduced to the refusal of our consent to error or confused thoughts. In the second, its meaning changes; it is positive agreement, but then the will loses its autonomy, and the great clarity existing in the understanding permeates and determines the will." *Op. cit.,* p. 328.

had other ambitions than Descartes the scientist and the Platonic philosopher.[3]

Descartes, Sartre believes, was too much of a dogmatist in his pursuit of science and too good a Christian to be able to understand himself and his own thought. Poor Descartes let himself be crushed to death by a pre-existing order of eternal truths and an eternal system of values created by God. Now, if man himself does not invent the good and does not himself create science, he is only nominally free.

According to Sartre, Descartes simply takes over the false Christian concept of freedom: man is free for error and evil but not for truth and the good; God leads man to the true and good which He has chosen for man; man has merely to give God a free hand; and all credit for man's progress in truth and goodness belong to God. Only to the extent that man is "nothingness" does he escape from God's grasp. Man is free to let God's hand go, but then he condemns himself to producing "nothing." The universal, divine order is not disturbed thereby.[4]

This, Sartre thinks, is what the text says according to the letter, but it is not what Descartes actually wants to say. For, according to Descartes, there is no essential difference between human and divine freedom. "The 'Yes' of man is not different from the 'Yes' of God."[5] Hence what Descartes says about divine freedom, he would unqualifiedly have affirmed about human freedom if he had not become the victim of his dogmatism and Catholicism.[6] Now the God of Descartes is the freest being that it is possible for man to conceive. He is the absolute Creator, who is not subject to any principles. He has created both the beings and their essences, the world and its laws, individuals and first principles. God decreed the mathematical truths and established the laws of nature. He is as free to make mathematical truths un-true as He is to refrain from creating the world. No truth is antecedent to God's knowledge, for to will and to know are one in God; hence by willing something, He knows it and it is true because He wills it.[7]

---

[3] *Op. cit.*, p. 329
[4] *Op cit.*, pp. 330 f.
[5] *Op. cit.*, p. 318.
[6] "Accordingly, it is of his own freedom, as he would have conceived it if he had been untrammeled by Catholicism and dogmatism, that he speaks when he describes God's freedom." *Op. cit.*, p. 331.
[7] *Op. cit.*, pp. 331 f.

Now this, says Sartre, is what Descartes really wished to say about human freedom. Divine freedom is freedom only when it is conceived as absolute autonomy; freedom and creation are one. God's "freedom is the foundation of truth, and the rigorous necessity that is found in the order of truths, is based on the absolute contingency of a creative free will."[8] The good likewise is absolutely good in virtue of the creative decision of the same free will.[9]

According to Sartre, it was necessary that centuries should go by, centuries marked by crisis of faith and science, before *man* would claim that freedom for himself. Centuries had to pass before man would begin to suspect the fundamental truth of humanism, viz., man is the being whose presence makes the world be.[10] Whatever Descartes said about God's own freedom he really wanted to affirm about man's own freedom, but the situation in which he lived made it impossible. Nevertheless, Sartre argues, humanism in the Sartrian sense was already present, though only in a vague way, in Descartes.[11]

All this does not tell us what Descartes actually thought about human freedom. But the way Sartre speaks about Descartes leaves no doubt about Sartre's ideas concerning freedom: freedom is nothing else but absolute and creative autonomy. Let us see how he develops that idea.

B. *Wavering Intentionality?*

If we consider only Sartre's definitions of man as subject, we inevitably get the impression that, whenever Sartre speaks of man, he is thinking of an intentional, existent subject that is really involved in the world.[12] And if we pay attention only to Sartre's phenomenological analysis of the human body, we cannot imagine that Sartre would still be able to separate the subject from the facticity of the body and the world.[13] A really intentional subject would then have to be understood as an intentional, that is, relative freedom, a

---

[8]*Op. cit.*, p. 333.
[9]*Ibid.*
[10]*Op. cit.*, p. 334.
[11]"But, on the other hand, there is nothing more contained in this freedom than in human freedom." *Op. cit.*, p. 333.
[12]"All consciousness, as Husserl has shown, is consciousness of something." Sartre, *Being and Nothingness*, p. LI.
[13]"We know that there is not a for-itself on the one hand and a world on the other as two closed entities for which we must subsequently seek some explanation as to how they communicate." *Op. cit.*, p. 306.

freedom that becomes meaningless when it is not involved in the facticity of the body and the world. With respect to such a subject there could be no question of an absolute, creative autonomy, for an intentional subject presupposes the facticity of that which the subject is *not*, namely, body and world.

However, the way Sartre speaks about worldly *things* makes us fear the worst. Sartre calls the worldly thing an "in itself." This thing is "massive," being in the proper sense, the only being deserving the name of being. It is "opaque to itself," "filled with itself," "full positivity." It "is what it is," entirely identical with itself. It "does not enter into any connection with what is not itself"; it contains no negation of any kind, "never posits itself as other than another being." It is, and "when it gives way, one cannot even say that it no longer is." It cannot be deduced from the possible or traced back to the necessary. "Uncreated, without reason for its being, without any connetion with another being, being in itself is 'superfluous' (*de trop*) for eternity."[14]

The meaning of those descriptions becomes somewhat clear when we reflect that Sartre's "in itself" is not a conscious being. Now, relations, to be other, reason for being, to be no longer, to be reduced, and so on, presuppose consciousness. The "in itself" lacks consciousness; hence, says Sartre, the "in itself" has no relations, is not other than another being, has no reason for its being, and so forth.

But the attentive reader also notices what is happening. The so-called description of the "in itself" is totally in terms of the "in itself for us." Sartre sees very well that the "in itself for us" is not full positivity, that it does have relations, that it is other than something else, that it is no longer after it has gone, and so forth. But he imagines that he can describe the "in itself" by simply assigning to it the opposite of the qualities of the "in itself for us." The "in itself, is not for us"; therefore, Sartre argues, in order to define the "in itself" all the qualities of the "in itself for us" must be replaced by negations.

Here, however, a question comes up which deals a crucial blow to Sartre's phenomenology. If the "in itself" is, in spite of everything, a reality that is separate from the subject, how can the subject *really* be an intentional subject? When the correlate of the intentionality is divorced from the intentional subject, doesn't it follow also that the

---

[14]*Op. cit.,* pp. LXV-LXVI.

subject is divorced from its correlate? But in that case there is no *real* correlation, so that the freedom of the subject is an absolute freedom.

For Sartre, as for all phenomenologists, to be subject means to be free.[15] For Sartre, it is inadmissible that the subject could be the deterministic result of thing-like processes and forces. Perhaps this is one of the reasons why Sartre calls the subject "Nothingness" (*Néant*). For if the term "being" is reserved for the being of a *thing,* there is then no other term to designate the being of the *subject* than the terms "Nothingness," if one wishes to stress the idea that the subject, unlike a thing, is *not* the deterministic result of thing-like processes and forces.[16]

The way a philosopher conceives the *subject* is decisive in determining the form freedom will take in his philosophy. As we have seen, Sartre, on the one hand, stresses the intentionality of the subject but, on the other, he takes that intentionality away. Hence it is to be expected that his thought about freedom will also vacillate. The question is, of course, which of the two sides will prevail.

C. Toward Absolute Freedom

It is not difficult to quote texts in which Sartre expresses the situated character of freedom. All ends, he says, "in fact are pursued in terms of a particular empirical situation";[17] "freedom is the choice of an end in terms of the past."[18] We must say, then, that the subject as freedom appears only as involved in a certain facticity, which means that the subject as project is affected by a certain restriction in respect to the field within which he can act.[19]

It is for this reason that the real world of freedom is distinguished from the dream world. To be able to *realize* a project belongs to being free, and requires more than the mere project. If the realization of a project required only that the project be conceived, there would be no difference between the real world and the dream world.[20] But there is a difference between them. The real world is

---

[15]"We have shown that freedom is actually one with the being of the For-itself." *Op. cit.,* p. 453.

[16]"These abortive attempts to stifle freedom under the weight of being . . . show sufficiently that freedom in its foundation coincides with the nothingness which is at the heart of man." *Op. cit.,* p. 440.

[17]*Op. cit.,* p. 567.

[18]*Op. cit.,* p. 497.

[19]*Op. cit.,* p. 567.

[20]*Op. cit.,* p. 482.

indispensable to freedom. The resistance of the world's facticity results only in enabling it (the subject) to arise as freedom. The subject is "only as engaged in a resisting world."[21]

To be free, however, is not the same as attaining what one wants to attain, but rather the self-determination to will and choose, the autonomy of choice. But the reality of that autonomy of choice, as distinguished from a dream and a pure wish, is manifested only in action. In fact, free choice and action are identical; the distinction between a free choice and the dreams or simple wish always presupposes a beginning of realization.[22] A prisoner does not have the freedom to leave his cell but "he is free to try to escape." This freedom, however, is real, and not a dream or pure wish, only to the extent that there is a "commencement of realization." This shows that there is no distinction between free choice, the free project and the action. Intentions, aims and choices can no more be divorced from the act than thought can be divorced from language. The action teaches us what we *really* intend and choose.[23]

Facticity and Freedom. What we have said indicates with all possible clarity that Sartre conceives the subject, his free project and its execution, his free action, as intentional. It is necessary to conclude, Sartre believes, that no factical situation ever has any meaning "in itself"; hence it can never exercise a unilateral, deterministic influence on the subject.[24]

Everyone who looks at things without prejudice is ready to agree with Sartre on that point, for it is evident that the meaning of a factical situation is co-determined by the project emanating from the subjectivity.[25] A rock on a mountain pass has its meaning of being scalable or not scalable only in virtue of the project of the alpinist.[26] It has a totally different meaning within the project of a pure aesthetic; and it is only within the project of moving it that the rock assumes the meaning of a heavy obstacle.[27] Likewise, the conditions of life of a laborer have no meaning in themselves. The real meaning of that facticity depends on the particular subject as

---

[21] *Op. cit.,* p. 483.
[22] *Ibid.*
[23] *Op. cit.,* pp. 483 f.
[24] *Op. cit.,* pp. 486 f.
[25] "From the start the environment conceived as a situation refers to the for-itself which is choosing, just as the for-itself refers to the environment by the very fact that the for-itself is in the world." *Op. cit.,* pp. 572 f.
[26] *Op. cit.,* p. 488.
[27] *Op cit.,* p. 482.

project the laborer is. The proletarian can lead a humiliated or proud existence accordingly as he chooses resignation or revolt. His facticity does not determine him to anything. The same holds true in respect to illness; it is never *per se* unbearable but can also be desirable, interesting or useful.

Similar ideas apply to the past. The past never has a meaning in itself. Whether a crisis at the time of puberty is "a pure accident . . . or a first sign of a future conversion" depends on the subject. Whether a time of imprisonment is fruitful or harmful, depends on the subject's decision to "give up stealing or become hardened."[28]

From the same point of view we can say also that the taking of the Bastille has no closed and definitive meaning.[29] No situation has ever a meaning in itself and the situation never exercises a unilateral, deterministic influence on the subject.[30]

That idea, in itself, is very true and authentically phenomenological, but Sartre develops it in an unbalanced way. When above we reproduced his rejection of views which consider the situation as an "in itself," we had to close our eyes to expressions which, to say the least, could easily be misunderstood. He says, for instance: "It is our freedom which constitutes the limits which it will subsequently encounter,"[31] and: "[The rock] will discourage me if I have freely fixed limits to my desire of making the projected climb."[32] Although it is possible to give a correct interpretation to those words, they can also be very easily misunderstood. Or should we say perhaps that we have to do here with an exaggerated notion of the significance of the subject? In other words, is Sartre surreptitiously absolutizing freedom? We are convinced that this is the case, and we shall justify our assertion by explaining Sartre's theory of freedom in reference to the passions and emotions.

"The existentialist," says Sartre, "does not believe in the power of passion. He will never regard a grand passion as a destructive torrent upon which a man is swept into certain actions as by fate and which, therefore, is an excuse for him. He thinks that man is responsible for his passions."[33] To depict a state of affairs in which

---

[28]*Op. cit.,* p. 489.
[29]*Op cit,* p. 501.
[30]"There is freedom only in a *situation,* and there is a situation only through freedom." *Op. cit.,* p. 489.
[31]*Op. cit.,* p. 482.
[32]*Op. cit.,* p. 488.
[33]Sartre, *Existentialism and Humanism,* London (Methuen), 1948, p. 34.

autonomy of freedom is attributed to the will but is denied to the passions is erroneous, Sartre believes.[34] Why? Is there, then, no difference between an act of will and passion?

Sartre does not deny the difference, but he considers it unimportant in connection with freedom because freedom precedes the act of the will and the passion. For freedom resides in the subject as project, since a situation has no meaning in itself but only within a free project. For this reason, argues Sartre, it is no longer possible to say, for example, that a threat determines me to take a passional flight, for a threat is a threat only in reference to my free project to save my life. I can execute this project either by a passional flight or by a rational resistance to the threat. I *myself* choose between the two possibilities.[35] I choose the volition or the passion. Whether the world is a rational world (object of my volition) or a magic world (object of my passion) depends *exclusively* on my choice.[36]

Divorce of Freedom from Situations. Here Sartre's lack of balance comes clearly into view. We readily agree that motives and incentives have no meaning in themselves. They appear as such only in virtue of a project. But Sartre should at least stress the fact that freedom as project is "situated," i.e., that all projects are possible only within definite limits, for example, within the limits imposed upon the freedom as project by passions and emotions. In that case we have once more the question that occupies Sartre—namely, whether it is unthinkable that passions and emotions are so strong that at a certain moment we can no longer speak about making a project in the authentically human sense of the term.

Sartre rejects such a possibility. The fear of a threat can never determine me, he says, for something or someone appears to me as a threat only in reference to my project to save my life. This means for Sartre that the threat derives its meaning exclusively from my subjectivity.[37] The subjectivity of the factical situation is thereby isolated and absolutized as project. It makes no difference for the

---

[34]"And if nihilation is precisely the being of freedom, how can we refuse autonomy to the passions in order to grant it to the will?" Sartre, *Being and Nothingness*, p. 443.

[35]"Shall I act by volition or by passion? Who can decide except me?" *Op. cit.*, p. 444.

[36]*Op. cit.,* p 445.

[37]"Actually, causes and motives have only the weight which my project— i.e., the free production of the end and of the known act to be realized— confers upon them." *Op. cit.*, pp. 450 f.

freedom of an action whether the subject reacts with an impassioned or a free action; the passionate action is also free, for it is executed in function of a completely free project. This completely autonomous project is executed either by the passion or by the volitional act.[38] Even if someone "breaks" under torture, his action, says Sartre, is a perfectly free act.[39]

Freedom and Responsibility

If man is absolute freedom, he also bears an absolute responsibility. Sartre draws this conclusion without the least hesitation or reservation. Man carries the weight of the whole world on his shoulders; he is responsible for himself and for the world, for he, and he alone, is the author of himself and of the world. Man makes himself and he makes a world be.[40]

It follows that man has never a right to complain, for nothing "foreign," nothing beside what he *himself* is, has decreed anything about what he feels, experiences, and is. Whatever happens to man is his *own*. The most cruel situations of war and the most severe tortures create no situations that lie beneath the level of what is human. And if there are situations that lie below that level, it is then exclusively because man has freely chosen to have them that way; hence he is responsible for them.[41]

When I am called up to go to war, the war is *my* war; I deserve it. I deserve it because I can always withdraw from it by suicide or desertion. If I do not do that, I then *choose* the war. Hence I am not merely an accomplice in it, but I am totally responsible for the war. There are no innocent victims in a war. Nothing can force me because violence exists only in function of my own project to let

---

[38]*Op. cit.*, pp. 446-452.
[39]*Op. cit.*, p. 524.
[40]These words connect Sartre's argument with his article on Descartes. In that article Sartre explicitly states as *his* opinion that a *divine* freedom belongs to man. For this reason it is not possible to give a benign interpretation to what he says about responsibility. Existential phenomenology undoubtedly sometimes uses expressions which are similar to those of Sartre. However, its expressions have a *radically different* meaning because existential phenomenology never attributes absolute autonomy or creative freedom to the subject which it calls free. In this matter therefore Sartre is not at all an existential phenomenologist. His view undeniably jeopardizes the ontological autonomy of meaning. However, it would be unfair to attribute this error to existential phenomenology, as De Petter does. To absolutize the meaning of the subject and his free projects goes against the fundamental ideas which inspire existential phenomenology.
[41]*Op. cit.*, pp. 554 f.

myself be forced. I am therefore responsible for the war, *as if I had personally declared war.*[42] Without remorse, regret or excuse, man all alone carries the weight of the world and no one can lighten his burden. It is even impossible for man to remain passive, to refuse to act, for "to refuse to act upon things" is still "to choose myself." Even suicide is a mode "of being in the world."[43] Man cannot not choose.

In this sense man also has chosen to be born, for his birth never appears to him as an "in itself" but solely within the perspective of a free project of his subjectivity. That is why my birth means something in reference to which I am ashamed, delighted, or astonished, or of something of which I would like to rid myself. But it is clear that I *myself* decide about that by the free project of my life. I never meet anything other than myself and my own responsibility; hence I can never ask why I was born; nor can I curse the day of my birth or declare that I did not ask to be born.

The fact that man is thrown into an absolute responsibility for himself and the world fills him with anguish. He who realizes that this anguish results from his being thrown into his condition knows neither remorse, regret nor excuse. But man, "most of the time flees from his anguish in bad faith."[44]

Freedom and Morality

In philosophy everything refers to everything else. It is to be expected, then, that, if Sartre absolutizes the subjectivity of freedom, this absolutism will reveal itself also in other questions. And this is exactly what happens when he speaks about the moral life.

Sartre creates difficulties for his readers because he constantly confuses *different* theses and imagines that he is justified when he applies what he was right or partly right in maintaining regarding one point to a totally different question in order to draw conclusions from it. We have seen examples of this procedure in the preceding page. Sartre is right when he stresses the fact that no situation possesses a meaning in itself. But he makes constant use of that thesis to proceed much farther and place the meaning of the situation in the hands of the absolutely autonomous, creative subject.

---

[42]*Op. cit.,* p. 555.
[43]*Op. cit.,* p. 556.
[44]*Op. cit.,* pp. 555 f.

General Norms of Morality are Meaningless. Regarding morality, Sartre asserts that there are no universal norms or universal values. There are no universal norms because there is no God who wrote such laws in heaven.[45] Sartre finds it "very annoying" that God does not exist but, since there is no God, someone else has to invent values, for life has no *a priori* meaning.[46] Man as subject must give meaning to life by inventing values.

Values, after all, do not exist or have any meaning in themselves in virtue of which they would be able to impose themselves on the will.[47] Values do not lie waiting like stones in an unexplored country. They always presuppose the subject. "It follows," says Sartre, "that my freedom is the unique foundation of values and that *nothing*, absolutely nothing, justifies me in adopting this or that particular value, this or that particular scale of values."[48] My freedom is the bottomless ground and foundation of all values.[49]

It follows, according to Sartre, that there is nothing stable to which we can cling in traditional Christian morality.[50] There are no signs by which a man can know what he ought to do. Sartre illustrates this by an example of a Jesuit whom he knew while he was a prisoner of war.

This priest's father died when the boy was still young, and the family fell into poverty. As a boarder in a school, he was made to feel that he had been accepted solely out of compassion, and for the same reason he was also refused certain honors due to his scholarly achievements. Later he failed to win the girl of his choice and similarly everything went wrong in his military service. But one day he saw all those events as signs of God's will and it became clear to him that he was called to work for the triumph of religion, for holiness and faith. So he became a priest.[51] Yet it is evident, Sartre remarks, that it was the man *himself* and he alone, who gave to those "signs" the meaning he wanted to give them. Why, for instance, did he not interpret those events as "divine signs" that God

---

[45]Sartre, *Existentialism and Humanism,* p. 33.

[46]"If I have excluded God the Father, there must be somebody to invent values. We have to take things as they are. And, moreover, to say that we invent values means no more nor less than this; that there is no sense in life *a priori*." *Op. cit ,* p. 54.

[47]Sartre, *Being and Nothingness,* p. 37.

[48]*Op. cit.,* p. 38.

[49]*Ibid.*

[50]Sartre, *Existentialism and Humanism,* p. 47.

[51]*Op. cit.,* p. 38

wanted him to become a carpenter? The reason was that he, the subject, did not desire it! Hence he was fully responsible for his decision.

Even if universal norms existed, they would be useless for man. This point Sartre also illustrates with an example. During the war one of his pupils came to ask his advice. He felt uncertain about what he should do: Should he go to England and enlist in the free French military forces or remain with his mother in order to give her support?[52] Sartre triumphantly asserts that there exists no system of universal norms of morality that can give an answer to that question. Christian ethics preaches love and recommends the hardest way. But what is love in this case? Does it mean to serve France or to give help to one's mother? Which of the two is the hardest way?

Kantian ethics, on the other hand, teaches that man must never treat his fellow-man as a means but always as an end. But he who remains with his mother uses his fellow soldiers as a means. He who joins his fellow soldiers uses his mother as a means.[53] It follows that general norms of morality are useless. "Even if God existed, that would make no difference."[54] "You are free, therefore, choose—that is to say, invent!"[55] Sartre says there are no universal values "in themselves"; *therefore,* man is the absolute and unique source of values. God has not written any general laws in heaven; *therefore,* there are no general laws. No moral system can tell us what has to be done here and now; *therefore,* all systems are superfluous. No sign from heaven gives man a guarantee that his actions are good, *therefore,* man must find his own norms with perfect autonomy. This is confusion confounded and leaves Sartre full freedom in his own view of morality.

Freedom as Norm of Morality. And yet, in spite of everything, Sartre holds that there is a universally valid morality and that it has a universally valid norm. That norm is freedom. Dostoevski has said that, if there is no God, then everything is permitted to man. "That," says Sartre, "for existentialism is the starting point."[56] Man must create values with perfect autonomy; he must invent

---

[52] *Op. cit.,* pp. 35 f.
[53] *Op. cit.,* p. 36.
[54] *Op. cit.,* p. 56.
[55] *Op. cit.,* p. 38.
[56] *Op. cit.,* p. 33.

norms of conduct and choose his morality.[57] "One can choose anything, but only if it is upon the plane of free commitment."[58] In
itself it makes no difference whether man tries to lead nations or
become a solitary drinker.[59] The choice of the latter could even be
morally superior when it is done with a higher degree of freedom in
the choice. Freedom is the universal norm.

The objection that there is no universal norm has been anticipated
by Sartre: Of course, a universal norm exists, but it is not written
in heaven. It is written in man as the truth, the reality, the objective
meaning of his human nature,[60] which is absolute freedom.

"But," the objector continues, "there is no human nature according to Sartre, for he has stated so explicitly."[61]

It is true that Sartre has said this, but, in his terminology, it
merely means that man is not a *thing* of nature. But, he says, there
is a "human universality of *condition*,"[62] a "human condition,"[63]
and this is the same thing as what other philosophies call the nature
or the essence of man,[64] without attaching any materialistic meaning
to those terms.

The universal moral law of absolute freedom is not written in
heaven, according to Sartre, but it is the expression of man's essence, of his absolute freedom. This enables him to judge the actions
of others. Those who renounce their absolute freedom by seeking a
guarantee for their deeds in heavenly signs, or who try to find an
excuse for their acts in their passions, are in bad faith and live an
inauthentic, immoral life. They reject what they are, namely, absolutely free beings. They are "cowards" and "scum"![65]

But if so, is man free to choose living in bad faith? Sartre's
answer is definitely negative. "Here one cannot avoid pronouncing a
judgment of truth."[66] He who chooses to live in bad faith fails to

---

[57]*Op. cit.,* pp. 48, 51
[58]Sartre, *op. cit.,* p. 54.
[59]Sartre, *Being and Nothingness,* p. 627.
[60]"Here one cannot avoid pronouncing a judgment of truth." Sartre, *Existentialism and Humanism,* p. 51.
[61]*Op. cit.,* p. 52.
[62]*Op. cit.,* p. 46.
[63]*Op. cit.,* p. 47.
[64]"We are then in the opposite of the situation of the psychologists since we
start with the synthetic totality which man is and establish the essence of man
before we begin with psychology." Sartre, *Esquisse d'une théorie des émotions,*
Paris, 1948, p. 9.
[65]Sartre, *Existentialism and Humanism,* p. 52.
[66]*Op. cit.,* p. 51.

recognize the *truth* of his essence, which consists in freedom as absolute autonomy. We meet here the definition of man as a moral being: the being of man is a having to be which is bound by the objectivity of his essence. For Sartre, this essence is absolute autonomy. Certain kinds of choice are based on the truth of man's essence, others on failure to recognize this essence.[67] Man, then, can act rightly or wrongly. The truth of his essence imposes an obligation upon him. For this reason the objectively universal moral law is at the same time subjectively universal.[68]

We see from the foregoing that, for Sartre, freedom is absolute. He accepts no moral norms written in heaven because there is no God. The elimination of God makes morality possible. But one might ask whether it would not be better to say that Sartre's morality makes it *necessary* to reject God.

"The Devil and The Good Lord"

As is well known, Christian ethics has always emphasized the fact that the universal moral laws and norms are not written in heaven and that, likewise, they do not derive their validity from their predominance within the facticity of a particular society. The explicit character of a universal moral law is nothing else but an expression in which man lays down the unconcealedness for man of a particular aspect of his essence. That is why the universal moral "oughts" are said to be "written in man's heart."

The question that arises inevitably is: By whom are those norms written in man's heart? Christian ethics answers by affirming and explicitating the religious dimension of morality. That which man's essence prescribes in the moral realm is for the Christian the expression of God's will regarding man. In a Christian perspective of thought, the recognition of God and the recognition of the moral nature of man form a dialectical unity. They presuppose each other and call for each other in such a way that no one can proclaim his adherence to God if he explicitly refuses to fulfill what he clearly recognizes as a moral demand of his essence. In a Christian frame of thought the moral good is God's will.

---

[67]"In certain cases choice is founded upon an error, and in others upon the truth." *Op. cit.,* p. 50.

[68]"Thus although the content of morality is variable, a certain form of this morality is universal." *Op. cit.,* p. 52.

This aspect of morality is extensively discussed by Sartre, not in any theoretical work, but in his play *The Devil and the Good Lord*.[69] There are other themes in that drama concerning God and the Devil, such as the problem of Providence and suffering, but they remain peripheral to the play. The central problem is that of the moral good and evil in the Christian sense, seen in the light of God's will.

According to Sartre in that drama, what Christianity calls the moral good is something impossible. Even those who expressly will and try to do the good realize only evil. It is therefore senseless to view doing the good as accomplishing God's will, for there exists no moral goodness. Hence God's will does not exist either. Man is alone, for the heaven above his head is empty. Man must act alone, and he must act without a justification for his deeds.

Sartre expresses his ideas through Goetz, the principal personage of the drama. Goetz has always done evil because it was evil and in order to provoke God. All that is good, he thinks, has already been done by God the Father; Goetz plans something new, viz., evil.[70] He will take the city of Worms which he now besieges and he will put its twenty thousand inhabitants to the sword to dare God. To Nasti, the prophet who tried to make him abandon his cruel plan Goetz, answers:

> But what do I care for mankind? God hears me; it is God I am deafening and that is enough for me, for He is the only enemy worthy of my talents. . . . It is God I shall crucify this night, through you, and through twenty thousand men, because His suffering is infinite and renders infinite those whom He causes to suffer. This city will go up in flames. God knows that. At this moment, He is afraid; I can feel it, I feel His eyes on my hand, His breath on my hair, His angels shed tears. He is saying to Himself: "Perhaps Goetz will not dare . . ." exactly as if He were a man. Weep, angels; I shall dare. In a few moments I will march in His fear and His anger. The city shall blaze; the soul of the Lord is a hall of mirrors, the fire will be reflected in a thousand mirrors. Then I shall know that I am an unalloyed monster.[71]

---

[69]*Le diable et le bon Dieu*, Paris, 1951; English ed., *The Devil and the Good Lord*, New York (Alfred H. Knopf., Inc.), 1960. Tr. from the French by Kitty Black. We refer to the English edition.

[70]*Op. cit.*, p 46.

[71]*Op. cit.*, p. 55.

The last preparations are made. The prophet Nasti must be put to the torture until he is prepared to make his confession before being hanged. "There is an act such as I love: with facets," says Goetz. "Is it good? Is it evil? The understanding is confused."[72] Catherine, the whore, is given to the stableboys. God does not interfere.

> Still no miracle. I'm beginning to believe that God is giving me a free hand. Thank you, God, I thank you very much. Thanks for the women violated, the children impaled, the men decapitated. . . . Listen, Nasti, I'm going to give you the answer: *God is making use of me.* You saw how it was to-night; well, He sent His angels down to start me up again. . . . Listen, I'm going to take a nice little bloodbath to oblige the Lord. But when all is over, He will stop His nose and cry that that wasn't at all what He wanted. Do you really not want it Lord? There is still time to prevent me. . . . Yes, Lord, you are completely innocent. . . . Hatred and weakness, violence, death, displeasure, all that proceeds from man alone. There, there—I take everything upon myself and I shall talk no more. On the Day of Judgment, silence, shut lips, I am too proud, I shall let myself be damned without uttering a word. But doesn't it embarrass You a little, Lord, a very little, to have damned the man who does work for you?[73]

Goetz wishes to be clearly distinguished from all others who do evil. All others who do evil do it through sensuality or self-interest. "I do evil for evil's sake."[74]

Goetz's bluff doesn't make the least impression on Heinrich, the priest. For what difference does it make that one does evil for this or that motive, *since it is certain that it is impossible to do anything but evil?*

> Completely impossible. Love is impossible! Justice is impossible! Why don't you try and love your neighbor? You can tell me afterward what success you have. . . . If you want to deserve Hell, you need only remain in bed. The world itself is iniquity; if you accept the world, you are equally iniquitous. If

[72]*Op. cit.,* p. 56.
[73]*Op. cit.,* pp. 60 f.
[74]*Op cit.,* p. 62.

you should try and change it, you become an executioner. The stench of the world rises to the stars.[75]

For Goetz this means a challenge, the challenge to do good. If no one has ever done good, he, Goetz, will do good. He decrees that the city of Worms will be spared. He gives the whore Catherine a purse of money and sends her away. He gives to poor farmers the lands which have been allotted to him by the Archbishop of Worms after the defeat and the death of his brother Conrad. They, Goetz and the farmers together, will establish a kingdom of peace and love in which goodness and nothing but goodness will reign.

But Nasti, the prophet, predicts nothing but misfortune for Goetz. In the City of the Sun, which Goetz wants to found, evil will be as prevalent as when Goetz was still living for evil. Goetz appeals to the light that God has given him. Nasti refuses to be convinced. "When God is silent, we can make Him say whatever you please."[76]

Evil is not long in coming; it already appears as a possibility of a peasant's rebellion on estates whose land was not distributed by their masters. Evil reappears, and Goetz once more faces Catherine who is now mortally ill and covered with sores. She dies because Goetz had cast her out of his life for the sake of doing good.

In the City of the Sun no one drinks or steals. Men are forbidden to beat their wives and parents are forbidden to strike their children; violence is unjust whatever be its source. And yet . . . there is evil; the City of the Sun is built on the misery of others. For the happiness that reigns in the City of the Sun has driven the farmers who are on other estates to despair. The masters plunder, rape and murder, but the inhabitants of the City of the Sun refuse to put an end to that because the use of violence is evil. They pray. When the rebellion begins, Nasti begs Goetz to take the leadership. Goetz refuses, for if he accepts, he will have to maintain discipline; that means, he will have to hang men, both the innocent and the guilty, to set an example. "God is against this revolt."[77] Goetz is ready to try to bring the farmers back to their senses. But they condemn his love as vice and call his gifts crimes. Then Goetz curses them and withdraws. He is alone with God.

---

[75]*Op. cit.*, pp. 62 f.
[76]*Op. cit.*, p. 71.
[77]*Op. cit.*, p. 118.

> Lord, Thou must guide me through the dark night. Since we must persevere despite frustration, let every frustration be to me a sign, every misery a piece of good luck, every accident a grace. Give me the good use of my misfortunes! Lord, I believe it; I must believe that Thou didst permit me to wind up outside the world because Thou didst desire to keep me for Thyself . . . I come, Lord, I come. I am walking in Thy night: stretch out Thy hand . . . I shall abase myself before all people, and Thou, O Lord, will take me in the nets of Thy night and raise me up above them. Blessed art Thou for Thy gift of light: I shall be able to see clearly.[78]

At dawn Goetz sees the City of the Sun lying in ruins. Peasants of the vicinity have ordered the inhabitants to fight side by side with them. They have refused. But they have refused also to defend themselves because it is wicked to use violence. They have all been murdered. But this doesn't grieve Goetz.

> Wash your hands of all this blood. We are nothing; we have no power over anything. Man dreams he can act, but it is God who leads him.[79]

Goetz withdraws to the forest where he fasts and practices mortification. He tries to annihilate the man in him. It is God's will that he decay.[80]

> I am not a man, I am nothing. There is only God. Man is an optical illusion.[81]

Heinrich, who had assured Goetz that the good is an impossibility, seeks for and finds him in his solitude, after his failure. He brings the news that the barons have defeated the peasants' army. Twenty-five thousand have lost their lives. But this is not the principal motive for his coming. He has come to reveal Goetz to himself, to show him that all his intentions were really wicked and that what he thought he was doing for good intentions was objectively speaking wicked. Goetz formerly violated and forced souls through tortures

---

[78]*Op. cit.,* pp. 124 ff.
[79]*Op. cit.,* p. 126.
[80]*Ibid.*
[81]*Op. cit.,* p. 132.

but later he did the same thing by doing good.[82] "Heinrich is the *Good* possible?"[83]

Goetz knows what Heinrich's answer will be, for Heinrich has already given it to him before Goetz decided to do good.

> Torture the weak or martyrize yourself, kiss the lips of harlot or a leper, die of privations or excesses: God doesn't give a damn.[84]

Goetz realizes that he has deceived himself. The orders which he thought he had received from God were apparently self-given. He has been living on illusions. Heinrich has made him see that he has done nothing but evil and that God had nothing to do with it. But Goetz now takes the initiative against Heinrich.

> I alone. I supplicated, I demanded a sign, I sent messages to Heaven, no reply. Heaven ignored my very name. Each minute I wondered what I could BE in the eyes of God. Now I know the answer: nothing. God does not see me, God does not hear me, God does not know me. You see this crack in the door? It is God again. You see that hole in the ground? That is God again. Silence is God. Absence is God. God is the loneliness of men. There was no one but myself. I alone decided on evil, and I alone invented Good. It was I who cheated, I who worked miracles, I who accused myself today, I alone can absolve myself; I, man. If God exists, man is nothing; if man exists ... where are you going?[85]

Heinrich wants to leave suddenly, for he is afraid of the conclusion which Goetz will draw from the premises that he, Heinrich, has given him. He does not want to hear that conclusion, for, if God does not exist, there is no means to escape from men. If God does not exist, man will not be judged by an infinite being but by men. If God does not exist, only men exist. Goetz has not lost the trial for which Heinrich made the indictment; there was no trial because there was no judge.

> Heinrich, I am going to tell you a colossal joke; God doesn't exist. He doesn't exist. Joy, tears of joy, Halleluia! Fool! Do

---

[82] *Op. cit.*, p. 138.
[83] *Op. cit.*, p. 140.
[84] *Op. cit.*, p. 141.
[85] *Ibid.*

not strike me, I have delivered us. No more Heaven, no more Hell; nothing but earth. . . . God is dead. . . . Alone at last.[86]

Everything begins anew for Goetz. He stabs Heinrich when the latter, in despair tried to oppose him. Goetz will no longer do evil to dare God and he will not do good any more in obedience to God's will, for God does not exist, and on this earth and at this time good and evil are inseparable. He wants to be with men, but he will not shrink from playing the role of executioner or fear to slaughter when love demands it. He reassumes the command. He will remain alone with the empty Heaven above his head, for there is no other way to be with all.

As we have noted, for Sartre absolute freedom serves as a universal norm of morality; it is a consequence of the fact that God does not exist. However, he doesn't discuss the non-existence of God thematically in connection with absolute freedom, but presupposes it. In *The Devil and the Good Lord,* however, he goes farther. Here Sartre tries to show that God has nothing to do with good and evil in the Christian sense, and that the man who realizes this must come to the conclusion that God does not exist at all.

In all that Sartre has not yet spoken *directly* about God. But he is not satisfied with that, and wants to speak thematically about God. This might astonish us, for, after all, Sartre is an atheist. Yet the reader must have noted that God is not *absent* from the work of Sartre.[87] The opposite is true: God is present everywhere in it, but only for the sake of being rejected over and over again.[88]

D. God

Sartre rejects all dependence of man upon God. God is not the king of men, for man is free. If God had wished to exercise dominion over man, He should not have created him free. At the moment when God created man as a free being, this freedom turned against God; man as freedom no longer belongs to God. There is, then, no longer anyone to give orders to man. Man has only one law, his own, and this is his freedom.[89] The gods also know this; it is their

[86]*Op. cit.,* pp. 141 f., 143.

[87]This is true until the publication of Sartre's *Critique de la raison dialect-ique* (Paris, 1960).

[88]Cf. H. Paissac, *Le Dieu de Sartre,* Arthaud, 1950, pp. 9-71.

[89]Sartre *"Les Mouches." Thèâtre,* Paris, 1947, pp. 84, 86.

painful secret. Once freedom has arisen in man, the gods can no longer do anything against such a man.[90] They can destroy man but they cannot cause man, in his *freedom,* to belong to the gods.

Sartre's idea is clear: God does not exist because man is free. If God really existed, He would crush man as freedom. But it is undeniable that man is free. Therefore, God does not exist.[91]

Although Sartre has, properly speaking, only one argument against the existence of God, he develops it in a threefold way. Let us see what he has to say.

God as "Superior Artisan"

Traditionally, God has always been thought of as the Creator of man. The creation of man is conceived by analogy with the making of an object by a workman. When a workman makes an object, he first has an idea of it and then executes the object in conformity with that idea. The essence of a paper-knife precedes the production of it and its real existence, for it exists *first* in the mind of the workman and is already fixed in his plan.[92]

This, says Sartre, is exactly the way we speak about the creation of man by God. God is conceived as a superior artisan. Before He creates, He knows precisely what He will create and in conformity with His idea, He makes man be. The idea "man" is to God's mind what the idea "paper-knife" is to the mind of the workman, and God produces man as the workman produces a paper-knife. Man's being, then, is fixed and settled beforehand and, since God's creation covers the whole life of man, man's entire life is fixed beforehand. According to such a view, man is nothing else but a fixed example of a fixed species, and his life is somewhat like the growth and filling-out of a pea.[93]

Sartre rejects such a doctrine because man appears in it as "being a mere thing." No doubt, man has thing-like aspects; he has an essence, that is, a definite facticity that makes him resemble things. However what is *proper* to man consists *precisely* in this that he has a priority over his *essence,* by the fact that he is existence, i.e., a self-realizing subject, and that as subject, that is, as freedom,

---

[90] Sartre, *op. cit.,* pp. 111-113.
[91] Cf. Paissac, *op cit.,* pp. 16 f.
[92] Sartre, *Existentialism and Humanism,* p. 26.
[93] *Op. cit.,* p. 27.

he gives meaning to that essence and thus "makes" himself.[94] Hence there is no such thing as a "man-idea," nor can man be defined, for nothing can be said about man except *a posteriori* in function of the way in which the subject has realized himself. One who wishes to speak about man must begin with subjectivity,[95] for existence precedes the essence.[96] This simply means, says Sartre, that man has a greater dignity than a stone, a chair, a cauliflower, a kind of moss or a fungus.[97]

Accordingly, Sartre finds it impossible to reconcile the existence of a Creator God with man as freedom, project, and history. But we cannot deny the reality of man; hence no reality can correspond to the idea of a Creator God.

God as the Other Par Excellence

Sartre's theory of intersubjectivity likewise makes it necesssary for him to reject the existence of God. Those who accept God's existence conceive Him as the Other *par excellence*. But *every* "other" means the death of my subjectivity and my only defense against the other is to destroy his subjectivity. In the same way, man's only defense against God is to reject Him.

The Other is "The One Who Looks at Me"

The other is immediately present and accessible to me through his look. He is essentially the one who looks at me."[98] But there is only one way to describe accurately the other's look: I must describe *myself* and precisely as being looked at, just as one who, looking through a keyhole of a hotel-room and suddenly hearing steps in the corridor followed by silence, senses that he is being looked at.[99]

In my being looked at by the other, the other's subjectivity reveals itself, but exclusively as the decomposition of my own subjectivity. Under the other's look, my subjectivity is reduced to a

---

[94]"Man is nothing but that which he makes of himself." *Op. cit.,* p. 28.

[95]*Op. cit.,* p 26.

[96]*Ibid.*

[97]*Op. cit.,* p. 28. If this expression really did not mean anything else, no one could object to it. As we have seen, however, Sartre recklessly exaggerates the relative priority of the subject.

[98]Sartre, *Being and Nothingness,* p. 257.

[99]"To apprehend a look is not to apprehend a look-as-object in the world (unless the look is not directed upon us); it is to be conscious of being *looked at.* The look which the *eyes* manifest, no matter what kind of eyes they are, is a pure reference to myself." *Op. cit ,* p. 259.

thing; for the other as subject I am an object in his world. As soon as there is *someone,* whoever he might be, by the very fact that his subjectivity arises before me, I have an "outside." I have a "nature," I am an "object." "My original fall is the existence of the other."[100]

As subject, I am the origin of meaning of my world. But my subjectivity is lost under the other's look, so that my world offers me a totally different countenance, a countenance which is beyond my grasp and correlated with the subjectivity of the other as source of meaning.[101] As subject, I am project, hence I am not what I am and am what I am not. But under the look of the other, the project that I am is totally destroyed, and I am what I am just as a *thing* is what it is. Under the look of the other I *am* indiscreet, just as a tafel is square.[102] As subject, I am the free execution of the project which I am, a constant movement by which I transcend myself. Under the other's look my transcendence freezes, and my freedom becomes petrified.[103] The other's look is the death of my subjectivity. The others are my Hell: *"L'enfer, c'est les Autres"* (*Huis-Clos*).

It is clear then that, according to Sartre, man has but one way of saving or regaining the subjectivity which is of necessity lost under the look of the other. I am object for the other as subject; I am never an object for an object. In order to free myself from being an object, I must make a gigantic effort and try to reduce the other to an object by my look at him.[104] For, as soon as the other appears to me as an object, his subjectivity is transformed into a "property" of the object, the appearance of which made me his victim. His subjectivity becomes a "property," for instance, of his eyes, just as being blue and being ugly are their properties. The other "has" his subjectivity, as a box "has" an inside. And "in this way I recover myself."[105]

In this fashion, all concrete human relations are fundamentally determined for Sartre. Either the other rejects me and reduces me

---

[100] *Op. cit.,* p. 263.
[101] "With the other's look a new organization of complexes comes to superimpose itself on the first." *Ibid.*
[102] *Op. cit.,* p. 262.
[103] "Thus for the other I have stripped myself of my transcendence." *Ibid.*
[104] "The objectivation of the other . . ., is a defence on the part of my being which, precisely by conferring on the other a being for me, frees me from my being-for the other." *Op. cit.,* p. 268.
[105] *Op. cit.,* p. 289.

to a thing in his world, or I hold his subjectivity in my power by making it an object for me. There are no other possibilities. Hence no intersubjectivity is possible if we mean by it a subject to subject relation. And yet man will continue to strive for such a goal. Love, masochism, desire, hate, sadism, are so many attempts to realize the intersubjectivity about which men dream.[106] But such attempts are useless.[107] Human relations can exist only in two ways: to transcend the other or to let the other transcend me. The essence of the relations between men is not a "being with" (*Mitsein*), as Heidegger calls it, but conflict.[108]

God, the "Unstared Stare." It follows that God's existence cannot be admitted unless man wants to sacrifice and lose his subjectivity.[109] God is the Other *par excellence*, i.e., He is the one who looks at all subjects, the one for whom they experience themselves as objects, the one whose presence is intolerable to any subject. God is the being who looks at all and cannot be looked at by anyone.[110] He is the "unstared stare." To accept God would thus be to accept being a thing. To accept God would imply to exist in alienation, to be estranged from my being man as freedom.[111] But is it true that I must accept God and that my freedom is an illusion? No, for man is free; he must therefore rise up against God; he must reject God if he wants to continue to exist as freedom. Man owes it to his being human to reject God.

Those ideas remind us of Nietzsche's viewpoint. Nietzsche said that it would be absolutely unbearable for him that there should be a God and that he, Nietzsche, would not be that God. Must we not say the same thing about Sartre?

Sartre's One-sidedness. It is hardly necessary to remark that men's thinking assumes a totally different orientation if the thinker is somewhat sensitive to the fact that intersubjectivity contains far more possibilities than Sartre imagines. Sartre is convinced that he

---

[106]*Op. cit.,* pp. 361-430.

[107]"We should hope in vain for a human 'we' in which the intersubjective totality would be conscious of itself as a unified subjectivity." *Op. cit.,* p. 428.

[108]*Op. cit.,* p. 429.

[109]"God here is only the concept of the other pushed to the limit." *Op. cit.,* p. 266.

[110]*Op. cit.,* p. 493.

[111]"The position of God is accompanied by a reification of my objectness. Or better yet, I posit my being an object for God as more real than my 'for itself'; I exist alienated and I cause myself to learn from outside what I must be. This is the origin of fear before God." *Op. cit.,* p. 290.

has unfolded the meaning of *the* "look," but he is wrong. All he knows is the hateful look, the attitude of a subject who cannot tolerate that the other should also be a subject and be his own source of meaning, a subject who projects his own world and makes his own history. But this hateful attitude is not the only possible or the only real attitude of a subject toward other subjects.

There is also the attitude of love, as "will of promotion,"[112] i.e., the attitude of accepting, willing, sustaining and fostering the subjectivity of the other. This attitude is not destructive but creative in reference to the other's subjectivity. It makes the other be; it *makes* the other be a subject, enabling him to attain a height in the planning of his world and the execution of his projects which he would never have attained if he had been left to himself alone.

There is really only one word to express what love is: it is a grace. Therefore, when God "sees" man, can His love have no other meaning than that He crushes man's subjectivity? Is it not possible for God to look at man with love and grace? If so, God does not crush man's subjectivity but rather *gives* man his subjectivity by a simple regard. Unfortunately, no one will be able to explain this to Sartre as long as the only look he knows is that of hatred.

The Idea of God is a Contradiction

For Sartre, God is not only merely the Destroyer of human freedom and the intolerable and unbearable Look. The idea of God, as an expression of *reality* proposed by religion, cannot possibly correspond to any reality, for it contains an internal contradiction.

By means of his fundamental concepts of "in itself" and "for itself," Sartre attempts to speak about the Being whom religion calls "God." Since we have already explained what Sartre means by "in itself," there is no need to repeat that description fully, the more so because Sartre does not use all the characteristics of the "in itself" in his discussion of God. The "in itself," unlike consciousness, is not a being that refers to itself; it is not a being that is "concerned with its being." To use Heidegger's expression, it is not characterized by relation to being (*Seinsverthältnis*), by understanding of being (*Seinsverständnis*). It lies "crushed on itself," that is, it does not show the nihilating distance which characterizes consciousness; hence it does not imply negativity but is total positivity.[113] It *is*, in

---

[112]M. Nédoncelle, *Vers une philosophie de l'amour,* Paris, 1946, p. 11.
[113]Sartre, *Being and Nothingness,* p. 77.

the full sense of the word; it is the fullness of being and needs nothing else in order to be what it is.[114]

This suffices, says Sartre, to realize that God, about whom the various religions speak, must be an "in itself." For, God is conceived as a Being to whom the fullness of "to be" belongs, a Being who is perfectly self-sufficient, who needs nothing else in order to be what He is.[115] But God is at the same time conceived as "for itself," as consciousness.[116] The general description, however which Sartre gives of the "for itself" opposes the "for itself" diametrically to the "in itself": the "for itself" is nothing but negativity; by definition it needs the "in itself" in order to be able to be "for itself"; hence it is never self-sufficient.

The contradiction is evident: God would have to be the identity of the "in itself" and the "for itself," the identity of pure positivity and pure negativity, of being self-sufficient and being not self-sufficient, of independence and dependence. God would have to be an intentional being which at the same time is not intentional. The idea of God, therefore, contains an inner contradiction; no reality can correspond to it.[117]

Critique. Sartre's so-called contradiction makes little impression on genuine phenomenologists, for it results from the evident fact that he betrays the phenomenological dimension of thought, viz., the unity of the mutual implication of subject and object. Sartre accepts that dimension of thought in his phenomenological descriptions, but disregards it completely in his ontology. What is the meaning of the "fullness of being" attributed to the "in itself," when one accepts that it is only about the "in itself for us" that we can speak meaningfully? The "in itself for us" certainly does *not* appear as fullness of being. Are we, then, permitted to withdraw the intentional movement of consciousness and maintain that the "in itself" nonetheless is the fullness of being? The various religions call God the Supreme Being, the Fullness of Being, but when He is identified with the "in itself" as fullness, an unbridgeable abyss is opened between Sartre and religion. Sartre imagines that the definition of God is self-contradictory. In reality his attempt to speak about the "in itself" contains a self-contradiction.

---

[114]*Op. cit.,* p. LXVI.
[115]"Is not God a being who is what he is—in that he is all positivity and the foundation of the world...?" *Op. cit.,* p. 90.
[116]*Ibid.*
[117]*Op. cit.,* pp. 90 f., 615.

Similar remarks apply to the "for itself." The religions maintain that God is the highest Being and that He is, therefore, on the level of consciousness. But Sartre robs consciousness of all positivity, refuses to give to it the value and significance of the highest form of being,[118] and conceives it as pure "nihilation"; hence his declaration that religion conceives God as a "for itself" opens another abyss between the two affirmations.

More important even is that religion calls God unqualifiedly a "conscious subject." No doubt, God is conceived as a conscious Subject but not without a qualification. The conscious subjects encountered by man are intentional subjects; and God, as conceived by religion, is *not* an intentional subject. Hence one cannot say *unqualifiedly* that religion conceives God as a "conscious Subject," for God is *not* an intentional subject. Religion does not conceive God as both an "in itself" and a "for itself," He is conceived neither as "in itself" nor as "for itself." In other words, what Sartre rejects is something quite different from what is held by the religious man.

Man as Project to Be God

The way in which Sartre makes the idea of God contain a contradiction has serious consequences for his view regarding man. The existence of an "in itself for itself" is a contradiction; but it cannot be denied that the two meet in man. For man is an oppositional unity of subjectivity and facticity, of "for itself" and "in itself," to use Sartre's terminology. The "in itself" is totally contingent; it just *is* without necessity, foundation or reason. For "foundation" and "reason" always refer to the "for itself," to consciousness, and the "in itself" has no consciousness. It follows that man must be conceived as the emergence of consciousness in the compact density of a contingent groundless "in itself." It is as if the "in itself," which is groundless, decompresses itself,[119] breaks its density, and produces a certain distance in relation to itself, i.e., it gives itself the modifica-

---

[118]"This presence to itself has often been taken for a plenitude of existence, and a strong prejudice prevalent among philosophers causes them to attribute to consciousness the highest rank of being." *Op. cit.*, p. 77.

[119]"Ontology furnishes us two pieces of information...; first, that every process of a foundation of the self is a rupture in the identity-of-being of the in-itself, a withdrawal by being in relation to itself and the appearance of presence to self or consciousness." *Op. cit.*, p. 620.

tion of a "for itself," in order to find a ground for its groundlessness.[120] This adventure is called "man."

Thus man is a "foundation project." Sartre conceives this project
as the attempt of the "for itself" to eliminate the distance which
separates it from the "in itself." Not being what it is, and being
what it is not,[121] the "for itself" would like to be what it is. The
"for itself" would like to give itself the fullness, massiveness, and
density of the "in itself" while maintaining its status as a "for itself." If man were successful in his attempt to make the "for itself"
identical with the "in itself" in himself, to make them coincide in
him, he would have overcome the contingency of his being man, that
is, man would have put his existence on a foundation by raising
himself to the dignity of the Being who is the cause of himself (*Ens
causa sui*). He would have become his own cause.[122] But "to be
one's own cause," the identity of "in itself" and "for itself," is nothing else but the definition of God. Hence the "foundation project"
which constitutes man is the desire to be God.[123]

Man tries to execute that project in his transcendence. As not
being what he is and being what he is not, as oppositional unity of
facticity and ability to be, man by his actions tends to the fulfillment
of the possibilities that are anchored in his facticity. Once it is made
real, the newly established meaning remains as an "in itself." This
opens new possibilities, each of which, in turn, being realized and
remaining as an "in itself" is "nihilated" by the "for itself." The
"for itself," which is a non-being, constantly haunts the "in itself"
which of itself is fullness of being,[124] without ever being able to
identify itself with the "in itself." Man is essentially a hole, a crack,
a breach in being, which is not overcome by his transcendence. Man
is truly a "sickness of being."

What does this mean but that the execution of the "foundation
project" which constitutes man is doomed to failure? For the "for
itself" is an unconquerable nihilation of the "in itself," so that there
continues to exist an infinite distance between the "in itself" and the

---

[120]"Ontology will therefore limit itself to declaring that *everything takes
place as if* the in-itself in a project to found itself gave itself the modification
of the for-itself." *Op. cit.*, p. 621.

[121]*Op. cit.*, p. 566.

[122]*Op. cit.*, p. 615.

[123]"Thus the best way to conceive of the fundamental project of human
reality is to say that man is the being whose project is to be God." *Op. cit.*, p.
566.

[124]*Op. cit.*, p. 12.

"for itself."[125] Man would like to overcome that infinite distance by means of his transcendence, in order to give a foundation to his being, but this is doomed to failure. The "human reality" as "foundation project" is an absurdity. How could it be otherwise? For the attempt to make the "for itself" identical with the "in itself" is the attempt to realize the definition of God. But the definition of God contains a contradiction.[126]

If man reached his ideal, he would lose himself, for no more distance would remain between "for itself" and "in itself," and that means that man would no longer be man.[127] Human consciousness is then an "unhappy consciousness," and there is no remedy for this unhappiness. Man will never be able to be more than an "abortive God."[128] Thus man's passion is the opposite of that of Christ, for man desires to lose his being man in order that God may be born. But the idea of God is self-contradictory and man loses himself in vain. "Man is a useless passion."[129]

In the Middle Ages reflection on the meaning of life was permeated with reflection upon God. This is true of Sartre also, with this difference that Sartre's philosophy ends with total negativity. In medieval thought the reality of God was seen as the final end of human transcendence. That is why medieval man could consent to his own existence. In Sartre we find almost the opposite. God does not exist and life is meaningless. Nevertheless, it would not be right to conclude that Sartre's thought has no value. Sartre really has "seen" something. As to what this "something" is, we shall come back to this point later after we have studied the atheism of Merleau-Ponty.

2. The Atheism of Merleau-Ponty

The reader must have noted that existentialistic atheism has much more profound foundations than, for example, the atheism of Marx. In the latter we find practically no speculative basis, for Marx was certain, before he even raised the question whether and how God's

---

125 *Op. cit.,* p. 620.
126 "Of course this *ens causa* sui is *impossible,* and the concept of it, as we have seen, includes a contradiction." *Op. cit.,* p. 622.
127 *Op. cit.,* p. 90.
128 "Everything happens as if the world, man, and man-in-the-world succeeded in realizing only a missing God." *Op. cit.,* p. 623. "A missing God" seems to be a less fortunate translation of *"un Dieu manqué."* Tr.
129 *Op. cit.,* p. 615.

existence can be affirmed. Only at a much later date did he incorporate the denial of God in a theory of man and a philosophy of history, but Marx would never have been able to write this part of his philosophy if he had not considered atheism to be true *a priori*. Hence Marx's atheism is based more on psychological than on philosophical grounds. Even in his junior years Marx was hurt by what he considered to be religion.[130] Let us add, however, that there were many in Marx's time who defended the concept of religion which Marx so passionately rejected. The same is true of Lenin. Lenin's rejection of God has not a single philosophical basis; it starts solely from what Christianity calls a misuse of religion and superstition.[131]

The situation is different in existentialistic atheism. Here atheism has deep philosophical roots. What Sartre says, in *The Devil and the Good Lord* about man's attitude toward God regarding the problem of good and evil, cannot be dismissed by the theist as worthless. We may perhaps add that henceforth it will be impossible to study that problem as if Sartre had never said anything about it. Since Kant's criticism of the proofs for God's existence we can no longer manipulate these proofs as recklessly as was done before Kant. And it seems to us that something similar must be said in respect to existentialistic atheism. The traditional topic "About the Names of God" can no longer be treated without reference to the criticism made by Sartre and Merleau-Ponty. We must now consider the critique of the latter.

Authentic Philosophizing

Anti-Theism and Atheism. Merleau-Ponty first notes the fact that contemporary philosophers scarcely, if ever, attempt to prove God's existence in the way it was done by St. Anselm, St. Thomas, or Descartes. Today one assumes that God's existence is proved and limits oneself to the refutation of those who deny His existence. For that purpose one tries to find in the new philosophies which reject the existence of God a crack through which the ever presupposed notion of the Necessary Being is re-introduced. And if that method fails, those philosophies are simply disqualified as being atheistic.[132]

---

[130] I. Lepp, *Psychanalyse de l'athéisme moderne,* Paris, 1961, pp. 87-9.

[131] A. Dondeyne, "L'expérience préphilosophique et les conditions anthropologiques de l'affirmation de Dieu," *L'existence de Dieu (Cahiers de l'actualité religieuse),* 1961, p. 162.

[132] *Eloge de la philosophie,* p. 58.

Those critics, says Merleau-Ponty, thus begin with the assumption that every philosophy ought to lead to the Necessary Being, and they feel certain that any philosophy that does not do it is atheistic by that very fact. In this way a philosophy is *defined* by means of a *negation,* viz., the rejection of God. But that means that they neglect to consider what philosophizing actually is.[133]

De Lubac and Maritain have spoken about atheism in the manner of those critics. They have assumed that a philosophy must end with the affirmation of God. They have shown that atheism dismisses God but later reintroduces a pseudo-god in order to give an ultimate explanation of all that is. They have shown that atheism murders one God to make room for another and that atheism thus lives by an "inverted act of faith."[134]

Merleau-Ponty knows, of course, that such a kind of anti-theism exists, but he refuses to call it philosophy; it is, according to him, an inverted theology, and Nietzsche is a classical example of it. As long as man continues to assume that it is necessary to give the ultimate, all-embracing and definitive explanation of all that is, individuals will continue to accuse one another of estrangement in their thinking. In the meantime they forget to ask themselves whether there are no other alternatives than theism on the one hand and the "apocalypse of Wonderland" on the other.[135]

In fact, says Merleau-Ponty, we are not justified in reducing a philosophy to some form of atheism because it happens to be non-theistic. Merleau-Ponty has always objected to having his philosophy branded as atheistic. For in this way the positive meaning of authentic philosophizing is transformed into a negation.[136]

The Positive Meaning of Philosophy. What then is the positive significance of philosophizing? "To philosophize means to seek, with the conviction that there is something to be seen and something to be said."[137] But in virtue of what is something to be seen and to be said? That there is something to be seen and to be said presupposes

---

[133]"Philosophy is side tracked...if it is defined as atheism." *Op. cit.,* p. 631.

[134]*Op. cit.,* p. 59.

[135]*Op. cit.,* pp. 59 f.

[136]"I do not spend my time in calling myself an atheist because that is not a pursuit and, moreover, it would transform into a negation a wholly positive effort of philosophical consciousness." Merleau-Ponty, "L'homme et l'adversité." and "Deuxième entretien privé," *La connaissance de l'homme au XX* siècle, Rencontres internationales de Genève,* 1951, p. 250.

[137]*Eloge de la philosophie,* p. 57.

the marvel which the emergence of subjectivity is. There is something to be seen and to be said because, through the emergence of subjectivity, there is meaning, in the form of truth and value. To speak with Heidegger, there is something to see and something to say because of the marvel of all marvels: "being is."[138]

This supreme marvel points to man as subject. There is meaning, in the form of truth and value, within the dialogue of subject and world. There is no meaning in a world in itself separated from the subject, nor in a "for self" separated from the world. There is meaning in a world for us that is made into a human world in a common history of human subjects.[139] Within the dialogue of subject and world, truth and value are undeniable, and there is truth and untruth, good and evil. But the term "is" has meaning precisely because, and to the extent that, the subject does not seek an absolute "in itself," and absolute "for itself".[140] He who searches for it anyhow, has already beforehand murdered the real life of truth and value.[141]

How are we to explain that marvelous emergence of subjectivity? This marvel makes true thinking and true acting possible, but don't we have to question that marvel itself? According to Merleau-Ponty, such a question is no longer meaningful, and any attempted answer is pure nonsense. Explanations are made in the "sciences."[142] An explanation consists in this that we try to reduce a being to its antecedents, that is, to the forces and processes which are its causes. Explanations are in order in the domain of natural things with their actions and reactions, i.e., in the realm where determinism reigns supreme. The being of a thing of nature is a being necessitated by processes and forces, and for this reason explanations are possible.

It is evident, however, that man as subject cannot be explained in any way. For whatever we might wish to bring in as an explanation is always a definite meaning, and every meaning *presupposes* the subject which man is. This implies that the subject can never be

---

[138]M. Heidegger, *Was ist Metaphysik?*, Frankfurt a.M., 7th ed., 1955, pp. 46-47.

[139]Merleau-Ponty, *Phenomenology of Perception*, pp. 61-63, and *Sens et non-sens*, p. 187.

[140]"There is something undeniable in knowledge and action, there is truth and falsehood, good and evil, precisely because I do not claim to find absolute evidence in them." *Sens et non-sens*, p. 191.

[141]"Metaphysical consciousness dies when it touches the absolute." *Ibid.*

[142]"I have taken the term 'explanation' in the current sense it has in philosophical German, which opposes 'erklären' and 'verstehen'." Merleau-Ponty, "Deuxième entretien privé," *op. cit.* (in footnote 136), p. 246.

explained, for the subject acts always primarily as the one that is presupposed before all explanation. The being of man as subject is not a being necessitated by processes and forces; it is a being contingent, a being free.[143]

Merleau-Ponty knows, of course, that many sciences have tried to explain man and to consider him as a moment, a phase, or a particle pertaining to the world of natural things.[144] But he considers all those explanations naive and dishonest, because they always take for granted the being in the world of the subject as *Cogito*. They all take it for granted without mentioning it; yet it is evident that, by virtue of this presupposition, i.e., through the existence of the subject, there begins to be a world of meaning, even of scientific meaning, around and for the subject.[145] How, then, would it be possible to explain through any meaning what is *presupposed* before all meaning?

Man's Contingency. Here we find the positive meaning of philosophy, as Merleau-Ponty understands it. The philosopher does not say that there is no God, but he affirms the contingent freedom of the subject in the world.[146] Through his contingency man transcends the process-like necessity that reigns in the order of natural things, and it is this contingency that makes *human* life possible. It makes possible the life of truth and value, human life as *history*. Hence history should not be conceived as a thing-like process. Man makes history, but not in the way a physical force starts a process, but as subject, that is, as the contingent, free source of meaning. That is why man is not "guaranteed." Man cannot rest his hope on this or that decree of fate, be it a favorable one, but only on the contingency of our history."[147] Progress is not something that comes about necessarily. It is even possible for mankind to fail on its way—like a grammatical sentence that remains unfinished.[148] For

---

[143]"Everything in man is contingency in the sense that this human manner of existence is not guaranteed to every human child through some essence acquired at birth, and in the sense that it must be constantly reforged in him through the hazards encountered by the objective body. Man is a historical idea and not a natural species." *Phenomenology of Perception*, p. 170.

[144]*Op. cit.*, p. IX.

[145]*Ibid.*

[146]"To finish, if we had to express our preceding remarks in a philosophical formula, we would say that our time, more perhaps than any other, has experienced and still experiences contingency." "L'homme et l'adversité," *op. cit.* (footnote 136), p. 70.

[147]*Eloge de la philosophie*, p. 61.

[148]"L'homme et l'adversité," *op. cit.* (footnote 136), p. 71.

man is not a "force" but a "weakness" in the heart of the thing-like
being of nature. He is not a cosmological factor, but a place where
all cosmological factors change their meaning and become history.[149]
Man can never be "explained," and nothing that is human is "explained" by *man*.

This thought makes one dizzy. As could be expected, Merleau-
Ponty was asked whether it was possible to live in such dizziness.
His answer was as clear as one could wish it to be: "Philosophy is
not a hospital."[150] When a man feels dizzy he can take medicine for
it. This he can do also when his being man makes him vertiginous.
But then, this means man's retreat from himself; it means a refusal
to acknowledge his being man. Fascism and occultism are retreats
from contingency.[151] But Merleau-Ponty accuses especially the
Marxism of contemporary Marxists and religion, especially Catholic
Christianity, of such treason against being-man and philosophy. We
must now consider the latter accusation.

The Basis of Merleau-Ponty's Rejection of God

Causality and Contingency. The authentic philosopher begins with
wonderment about the wonder of all wonders: that meaning exists.
He places himself at the heart, the source of that marvel, viz., in the
subject who is the source of meaning, and tries to express what he
sees. He refuses to give an explanation of that source of meaning
because every explanation destroys the wonder. The subject is contingent freedom.

This refusal to give an explanation of the subject as contingent
freedom, says Merleau-Ponty, also demands the denial of God.
Catholic theology is familiar with the idea of contingency. But
"theology establishes man's contingency only for the purpose of deriving it from a Necessary Being. It thereby *does away with* this
contingency. It makes use of philosophical wonderment solely in
order to give a reason for an affirmation which determines," i.e.,
puts an end to, that wonderment.[152] One who affirms God's existence as the Necessary Being, and conceives the Necessary Being as
the "cause" of man's contingency, implicitly reduces the being of

---

[149]*Eloge de la philosophie*, p. 61.
[150]"Deuxième entretien privé," *op. cit.* (footnote 136), p. 247.
[151]"L'homme et l'adversité," *op. cit.* (footnote 136), p. 73.
[152]*Eloge de la philosophie*, p. 61.

man to being necessitated. This puts an end to all wonderment, for wonderment precisely presupposes the contingency of the subject.

According to Merleau-Ponty it is absolutely impossible to speak of a theistic existentialism. He knows, of course, that there are existentialists who defend theism. But, according to Merleau-Ponty, the Pope was perfectly right from his standpoint when he condemned existentialism. An existentialist can remain a theist only if he is illogical.[153] Merleau-Ponty names Gabriel Marcel as an example.[154]

De Lubac has accused Merleau-Ponty of going so far as to take away the very problem from which the affirmation of God's existence is born.[155] Merleau-Ponty replies that he does not evade the problem but "makes it radical and puts it above 'solutions' that would stifle it."[156] The subject's contingency is stifled not only when a naturalistic explanation is given for it, but also when the contingency is bound up with a Sovereign Necessity.[157] And this, according to Merleau-Ponty, is done in Christian thinking.

Maritain, has made it clear that the essence of Christianity demands the constant rejection of idols. The saint is an "integral atheist" in respect to a God who is merely the guarantee for a natural order, who sanctions all good and all evil in the world, who justifies slavery, injustice, the tears of children and the agony of the innocent, who sacrifices man to the cosmos, and who is nothing else but the absurd "Emperor of the World." Such concepts of the divinity are foreign to the God of Christianity who hears the prayers of men.

Merleau-Ponty recognizes that the rejection of pseudo-gods belongs to the essence of Christianity. But he asks himself whether the idea of God as a Necessary Being does not unavoidably imply and include the idea of an Emperor of the World. He asks himself whether Christians would still call God the Maker of the world if they did not acknowledge God as this Emperor. If the reply is negative, philosophy alone, and not Christianity, would seriously reject false gods.[158]

---

[153]"Deuxième entretien privé." *op. cit.* (footnote 136), p. 246.
[154]*Ibid.*, p. 247.
[155]*Eloge de la philosophie*, p. 62.
[156]*Ibid.*
[157]*Op. cit.*, p. 63.
[158]*Op. cit.*, pp. 64 f.

Merleau-Ponty is not unaware of the fact that, especially in French Catholicism, a current of thought has developed which makes the modernism of the early twentieth century look like vague sentimentalism. This is undeniable. But, according to Merleau-Ponty, in spite of that undeniable fact, the hierarchy continues to make use of the worn and antiquated terms of explanatory theology. This, he says, shows once more that the contingency of man as subject cannot coexist with a "Thought that is infinite and Creator of the world." Of course, he continues, we should not expect a religion to conceive history as a contingent melody of meaning. And in fact the hierarchy does not do so. Adherence to the categories of explanatory theology means a divorce between the "heaven of principles" and the "earth of existence," a divorce between the history which is already completed in God and the real history of the contingent birth and growth of meaning. For such people philosophical wonderment is a bare formality. The resistance encountered by history is called Satan, but Satan is already overcome. "Occultist thought shows its mark."[159]

The philosopher does not begin with the declaration that God does not exist. He does not begin by defining philosophy as atheism. One who does it anyhow, thereby takes a viewpoint which is not his own but that of another. He who defines philosophy as atheism looks at philosophy through the eyes of a theologian. The true philosopher dwells in the wonder which the dawn of meaning is for the subject. If he remains faithful to that attitude, he will reject everything that would make such an attitude impossible. In such a case the affirmation of God's existence does not even come into consideration. Thus philosophy preserves its positive tension. That is why Merleau-Ponty refuses to call himself an atheist. He does it only when he is provoked.[160]

Merleau-Ponty's Idea of Causality. It might be well to pause here briefly and to reflect on Merleau-Ponty's way of thinking to prevent his ideas from becoming wholly unintelligible to some. This danger is not imaginary. The opinion that God's necessary being is the cause of the contingency of the existent subject is, according to Merleau-Ponty, identical with the idea that the subject is not con-

---

[159]"L'homme et l'adversité," *op. cit.* (footnote 136), p. 74.
[160]M. Merleau-Ponty, "Deuxième entretien privé," *op. cit.* (footnote 136), p. 250.

tingent. Subjectivity, he believes, is stifled when it is conceived as "caused" by the Necessary Being of God.

Anyone can see immediately that a particular concept of "causality" underlies Merleau-Ponty's position. When theology calls God a cause, Merleau-Ponty thinks of a kind of causality which eliminates the possibility that a contingent subject can be a true subject. Hence we must ask ourselves what Merleau-Ponty understands by causality. Is he thinking of the creative causality of love?

Everybody knows nowadays that it is simply impossible for man to live an authentic human life without the love of his fellow-man. Psychologists have observed that fact over and over again, and philosophers have given philosophical depth to it. For it is undeniable that the being of man is a "being together." Man is all that he is *with* and through his fellow man. We may say therefore that man, to a certain extent, is the "cause" of his fellow-man's being because "cause" originally means nothing else but "to exercise influence on" "to be," and "to be caused" means merely "to be through the influence of" something or someone.

This influence is realized on many levels of coexistence and in a special way on the intersubjective level. The loving attention of subject to subject causes the subject which the other is to be, *makes* him *be*, which is precisely to be a *subject*. Love, then, is creative to some extent; it is "at work," it has an "effect." When we now ask ourselves what it is that love "effects," the answer is: a certain fullness of the other's "being a *subject*." Hence we are permitted to say that love is the "cause" of the fullness of the other's "being a subject," that the fullness of the "being a subject" of the other is "caused," for to be caused means "to be through the influence of."

Of course, no one will make the mistake of conceiving the term "cause" here in the sense in which causality is spoken of when we ask what causes heavenly bodies to move or what causes water to boil at a given temperature and a given pressure. These causes operate unilaterally and deterministically. In the "causality" of love, on the contrary, the preponderant aspect is the reciprocity of the subjects, and the "effect" is not that of being determined but precisely that of being free.[161]

Merleau-Ponty's ideas would be wholly unintelligible to anyone who has the "causality" of love in mind and reads in this phil-

[161]Luijpen, *Existential Phenomenology*, pp. 225-228.

osopher that conceiving God as cause of subjectivity would stifle and destroy this subjectivity. For, when Merleau-Ponty speaks about God as "cause," he is thinking of the unilateral and deterministic influence a thing of nature exercises on the being of another thing of nature. And precisely because he has that idea in mind, he is able to reject God as "cause," for it is evident that a *subject* cannot be caused by a natural force in a natural process. That is also the reason why Merleau-Ponty rejects all "explanations" of the subject. Only a thing of nature can be "explained," because for Merleau-Ponty "to explain" is "to connect with unilateral and deterministic antecedents." For Merleau-Ponty to give a natural explanation of the subject is the same as to connect the contingent subject with the Necessary Being of God as "Cause" of the subject, for he conceives God as "Cause" in the sense of a *"force"* and his *"causality"* as a *"process."*[162] In Merleau-Ponty's view "explanatory" theology uses the same concept of cause as physical science.

Merleau-Ponty and Christianity

"Understanding" and *"Accepting"* Christianity. Merleau-Ponty does not begin with the rejection of God. He begins by putting himself within the wonder that meaning emerges, and in this context God does not come into consideration. What comes into the discussion is religion, but solely as one of the many *expressions* of the marvel of the apparition of meaning. In this sense religion is understood. But to "understand" religion is quite different from "accepting" it. It is almost exactly the opposite.[163] Socrates "understood" the religion of his city but this did not imply that he accepted it. Merleau-Ponty takes the same attitude. He "understands" religion but does not accept it. For the idea of a Necessary Being, just as the idea of "eternal matter" or of the "total man," seems to him wholly prosaic in comparison with the recognition of the marvel which is the emergence of meaning on all levels of the world, a marvel which is talked out of existence by those who accept the Necessary Being.[164]

---

[162]Remy C. Kwant, *The Phenomenological Philosophy of Merleau-Ponty,* Pittsburgh, 1963, pp. 132 ff.

[163]"In this situation [the philosopher] is quite able to understand religion as one of the central phenomon's expression, but as Socrates' example reminds us, to understand religion is not the same but almost the opposite of positing it." *Eloge de la philosophie,* p. 62.

[164]*Ibid.*

Merleau-Ponty develops this idea and applies it to two aspects of man as existence, namely, the search for truth and the establishment of value. On these points Merleau-Ponty explicitly confronts Christian thought. And he concludes that the Christian is not an authentic partner in man's historical search for truth and value.

The Essential Equivocity of Christianity. When Merleau-Ponty determines his position toward Christianity, he is not concerned with a question of fact but with a "quaestio juris." It is not a question of establishing the fact that in certain periods and particular places some Christians did or did not side with man in his search, did or did not foster the progress of history or take their place in the ranks of revolutionaries. Merleau-Ponty knows, of course, about all kinds of writings of historical deeds which show that certain Christians stood on the side of *man* and were intensely involved in a search for meaning, truth and value. But there are other texts and other deeds that tell a totally different story. Hence the debate with Christianity is not even really started if it is confined to the realm of *facts*.

What must be examined is the very essence of Christianity, for only on that condition can a philosopher determine his fundamental position toward it. If we remain within the field of facts, the Christian can always disavow a certain past as an unfortunate incident and call it something that should not have happened. "He will plead guilty for the past and innocence in regard to the future"[165] on the basis of his principles. This, according to Merleau-Ponty, is the position taken by Daniélou who appeals to principles in arguing against Hervé, whereas Hervé continues to appeal to facts.[166]

According to Merleau-Ponty the historically observable equivocity of Christians belongs to the very essence of Christianity. For the human "body," i.e., the facticity of existence, bears witness to what man is; body and spirit express each other and they are inseparable from each other. The factual ambiguity and equivocity of Christianity must be traced to a fundamental ambiguity and equivocity that belongs to the very essence of Christianity.[167]

The "Internal" God and the "External" God. Merleau-Ponty thinks that he can point to such a fundamental ambiguity in Catholicism. For, the Catholic believes simultaneously in an internal and

---

[165]*Sens et non-sens*, p. 353.
[166]"Hervé's critique is incomplete. . . . It transfers the debate from the level of principles to that of facts." *Ibid.*
[167]*Op. cit.,* p. 354.

an external God;[168] his religion is simultaneously a "religion of the Father" and a "religion of the Son."

The Catholic finds the internal God by turning away from things. He finds God in his inner self, for God is "more intimate to him than man is to himself." Only the testimony which God gives about Himself in man has value. Because God is within man, no one can be compelled to believe by external force. Faith in an internal God has a dimension of eternity which makes it invulnerable.[169]

From the standpoint of faith in an internal God with its eternal dimension, the temporal has *no real significance.* The believer can act against his conscience, and in that case he ceases to be himself, to be a true interiority; but he does not do anything positive, for evil is only the absence of good. In this sense sin is something unreal. But the good also has no *real significance.* For, the good dwells in man's inner self, that means ultimately in God since God is more intimate to man than man is to himself. But God is the infinite, eternal Goodness to whom man cannot add anything, Hence there is no longer any good that man could do.[170]

Man's fate here on earth is unimportant when seen in the perspective of belief in an internal God. Man has merely to take his fate as it comes with or without happiness: "Thy will be done." But man's lot in the hereafter is likewise without any significance, for God is, some way or other, adorable: *"Let us repose in Him."* By faith in an internal God man divests himself of his life. In that perspective human history has no consistency, no importance, no reality. Faith in an internal God is nothing but quietism.[171] This, according to Hegel's expression is "the reign of the Father."[172]

But everything changed when God became incarnate in history. The Incarnation is the beginning of faith in an external God, the beginning of the "religion of the Son." God is no longer found in man's interior, but in the exteriority of history: He has been seen in a definite place, at a definite time, and He has left behind words and signs. From the time that God enters the world, the world is

---

[168]*Ibid.*

[169]*Op. cit.,* p. 356.

[170]"To do good—the expression no longer makes much sense since the good resides in the spirit alone, and ultimately in God who is eternal. . . . If God 'is,' perfection is already realized on this side of the world; it cannot be increased; and there is, literally, nothing to be done." *Ibid.*

[171]*Ibid.*

[172]*Op. cit.,* pp. 356 f.

no longer seen as a fault or defect in an eternal diamond. History, with its searching and groping for truth and value, becomes important.

From the moment of the Incarnation it is as if the infinitely infinite God is no longer self-sufficient, as if something has changed in Him, as if man and the world are necessary for the attainment of a higher perfection instead of being waste products of an original perfection. God can no longer be fully God, and His creation cannot attain its perfection, unless man acknowledges God and, through faith, gives creation back to God. Man, the world, and history are no longer useless, for there is something to be *done*. Man can no longer withdraw from the world in order to live for God in his interiority and by his pure principles. Man involves himself in the world, in the ambiguity of good and evil. For that reason man cannot say that he "is" a Christian, as he can say that he is tall or short, for in his life he represents the contradiction of good and evil, which means that he also "is" a non-Christian. He lives simultaneously in light and darkness. That is why he does not fall away from his God and His Church, not even when at first he does not understand their decrees. He does not doubt about the sacraments, not even when he does not become happier through them.[173]

Merleau-Ponty imagines that the fundamental ambiguity contained in the attitude and conduct of Christians can be understood clearly through the distinction between faith in an internal God, the "religion of the Father", on the one hand, and faith in an external God, the "religion of the Son," on the other. "The paradox of Christianity, in particular of Catholicism, consists in this that the Catholic never clings either to the internal God or to the external God, but always takes a position that lies *in between* those two possibilities."[174]

This ambiguity finds expression in all kinds of circumstances. The Catholic is ready to lose his life, but by losing it he precisely regains it. Faith is a surrender in the dark but the Catholic knows to whom he surrenders and entrusts himself. To be a Catholic is a matter of faith but, according to the Syllabus, one is not a Catholic when he believes that it is impossible to give a rational proof for God's existence. The Catholic accepts that God is with him and yet not absolutely so. History is important and yet unimportant because the

---

[173]*Op. cit.*, pp. 357-360.
[174]*Op. cit.*, p. 360.

"Infinite Look" of the Father, which prevents man from having any secret, any freedom, any desire, or future, always oppresses him. Why, then, should a Catholic not use force against his fellow-men? He *knows* that they are merely wasting time with their ceaseless searching and groping, for Infinite Wisdom has already determined everything.[175]

Practical Consequences. All this explains, according to Merleau-Ponty, the Christian's equivocal attitude in politics. In line with their faith in the external God, Christians can be revolutionaries. But faith in the internal God makes them conservative. *Post factum* they can always say that evil has contributed to the good, but at the time when decisions are being made they may not say that, and evil remains something that is forbidden. *Post factum* the Christians will forgive all crimes committed in a revolution, but they are never permitted to buy revolutionary progress through a crime. That means that the Christians can join a revolution only after it has been a success; they must wait until the future becomes the past, for, until then, the revolution remains suspect. The Christian is a nuisance to the established powers because they cannot fail to realize that they cannot fully count on him. But for exactly the same reason the Christian is a nuisance to revolutionaries. Both as a conservative, and as a revolutionary, he is unreliable.[176]

There is only one case in which the Catholic Church prescribes revolution—namely, when the lawful authority violates the divine law. But in no case has the Catholic Church actually chosen sides against a lawful authority because the latter acted *unjustly*, nor has she ever taken sides in favor of a revolution because it was just. What has happened is that the Catholic Church has favored revolutionaries because they protected her tabernacles, ministers, and property. Only then will God have come really to earth when the Catholic Church will recognize no more obligations toward her ministers than toward other human beings, and when she will protest as much against the destruction of houses in Guernica as she does against the destruction of her temples.[177]

Actually, however, says Merleau-Ponty, the Church expects the faithful to practice heroism in her favor; she is conservative. More-

---

[175]*Op. cit.,* pp. 360-362.
[176]*Op. cit.,* pp. 360-363.
[177]*Op. cit.,* pp. 363 f.

over, Christianity says explicitly that man cannot serve two masters. But because Christians believe in the Incarnation, they can be near-revolutionaries, as "near" as revolutionaries might wish them to be. There are examples of that, and those who set that example were sincere. They said what they thought. But it was only a "secondary sincerity." The "primary sincerity" is not possible for Christians because it is impossible for them to banish equivocity from their essence.[178]

Summary. It may be useful to try to formulate here Merleau-Ponty's attitude toward the problem of God. Merleau-Ponty rejects God because to accept Him violates the authenticity of life and of philosophizing about life. Authentic philosophizing demands that the philosopher establish himself within the wonder of the dawn of meaning and give expression to that meaning. Meaning presupposes the subject, for whom and through whom truth and value arise for the subject. The existence of the subject himself is a contingent fact for which no explanation can be found; in fact it resists in principle any kind of explanation because every explanation presupposes the contingency of the subject. It is useless to take for granted that which has to be explained and to make use of it in the explanation. Moreover, every explanation destroys the contingency of the subject, because an explanation consists in establishing a necessary bond between that which must be explained and its necessary and necessitating antecedents. Hence in every explanation the contingent is conceived as necessitated, whereas, as contingent, it is precisely non-necessitated.

It makes no difference for Merleau-Ponty whether we connect the contingent subject with cosmological factors or with the Necessary Being of God, for in both cases the contingency of the subject is disregarded. Hence Merleau-Ponty rejects God because he refuses to reject man's authenticity. Only by rejecting God, he thinks, can the authenticity of human history, which has its source in the contingent subject, be saved. It is precisely because the subject is contingent that the search for truth and the foundation of values which occur in history are never guaranteed.

Christians have to deny the latter, says Merleau-Ponty, for God is Truth Itself. The Christian thinks that he possesses that Truth in

---

[178]"One does not see how they could posses that 'first sincerity,' which consists of casting out [all] equivocity." *Op. cit.,* p. 364.

faith and that he can look at man, the world and history in the light of that Truth. Hence he can sedately leave the search for truth to non-believers, for he is "one who knows." There is therefore no possibility of a dialogue with Christians, says Merleau-Ponty.[179]

Something similar must be said about the establishing of values. This also has little or no importance for Christians, for God is Goodness itself. But if this is true, man no longer has anything to do. The laborious construction of a good world becomes unimportant. True, the Incarnation has changed all that a little, but not sufficiently to remove equivocity from what the Christian does and permits. The Christian is not a man among men.

Merleau-Ponty's philosophical attitude presents itself as a serene kind of atheism. It has nothing of the Luciferan attitude that reveals itself so often in the work of Sartre. Merleau-Ponty does not insult anybody. His philosophy makes him confront questions that have been discussed over the years without being really reflected upon in a profound way. His philosophy is a challenge to theism. Theology cannot simply dismiss it.

C. *Critical Review*

Kant's critique of the proofs for God's existence almost caused a panic among the followers of traditional theistic metaphysics. In fact, they were so upset that they forgot to read Kant's *Critiques* carefully. It was only through Joseph Maréchal's work, *Le point de départ de la métaphysique*, that a change took place. Today's situation differs greatly from the one that existed at the time of that anxious defense against Kant. We now sincerely admit that we owe much to Kant precisely when it is a question of preventing us from affirming a pseudo-god.

We get a strong impression that something similar must be said regarding existentialistic atheism. Again there was a kind of panic and many appeared to feel that their theism was in jeopardy. But it would be too bad if the only reactions were those inspired by anxiety. In that case it might take a hundred years before the theists would realize that even existentialistic atheism can contribute something positive to theism. Dondeyne has shown that such a con-

---

[179]"How could there be a genuine exchange between 'he who knows' and 'he who does not know'?" Merleau-Ponty, "L'homme et l'adversité," *op. cit.* (in footnote 136), p. 74.

tribution is possible.[180] We would like to study the new problems in the spirit in which he deals with them.

First of all, we want to find a point of contact in Merleau-Ponty's objections against those who brand his philosophy as atheistic. Merleau-Ponty rejects this epithet because it starts from the *supposition* that there are two kinds of philosophy: one which gives an ultimate and all-embracing explanation of all things, and another which rejects such an explanation. The traditional opposition between theism and atheism, Merleau-Ponty says, is based on that *supposition,* which he refuses to admit. He himself does not start with the intention of presenting an all-embracing explanation or of rejecting its possibility. He starts from the contingent fact of the subject's existence and the "history of meaning" implied in it. In such a starting point God does not even enter into the picture. One who introduces Him anyhow into this starting point as the Necessary Being, in order to explain the existence of the subject, talks the subject out of existence.

Two Meanings of Contingency

How is it possible that contingency is the basis on which traditional metaphysics affirms the existence of God as the Necessary Being, whereas this same basis leads Merleau-Ponty to reject God as the Necessary Being? The reader immediately guesses that there must be some difference in the meaning which the opponents give to that term contingency. And we feel that this is the case.

Anthropological Sense of Contingency. What does Merleau-Ponty mean by contingency? For him contingency expresses the mode of being that is proper to the subject. The being of the subject is a "being contingent" because, and to the extent that, the subject is *not* the product of processes and forces that act with *necessity.* For if the subject were the result of such forces, he would be a *thing,* like all other products of processes and forces. But in that case there would be no more *meaning,* a thing is not a meaning for a thing. But there is meaning, for the contingent subject *is.* To be contingent, then, according to Merleau-Ponty, means *not* to be necessitated in the way the being of things is to be necessitated. To be contingent

---

[180]A. Dondeyne, "L'athéisme contemporain et le problème des attributs de Dieu," *Foi et réflexion philosophique,* Gembloux-Louvain 1961, pp. 462-480. This work is a reprint from *Ephemerides Theologicae Lovanienses,* 1961, pp. 389-596, and retains the original pagination.

means to be free. The being contingent of the subject has an anthropological significance.

Metaphysical Sense of Contingency. Traditional metaphysics, on the other hand, gives to the term "contingency" another, more profound and metaphysical meaning. The metaphysician calls be-ing as be-ing contingent, to signify that no be-ing whatsoever, precisely as be-ing, has the ground or reason of its being in itself. In an anthropological perspective of thought the being of the subject must be called a being contingent or a being free, and the being of a thing, a being necessitated. But in a metaphysical perspective both the subject and the thing considered *as* be-ings, viz., *as* not-nothing, are called contingent because, *as* be-ings, they do not have a ground or reason in themselves for their being. Accordingly, the same term assumes different meanings in different perspectives, as is clearly the case in the present controversy between Merleau-Ponty and traditional metaphysics. For Merleau-Ponty the contingency of the subject means "not being necessitated by processes and forces," i.e., to be free. The metaphysician, on the contrary, means by contingency that be-ing *as* be-ing does not find in itself any ground for its being, and this applies to both the subject and the things *as* be-ing, hence as not-nothing.

Consequences of the Distinction. Ths difference explains why metaphysicians continue to seek an all-embracing and all-explanatory principle, whereas Merleau-Ponty does not feel called to such a task. The metaphysicians *must* pursue their questioning, for their metaphysical affirmation of be-ing as be-ing reveals itself as impossible at a certain moment if they affirm nothing other than be-ing. For be-ing manifests itself as not having a ground or reason in itself. Be-ing, then, cannot be at all if there is nothing but be-ings. In this metaphysical perspective "nothing" shows itself at a certain moment to be much more simple than be-ing. But we cannot say that there is nothing, for be-ings are—and undeniably so. The metaphysicians therefore reach a point when they must either maintain that there is nothing or give a new dimension to their affirmation of be-ings, since be-ings are, but *cannot* be from themselves.

Merleau-Ponty does not use the term "contingency" in the sense in which it is used by the metaphysicians. He is a total stranger to the metaphysical attitude of asking questions, hence he cannot understand why the metaphysicians are so eager to find an all-embracing and all-explanatory principle. The fact that Merleau-

Ponty is a stranger to the authentically metaphysical question should not surprise us. As Kwant has shown, his analysis of philosophical rationality as well as of rationality in general is very incomplete. True, Merleau-Ponty speaks about human rationality; but when he does it is always in order to point out its impersonal, dark roots in the "body-subject." To search for these roots is not at all the same, of course, as to describe the *proper* character of rational thinking.

Since the studies of Merleau-Ponty no one will be tempted to follow Descartes in his description of rational thinking. On the other hand, however, since Descartes it is evident also that the "soul" cannot be reduced to the "body," viz., that rationality has characteristics of its own which distinguish it from the deep dimension of bodily being from which it emerges.

Merleau-Ponty gives an extensive description of the affirmation of the world in so far as this affirmation is an affirmation made by the "body-subject." However, this affirmation does not exhaust all of man's possibilities for affirming the world. One who confines himself to the affirmation of the world by the "body-subject" runs the risk of neglecting the level of authentic rationality. Although Merleau-Ponty does not neglect it, whenever he speaks about rationality, he always does it in order to point to its roots in the "body-subject." Obviously, this procedure does not tell us what the *proper* character of rationality is. Merleau-Ponty does not describe this proper character but he draws conclusions as if he had given a description of it.[181] Since he has not examined the true nature of human rationality, it is not surprising that he has also failed to reached the level of rational thinking proper to the metaphysician and that he has not come face to face with the dilemma: either there is nothing or there is an all-explanatory principle.

Sartre's Fundamental Attitude. Since we are speaking about the significance of metaphysics, it may be appropriate to discuss here also Sartre's fundamental position in the light of metaphysics. Sartre's atheism, in contrast to that of Merleau-Ponty, is Luciferan in character. Sartre's rejection of God is impassionate and appears in his works as a protest. The three reasons given explicitly by Sartre for his rejection of God will be discussed later, for at present we are concerned only with his fundamental attitude. It is expressed in his play *Les Mouches.*

---

[181]Kwant, *The Phenomenological Philosophy of Merleau-Ponty,* Pittsburgh, 1963, pp. 225 ff.

God, says Sartre, cannot exist, for otherwise man cannot be free in the way Sartre wants him to be free, namely, divinely. We answer, using the principle which Sartre himself adopts to describe the subjectivity of freedom: "Here, we cannot escape from a judgment of truth."[182] The truth regarding subjectivity as freedom is that the subject does not have in himself any ground for his being, for no be-ing can give "to be" to itself. There is one standpoint, namely, that of the metaphysician, from which man as subject appears to himself as an "impossibility," as being nothing, *of himself*. And yet man *is!* Man is the co-origin of the world's meaning, but in the light of metaphysics he is only a "second origin." Man in his action is co-origin of a new meaning, but his initiative is a "produced initiative." With man the world begins to be for man, but the beginning of the world, which man is, is a "begun beginning."[183] God is the Lord of the totality of all be-ings and before Him man must bow in adoration.[184]

Sartre considers it simply scandalous that man should consent to such a thing. But why is it so scandalous? Perhaps on the basis of a "judgment of truth"? Sartre suggests his answer when, describing Electra's submission to Jupiter, he lets her say: "I will be your slave and your thing."[185] To acknowledge God is, according to Sartre, the degradation of man to the rank of a mere thing. And this brings us back to Merleau-Ponty's line of thought. For he, too, maintains that the affirmation of the Necessary Being stifles subjectivity as freedom.

The Subject and the Necessary Being

Merleau-Ponty refuses to accept the necessity of looking for an all-explanatory principle because he does not think on a level which makes such a search necessary. However he goes beyond that fundamental refusal when he maintains that to accept God as a Necessary Being in order to explain contingency as freedom is to stifle that freedom. All explanations, according to him, stifle freedom.

"Explanation." We have already explained what "to explain" means for Merleau-Ponty. According to him, only a "thing" can be

---

[182]Sartre, *Existentialism and Humanism*, p. 51.
[183]*La personne incarnée*, Paris, 1947, p. 116.
[184]Sartre. "Les Mouches," *Théâtre*, Paris, 1947, p. 116.
[185]J. Daniélou, *Le Problème de Dieu et l'existentialisme*, Montreal, 1958, p. 27.

explained. An explanation can be given when one understands a thing or a phenomenon of nature by means of its antecedents, i.e., when one sees the thing or the phenomenon in reference to the unilateral, deterministic cause or causes which have influenced the thing or phenomenon in such a way that it is what it is.

It makes no difference for Merleau-Ponty whether the "explanation" of the subject as freedom is done in a naturalistic or a theological fashion. In both cases the subject as freedom is stifled, denied, rendered impossible. Regarding a naturalistic explanation, everyone has to agree with Merleau-Ponty and admit that such an explanation truly denies, renders impossible, and stifles the subject as freedom. The same cannot be asserted when there is question of a metaphysical and theological "explanation" of the subject. However, this point will be discussed later. First we wish to note that, to Merleau-Ponty's mind, metaphysical and theological "explanations" seem to be of the same kind as those that explain a thing or phenomenon of nature. God, the Necessary Being, as "Cause" means exactly the same thing for Merleau-Ponty as the unilateral, deterministic, causal influence of a thing on a thing. Obviously, if one conceives God's causality in that way, it must of necessity stifle freedom. But, we ask ourselves, who should become panic-stricken by Merleau-Ponty's atheism and whose theism is endangered by his theory? Evidently only those metaphysicians and theologians who have too loosely compared God's "causality" to the causal influence of a thing upon a thing.

Kant and Merleau-Ponty. With respect to causality and God's existence, Kant and Merleau-Ponty differ in the following way. Kant has shown on epistemological grounds that a *thing-like* idea of causality can never lead to God. Merleau-Ponty, basing himself on anthropological grounds, shows that God's "causality," conceived in a thing-like fashion, disregards man as subject. In both cases, it is evidently a physicalistic or causalistic concept of "cause" that is rejected.

There is a difference, of course, between Kant and Merleau-Ponty, for Kant is a theist and Merleau-Ponty an atheist. Moreover, Merleau-Ponty implies that the only possible way of conceiving a cause is the physicalistic and causalistic way. This is not true, for intersubjectivity reveals to us "causal influences" which do not show the least resemblance to the influence of thing upon thing. Merleau-

Ponty's thought regarding the concept of "cause" is very one-sided.[186] That is why a phenomenology of love is conspicuously absent from his works.

Missing the Point. One who understands Merleau-Ponty's presuppositions sees also that these presuppositions make it necessary to reply to Merleau-Ponty on the level on which he moves in his thinking. Contingency means freedom for him, understood as the being of the subject, as autonomy in reference to the results of cosmic processes and forces. That both the subject and the thing, as be-ings, have no ground or reason for their being in themselves, and are thus contingent in the *metaphysical* sense, lies outside the perspective of Merleau-Ponty's thought. "To explain" means for him *exclusively* to see a thing in relation to its deterministic antecedents. It does not dawn upon him that an authentic metaphysics uses the term "to explain" in a totally different sense. He maintains that theology is not able to explain the contingency of the subject in relation to God. But, if we keep in mind his presuppositions, this assertion means no more and no less than that freedom cannot be the result of a thing-like process. Of course, in this sense, the assertion is evident.

We do not have the impression that Merleau-Ponty's critics always give him a reply that is situated on the level of his own thinking. When, for example, De Lubac accuses Merleau-Ponty of not even recognizing *the problem itself* from which the affirmation of God's existence is born, he is thinking of the contingency of the being as be-ing, viz., the undeniable fact that no be-ing as be-ing finds the ground of its being in itself, and that therefore, *viewed in itself,* it *cannot* at all be. When Merleau-Ponty retorts that he makes contingency radical, he is thinking of the subject as freedom, which can never *be* the result of a thing-like process. In other words, there is no meeting of minds in the dispute.

If we are not mistaken, De Petter likewise fails to meet Merleau-Ponty on his own ground. De Petter considers it "incomprehensible" that Merleau-Ponty rejects God on the ground of contingency. "For if contingency or the 'gratuitousness' of be-ings demands the affirmation of the Creator, it is equally evident that, conversely, the affirmation of the Creator presupposes of necessity the radical contingency or 'gratuitousness' of being of the be-ings."[187] De

---

[186]Kwant, *op. cit.*, p. 133.
[187]"Le caractère métaphysique de la preuve de l'existence de Dieu et la pensée contemporaine," *L'existence de Dieu,* Tournai, 1961, p. 172.

Petter evidently conceives the contingency of be-ings in the metaphysical sense, for he defines it as the "gratuitousness of the being
of the be-ings" and also as the "impossibility for be-ings ... to account for, and give a basis to their being."[188] But Merleau-Ponty is
not concerned with that; hence we should not try to answer him as
if that is the point about which he speaks.

Speaking About God in Metaphysics and in Theology

A Faulty Way of Speaking About God. In spite of the above
misunderstandings, Merleau-Ponty's assertion that the affirmation of
God stifles the freedom of the subject has shocked metaphysicians
and theologians out of their complacency. They have come to realize
that their way of speaking about God is not completely secure
against the criticism of existentialistic atheism. We speak intentionally in a rather general way, for the criticism we now have in mind
was not expressed by Merleau-Ponty alone. Practically the same
thought can be found in Sartre. Merleau-Ponty conceives God's
"causality" as the influence of a kind of cosmic force, as a kind of
"sublimated natural energy."[189]

Sartre is closer to the usual concept of traditional metaphysics and
theology. He sees God's "causality" with respect to man as a creation,
but he conceives creation as analogous with the making of a utensil,
such as a paper-knife. God, then, is a kind of Superior Artisan and
man is like a utensil, like a paper-knife that is *prefixed* in the
thought of the maker. In this way Sartre develops the idea he had
already insinuated in *Les Mouches*. Describing Electra's submission
to Jupiter, he makes her say: "I will be your slave and your thing!"
The thought is clear; God makes man a thing and that means
slavery for man.

This thought is not foreign to philosophies that lie outside existentialism. For instance, Michael Verret states that "to make God
the Creator it is sufficient to merge the architect and the mason."[190]
For the architect supplies the idea which the mason makes real
through his labor.

As we have mentioned, the atheistic critique of the theology of
Creation was a shock to the theologians.   The way they had

---

[188]De Petter, *art. cit.,* p. 167.
[189]Dondeyne, *art. cit.,* p. 476.
[190]*Les marxistes et la religion, Essai sur l'athéisme moderne,* Paris, n.d., p. 39.

spoken about God was such that it gave the atheists a chance to deliver a punch which they could not ward off. If man exists, then theologians are not permitted to say what they please! Of course they hasten to admit that the relation between God and man should be conceived in a more personalistic way,[191] and they readily admit that categories borrowed from intersubjectivity are more appropriate for this purpose than those that refer to the fabrication of utensils.[192] All this, however, does not take away from the fact that for hundreds of years this point was not recognized and that this failure offered a golden opportunity to atheism.

The Source of this Failure. What is the reason, we may ask, why such a vital point continued to be overlooked? The answer, it seems, is not difficult to find. There was a lack of effective control of the concepts that were used with respect to God, and this led to their degeneration. As we have mentioned in Chapter Two, metaphysics should be exceedingly careful before it dares to say that God "is," for the term "is" applies to a be-ing, and God "is" not a be-ing. But even this assertion is not more than just words for one who is not *personally* involved in the quest of metaphysics. For only the man who is personally involved in asking the questions proper to metaphysics, sees what possibilities there are to make affirmations and what affirmations he is forced to make without being able to make them *as* they should be made. We spoke of the indirect and directional character of all the terms that are used to affirm the being of God. He who does not keep that in mind at all times will also fail to realize that the concepts he uses are shop-worn and deteriorated.

Generally speaking, this kind of deterioration can be prevented only if philosophers and theologians make constant efforts to keep alive the meaning of the terms they employ. When the "spoken word" begins to be at the disposal of a speaking community as a kind of "thing," the origin and, with it, the life of a term begins to disappear, and there is danger that in the end not much more will

---

[191]Schillebeeckx, "De zin van het mens-zijn van Jezus, de Christus," *Tijdschrift voor Theologie*, vol. II (1962), p. 131.

[192]When phenomenologists stress that the categories of intersubjectivity are more suitable for expressing the relationship of God and man, they do not at all want to claim that all problems concerning this relationship are thereby solved. Hence it is unfair to ascribe such a claim to them and then show that they "fail to make good" (Schillebeeckx, *art. cit.*, p. 130). The phenomenologists merely want to point out that the categories of intersubjectivity safeguard us from *fostering* atheism.

remain than lifeless verbiage. The origin of a word is *real* speech, the "speaking word," which is called *real* precisely because it expresses *reality*. But it is clear that this kind of speech implies a certain "seeing," i.e., a *personal* presence to a present reality. *Reality* is conceptualized in speech and the concept becomes incarnate in language. Speech is "intentional," it essentially refers to that which it itself is not, to a reality which in a personal act of "seeing" is embodied in words. We repeat once more what we have stressed in Chapter Two: this act is a personal act, for "seeing" is something that each man does for himself. If *he himself* does not see, then he does *not see*. When man does not keep the origin of the spoken word alive by personally following its intentionality, the word begins to have a kind of isolated existence. The word is, as it were, reified and is put at the disposal of the community as a kind of utensil which the community uses without *really* saying anything. Heidegger use the term "chatter" *(Gerede)* to indicate that empty use of words.[193] It is not much more than verbiage.

The immediate result of such "chatter" is that one no longer sees how every word that refers to man and things human can run through an endless scale of meanings. I can say of man that he is a subject and speak about love and sin, but what does all this mean if I fail to *see* that what I express by those words can be made real in numberless ways?[194] With respect to man and things human, all terms are used in an analogous sense. But the awareness of this fact weakens and fades away when we limit ourselves to manipulating the "spoken word."

A Twofold Analogy. If the meaning of every word is of a directional nature, the same is doubly true of the "Names" that are used for God. Because God is not a reality that is present to man, i.e., He is not a datum of experience, man has no terms to indicate concepts that directly express what God is. For this reason the philosopher has to use terms embodying concepts which directly refer not to God but to the reality that man can experience. Reality *itself* prompts man to a manner of "affirmation" which transcends his *direct* affirmations. If the directly affirmed reality *itself* did not point beyond itself and force man to transcend his *direct* affirmations, then

---

[193]"We do not so much understand the be-ing that is talked about, but already listen only to the talking as such." *Sein und Zeit,* p. 168; English ed., p. 212.

[194]Dondeyne, *art. cit.,* pp. 472-475.

all the indirect affirmations which he is forced to make because of his metaphysical thinking about reality would be mere projections. One who realizes that the indirect affirmation of God is not a projection must nevertheless keep in mind *at all times* that the "affirmation" of God is and *remains indirect.*

The word spoken by man is intentional; it refers to the reality expressed in the word. Within that intentionality no speaking can claim to be speaking about God. However, prompted by his metaphysical consciousness, man uses the intentionality of his words to express the reference of reality *itself* to God. But that does not mean that his words thereby acquire *themselves* an intentionality that transcends their reference to a present, perceptible reality. When man expresses the "Name of God," his words do not reach God as a present reality. The do not dwell with God, as human speech about perceptible reality dwells with reality. Nevertheless, man *has to* speak because his metaphysical thinking about reality *itself* forces him to do so. In other words, man is forced to speak inadequately, for he has no other concepts than those he uses in speaking about perceptible reality. His speaking about God is and remains indirect and "directional"; hence it is analogous in a second sense.

Affirmation and Negation. All speaking attains its ultimate form in the judgment. But the formulated judgment no longer makes us "see" the indirect and directional character of the terms. When I say that God *"is,"* I can understand this judgment correctly only if I keep in mind the implications of the metaphysical consciousness that lie at the basis of that judgment. This judgment can be properly understood only when it is seen in the light of a metaphysical "speaking word." Only in this light we see that to *every* positive judgment about God we must immediately add a negative judgment, to point out that metaphysical consciousness does not give a new dimension to the intentionality of "speaking" which would make man's speaking about God "adequate." Speech about God uses the intentionality of the human word that refers to perceptible reality; hence it must always be followed by a denial.

When we realize how easily the "speaking word" deteriorates into "chatter," we also readily understand that this is still more the case in respect to speech about God. This deterioration sets in when we acknowledge the principle that every positive judgment should be followed by a negative one and then neglect to do so because we consider it sufficient to acknowledge the principle. The omission of those negative judgments means that *de facto* solely the positive judgments remain. In this situation we are greatly tempted to lose sight of the reason why a negative judgment must be added to every positive one. And as soon as this is forgotten, we forget also that all "Names of God" have a purely directional character, and finally imagine that we *know* what we are talking about. Then we begin to manipulate the "Names of God" just as we can play with the "clear and distinct ideas" of geometry.[195]

A Protest Against an Uprooted Theism. The atheism of Sartre and Merleau-Ponty is not only a denial of God, but it is also a protest against an uprooted theism. When metaphysics concludes to the real existence of God as "Origin" of all that is, it simultaneously assumes the duty of "thinking" about God in such a way that beings are possible. The atheism of Sartre and Merleau-Ponty is a reproach to theism for having neglected this duty. Dondeyne explains as follows the spirit which prompted those atheists to make that accusation:

"When you, believers, have proved the existence of God, you quickly imagine that you have found a solution for all the antinomies which are met with by human thought when it tries to find a ground for and justify finite human existence. In reality you have merely relocated the difficulties, for it is not sufficient to prove that God is the foundation of everything. It is also necessary to reflect upon the co-existence of the necessary and infinite Being with the freedom and historicity of finite existences, and to find a ground for it. Now, at this stage of reflection all the difficulties reappear and the critical analysis of the attributes of God destroys what the proof of God has established. The second part of theodicy turns against the first part."[196]

Atheism undoubtedly demands too much from a theistic metaphysics when it requires metaphysics positively to ground the possibility of the co-existence of the Necessary Being and finite existences. However, when metaphysics deals with the "Names of God," it has the evident duty of avoiding the use of categories that virtually do away with man's freedom and historicity. Now it fails in this duty when it conceives God's "causality" in a physicalistic way and

---

[195]Dondeyne, *art. cit.*, p. 472.
[196]Dondeyne, *art. cit.*, p. 466.

"explains" the idea of creation by comparing it with the fabrication of a utensil.[197] It stands to reason that such misunderstandings can arise only when the "Divine Names" are not spoken as "speaking words." The importance of the twofold analogy which makes the use of those "Names" meaningful is then lost sight of by the speaker, and he is no longer *really* aware of the need to use also the "negative way."

We also ask ourselves whether the controversy between "Thomists" and "Molinists" would have been possible if both parties had expressed the Divine Names as "speaking words." For the issue became a dispute precisely because both parties assumed that they "knew" the meaning of the terms that were used in the formulations of the question. But one does not so readily assume this when one uses the terms as "speaking words," i.e., in the awareness that they imply a not-knowing.

Simone Weil had said that of two men who have no experience of God the one who denies God is perhaps closer to Him than the other.[198] Taken literally, this view disregards the metaphysical possibility for affirming God. Although this possibility is indirect it is nevertheless positive. But taken according to their intent, those words express the mentality that should animate the metaphysician if he does not want his speaking about God to be blasphemous.

"There is, Literally, Nothing to Do"

Christian Quietism. Because the subject is contingent, undetermined and free, success is never guaranteed to the search for truth and the establishment of values. According to Merleau-Ponty, Christians cannot admit this; and therefore, they cannot earnestly collaborate in this search. They are worthless for this world and it is impossible, or at least very difficult, to hold a dialogue with them.

We prefer to leave aside the models Merleau-Ponty uses to embody his thought and try to determine exactly what he wants to say. For this reason we shall not enter into a discussion regarding the question whether it makes sense to distinguish between what Merleau-Ponty calls the "religion of the Father" and the "religion of the Son." We abstain also from asking whether or not that distinction, if it is meaningful, can be defined in the way it is done by him. We can leave those questions aside because what Merleau-Ponty really

---

[197]"To think of oneself as a product would be again to think of oneself as a thing." Marcel, *L'homme problématique,* Paris, 1955, p. 66.
[198]Simone Weil, *La pesanteur et la grâce,* Paris, 1948, p. 132.

wishes to say comes down to the assertion that he who adheres to God cannot take the world seriously.

After all, God is called the Supreme Truth and the Supreme Goodness. Christians think they possess God. Hence, they have no longer any reason to take part in the contingent and often dizzying *search* for truth; still less have they a reason for becoming involved in the dangerous attempt to establish values. This idea can also be expressed in another way. If the history of truth and value is finished in God and the Christians are established in God and can say that they possess Him, there is then no longer any sense in desiring to *make* history. "There is, literally, nothing to do. What a Quietism!"[199] In the field of research such an attitude leads to intolerance.[200] And in the struggle for a more human world it leads to conservatism. Merleau-Ponty does not give an absolute meaning to that assertion, for he knows that the history of Christianity has also a different aspect. However, according to him, the fundamental ambiguity of Christianity is never overcome.

Let us begin by pointing out that the first Christians would have been quite puzzled if anyone told them that there was nothing left for them to do as soon as they had become Christians. They realized that everything had just now begun for them, that man and the world had received an entirely new meaning through God's entrance into human history, and that this new meaning provided motives for enabling their activity to develop with hitherto unheard of energy.[201]

Christian Ambiguity. Nevertheless, Merleau-Ponty is right when he thinks that there is a certain ambiguity in the existence of Christians. The Christian project of existence starts from the recognition of a multi-dimensional intentional movement of the subject which man is, namely, man's being directed to the world and his being directed to a Transcendent God. It stands to reason that this recognition will affect the Christian's conduct. It is clear also that the consequences of that recognition will immediately appear as a form of estrangement to those who cannot accept that multi-dimensionality. As a matter of fact, that is the accusation Merleau-Ponty makes: Christians do not take the world and its history seriously but are estranged from it. The Christians' acceptance of the multi-

---

[199]*Sens et non-sens,* p. 356.
[200]"I piously kill my enemies." *Op. cit.,* p. 190.
[201]A. De Waelhens, *Une philosophie de l'ambiguité, L'existentialisme de Maurice Merleau-Ponty,* Louvain 1951, p. 379, note 3.

dimensional character of their existence means that they are in a situation of tension which always remains a concrete task for them and which always includes a danger of estrangement. Even if theoretically there were no problem, practically a problem does exist. Theoretically the Christian does not live *between* the two intentional movements of his subjectivity,[202] but he develops and realizes himself *in* both.[203] But in practice this is always a task which will present itself in ever new forms and, *concretely* speaking, the Christian will never be satisfied with the solution.

The Question "de Jure." Merleau-Ponty does not want to deal with the question why one can never count fully upon the Catholic, regarding the *making* of history, as a question of fact but as a question of principle, a question *"de jure."* When the question of fact is raised, it is always possible to disavow the facts by an appeal to the principles; it is always possible to disavow past events as unfortunate accidents, as something that should not have taken place. The Christian will admit guilt with respect to the past, but proclaim his innocence in regard to the future by appealing to his principles.

According to Merleau-Ponty, the fact that Christians are now revolutionaries and then conservatives, that they are always bad revolutionaries and always bad conservatives, and that therefore one can never wholly count upon them, has its foundation in the very essence of Christianity, for Christianity conceives man as oriented to God. That reason settles the question *"de jure,"* because for Merleau-Ponty this orientation implies of necessity an estrangement. In his opinion, one could *fully* count upon Christians only if they were ready to give up their estrangement and define their existence as *nothing else* but an involvement in the world.[204]

But there is not the least doubt what the Christians answer with respect to their fundamental position will be. They are not prepared to define their existence as pure being in the world. Using Sartre's expression, they reply: "Here one cannot avoid a judgment of truth,"[205] though the meaning they give to it is different from that of Sartre.

---

[202]*Sens et non-sens*, p. 360.

[203]"The Christian is not 'always *between* one and the other' but always *in* one and the other." De Waelhens, *op. cit.*, p. 381.

[204]"But if we rediscover time beneath the subject, and if we relate to the paradox of time those of the body, the world, the thing, and other people, we shall understand that beyond these there is nothing to understand." *Phenomenology of Perception*, p. 365.

[205]*Existentialism and Humanism*, p. 51.

If the truth of human existence, viz., the true essence of man, reveals itself as both orientation to the world *and* orientation to God, the Christian will not offer any excuses for explicitly recognizing this truth, and he will try to draw the necessary conclusions from it. And if one of the conclusions is to the effect that the Christian cannot be ready to buy the progress of history at the price of a crime, he will likewise not excuse himself for accepting that consequence, and he will add that one cannot simply claim that what he thus refuses to realize is a *real* progress of history.

Does it follow, then, that our lot here on earth is of *no* importance?[206] that the Christian is *not* involved?[207] that he divest himself, as it were, of life?[208] All that would indeed be true if the Christian conceived existence as *nothing other than* the implementation of his orientation to his Transcendent God. But it is not right to accuse Christianity of that kind of exclusivism; at least Catholic Christianity should not be accused of it.[209]

The Question of Fact. Consequently, for the Christians only the "question of fact" remains to be debated with Merleau-Ponty. On the other hand, that debate is also particularly difficult. As we have stressed, the Christians do not live *between* their orientation to God on the one side and their orientation to the world on the other. They realize themselves *in* both intentional movements, which form a dialectical unit. For love toward God is not really authentic without love for man, that is, without readiness to humanize the world. On the other hand, the readiness to humanize the world is not of itself identical with the love for God. That is why we spoke of a dialectical unity, a unity of reciprocal implication.

When we realize what that means, we realize at the same time the ever threatening possibility that the Christian may become alienated from his essence. This possibility is rooted fundamentally in the Christian's nature as *man;* for man's being is a "having to be," a

---

[206]*Sens et non-sens,* p. 356.
[207]*Ibid.*
[208]*Ibid.*
[209]"Undoubtedly less exact is the conclusion which Merleau-Ponty draws from it and which is absolute quietism. If, he explains, faith makes us children of God and partakers of His glory, there is nothing left for us to do. 'If God is, perfection is already realized on this side of the world, it cannot be increased, there is, literally, nothing to be done. My kingdom is not of this world. Works result from religion as something over and above it.' But this is not what Christianity, at least Catholic Christianity, thinks." De Waelhens, *op. cit.,* p. 379.

task, on every level of his subjectivity as existence. But the execution of the task, which man himself *is*, is never guaranteed, for it is rooted in the contingent subject. For this reason self-criticism and self-control are indispensible for man and for the Christian, in order that he may prevent his estrangement as much as possible. That is why no one can refuse to admit that a distinction must always be made between a doctrine on the one hand and the practice of its adherents on the other. One who refuses to accept that distinction has no longer any other choice than either complete skepticism or permanent illusion regarding man, including himself.[210]

We said above that the discussion with Merleau-Ponty, in respect to the Christians' estrangement from the world, is particularly difficult even when the debate is concerned only with the question of fact. The reason is that the question for Christians regarding their *de facto* estrangement must consist in examining to what extent they have been faithful to their essence as a task, in regard to both their subjective orientation to God and to their orientation to the world. But Merleau-Ponty does not accept that the execution of man's orientation to God is a *real* task. The subject's multi-dimensional orientation means that for the Christian there is a tension which does not exist for Merleau-Ponty, because he accepts only one dimension of existence for man. Thus, the Christians cannot simply let themselves be guided by Merleau-Ponty when they question themselves regarding "the fact." The opponents in the debate do not stand on the same ground. This divergence reveals itself when one reads Merleau-Ponty's expressions which he has borrowed from Christianity and which he uses to characterize Christianity to his own satisfaction, such as, "Thy will be done,"[211] "Let us repose in Him,"[212] "It is not possible to serve two masters,"[213] "My kingdom is not of this world,"[214] "We must lose our life."[215] These expressions have another meaning for the Christian than for Merleau-Ponty when he uses them to describe Christianity to his own satisfaction. For Merleau-Ponty they signify *per se* "estrangement," but

---

[210]"And, in order not to reject a doctrine, is it necessary that this doctrine be found consistent with itself in the deeds and works that are supposed to express it? In that case we would have no other choice than that between skepticism and illusion about ourselves." De Waelhens, *op. cit.*, p. 381.

[211]*Sens et non-sens*, p. 356.

[212]*Ibid.*

[213]*Op. cit.*, p. 364.

[214]*Op. cit.*, p. 356.

[215]*Op. cit.*, p. 360.

for a Christian they refer to a tension and to a task that is more complicated than Merleau-Ponty is able to suspect.

A "Postulatory" Atheism. All this shows, we think, that the term atheism has a great variety of meanings. Existentialistic atheism is a "postulatory" atheism; it demands the rejection of God in order to make the affirmation of man possible.[216] Hence the form assumed by this kind of atheism depends on the way man is defined. Nietzsche denies God to make room for the affirmation of man as the creator of culture. Jeanson rejects Him—to express it paradoxically—in order to open up again for man the possibility to understand the Christian command of love. "I will choose to be free," says Jeanson, "that is, to exist, not for God, but for those who are my brothers, because they share in my being man although their share is often more wretched than mine. And in order not to run the risk of betraying that duty of solidarity I will refuse every other obligation. . . . I will discard every other justice and every other love than the justice and love toward them, and I will endeavor to the best of my ability to establish it even better in this life here on earth. If morality is a possibility, it will not lose by it, and if God exists I believe that He will find in that attitude what is due to Him."[217]

In the presence of that kind of "atheism" who would not be more inclined to remain silent than to start a discussion? But we ask ourselves: who were the Christians whose lives exemplified Christianity to Jeanson? Were they the worker priests or were they those who, to the "best" of their ability, oppose both these priests and the "other blind Christians who have become accomplices of atheistic communism?"[218]

God as Guarantee

"Inside" Knowledge of God's Plans. There is yet another special reproach implied in Sartre and Merleau-Ponty's rejection of God which we want to discuss more fully. It concerns the way in which some Christians are accustomed to use and dispose of God. They virtually maintain that they have, as it were, an insider's knowledge of the Divine Being and the Infinite Wisdom with which God has

---

[216]"For many atheism is a radical negation of theology in favor of anthropology." J. Lacroix *Le sens de l'athéisme moderne,* Tournai, 1958, p. 42.
[217]Jeanson, "Athéisme et liberté," *Lumière et vie,* vol. 13 (1954), p. 96.
[218]I. Lepp, *Psychanalyse de l'athéisme moderne,* Paris, 1961, p. 112.

ordered all things. Sometimes they go even so far as to think that this knowledge gives them a kind of immunity and a guarantee for their conduct, so that the contingency which belongs to any concrete action is jeopardized.

In this connection let us recall Sartre's interview with a French Jesuit who was his co-prisoner of war. The latter had seen a divine "sign" in all the misfortunes he had met with in the various phases of his life in the world and he had concluded from it that God called him to work for the triumph of religion and to foster faith and sanctity. Sartre rejected that conclusion, for it was clear to his mind that it is man *himself* and he *alone* who gives to the "sign" the meaning he himself chooses to give to it.[219] In other words, this young man's action was not sanctioned by any divine guarantee.

We find the same idea in Merleau-Ponty. "If I really think that I can believe in the evidence of being in touch with the absolute principles of all thought and evaluation, I have the right to withdraw judgments from the control of others, for my judgments then have the character of sacredness."[220] In the practical order that attitude "provides me with an escape hatch through which my actions are transfigured. Then the suffering which I have caused—[precisely because my action is and remains contingent]—is turned into good fortune, deceit becomes reason, and I piously kill my enemies."[221]

This was done also by Goetz in *The Devil and the Good Lord* when he had decided to do good; what *he* concretely saw as good he immediately presented as God's will. When it finally became evident that his actions were bad all the same, he first said that his actions had a much deeper meaning, that the suffering he caused was a good fortune, until he could no longer escape the overwhelming evidence to the contrary. God then had not guaranteed anything and "therefore" God does not exist.

Sartre and Merleau-Ponty demand the rejection of God because the attribution of a divine guarantee to *concrete* judgments and actions denies the contingency of judgments and actions and leads to

---

219"Who can doubt but that this decision as to the meaning of the sign was his and his alone? One could have drawn quite different conclusions from such a series of reverses—as, for example, that he had better become a carpenter or a revolutionary." *Existentialism and Humanism*, p. 38.

220*Sens et non-sens*, p. 190.

221 *Ibid.*

intolerance,[222] and because the rejection of God is the only means to honor contingency once more.[223] "I have nothing at my command but my own opinions when I wish to make judgments."[224]

Justified Criticism. We firmly believe that Sartre and Merleau-Ponty put their fingers here on a very weak spot in the existence of many Christians. The way Christians sometimes imagine to have God and His Providence at their "disposal" often amounts to a degradation of God's Transcendence. What is worse, such an attitude is often considered to manifest a "profound faith." To the example given by Sartre we may add another that is not pure fabrication.

Someone wakes up in the morning with the vague feeling that he has still to fulfill some obligation, but he cannot remember what it is and so he goes to work as usual. But he does not succeed; he cannot control his attention and has not the energy to force himself to concentrate, so that he is on the point of stopping his work for a while. He confesses to himself that he should attribute his discomfort to himself since he drank too much the night before. Just then he remembers his obligation. He has promised a friend some time ago that he would visit him. This morning seems an excellent occasion for it. He finds his friend and the latter's wife at home, but they seem to be close to a nervous crisis. One of their children is feeble-minded and they can no longer bear that situation. He comes thus as one sent by God, for the director of an institution that has recently been opened for such children has special obligations toward him. The case is settled within one hour; the child is accepted for three months to give the parents a breathing spell.

Here then, some might say, "God's finger" and His Providence manifest themselves in a palpable fashion. "Pious" people often reason that way. The individual in our example now "realizes" that God's guidance was already at work at the time when he did a service to the gentleman who later became the director of the institute. He "realizes" that God has drawn good from evil—namely,

---

[222]"It is not only tempting but urgent to restrain men when one *knows* that they are wasting their time in searching since 'on the other side' an infinite knowledge (*science*) has already settled everything." *Op. cit.*, p. 362.

[223]"The notion of a theist has many historical connotations attached to it; and therefore I do not speak of it. Nevertheless, I cannot refrain from saying that in my opinion philosophy can breathe [freely] only when it rejects infinitely 'infinitized' thought, in order to see the *world* in its strangeness." Merleau-Ponty, "Deuxième entretien privé," *La connaissance de l'homme au XXe siècle*, (*Rencontres internationales de Genève*, 1951), p. 251.

[224]*Sens et non-sens*, p. 189.

from the fact that the night before he drank too much and thus was too lazy to make an effort at his job the following morning. God's guidance is "visible," he thinks, and his conduct has a divine guarantee; he is a man of "profound faith."

Dangers of Such Claims. It is not at all our intention to deny God's guidance and Providence. But God is a Transcendent God, and we refuse to admit that any man can ever lay claim to having "inside" knowledge of God's Providence in the way described above. For such a claim represents God as a *man* who regulates everything. Is it then to be wondered at that such a "faith" frequently changes into "unbelief"? For it also happens that in similar circumstances things turn out quite differently than we had hoped. The child's medical treatment can lead to the opposite of what it was meant to accomplish. He could then have returned home, made his parents really suffer a mental collapse, lead them to bitter arguments and mutual infidelity. In that case the one who "saw" God's guidance and Providence in such *anthropomorphic* fashion must now logically conclude *in the same line of thinking* that God in His "Providence" has played a dirty trick on his unfortunate friends. When human initiatives have failed and man suffers the wretched consequences, people are generally willing to emphasize that God's "plans" and "guidance" are not to be measured by human standards. Why, then, should we not recognize this immediately from the start?[225]

In our critical reflection on Marxism we have stressed that not a single *concrete* economic, social or political activity of the Christian can lay claim to a divine guarantee by virtue of his belief in the divine origin of the command of love. Every concrete choice or measure brings with it the danger that the result might be harmful to man and humanity.[226] The Christian knows no more than the non-Christian in the field of economic, social and political activity. Prompted by the critique of Sartre and Merleau-Ponty, we must now extend that thought to every *concrete* action within man's being in the world. Not a singe *concrete* action can claim to be divinely guaranteed in virtue of man's faith in God and His Providence. Man has no "inside" knowledge of God's Transcendent Essence.

---

[225]"If I address myself to any God in order to thank Him for the gifts bestowed on me, why shouldn't I blame Him for the evils which He sends to me or my fellow-men?" Jeanson, *art. cit.*, p. 91.

[226]"Whether God exists or not, the adventure is the same, the risks are of the same kind, and the means are identical." Jeanson, *art. cit.*, p. 91.

Another Example. A last example may help to illustrate that Christians do not always keep this principle in mind even when they explicitly recognize its truth. In a symposium concerning the significance of contemporary non-religious humanism Schillebeeckx confronts this humanism with Catholic Christianity. By way of conclusion he wants to "show briefly" that God's grace is not inactive in reference to that humanism. And he would like to entitle his conclusion "God's occupation with non-religious humanism."[227]

We ask ourselves whence a theologian derives the possibility for determining that point and describing how God "occupies" Himself with a concrete and historical human initiative.[228] He who briefly shows that God busies Himself with humanism, at least gives the impression that he has an "inside" knowledge of God's "plans" and "guidance." And we then understand why Merleau-Ponty accuses the Christians of claiming "to know that others waste their time in searching since an infinite Knowledge has already settled everything."[229] And must not the humanists also conclude that they are wasting their time in searching, since theology is capable of showing that God Himself "is busy" with humanism and of describing how this is done?

We consider this a dangerous way of thinking. Suppose that half a century later non-religious humanism would have displaced Catholicism in a particular country—what would theology have to say? Fifty years earlier, it had certified that God Himself was busy with humanism! Continuing *in the same line of thought,* would it not be necessary to conclude that God had played a dirty trick on Catholicism? Of course, the answer then would be that God's plans and "guidance" are not to be measured by human standards. But why not recognize this truth at once? Is the reason perhaps the dislike of giving up certain claims of having "knowledge"? Let us never forget that "I have only my own opinions at my disposal for judging things."

---

[227]E. Schillebeeckx, "De betekenis van het niet-godsdienstige humanisme voor het hedendaagse katholicisme," *Modern niet-godsdienstig humanisme,* Nijmegen, 1961, pp. 105 f.

[228]"It seemed to me that in a Christian perspective the attitude of man with respect to God could provide a certain understanding of History in its entirety, but in no case a method to explain particular historical events." Jeanson, *art. cit.,* pp. 87 f.

[229]*Sens et non-sens,* p. 362.

Is Man an Abortive God?

Sartre Does Not "Call God Back." Nietzsche's reason for rejecting God is the divine character of the man of the future. But when Nietzsche describes what it means for the man of the future that he has to live without God, he paints a picture that is precisely the opposite of a "liberation." It is a stark picture of nihilism. In utter despair Nietzsche finally calls God back.

Sartre's starting point is closest to that of Nietzsche's philosophy: man, he believes, is free in a divine way. The course of Sartre's thinking, however, is affected by an ambiguity which at the end brings him very close again to the finale of Nietzsche's thought. To Sartre's mind man is an abortive God, and man's "passion," in his attempt to identify the "for itself" with the "in itself" in his existence, that is, to realize the contradictory definition of God, is a useless passion. Does Sartre also call God back when he becomes aware of what this useless passion means?

When we confine ourselves to Sartre's explicit statements, we must conclude that he does not. The uselessness of the passion of human existence is, for Sartre, not even a reason for despair. Authentic "human life begins beyond despair."[230] The authentic man is not a nihilist;[231] he even renounces despair,[232] because he who despairs betrays through his attitude that he is still living on the basis of the contradictory ideal of identifying the "for itself" with the "in itself" in his existence. The authentic man accepts himself as a "lack of being," for the negativity of his subjectivity as *Volo* is invincible. Sartre does not call God back. Yet we have to look beyond his explicit statements.

Man As a Search for Ground. The "for itself," in its transcendence, tries to identify itself with the "in itself," in order to find a ground for its "groundlessness." For, according to Sartre, the "for itself" would find its own ground—it would, in fact, *be* its own ground—if man could attain the identification of the "for itself" with

---

[230]Sartre, "Les Mouches," *Théâtre*, Paris, 1947, p. 114.

[231]S. de Beauvoir, *Pour une morale de l'ambiguité*, Paris 1947, p. 75.

[232]"But to the extent that this attempt still shares in the spirit of seriousness and that these men can still believe that their mission of effecting the existence of the in-itself-for-itself is written in things, they are condemned to despair; for they discover at the same time that all human activities are equivalent (for they all tend to sacrifice man in order that the self-cause may arise) and that all are on principle doomed to failure." *Being and Nothingness*, p. 627.

the "in itself," i.e., if man were able to realize the contradictory definition of God in his human existence. We have already pointed out that God cannot be conceived as an identity of the "for itself" and the "in itself." It follows therefore, that man also, as the opposional unity of the "for itself" and the "in itself" cannot be conceived as a project for being God.

And yet man is a seeker of "Ground." It is this that Sartre has "seen" and it is this which has led him to where he does not want to go. So now we have merely to ask ourselves what that "seeking" for a "Ground" really means if it is not man's desire to make himself God.

That this search is the meaning of being man Sartre concludes from what he calls an "existential psychoanalysis." [233] This kind of analysis does not consist of drawing up a list of ways of human behavior, of urges and tendencies, but of trying to decipher them.[234]

Basing ourselves on a pre-ontological comprehension of what man is and on the unreflective presence of man to his own essence, it is possible to decipher those individual ways of behavior and tendencies as manifestations of what man is in his innermost essence. For Sartre the conclusion from this analysis is that "man is a useless passion." Man is an attempt to make the "for itself" and the "in itself" coincide. This, however, is an impossible attempt because the "for itself" is nothing but "nihilation," the creation of distance between the "in itself" and the "for itself."

He who rejects the conclusion of Sartre's existential psychoanalysis and his way of explaining things, could try to "interpret" once more man's conduct, urges and tendencies as manifestations of what is his innermost essence. For this purpose it would not be necessary to cast doubt on the realities discovered by Sartre's phenomenological description of man as transcendence. But he should try to look beyond the text, read between the lines, and express what Sartre really "sees" when he says that man is a "search for ground."

There is, however, also another way, which perhaps casts more light on what man is in his innermost essence or on what Sartre has "seen." We mean an examination of what Sartre *really* rejects when he claims to reject God.

---

[233]"Existential psychoanalysis is going to reveal to man the real goal of his pursuit, which is being as a synthetic fusion of the in-itself with the for-itself." *Op. cit.,* p. 626.
[234]*Op. cit.,* p. 568.

What Sartre Really Rejects in His Denial of God. Sartre refers to the man who adheres to God as the "grave man." The grave man is a coward, for he hides his absolute freedom to himself.[235] He is one who interprets his own being as a thing among things; he renounces his being man in favor of the world.[236] He attributes to himself the manner of being of a rock, the firmness, inertia, and opacity of a thing in the world.[237] Marx is the typical "grave" man, for he affirms the priority of the object over the subject, and man is "grave" when he looks upon himself as an object.[238] But he is in bad faith, since he buries in the depths of himself the consciousness of his freedom.[239]

Sartre's analysis of bad faith enables us to go a step further. It sounds strange but, according to him, everyone who strives for sincerity is in bad faith. For what else is that striving except the attempt to be for oneself what one is?[240] But this is precisely the definition of the "in itself," of a thing.[241] It follows that such a striving is always and necessarily hypocritical, for man is a be-ing who in his being is concerned with his being, and this means that man "nihilates" what he *is*.[242] Man unavoidably escapes from what he is, and the ideal of sincerity is a hopeless task, for it is in contradiction with the nihilating structures of the "for itself."[243] The striving for sincerity is the attempt to be like a thing.[244]

The "grave" man therefore is in bad faith because he ascribes to himself the manner of being of a thing. And this, precisely, is the case of him who accepts God. What, we may ask, does Sartre mean by that?

When man attributes to himself the manner of being of a thing, he thereby rejects his freedom as distance and precisely for this reason he is in bad faith. As we have seen, the distance inherent in the fact that subjectivity is involved in facticity is to be conceived in

---

[235]*Existentialism and Humanism,* p. 52.

[236]*Being and Nothingness,* p. 580.

[237]"He has given himself the type of existence of the rock, the consistency, the inertia, the opacity of being-in-the-midst-of-the-world." *Ibid.*

[238]*Ibid.*

[239]*Ibid.*

[240]"Now what is the ideal to be attained in this case. It is necessary that a man be *for himself* only what he *is*, in a word, that he is fully and solely what he *is*." *Op. cit.,* p. 98. The second half of the last sentence is missing in the English translation.

[241]*Ibid.*

[242]*Op. cit.,* p. 45.

[243]*Op. cit.,* p. 62.

[244]*Op. cit.,* p. 63.

two ways. It implies "nihilation" on the cognitive level, but also "nihilation" on the level of affectivity. The distance of the subject as *Volo* with respect to facticity is an essential aspect of being man. Man is unable to consent fully and without reservation to any kind of worldly facticity. This means that all fullness is permeated by emptiness, all being filled and being satisfied is affected by non-fulfillment and non-satisfaction; all rest, peace and happiness are mingled with unrest, strife and unhappiness. When man refuses to acknowledge his non-being, he thereby rejects his being man; he is in bad faith.

This is the kind of man that Sartre rejects, and rightly so. Man should not be satisfied with any kind of being in the world; He must not say absolutely and definitively "Yes" to any worldly reality. Yet this is precisely what the grave man *does*.[245] In his case the affective distance between the subject-as-*Volo* with respect to facticity is buried, and man gives himself the mode of being of a thing, for a thing is compact density, it lies "crushed on its own self."

That is why Sartre says that the grave man renounces his being man in favor of the *world,* that he is "of the world."[246] Simone de Beauvoir, Sartre's most slavish disciple, calls the grave man the "sub-man" in an allusion to Nietzsche's "superman." The "sub-man" loses himself in the object,[247] he clings firmly to his facticity and thus puts an obstacle in the way of the expansion of the kingdom of man, of the unfolding of freedom.[248] But the "sub-man" is bored and the world is a desert to him.[249] He is in bad faith.[250]

This helps us to see what Sartre *really* rejects when he imagines he rejects God. The man who accepts God is a *grave* man; he renounces his being man in favor of the *world*. God is thus thought of as a "worldly" reality, to which man nonetheless adheres unreservedly. Now such a God must surely be rejected, for he is not a God.

Simone de Beauvoir gives unambiguous examples to illustrate that "gravity," i.e., the acceptance of God which she herself and Sartre

---

[245]"The grave man, if there is any, is the man of but one thing to which he says 'Yes'." Merleau-Ponty, *Eloge de la philosophie,* p. 79.

[246]*Being and Nothingness,* p. 580.

[247]"The attitude of the 'sub-man' logically passes into that of the grave man: he makes an effort to engulf his freedom in the contents which it receives from his society, he loses himself in the object in order to destroy his subjectivity." S. de Beauvoir, *Pour une morale de l'ambiguïté,* Paris 1947, p. 65.

[248]De Beauvoir, *op. cit.,* p. 64.

[249]De Beauvoir, *op. cit.,* p. 65.

[250]"The bad faith of the grave man comes from the fact that he is obliged constantly to renew the denial of that freedom." De Beauvoir, *op. cit.,* p. 68.

so greatly detest. The officer for whom the army is Everything, the colonist who sacrifices the life of the natives to the Road he wants to build, the revolutionary who sees nothing but the Revolution—they are grave men because they are servants of "divinities."[251] But what are those divinities? They are worldly realities to which a transcendent dignity is assigned. The man who unreservedly consents to them thereby rejects the negativity that affects his existence and he crushes his freedom. He will necessarily be disillusioned by life, for his gravity is the impossible attempt to realize the "contradictory synthesis of the 'in self' and the 'for self'."[252] This Sartrian definition of God is discussed by Simone de Beauvoir immediately after her examples of gravity.

It is evident that God is conceived here as a reality within the world, and the man who adheres to God appears as a be-ing who makes a relative be-ing and his own relativity absolutes. It must be admitted that in such a case, man's *proper* being dies in contact with *that* absolute.[253]

Value of Sartre's Description of Man's Essence. It would really be unnecessary to add that all this has nothing to do with the true God and an authentic acceptance of God. This is so true that Christian religions call "sin" the very thing that Sartre conceives as "acceptance of God." Sin, in the strict sense, is precisely giving absoluteness to a worldly reality. Sin is the "grave man's" way of making an affirmation; and the human struggle against evil is precisely the struggle against such an affirmation to which man is tempted by the world.

But the way Sartre rejects the massive affirmation of the world and the subject's "being of the world" is so penetrating that his insight can be called a lasting acquisition of philosophy. The deepest ground of the "having to be" that characterizes man has perhaps never been so clearly revealed as it is in the philosophy of Sartre. That ground is the negativity that belongs to the very core of being man. Perhaps never before has it been shown with such clarity that "having to be" constitutes the innermost essence of man. Sartre's insight is the result of what he calls an "existential psychoanalysis."

---

[251]De Beauvoir, *op. cit.,* pp. 70-73.

[252]"Gravity is one of the ways to try to realize the impossible synthesis of the in-itself and the for-itself." De Beauvoir, *op. cit.,* p. 74.

[253]"Metaphysical and moral consciousness dies when it comes in contact with the absolute." Merleau-Ponty, *Sens et-non-sens,* p. 191.

This analysis starts from a preontological and fundamental consciousness of, and insight into, the essence of the human person for the purpose of expressing that essence in clear concepts.[254]

Sartre's conclusion is that man is "the desire to be God."[255] But this can be said only in virtue of a false notion of God. However, if we reject Sartre's *interpretation* of man's innermost essence, we do not mean thereby that we cannot accept the real value of his *description*. For this description is very penetrating. The subject as *Desidero* is really such that no wordly reality is capable of satisfying him. So long as man lives locked up in the world, he cannot consent definitely to his subjectivity as "having to be," for all such consent to himself is in function of the fulfillment which his subjectivity finds as "having to be." When man seeks the ground of his existence, he looks for the possibility of being able to consent *definitively* to his subjectivity as "having to be."

Within the dimension of the world that is not possible. The grave man, the "sub-man," gives proof of it. He is in bad faith. He is bored in a world which is like a desert to him. It is a boredom that has metaphysical dimensions. It reveals the true nature of the subjectivity in the world, understood as "natural desire"; it shows that the "longing," which subjectivity in the world really is, must be understood as "desiring much more than worldly things," as "really desiring something totally different." That "something totally different" Christians call the Transcendent God. But God is not a "reality" just as worldly things are realities. That is why God can *never* be "affirmed" *just as* the world is affirmed. Any attempt to do so degrades God's Transcendence and fails to recognize the true dimension of the human subject as *Desidero*.

A "Theology Without God." The being of man is indeed a "foundation project." It is the search of the subject for the possibility to consent definitively to himself. A definitive consent to himself is not possible on the basis of his "Yes" to the world, because this "Yes" is essentially and therefore invincibly affected by a "No."

---

[254]*Being and Nothingness,* p. 568.

[255]"The fundamental value which presides over this project is exactly the in-itself-for-itself; that is, the ideal of a consciousness which would be the foundation of its own being-in-itself by the pure consciousness which it would have of itself. It is this ideal which can be called God. Thus the best way to conceive of the fundamental project of human reality is to say that man is the being whose project is to be God." *Op. cit.,* p. 566.

However, we must ask, is it possible that a "Yes" to God could be the foundation for a definitive consent of man to his own subjectivity? In the perspective of Sartre's *explicit* theories that question is meaningless, for Sartre rejects God and considers every definitive "Yes" a form of estrangement. But what happens if we radically distinguish God as Transcendent from the world—and we cannot do anything else without denying God and thus also denying the human subject as *Desidero*? In that case one cannot still claim that a definitive "Yes" to God implies "gravity," for the grave man unreservedly affirms the *world*. His affirmations do not give any definitive meaning to life; it is a "useless passion."[256]

Once man is convinced that such an affirmation of the world is unsatisfactory, the search for the meaning of life and the attempt of the subject to find a ground for his groundlessness appear in their *proper* dimension. Sartre has not supplied the answer because the possibility of this twofold question did not even occur to him. Nevertheless, it is perhaps not an exaggeration to say that Sartre's *implicit* doctrine is a theology without God.[257]

CONCLUSION

When Nietzsche realized what it would mean for the man of the future to have to live without God, he called God back. The future foreseen by Nietzsche is today's actuality. Does contemporary man possess the profound understanding of his existence that Nietzsche had in his vision of the future man? Has modern man already reached the stage when he calls God back?

The Persistence of Pseudo-Gods. We have the impression that this is not yet so. And there are many reasons for it. Not the least, it seems to us, is the fact that many pseudo-gods still remain insufficiently unmasked. The task of doing it belongs primarily to the believer. But he receives valuable assistance from atheism, on condition that the voices of the atheists do not sound in his ears as if they were coming from distant lands and strange times. He should understand those voices as coming from his own existence, as a protest of what is best in his own essence against his own worship of

---

[256]Cf. Fr. Jeanson, "La conduite humaine selon J. P. Sartre," *Morale chrétienne et requêtes contemporaines*, Tournai, 1954, p. 176.

[257]E. Vietta, *Theologie ohne Gott, Versuch über die menschliche Existenz in der modernen französischn Philosophie*, Zurich, 1946.

pseudo-gods, both in theory and in practice. Are the believers ready to listen to those voices?

A great number, unfortunately, do not want to listen. Some continue to refuse to reflect at all. Others confine themselves to "guarding the purity of doctrine," cast suspicion on the "atheism" of those who actually give thought to the matter, accuse and denounce them. They do all this without analyzing themselves to discover what are the *real* motives that animate their actions.

Others, again, think they have done enough by tracing the calamities of history and particularly the unrest, the loneliness, the disorientation and despair of our time to the fact that man has forsaken God. They are firmly convinced that "pagan humanism" is a deadly poison for the human person and that it must inevitably lead to destruction and ruin. Man himself is bound to become the victim of his own denial and his rebellion, and his works will turn against him. "This is God's revenge."[258] When this has been said, these critics feel safe, for they have the illusion that they can pronounce judgment on atheism "in God's name." Apparently they do not realize that such a judgment once more implies a worship of a pseudo-god and that their attitude feeds the fire of atheism.

This brings us to the conclusion that it is all to the good that in the present phase of history, atheism is no longer the sociological impossibility which it was formerly. The mistakes of believers compromise the "cause of God," and modern atheism is merciless in castigating their faults.

The Recall of God. Modern man, then, will not, without more ado, call God back, when the time for it has arrived. Jupiter and Thor, after their fall, have never been restored to their altars, and rightly so. So also will the man of the future not call back a "God" who has to make up as a sort of physical energy, for the loss of energy in the macrocosm, who has to justify the injustices of the mighty of this world, who has to make the poor accept their wretched lot on earth, who must keep the oppressed in their social and political state of degradation. He will not be a God who acts like a French king or a German emperor, who can be inspected as a factor in an Oedipus-complex, who is a kind of "unstared stare" and pursues man with his threats, who produces man as a kind of utensil, who makes man's cultural activity superfluous. He will

---

[258]Fr. Jeanson, "Athéisme et liberté," *Lumière et vie,* vol. 13 (1954), p. 87.

not be a God who lets theologians have a look at the maps of His Providence, who lets Himself be invoked as a meteorological and agricultural factor.   He will not be a super-economist, a super-physician, a super-psychiatrist who puts all economists, physicians, and psychiatrists in the shade, who so greatly prompts man to forget his fellow-man that charity becomes unimportant. The man of the future will call God back, but this call will be only for the true God. With the heaven above his head empty of pseudo-gods, he will walk through the world and history, calling for a Transcendent God.

God has already heard that cry and has entered history. He has made His word speak to men. He has spoken about Himself and about man. The believer is called to unfold His word. What we have written here about atheism is merely a preparation for the new work of reflection that begins here.

INDEX OF NAMES

INDEX OF SUBJECT MATTER

Imprimatur

M. Oomens, vic. gen.
Buscoduci, die julii, 1963